Global Environmental Politics

Dilemmas in World Politics

Dilemmas in World Politics offers teachers and students in international relations a series of quality books on critical issues, trends, and regions in international politics. Each text examines a "real world" dilemma and is structured to cover the historical, theoretical, practical, and projected dimensions of its subject.

BOOKS IN THIS SERIES

FOURTH EDITION

Global Environmental Politics

PAMELA S. CHASEK

DAVID L. DOWNIE

JANET WELSH BROWN

Westview PRESS

A Member of the Perseus Books Group

Dilemmas in World Politics

Westview Press books are available at special discounts for bulk purchases in the United
States by corporations, institutions, and other organizations. For more information, please
contact the Special Markets Department at the Perseus Books Group, 11 Cambridge
Center, Cambridge MA 02142, or call (617) 252-5298 or (800) 255-1514, or e-mail
special.markets@perseusbooks.com.

Designed by Brent Wilcox

Library of Congress Cataloging-in-Publication Data

Chasek, Pamela S., 1961–
    Global environmental politics.— 4th ed. / Pamela S. Chasek, David L. Downie,
Janet Welsh Brown.
        p.   cm. — (Dilemmas in world politics)
    Rev. ed of: Global environmental politics / Gareth Porter, Janet Welsh Brown,
and Pamela S. Chasek. 3rd ed. 2000.
    Includes bibliographical references and index.
    ISBN-13: 978-0-8133-4332-7 (pbk. : alk. paper)
    ISBN-10: 0-8133-4332-1 (pbk. : alk. paper)
    1. Environmental policy.   I. Downie, David L.   II. Brown, Janet Welsh.   III. Porter,
Gareth, 1942– Global environmental politics.   IV. Title.   V. Series.
GE170.P67   2005
363.7'056—dc22
                                                                                    2005022567

06 07 08 / 10 9 8 7 6 5 4 3 2 1

Contents

Illustrations

Photos

Cartoons

Acknowledgments

This book has been made possible by the inspiration, encouragement and assistance of many colleagues. Most important, we thank Gareth Porter and Janet Welsh Brown for their contribution to the study of global environmental politics by initiating and writing the earlier editions of this book and then entrusting us to carry on with this edition. We also want to thank our editor, Steve Catalano, for his endless support and positive attitude throughout this process.

In addition to all our colleagues who were thanked in earlier editions of this book, we thank Stefan Ekernas, Blair Lampe, Martin Mendez, Nicole Pollio, Todd Osmundson, and Kari Schmidt for their research assistance with the case studies in chapter 3. We are also grateful to the following colleagues and friends who reviewed portions of the manuscript for accuracy or clarity or provided other valuable assistance: Soledad Aguilar, Andrew Baldwin, Perinaz Bhada, Alice Bisiaux, Emily Boyd, Kate Brash, Ian Fry, Mark Halle, Elisa Morgera, Adil Najam, Lisa Schipper, Nicole Eckley Selin, Anju Sharma, Chris Spence, Jennifer Stamatelos, Elsa Tsioumani, Laura Whitman, Hugh Wilkins, and the staff of the *Earth Negotiations Bulletin*.

Last, but certainly not least, David Downie thanks his family—Laura Whitman, William Downie, and Lindsey Downie—for making all the good things in his life possible. Pamela Chasek thanks her family—Kimo, Sam, and Kai Goree—for all of their patience, support and love.

Pamela Chasek
David Downie

Acronyms

ACP	Africa, the Caribbean and the Pacific
AGBM	*Ad Hoc* Group on the Berlin Mandate
AOSIS	Alliance of Small Island States
ARPA	Amazon Regional Protected Area Program
APEC	Asia-Pacific Economic Cooperation
BIO	Biotech Industry Organization
BCRC	Basel Convention Regional Centers
BCSC	Business Council on Sustainable Development
CAFÉ	Corporate Average Fuel Economy Standards (U.S.)
CBD	Convention on Biological Diversity
CCAD	Central American Commission on Environment and Development
CDM	Clean Development Mechanism
CFCs	chlorofluorocarbons
CITES	Convention on International Trade in Endangered Species of Wild Fauna and Flora
COFI	Committee on Fisheries (FAO)
COFO	Committee on Forestry (FAO)
COICA	Coordinadora de Organizaciones Indigenas de la Cuenca Amazonica (Coordinating Council of Indigenous Organizations of the Amazon Basin)
COP	Conference of the Parties
CPF	Collaborative Partnership on Forests
CSD	Commission on Sustainable Development
CSE	Center for Science and Environment
CTE	Committee on Trade and Environment (WTO)
CUEs	critical-use exemptions
EC	European Community
ECE	United Nations Economic Commission for Europe
ECOSOC	United Nations Economic and Social Council
EEB	European Environmental Bureau
EEC	European Economic Community
EEG	Energy and Environment Group (UNDP)
EEZs	exclusive economic zones
ESMAP	Energy Sector Management Assistance Programme

ETMs	environmental trade measures
EU	European Union
FAO	Food and Agriculture Organization of the United Nations
FIELD	Foundation for International Environmental Law and Development
FOEI	Friends of the Earth International
FRG	Federal Republic of Germany (former)
FSC	Forest Stewardship Council
FTA	financial and technical assistance
G–77	Group of 77 (developing country negotiating bloc)
GATT	General Agreement on Tariffs and Trade
GCIP	Global Climate Information Project
GEF	Global Environment Facility
GEOSS	Global Earth Observation System of Systems
GHGs	greenhouse gases
GM	genetically modified
GMOs	genetically modified organisms
GNP	gross national product
GPA	Global Programme of Action for the Protection of the Marine Environment from Land-Based Activities
GRID	Global Resource Information Database
GWP	gross world product
HCFCs	hydrochlorofluorocarbons
HFCs	hydrofluorocarbons
HIPC	Heavily Indebted Poor Countries
IBA	Industrial Biotechnology Association
IDB	Inter-American Development Bank
IFCS	Intergovernmental Forum on Chemical Safety
IFF	Intergovernmental Forum on Forests
IGOs	intergovernmental organizations
IIED	International Institute for Environment and Development
IISD	International Institute for Sustainable Development
IMF	International Monetary Fund
IMO	International Maritime Organization
INC	Intergovernmental Negotiating Committee
INCD	Intergovernmental Negotiating Committee on the International Convention to Combat Desertification
INGOs	international nongovernmental organizations
IOs	international organizations
IOMC	Inter-Organization Programme for the Sound Management of Chemicals
IPCC	Intergovernmental Panel on Climate Change

IPCS	International Programme on Chemical Safety
IPEN	International POPs Elimination Network
IPF	Intergovernmental Panel on Forests
IPM	integrated pest management
IPR	intellectual property rights
IRPTC	International Register of Potentially Toxic Chemicals
ITTA	International Tropical Timber Agreement
ITTO	International Tropical Timber Organization
IUCN	International Union for the Conservation of Nature and Natural Resources/World Conservation Union
IUU	illegal, unreported, and unregulated (fishing)
IWC	International Whaling Commission
JI	Joint Implementation
JPOI	Johannesburg Plan of Implementation
LMOs	living modified organisms
LPG	liquid petroleum gas
LRTAP	Convention on Long-Range Transboundary Air Pollution
MAI	Multilateral Agreement on Investment
MARPOL	International Convention for the Prevention of Pollution from Ships
MDBs	multilateral development banks
MDGs	Millennium Development Goals
MEAs	multilateral environmental agreements
MIKE	Monitoring of Illegal Killing of Elephants
MMPA	Marine Mammal Protection Act (U.S.)
MOP	Meeting of the Parties
MSC	Marine Stewardship Council
NAFO	Northwest Atlantic Fisheries Organization
NAFTA	North American Free Trade Agreement
NASA	National Aeronautics and Space Administration (U.S.)
NEPA	National Environmental Policy Act (U.S.)
NEPAD	New Partnership for Africa's Development
NGOs	nongovernmental organizations
NIEO	New International Economic Order
NRDC	Natural Resources Defense Council
NWF	National Wildlife Federation
OAS	Organization of American States
OAU	Organization of African Unity (former)
ODA	official development assistance
ODS	Ozone Depleting Substance(s)
OECD	Organization for Economic Cooperation and Development
OPEC	Organization of the Petroleum Exporting Countries

PACD	Plan of Action to Combat Desertification
PIC	prior informed consent
POPs	persistent organic pollutants
PPMs	process and production methods
PRSPs	Poverty Reduction Strategy Papers
RGGI	Regional Greenhouse Gas Initiative
RMP	Revised Management Procedure
RMS	Revised Management Scheme
SAICM	Strategic Approach to International Chemicals Management
SEEN	Sustainable Energy and Economy Network
SPREP	South Pacific Regional Environment Programme
TEDs	turtle excluder devices
TRAFFIC	Trade Records Analysis of Flora and Fauna in Commerce
UNCCD	United Nations Convention to Combat Desertification
UNCED	United Nations Conference on Environment and Development
UNCHE	United Nations Conference on the Human Environment, 1972
UNCTAD	United Nations Conference on Trade and Development
UNDP	United Nations Development Programme
UNEP	United Nations Environment Programme
UNFCCC	United Nations Framework Convention on Climate Change
UNFF	United Nations Forum on Forests
UNFPA	United Nations Population Fund
UNGA	United Nations General Assembly
UN-HABITAT	United Nations Human Settlements Programme
VOCs	volatile organic compounds
WALHI	Wahana Lingkungan Hidup (Indonesian Environmental Forum)
WCMC	World Conservation Monitoring Center
WHO	World Health Organization
WMO	World Meteorological Organization
WRI	World Resources Institute
WSSD	World Summit on Sustainable Development
WTO	World Trade Organization
WWF	World Wildlife Fund (U.S.) or Worldwide Fund for Nature (International)

1

The Emergence of
Global Environmental Politics

Until the 1980s, most governments regarded global environmental problems as minor issues; marginal to their core national interests and to international politics in general. This situation has changed. The rise of environmental movements in the industrialized countries and the appearance of well-publicized global environmental threats that could profoundly affect the welfare of all humankind—such as the depletion of the ozone layer, global climate change, and depletion of the world's fisheries—have awarded global environmental issues a much higher status in world politics. These issues are no longer viewed as merely scientific and technical but as important in their own right and intertwined with central issues in world politics: the international system of resource production and use, the liberalization of world trade, North-South relations, and even international conflict and internal social and political stability.

Growing international concern about the environment is no historical accident. It developed in response to alterations in major components of the biosphere, including the atmosphere, the oceans, soil cover, the climate system, and the range of animal and plant species. Many byproducts of economic growth—the burning of fossil fuels; the release of ozone-destroying chemicals; emissions of sulfur and nitrogen oxides; the production of toxic chemicals and other wastes and their introduction into the air, water, and soil; and the elimination of forest cover, among others—have caused cumulative stresses on the physical environment that now threaten human health and economic well-being. The costs of these activities to future generations

1

will be much higher in developing as well as highly industrialized countries than they are to the world's current population.

The past three decades have seen an enormous increase in scientific understanding of global environmental issues. Realization that environmental threats have serious socioeconomic and human costs and that they cannot be solved by the unilateral decisions of states has given impetus to increased international cooperation in halting or reversing environmental degradation. That realization has also unleashed a new political force, a global environmental movement that undertakes increasingly effective transnational action on various issues. But some states, and certain economic interests, have opposed strong international actions to reduce or eliminate activities that threaten the global environment.

The result is an intensifying struggle over global environmental issues. As global negotiations multiply on issues affecting a wide range of interests around the world, the stakes for all the participants in the struggle continue to grow. As an introduction to global environmental politics, this chapter highlights the economic and environmental trends underlying the emergence of environmental politics as a major issue area, defines the scope of the issue area, and outlines some of its major characteristics. The chapter also traces some of the major intellectual currents and political developments that have contributed to the evolution of global environmental politics.

GLOBAL MACROTRENDS

Global economic, demographic, and environmental macrotrends describe key changes that drive global environmental politics. Indeed, the rise of global environmental politics can be understood only within the context of the major changes in the physical environment produced by the explosive growth in economic activity and population during the past fifty years.

The measure of total potential stress on the global environment is not total world population alone but total population multiplied by per capita consumption. The per capita gross world product (GWP)—the total of goods and services produced and consumed per person throughout the world—has been growing faster than world population for decades. Consumption of natural resources by modern industrial economies remains high: from 45 to 85 metric tons per person annually when all materials (including soil erosion, mining wastes, and other ancillary materials) are counted. About 300 kilograms of natural resources are currently required to generate $100 of income in the world's most advanced economies. Given the size of these economies, this represents a massive scale of environmental alteration.[1]

The cumulative effect of resource-intensive production has produced serious environmental harm. Specifically, this type of production usually requires moving or processing large quantities of primary natural resources, much of which does not end up in the final product. For example, manufacturing automobiles and other metal-intensive products in Japan requires mining and processing a yearly per capita equivalent of more than 10 metric tons of ore and minerals. Food production in the United States causes millions of tons of soil erosion annually. In Germany, producing the energy used in a year requires removing and replacing more than 29 metric tons of coal overburden for each German citizen, quite apart from the fuel itself or the pollution caused by its combustion. These hidden material flows from mining, earth moving, erosion, and other sources, which together account for as much as 75 percent of the total materials that industrial economies use, are easy to ignore because they do not enter the economy as commodities bought and thus are not accounted for in a nation's gross domestic product; but because they represent a massive scale of environmental alteration, they are important to the total environmental impact of industrial activities.[2]

But although environmental problems have been the starting point for many critiques of consumption patterns in the West, the growing gulf in consumption levels within and between countries also draws attention. Although in recent decades the world has seen a consumption explosion—household spending has grown fourfold, from $4.8 trillion in 1960 to more than $20 trillion in 2000 (in 1995 dollars)[3]—the benefits have not been uniform. The world's richest countries make up only a fifth of global population but accounted for 34 percent of all meat consumption in 1999 (see fig. 1.1).[4] The richest countries account for 58 percent of total energy use, 84 percent of paper use, and 87 percent of vehicle ownership.[5] At the other end of the spectrum, 2.8 billion people—two out of five—live on less than $2.00/day; 1.1 billion people—the poorest fifth of the world's population—do not have access to safe drinking water; and 2.4 billion live without basic sanitation. Providing adequate food, clean water, and basic education for the world's poorest could be achieved for less than people spend annually on makeup, ice cream, and pet food.[6] By some estimates, basic health care and nutrition for the world's poor would cost about $13 billion a year, less than the $17 billion that is spent on pet food in Europe and the United States.[7] (See table 1.1.)

FIGURE 1.1   **Regional Meat Consumption**

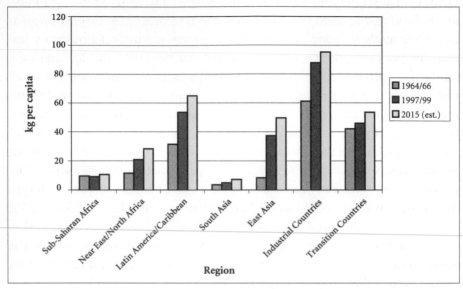

Data Source: Food and Agriculture Organization, *World Agriculture Towards 2015/2030: An FAO Perspective* (London: Earthscan, 2003).

TABLE 1.1   Annual Expenditure on Luxury Items Compared with Funding Needed to Meet Selected Basic Needs

Product	Annual Expenditure	Social or Economic Goal	Additional Annual Investment Needed to Achieve Goal
Makeup	$18 billion	Reproductive health care for all women	$12 billion
Pet food in Europe and the United States	$17 billion	Elimination of hunger and malnutrition	$19 billion
Perfumes	$15 billion	Universal literacy	$5 billion
Ocean cruises	$14 billion	Clean drinking water for all	$10 billion
Ice cream in Europe	$11 billion	Immunizing every child	$1.3 billion

Source: World Watch, *State of the World 2004* (New York: W.W. Norton, 2004), p. 10.

Population growth worldwide also has a major impact on the environment. Global population doubled between 1950 and 1987 (from 2.5 billion to 5 billion) and reached the 6-billion mark in October 1999. World population is currently growing at a rate of 1.2 percent annually, significantly less than the peak growth rate of 2.04 percent in 1965–1970, and less than the rate of 1.46 percent in 1990–1995. These figures imply a net addition of 77 million people per year. Six countries account for half of that annual increment: India for 21 percent; China for 12 percent; Pakistan for 5 percent; Bangladesh, Nigeria, and the United States of America for 4 percent each.[8] Projections of future population growth depend on assumptions made about fertility trends, which will be affected strongly by actions undertaken in the coming years. If fertility remains constant in all countries at current levels, the global population could more than double, reaching 12.8 billion by 2050 (see fig. 1.2). Whereas the most significant increases to date in consumption have occurred in the richest and most highly industrialized countries, the population growth rate of less-developed regions is increasing nearly six times as fast as that of industrialized countries.[9]

Population growth and consumption patterns contribute to environmental degradation at the global and national levels by increasing stress on natural

FIGURE 1.2   World Population, 1950–2050 (projected)

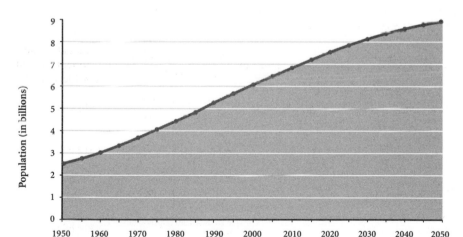

Source: United Nations Population Fund, *State of the World Population 2004* (New York: United Nations Publications, 2004).

resources and vital support services, such as the ozone and climate systems. The increasing numbers of people and their needs for refrigeration, transportation, and manufactured goods have far-reaching implications for **climate change,** pollution, energy use, and the natural resource base, especially with regard to agricultural land, forests, and fisheries.

Today, the world's richest people use on average twenty-five times more energy per person than the poorest ones; the richest comprise only 15 percent of the world's population, but they use more than half its energy.[10] (See fig.1.3.) The average American consumes five times more energy than the average global citizen, ten times more than the average Chinese, and nearly twenty times more than the average Indian.[11] However, energy consumption in developing countries is increasing rapidly, driven by industrial expansion and infrastructure improvement, high population growth and urbanization, and rising incomes, which, in turn, enable families to purchase energy-consuming appliances and cars (see fig. 1.4). China is already the world's top coal consumer and the third-largest oil user; Brazil is the sixth-largest oil consumer, India the eighth, and Mexico the tenth.[12]

If present trends in energy and fossil fuel consumption continue, energy-related emissions of carbon dioxide will be more than 60 percent higher by 2030 than they are today. More than two-thirds of the projected increase in emissions will come from developing countries, and they will remain big users of coal—the most carbon-intensive of fuels. Power stations, cars, and trucks will be responsible for most of the increases in energy-related emissions.[13] Further increases in energy efficiency in production processes will need to be combined with shifts in consumption patterns toward goods and services that are inherently less energy- and resource-intensive if **greenhouse gas** emissions are to be stabilized.

Almost three out of five people in developing countries—some 3 billion—live in rural areas. But most of the land available to meet current and future food requirements is already in production. Further expansion will involve fragile and marginal lands. As land becomes increasingly scarce, farmers are forced to turn to intensive agriculture; the dramatically higher levels of irrigation and chemicals will, in turn, contribute to soil erosion, salinization, deteriorating water quality, and desertification. Population growth and development are converting forests into agricultural land and urban areas.

Overall, the convergence of population growth, rising demand for lumber and fuelwood, and the conversion of forests to agriculture are putting increasing pressure on the world's forests, especially in developing countries. At the beginning of the twentieth century, the world contained about 5 billion

FIGURE 1.3   Global Energy Use, 2002

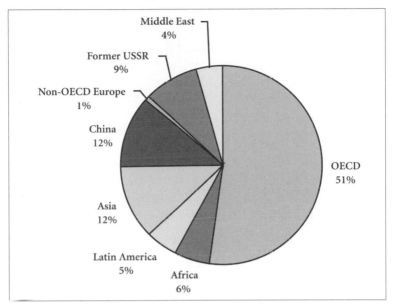

Data Source: International Energy Agency, *Key World Energy Statistics, 2004*
(Paris: International Energy Agency, 2004).

hectares of forested area; now less than 4 billion hectares remain.[14] Deforestation, in turn, has contributed to the loss of **biodiversity** (variety of living
things), including the extinction of species and the loss of genetic diversity
within species. Biodiversity is being lost at a historically unprecedented rate.
Scientists began warning in the 1980s that the destruction of tropical forests,
which hold an estimated 50 to 90 percent of all species, could result in the
loss of one-fourth, or even one-half, of the earth's species within a few
decades. However, the earth's biodiversity is not confined to the tropical
forests: About 12 percent of the world's nearly 10,000 bird species are vulnerable or in immediate danger of extinction, as are 24 percent of the world's
4,800 mammal species and an estimated 30 percent of all fish species.[15]

Many of the world's major fisheries are overfished or on the edge of collapse. Because the waters and biological resources of the high seas belong to
no nation, it is not surprising that overfishing has become a serious problem.
According to the Food and Agriculture Organization of the United Nations,
an estimated 75 percent of major marine fish stocks are fully exploited, overexploited, or significantly depleted. Among the stocks considered depleted,
the Northeast Atlantic and the Mediterranean and Black Seas contain stocks

FIGURE 1.4   Past and Projected Trends in Energy Consumption, 1973–2030

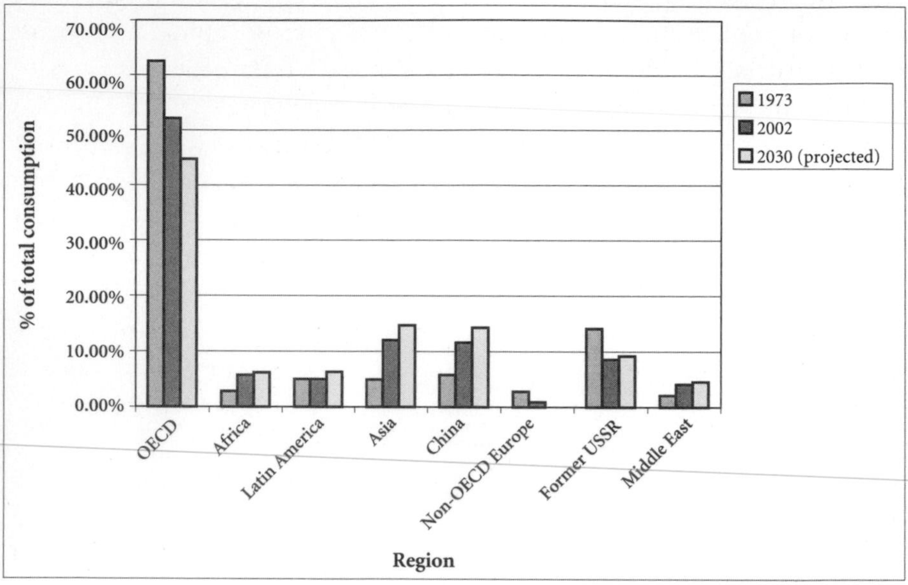

Data Source: International Energy Agency, *Key World Energy Statistics, 2004*
(Paris: International Energy Agency, 2004).

with the greatest need for recovery, followed by the Northwest Atlantic, the
Southeast Atlantic, the Southeast Pacific, and the areas comprising the
Southern Ocean. Of the top ten species that account for about 30 percent of
the world capture fisheries production, seven are considered fully exploited
or overexploited (anchoveta, Chilean jack mackerel, Alaska pollock, Japanese
anchovy, blue whiting, capelin, and Atlantic herring).[16] Staples such as tuna,
swordfish, Atlantic salmon, and even cod could soon be on the endangered
list. The industries they support will be crippled. Inefficient fishing practices
waste a high percentage of each year's catch; furthermore, 20 million metric
tons of **by-catch** (unintentionally caught fish, seabirds, sea turtles, marine
mammals, and other ocean life) die every year when they are carelessly swept
up and discarded by commercial fishing operations.[17]

In addition to overfishing, the marine environment is under siege from
land-based sources of marine pollution, believed to account for nearly 80
percent of the total pollution of the oceans. The major land-based pollutants
are synthetic organic compounds; excess sedimentation from mining, deforestation, or agriculture; biological contaminants in sewage; and excessive nutrients from fertilizers and sewage.

The world's freshwater resources are also under serious stress. Global water consumption rose sixfold between 1900 and 1995—more than double the rate of population growth—and continues to grow rapidly as agricultural, industrial, and domestic demand increases.[18] Today, 450 million people in twenty-nine countries suffer from water shortages. A 2002 United Nations Environment Programme assessment estimated that two out of three people will live in water-stressed areas by the year 2025. In Africa alone, an estimated twenty-five countries will experience chronic water stress by 2025.[19] Population growth and socioeconomic development drive the rapid increase in water demand, particularly in the industrial and household sectors. Agricultural water use accounts for about 75 percent of total global consumption, mainly through crop irrigation. Industrial use accounts for about 20 percent. The remaining 5 percent is used for domestic purposes.[20] (See fig. 1.5.)

Environmental quality in urban areas is also a major problem. The world's urban population is currently growing at double the rate of the total world population. As a consequence, about 3 billion people, or 48 percent of humankind, now live in urban areas.[21] By 2030, 5 billion people are expected to live in urban areas;[22] that is, almost two-thirds of the world's population will live in towns and cities, implying heavier water and air pollution and a higher rate of consumption of natural resources (see fig. 1.6). The number of cities supporting 5 million inhabitants or more is projected to rise from forty-six in 2003 to sixty-one in 2015. Among these, the number of mega-cities (supporting 10 million inhabitants or more) will increase from twenty in 2003 to twenty-two in 2015. Most of these large cities are located in developing countries.[23] The current pace and scale of urbanization often strain the capacity of local and national governments to provide even the most basic services to urban residents. According to the United Nations Human Settlements Programme, if nothing is done to check the current trend, the number of people living in slums, with little or no access to fresh water, sanitation, or refuse collection, will rise from 1 billion today to some 1.5 billion by 2020.[24] Environmental quality and human health and well-being are so much at risk in these situations that the Millennium Development's target of significantly improving the lives of at least 100 million slum-dwellers by 2020 will be difficult to achieve.

These major changes in the global environment, which have resulted from intense economic development, population growth, and inefficient production and consumption patterns in the latter half of the twentieth century and the beginning of the twenty-first, are the forces that shape global environmental

Figure 1.5 Evolution of Global Water Use

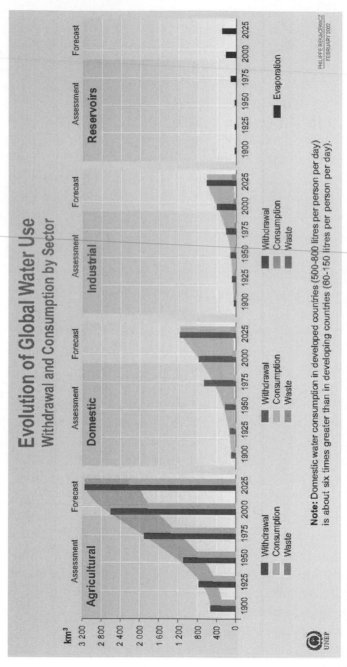

Source: Igor A. Shiklomanov, State Hydrological Institute (SHI, St. Petersburg) and United Nations Educational, Scientific and Cultural Organisation (UNESCO, Paris), 1999. Reprinted with permission UNEP, *Vital Water Graphics—An Overview of the State of the World's Fresh and Marine Waters*. (Nairobi: UNEP, 2002)

FIGURE 1.6   Percentage of Population Residing in Urban Areas by Major Areas of the World: 1950, 1975, 2003, and 2030

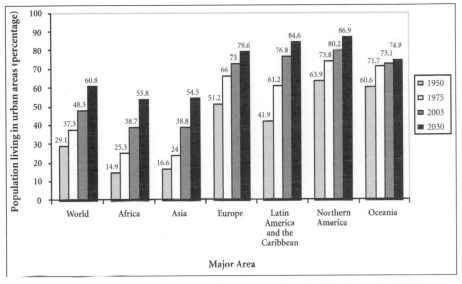

Data Source: United Nations Department of Economic and Social Affairs/Population Division, *World Urbanization Prospects: The 2003 Revision* (New York: United Nations, 2004).

politics. Thus, with this as a backdrop, it is time to look at the issues and politics that revolve around natural resources and the environment.

AN INTRODUCTION TO
GLOBAL ENVIRONMENTAL POLITICS

As the previous section has demonstrated, environmental problems do not respect national boundaries. Transboundary air pollution, the degradation of shared rivers, and the pollution of oceans and seas are just a few examples of the international dimensions of environmental problems. Population growth, in combination with resulting urbanization and industrialization, has increased the amount and frequency of major international environmental problems. The cumulative impact that human beings have had on the earth, together with an increased understanding of ecological processes, means that the environment cannot be viewed as a relatively stable background factor; indeed, the interaction between economic development and the complex, often fragile, ecosystems on which that development depends has become an international political and economic issue.[25] Thus, global environmental politics can be defined by two dimensions: the environmental consequences of the economic activity in question and the states and non-state actors involved. If the consequences are global, or if the actors transcend one region, we consider it a global environmental issue.[26]

Global environmental issues can be observed in many ways. From the economist's point of view, global environmental problems are the result of resource misallocation caused by "externalities"—the unintended consequences or side effects of one's actions that are borne by others. Externalities have always existed, but when the use of polluting technologies such as CFCs, synthetic fertilizers, pesticides, herbicides, and plastics keeps pace with a more crowded world and its resulting rise in per-capita consumption, they become more critical.[27]

In this sense, the externalities that lead to environmental degradation are similar to the "tragedy of the commons." Garrett Hardin observed that over-grazing unrestricted commonlands, prior to their enclosure, was a metaphor for the overexploitation of the earth's common property: land, air, and water resources. The root cause of overgrazing was the absence of a method for obliging herders to take into account the harmful effects their own herds' grazing had on the other herders who shared the common. The solution lay in assigning property rights so that owners could limit the use of the commons. Yet, Hardin also recognized that air, water, and many other environmental resources, unlike the traditional commons, couldn't readily be fenced and parceled out to private owners who would be motivated to preserve them. This observation raised a central question: How can we oblige users to internalize the damages they inflict on environmental resources that, by their very nature, cannot be owned by anyone?[28]

Oran Young, a political scientist, groups international environmental problems into four broad clusters: commons, shared natural resources, transboundary externalities, and linked issues.[29] Young describes the **commons** similarly to Hardin as the natural resources and vital life-support services that belong to all humankind rather than to any one country. These include Antarctica, the high seas, deep seabed minerals, the stratospheric ozone layer, the global climate system, and outer space. They may be geographically limited, as in Antarctica, or global in scope, such as the ozone layer and the climate system. Shared natural resources are physical or biological systems that extend into or across the jurisdiction of two or more states. These include nonrenewable resources, such as pools of oil beneath the surface; renewable resources, such as migratory species of animals; and complex ecosystems that transcend national boundaries, such as regional seas or river basins.

Young's concept of transboundary externalities refers to activities that occur wholly within the jurisdiction of individual states but produce results affecting the welfare of those residing in other jurisdictions.[30] Transboundary externalities include the consequences of environmental accidents, such as the 1986 explosion at the Chernobyl nuclear power plant in the former Soviet Union, and the loss of biological diversity, measured in the potential for the development of new pharmaceuticals, caused by the destruction of tropical forests. Linked issues refer to cases where efforts to deal with environmental concerns have unintended consequences affecting other regimes, and vice versa. The most controversial issue of this type is the link between efforts to protect the environment and to promote economic development within countries or trade between countries. For example, does the protection of the stratospheric ozone layer and the global climate system mean that developing countries must forgo the use of products or resources, such as fossil fuels, that have played key roles in the development of industrialized societies?[31]

All sectors of the international community are involved in addressing these clusters of global environmental issues. There are multilateral agreements aimed at reducing environmental threats. The policies and actions of various international institutions affecting the environment are an integral part of the issue area. The development-assistance agencies of large donor countries, United Nations agencies such as the United Nations Development Programme (UNDP) and the Food and Agriculture Organization (FAO), multilateral financial institutions such as the World Bank and International Monetary Fund (IMF), and the World Trade Organization (WTO) make decisions that have impacts on the environment. These institutions are the targets of lobbying and pressure not only from states but also from nonstate actors, including nongovernmental organizations (NGOs) and multinational actors.

States have different combinations of internal economic and political forces that influence their policies toward environmental issues. Because the actual costs and risks of environmental degradation are never distributed equally among all states, some are less motivated than others to participate in international efforts to reduce environmental threats. Nor do states have the same perceptions of equitable solutions to environmental issues. Yet, despite these disparate interests, states must strive for consensus, at least among those that significantly contribute to and are significantly affected by a given environmental problem.

One of the distinctive features of global environmental politics is the importance of veto power. For every global environmental issue there exists one state or group of states whose cooperation is so essential to a successful agreement for coping with the problem that it has the potential to block strong international action. When these states oppose an agreement or try to weaken it, they become **veto** or **blocking states** and form **veto coalitions**.

The role of veto coalitions is central to the dynamics of bargaining and negotiation in global environmental politics. On the issue of a whaling moratorium, for example, four states, led by Japan, accounted for three-fourths of the whaling catch worldwide; they could therefore make or break a global regime to save the whales. Similarly, the "Miami" group (Argentina, Australia, Canada, Chile, the United States, and Uruguay), which consists of major grain exporters, blocked consensus on a Biosafety Protocol under the Convention on Biological Diversity in February 1999 for fear that the proposed provisions on trade in genetically modified crops would be too stringent and would hamper grain exports.[32]

Veto power is so important that even economically powerful states are not free to impose a global environmental agreement on much less powerful states if the latter are strongly opposed to it and critical to the agreement's success. For example, industrialized countries could not pressure tropical forest countries such as Brazil, Indonesia, and Malaysia to accept a binding agreement on the world's forests during the 1992 United Nations Conference on Environment and Development (UNCED), also known as the Earth Summit. Moreover, in global environmental negotiations, weaker states can use their veto power to demand compensation and other forms of favorable treatment. This occurred during the expansion of the ozone-layer regime when India and China led a coalition of developing countries that successfully demanded a financial mechanism that would provide resources to assist them in meeting the higher costs of using the alternative chemicals.

A second characteristic of global environmental politics is that the political dynamics of issues often reflect the roles of state actors in the international trade of a particular product. The issue of international hazardous waste trading, for instance, is shaped by the relationship between industrialized countries that are exporting the waste and developing countries that are potential importers. The issue of international trade in endangered species is defined by the roles of the developing countries that export illegal wildlife products and the major economies that import them. And trade relations between tropical timber exporters and consuming nations are critical to the dynamics of tropical deforestation.

For each of these issues, the roles and relative bargaining influences tend to be defined by a country's position in international trade in the product. In some cases, producing-exporting countries have veto power; in others, the importing countries have it. For tropical deforestation, producers and importers have roughly equal veto power within the context of the International Tropical Timber Council. But industrialized states and developing states do not have equal veto power in most global environmental regimes. Although some developing states may be able to prevent an agreement from being reached or to bargain for special treatment on some environmental issues, the major economic powers can wield veto power on most of the regimes they negotiate. This broader veto power results from their important economic role in production and consumption as well as their ability to deny funding for a regime if they oppose it.

A third characteristic of global environmental politics is that economic power can affect the positions of states, and even the outcome of bargaining on international agreements in some circumstances, whereas military power is not useful for influencing such outcomes. The ability of a country to give or withhold economic benefits, such as access to markets or economic assistance, can persuade states dependent on those benefits to go along with that power's policy if the benefits are more important than the issue at stake in the negotiations. Thus Japan and the Republic of Korea have accepted international agreements on drift-net fishing and whaling because they feared the loss of fishing benefits from the United States. And Japan succeeded in ensuring the support of some small non-whaling nations for its pro-whaling position by offering assistance to their fishing industries.

Military power has not affected negotiations on global environmental issues. Global environmental politics do not give rise to a **hegemonic** power in the traditional sense; that is, when a state enjoying superior military power coerces other states into accepting the hegemon's position. No positive correlation exists between dominant military power and leadership on global environmental issues, and there may be a negative correlation between the two in that high levels of military spending divert financial resources from environmental issues. Moreover, it is almost universally accepted that global environmental threats can be successfully addressed only through the active cooperation of the key actors. Using military force to enforce an environmental agreement would be impractical even if it were politically acceptable.

The fourth characteristic of the politics surrounding global environmental issues is that, despite the obstacles of veto power and sovereignty, the outcomes of multilateral bargaining processes usually result in cooperative efforts at curbing environmental threats. The overarching international political system encompassing negotiations on global environmental issues is a decentralized system in which sovereign states are free to act on their own definition of national interest. But during the past three decades, ever larger numbers of states have reached agreement in addressing global environmental problems, sometimes giving up freedom of action in the process. The ways in which sovereign states with divergent interests are able to act collectively is one of the major themes of this book.

The fifth characteristic of environmental politics is the importance of public opinion and nonprofit NGOs, especially environmental NGOs, which are national and international in scope. Environmental issues, like human rights issues, have mobilized the active political interest of large numbers of citizens in key countries, inducing shifts in policy that helped turn the tide in various environmental issues. Public opinion, channeled through electoral politics and NGOs, has had a substantial, if not decisive, influence on the outcomes of global bargaining on whaling, endangered species, hazardous wastes, ozone depletion, and climate change. Public opinion has not played comparable roles in the security and economic issue areas, which tend to be much more heavily dominated by bureaucratic or economic elites. This situation may be changing, however, as indicated in the recent international action taken to ban land-mines, and in popular votes rejecting further integration within the European Union.

INTERNATIONAL REGIMES
IN ENVIRONMENTAL POLITICS

The Concept of International Regimes

Understanding the nature of global environmental politics entails recognizing the importance of **international regimes.** The concept of international regime has been defined in two very different ways. According to the first definition, a regime is a set of norms, rules, or decisionmaking procedures, whether implicit or explicit, that produces some convergence in the actors' expectations in a particular issue area. In this broad definition, the concept may be applied to a wide range of international arrangements, from the coordination of monetary relations to superpower security relations. This way of conceiving regimes has been strongly criticized for including arrangements that are merely agreements to disagree and have no predictability or stability.[33] Although a set of norms or rules governing international behavior may exist in some issue areas in the absence of a formal international agreement, it is difficult to identify norms or rules in the global environmental area that are not defined by an explicit agreement.

The second definition of regime—and the one used in this book—is a system of principles, norms, rules, operating procedures, and institutions that actors create or accept to regulate and coordinate action in a particular issue area of international relations. Principles are beliefs of fact, causation, and rectitude. Norms are standards of behavior. Rules are specific prescriptions or proscriptions for action. Operating procedures are prevailing practices for work within the regime, including methods for making and implementing collective choice. Institutions are mechanisms and organizations for implementing, operating, evaluating, and expanding the regime and regime policy.[34]

Regimes are found in many areas of international relations, including trade, money, environment, human rights, managing the commons, communications, travel, and even security. As a result, regimes receive a good deal of theoretical and empirical attention from scholars of international relations and are one of the most significant recent offshoots of the longstanding inquiry into "cooperation under anarchy."[35] One important line of progenitor theories is marked by concern for the impact and mitigation of structural anarchy (the absence of a hierarchical structure governing international politics). A second flows from the constitutionalists, who studied treaties and the formal structure of international organizations, and from researchers employing the Institutional Process approach, which concentrates on an organization's actual operation.[36]

A third line of antecedents starts with the premise that, despite structural anarchy, extensive common interests exist among states and their people and that scholars and statesmen must learn how these interests can be realized. Present in eighteenth-century enlightened optimism, nineteenth-century liberalism and twentieth-century Wilsonian idealism, this view has more recently informed nonpositivist legal scholarship concerned with world order and argued that custom, patterned interaction, and the needs and wants of civilian populations are important sources of international law and require the respect of states.[37]

Functionalists began a fourth important line of predecessors. Functionalism, often associated with the work of David Mitrany, argues that the scholarly and political focus of international cooperation must center not on formal interstate politics but rather on providing opportunities for technical (nonpolitical) cooperation among specialists and specialized organizations

to solve common problems.[38] Functionalists argue that such technical cooperation can begin a process in which increasing interdependence and "spillover" (technical management in one area begetting technical management in
another) will present opportunities for organizing more and more government functions internationally and technically rather than nationally and
politically—a process that will slowly erode or bypass domestic regulators in
favor of global institutions.

Functionalism alone proved inadequate to explain action in an international
system in which politics is always a factor, states do not want to relinquish control, and technological determinism has not responded automatically to increasing interdependence. However, functionalist insights did influence
several important theoretical approaches, including neofunctionalist integration theory, transnational relations theory, turbulent fields, complex interdependence, and regimes.[39]

Neofunctional integration theory critiqued and extended functionalism,
arguing that gradual, regional integration is most important for understanding and creating effective international governance.[40] The approach added
politics (including the importance of states and individual political figures)
and regional encapsulation to functionalist strategies emphasizing spillover
and managed incremental advancements. This approach also lost favor, particularly when Ernst Haas, formerly a leading proponent, argued that focusing exclusively on regional encapsulation had become inadequate for
addressing new, "turbulent" issue areas of international relations characterized by competing interests and high degrees of complexity and interdependence. Haas argued that the interplay of knowledge, learning, and politics is
most important in managing turbulent issue areas and the conduct and
adaptability of international organizations.[41]

Research on transnational relations—nongovernmental interconnections
and interactions across national boundaries—argued similarly that interdependence can fracture international politics into distinct issue areas and that
states are neither the only important actors in international politics nor even
totally "coherent" actors.[42] These insights culminated in "complex interdependence," an alternative to realism as a paradigm for understanding international relations.[43] Regimes are the result of these concerns. If international
relations are increasingly interdependent, influenced by new types of actors
and interactions and fractured into issue areas across which power and interests vary, then how actors choose to manage these issue areas—the regimes
they create to manage them—is important to the conduct and study of international politics.

John Ruggie is often credited with introducing international regimes as "set[s] of mutual expectations, rules and regulations, plans, organizational energies and financial commitments, which have been accepted by a group of states."[44] Ernst Haas initially defined regimes as "collective arrangements among nations designed to create or more effectively use scientific and technical capabilities."[45] Robert Keohane and Joseph Nye first defined regimes instrumentally: "[B]y creating or accepting procedures, rules or institutions for certain kinds of activity, governments regulate and control transnational and interstate relations. We refer to these governing arrangements as international regimes." In the same work they defined a regime as a "network of rules, norms, and procedures that regulate behavior."[46] In 1983, a group of leading scholars working with Stephen Krasner attempted to standardize and extend regime study. Most definitions, including the one used in this volume, are variants of the definition developed in that study.[47]

There are international regimes for whaling, climate change, protection of endangered species, the prevention of ozone depletion, and many other environmental issues. Regimes are always created and operated through multilateral negotiations. Negotiations take place when states consider the status quo unacceptable. Quite often, states anticipate high costs, even crisis, if existing trends continue. Although reaching agreement on how to manage the problem is in a state's best interest, it is also in its interest to gain as much as possible while giving up as little as possible. Nevertheless, the expected value of the outcome to each state, and hence the total value of the outcome, must be positive or else there would be no incentive to negotiate or to accept the outcome. In multilateral negotiations, all states must win (or be better off than with no agreement) or they will not come to agreement.[48]

Most regimes take the form of a binding agreement, or legal instrument. On global environmental problems, the most common kind of legal instrument is the **convention;** this may either contain all the binding obligations expected to be negotiated or be followed by a more detailed legal instrument elaborating on its norms and rules. Because the members of international regimes, according to this definition, are states, the rules of the regime apply to the actions of states. However, the parties that engage in the activities governed by regimes are frequently private entities such as multinational corporations, banks, timber companies, and chemical companies. States participating in international regimes must therefore assume responsibility for ensuring that these entities comply with the norms and rules of the regime.[49]

If a convention is negotiated in anticipation that parties will negotiate one or more subsequent elaborating texts, it is called a **framework convention.**

Framework conventions usually establish a set of general principles, norms, and goals for cooperation on the issue (including a regular Conference of the Parties, or COP, to make policy and implementation decisions) rather than impose major binding obligations on the parties. A framework convention is followed by the negotiation of one or more **protocols**, which spell out specific obligations of the parties on the overall issue in question or on a narrower subissue. The negotiation of a framework convention and protocols may take several years, as they did for transboundary acid rain, ozone depletion, and climate change.

A nonbinding agreement could also be viewed as a regime to the extent that it establishes norms that influence state behavior. In global environmental politics, nonbinding codes of conduct and guidelines for global environmental problems such as land-based sources of marine pollution or sustainable forest management, which are referred to as **soft law,** could be considered regimes with varying degrees of effectiveness. And Agenda 21, the plan of action adopted at the 1992 Earth Summit, also could be considered an "umbrella regime" for worldwide sustainable development because it defined norms of behavior for a wide range of environment and development issues. Although such nonbinding agreements do influence state behavior to some extent, regimes based on legal instruments are usually more effective. That is why some countries become dissatisfied with a given nonbinding code of conduct or other soft-law agreement and insist that it should be turned into a legally binding agreement.

An Overview of Global Environmental Regimes

Thus far, global environmental regimes have been negotiated on a wide variety of issues from whale protection to climate change to desertification. These regimes vary from weak to quite strong in their effectiveness. The regime for whales grew out of the International Convention for the Regulation of Whaling (1946), which was not originally intended to be a regime for conserving whales but grew into a ban on whaling in 1985. The regime for marine oil pollution was originally the International Convention for the Prevention of Pollution of the Sea by Oil (1954), which was limited to a zone within 50 miles (80 kilometers) of the nearest coast, allowed significant deliberate oil spillage, and had no reliable enforcement system.[50] It was so ineffective that it was replaced by the International Convention for the Prevention of Pollution from Ships (1973), also known as the MARPOL Convention, which limited oil discharges at sea, prohibited them in certain sensitive zones, and set minimum distances from land for the discharge of various pollutants. The MARPOL Convention was so strongly opposed by shipping interests in crucial maritime states that it did not enter into force until a decade later.

The Convention on the Prevention of Marine Pollution by Dumping of Wastes and Other Matter, or London Convention (1972), established a regime to prohibit the dumping of some substances, including high-level radioactive wastes, and to require permits for others. It was the first marine-pollution agreement to accept the right of coastal states to enforce prohibitions against pollution. It became an important forum for negotiating further controls on ocean dumping.

Until the 1970s, virtually all international treaties relating to wildlife conservation were lacking in binding legal commitments and were ineffective in protecting migratory birds and other species. The first global convention on wildlife conservation that had strong legal commitments and an enforcement mechanism was the Convention on International Trade in Endangered Species of Wild Fauna and Flora, or CITES (1973). It set up a system of trade sanctions and a worldwide reporting network to curb the traffic in endangered species, but it also contained loopholes that allowed states having interests in a particular species to opt out of the controls on it.

The original regime to regulate acid rain that crosses borders before falling was the Convention on Long-Range Transboundary Air Pollution (1979), a framework convention that did not commit the signatories to specific reductions in their emissions of the compounds. Later, however, the regime was strengthened by the addition of eight protocols that address long-term financing for the Cooperative Programme for Monitoring and Evaluation of the Long-Range Transmission of Air Pollutants in Europe (1984), the reduction of sulfur emissions (1985 and 1994), the control of nitrogen oxides (1988), the control of emissions of volatile organic compounds (1991), heavy metals (1998), persistent organic pollutants (1998), and the abatement of acidification, eutrophication, and ground-level ozone (1999).

Similarly, the initial framework convention for the ozone regime, the Vienna Convention for the Protection of the Ozone Layer (1985), did not commit the parties to reduce the consumption of ozone-depleting chemicals. The Montreal Protocol (1987) represented the first real step toward protecting the ozone layer by requiring reductions in the consumption of certain chlorofluorocarbons (CFCs). The regime was subsequently strengthened significantly by a series of amendments and adjustments, beginning in 1990, so that it now mandates phasing out the use of CFCs and almost all other ozone-depleting substances.

The agreement establishing a regime on transboundary shipments of hazardous wastes is the Basel Convention on the Control of Transboundary Movements of Hazardous Wastes and Their Disposal (1989), which does not prohibit the trade but establishes conditions for it. But dissatisfaction with the agreement on the part of developing countries, especially in Africa, resulted in an agreement by the parties to the Basel Convention on a complete ban on waste exports. The international regime on fisheries is composed of a number of different agreements. Key components include the 1995 United Nations Agreement for the Implementation of the Provisions of the United Nations Convention on the Law of the Sea of 10 December 1982 Relating to the Conservation and Management of Straddling Fish Stocks and Highly Migratory Fish Stocks, as well as two nonbinding agreements, the 1995 FAO Code of Conduct for Responsible Fisheries and the 1999 FAO International Plan of Action for the Management of Fishing Capacity, and numerous regional fisheries agreements.

A regime for biodiversity conservation was established with the signing of the Convention on Biological Diversity (1992). Although the biodiversity convention does not obligate parties to measurable conservation objectives, it requires development of national strategies for the conservation of biodiversity.

A global regime to control toxic chemicals centers on the 1998 Rotterdam Convention on the Prior Informed Consent Procedure for Certain Hazardous Chemicals and Pesticides in International Trade (PIC) and 2001 Stockholm Convention on Persistent Organic Pollutants (POPs). It can also be thought to include the Basel Convention as well as long-standing activities associated with the International Programme on Chemical Safety, the Inter-Organization Programme on the Sound Management of Chemicals, the Intergovernmental Forum on Chemical Safety, and the nascent Strategic Approach to International Chemicals Management initiative. But despite years of international activity in this area, only the Stockholm Convention includes specific and binding restrictions on the production and use of certain toxic chemicals, provisions that significantly strengthen the chemicals regime.

The regime for climate change, the Framework Convention on Climate Change (1992), did not originally impose targets and timetables for emissions of greenhouse gases. With the adoption of the Kyoto Protocol (1997), however, parties agreed to reduce their overall emissions of six greenhouse gases by at least 5 percent below 1990 levels between 2008 and 2012. The Convention to Combat Desertification (1994), which established a regime to address the problem of **desertification,** the desert-like conditions that result from the destruction of formerly productive lands' biological potential, calls for countries to draw up integrated national programs in consultation with local communities.

Theoretical Approaches to International Regimes

Several major theoretical approaches have been used to explain the concept of international regimes, how they come into existence, and why they change.[51] These include the structural, the game-theoretic, the institutional bargaining, and the epistemic communities approaches. Each may help explain one or more international regimes, but each fails to account for all the regimes described and analyzed in this book. The structural—or hegemonic power—approach holds that the primary factor determining regime formation and change is the relative strength of the state actors involved in a particular issue and that "stronger states in the issue system will dominate the weaker ones and determine the rules of the game."[52] This approach suggests that strong international regimes are a function of a hegemonic state that can exercise leadership over weaker states and that the absence of such a hegemonic state is likely to frustrate regime formation.

The structural approach can be viewed in two ways, one stressing coercive power, the other focusing on "public goods." In the coercive power variant, regimes are set up by hegemonic states that use their military and economic leverage over other states to bring them into regimes, as the United States did in setting up trade and monetary regimes immediately after World War II.[53] The second variant views the same postwar regimes as the result of a hegemonic power's adopting policies that create public goods; that is, benefits open to all states who want to participate, such as export markets in the United States and the dollar as a stable currency for international payments.

However useful the structural approach has been to explain the post–World War II global economic systems, it cannot explain why global environmental regimes have been negotiated. The international regimes negotiated since the 1980s, including environmental regimes, have come about even though the United States, which had been the hegemon in the past, has been constrained by two factors: the rise of competing economic powers in Japan and Europe and, from 1981 to 1993, and again since 2001, a U.S. ideological hostility toward international environmental regulation. The successfully negotiated environmental regimes have depended on wide consensus among a number of states, not on imposition by the United States.[54]

Another approach to regime creation is based on game theory and utilitarian models of bargaining. In game theory, bargaining is distinguished by the number of parties involved, the nature of the conflict (zero-sum or non-zero-sum), and an assumption that the actors are rational (they cannot pursue their own interests independently of the choices of other actors). This approach suggests that small groups of states or coalitions are more likely to be successful in negotiating an international regime than a large number because each player can more readily understand the bargaining strategies of other players. Fen Osler Hampson took this approach into account when he analyzed the process of regime creation as an effort by a small coalition of states to form a regime by exercising leadership over a much larger number of national actors.[55]

Because of the importance of veto power in global environmental politics, however, relatively small groups of states are no more likely to form regimes than much larger ones. If veto states are included among a small group, they will be just as prone to opposition as they would have been in a large group of states. If veto states are left outside the small group, they will still be in a position to frustrate regime formation when it is enlarged.

A third approach, which has been called the institutional bargaining model of regime creation, hypothesizes that because states are ultimately concerned with protecting national security and maintaining economic growth, they may be incapable of adequately addressing the fundamental problems that have given rise to environmental issues. The international community's ability to preserve the quality of the planet for future generations depends on international cooperation, which, in turn, requires effective international institutions to guide international behavior. Under this approach, institutions can be defined as "persistent and connected sets of rules and practices that prescribe behavioral roles, constrain activity, and shape expectations."[56] They may be bureaucratic organizations, regimes, or conventions.

The global environmental negotiations that have resulted in the formation of regimes suggest, however, that lack of clarity about the interests of the actors is seldom, if ever, the factor that makes regimes possible. As will be shown in chapter 3, environmental issues do not arise from imperfect information about the problems but from factors that have induced veto states to make the necessary concessions for the establishment or strengthening of regimes.

A fourth approach is the epistemic communities model, which emphasizes the impact of international learning and transnational networks of experts and bureaucrats, primarily on the basis of scientific research on a given problem, as a factor influencing the evolution of regimes.[57] This approach, advanced initially to explain the adherence to and compliance with the Mediterranean Action Plan, identifies intra-elite shifts within and outside governments as the critical factor in the convergence of state policies in support of a stronger regime. The shifts empowered technical and scientific specialists allied with officials of international organizations. These elites thus formed transnational epistemic communities, that is, communities of experts sharing common values and approaches to policy problems.

The importance of scientific evidence and scientific expertise in the politics of some key global environmental issues cannot be ignored. Global warming and ozone depletion, involving threats that cannot always be detected, much less understood, without scientific research, have been defined to an extent by the judgments of scientists. A significant degree of scientific consensus has sometimes been a minimum condition for serious international action on an issue. A 1985 agreement to reduce sulfur dioxide emissions by 30 percent of 1980 levels was made possible by mounting scientific evidence of the damaging effects on European forests. The impetus for an agreement to phase out CFCs in 1990 was scientific evidence that the ozone layer was much thinner than had previously been thought. The Kyoto Protocol to the Framework Convention on Climate Change was made possible, in part, by the Second Assessment Report of the Intergovernmental Panel on Climate Change (IPCC), which found that the earth's temperature had increased and that there is a "discernible human influence" on climate.

But although scientific elites may play a supportive and enabling role in certain environmental negotiations, on other issues they remain divided or even captured by particular government or private interests. And on some issues, such as the whaling ban, the hazardous waste trade, the Antarctic, the loss of biodiversity, and the ocean dumping of radioactive wastes, scientists have contributed little to regime formation and/or strengthening. Either scientific elites were not particularly influential in policymaking or else key actors explicitly rejected scientific findings as the basis for decision.[58]

The case studies presented in chapter 3 suggest that theoretical approaches based solely on a **unitary actor model** (one suggesting that state actors can be treated as though they are a single entity encompassing one internally consistent set of values and attitudes), ignoring the roles of domestic sociopolitical structures and processes, are likely to be poor bases for analyzing and predicting the outcomes of global environmental bargaining. Negotiating positions usually reflect domestic sociopolitical balances and may change dramatically because of a shift in those balances. Although the structure of an issue in terms of economic interests may indicate which states are most likely to join a veto coalition, domestic political pressures and bargaining usually tip the balance for or against regime creation or strengthening. A theoretical explanation for global environmental regime formation or change, therefore, must incorporate the variable of state actors' domestic politics.

A theoretical model of regime formation and strengthening, therefore, should link international political dynamics with domestic politics and view the whole as a "two-level game." While representatives of countries are maneuvering the outcome of bargaining over regime issues, officials must also bargain with interest groups within their domestic political systems. Because the two processes often take place simultaneously, the arenas influence each other and become part of the games going on at each level.[59]

A theoretical explanation for the formation of global environmental regimes must also leave room for the importance of the rules of the negotiating forum and the linkages between the negotiations on regimes and the wider relationships among the negotiating parties. The legal structure of the negotiating forum, the "rules of the game" regarding who may participate and how authoritative decisions are to be made, are particularly important when the negotiations take place within an already established treaty or organization. The whaling case illustrates how these rules can be crucial in determining the outcomes of the negotiations.

Economic and political ties among key state actors can also sway a veto state to compromise or defect. Particularly when the global environmental regime under negotiation does not involve issues that are central to the economy of the states that could block agreement, the formation or strengthening of a regime is sometimes made possible by the potential veto state's concern about how a veto would affect relations with states that are important for economic or political reasons.

Building a theoretical approach that accounts for actual historical patterns of regime formation and regime strengthening and that can predict most outcomes will require advancing a series of testable hypotheses encompassing multiple variables rather than relying on a single-variable approach. Because such explicit hypotheses have yet not been generated and tested, the study of regime formation in this book will focus primarily on identifying some common patterns through case studies. A phased process approach will be used to analyze the negotiations that result in the establishment of environmental regimes.

PARADIGM SHIFT AND ENVIRONMENTAL POLITICS

In all issue areas, public policy and regimes are shaped not only by impersonal forces, such as technological innovation and economic growth, but also by people's, governments', and institutions' perception of reality. In times of relative social stability, there is a dominant social **paradigm,** a set of beliefs, ideas, and values from which public policies and entire systems of behavior flow logically. A view of the world emerges as the dominant social paradigm within a society because it has been the most useful way of thinking about and solving certain problems and is transmitted across social sectors and generations by various socialization processes. Every dominant paradigm is ultimately challenged, however, as its anomalies—the contradictions between its assumptions and observed reality—multiply and its usefulness wanes. Finally, it gives way to a new paradigm through a process known as a paradigm shift.[60] The hypothesis that an alternative paradigm, one showing more sensitivity to environmental realities, may be on the horizon provides a lens through which to view the issues discussed in the rest of this book.

The Dominant Social Paradigm

Because economic policy and environmental policy are so intertwined, the social paradigm that has dominated public understanding of environmental management during the period of rapid global economic growth has been essentially a system of beliefs about economics. It has been referred to as the exclusionist paradigm because it excludes human beings from the laws of nature. It has also been called frontier economics, suggesting the sense of unlimited resources that characterizes a society living on an open frontier.[61]

In capitalist societies, this dominant social paradigm has been based primarily on the assumptions of **neoclassical economics:** first, that the free market will always maximize social welfare; and second, that there exists an infinite supply not only of natural resources but also of "sinks" for disposing the wastes that accrue from exploiting those resources—provided that the free market is operating. Humans will not deplete any resource, according to this worldview, as long as technology is given free rein and prices are allowed to fluctuate enough to stimulate the search for substitutes; in this way, absolute scarcity can be postponed to the indefinite future.[62] Waste disposal is viewed as a problem to be cleaned up after the fact but not at the cost of interference with market decisions.[63] Because conventional economic theory is concerned with the allocation of scarce resources, and nature is not considered a constraining factor, this paradigm considers the environment irrelevant to economics.

(Despite a different economic and political ideology, the former Soviet Union and other Communist states also shared this assumption.) The traditional legal principles of unrestricted freedom of the seas and open access to common resources such as the oceans and their living resources buttressed the exclusionist paradigm and weakened the impulse toward international cooperation for environmental protection.

In the early 1960s, the dominant paradigm came under steadily mounting attack, starting in the United States, where the critique of the dominant paradigm was first articulated, and then spreading to Europe and other regions. The publication in 1962 of Rachel Carson's *Silent Spring*, which documented the dangers to human health from synthetic pesticides, was the beginning of an explosion in popular literature reflecting the new scientific knowledge about invisible threats to the environment, among them radiation, heavy metal toxic wastes, and chlorinated hydrocarbons in the water. Research and writing on these subjects helped raise awareness that public policies based on the exclusionist paradigm carry high costs to societies. The first mass movement for environmental protection, which focused on domestic issues, developed in the United States. Parallel changes in public concern about air, soil, and water pollution also occurred in other non-Communist industrialized countries. One result of the burst of environmental activism in the United States was the passage of the National Environmental Policy Act of 1969 (NEPA), which directed federal agencies to support international cooperation in "anticipating and preventing a decline in the quality of mankind's world environment."[64]

As a result of a 1967 Swedish initiative supported by the United States, the first worldwide environmental conference in history, the United Nations Conference on the Human Environment, was convened in Stockholm in 1972. The Stockholm Conference, attended by 114 states (not including the Soviet bloc states), approved a declaration containing twenty-six broad principles on the management of the global environment along with an action plan containing 109 recommendations for international cooperation on the environment. On the recommendation of the conference, the UN General Assembly in December 1972 created the United Nations Environment Programme to provide a focal point for environmental action and coordination of environmentally related activities within the UN system.

The Rise of an Alternative Social Paradigm

The rapid rise of environmental consciousness in the 1960s and early 1970s attacked the dominant paradigm but did not yet produce an alternative set of assumptions about physical and social reality that could become a competing worldview. The essential assumptions of classical economics remained largely intact. Confronted with evidence that existing patterns of resource exploitation could cause irreversible damage, proponents of classical economics continued to maintain that such exploitation was still economically rational.[65]

During the 1970s and 1980s, however, an alternative paradigm challenging the assumptions of classical economics began to take shape. Two of the intellectual forerunners of this paradigm were the *Limits to Growth* study by the Club of Rome, published in 1972, and the *Global 2000 Report to the President,* released by the U.S. Council of Environmental Quality and the Department of State in 1980.[66] Both studies applied global-systems computer modeling to the projected interactions among future trends in population, economic growth, and natural resources. They also predicted the depletion of natural resources and the degradation of ecosystems. Because each of the studies suggested that economic development and population growth were on a path that would eventually strain the earth's "carrying capacity" (the total population that the earth's natural systems can support without undergoing degradation), the viewpoint underlying the studies was generally referred to as the limits-to-growth perspective.

These studies were widely criticized by defenders of the dominant paradigm, among them Herman Kahn and Julian Simon, for projecting the depletion of nonrenewable resources without taking into account technological changes and market responses. These critics argued that overpopulation would not become a problem because people are the world's "ultimate resource," and they characterized the authors of studies based on global-systems models as "no-growth elitists" who would freeze the developing countries out of the benefits of economic growth. They argued that human ingenuity would enable humanity to leap over the alleged limits to growth through new and better technologies.[67]

The development of an alternative paradigm regarding the world society and environment was set back in the United States in the early 1980s when the Reagan administration enthusiastically embraced the exclusionist paradigm. But meanwhile, knowledge about ecological principles and their relationship to economic development was spreading and the web of specialists on these linkages was thickening worldwide. A global community of practitioners and scholars was emerging, allied by the belief that economic policies based on the dominant paradigm had to be replaced by ecologically sound policies.

By the early to mid–1980s, **sustainable development** was emerging as the catchword of an alternative paradigm. It was being heard with increasing frequency in conferences involving NGOs and government officials in the United States and abroad.[68] The publication in 1987 of *Our Common Future,* the Report of the World Commission on Environment and Development (better known as the Brundtland Report after the commission's chair, former Norwegian prime minister Gro Harlem Brundtland) popularized the term *sustainable development* and gave the new paradigm momentum in replacing the dominant paradigm.[69] Drawing on and synthesizing the views and research of hundreds of people worldwide, that report codified some of the central beliefs of the alternative paradigm.

The Brundtland Report defined sustainable development as development that is "consistent with future as well as present needs." Its central themes criticized the dominant paradigm for failure to reconcile those needs. It asserted that the earth's natural systems have finite capabilities to support human production and consumption and that the continuation of existing economic policies carries the risk of irreversible damage to the natural systems on which all life depends.

The sustainable development paradigm emphasizes the need to redefine the term *development*. It posits that economic growth cannot continue at the expense of the earth's natural capital (its stock of renewable and nonrenewable resources) and vital natural support systems such as the ozone layer and climate system. Instead, the world economy must learn to live off its "interest." That means reducing the amount of energy used per unit of gross national product and shifting from fossil fuels to greater reliance on renewable energy sources over the next several decades. It implies a rapid transition to sustainable systems of renewable natural resource management and efforts to stabilize world population at the lowest possible level.[70] This viewpoint also suggests, although not always explicitly, the need to impose limits on total worldwide consumption.

The sustainable development paradigm assumes the need for greater equity not only between wealthy and poor nations but also within societies and between generations (**intergenerational equity**). Highly industrialized countries such as the United States, which use a disproportionate share of the world's environmental resources, are seen as pursuing economic growth that is inherently unsustainable, as are societies in which the distribution of land and other resources is grossly unequal. Sustainable development further holds that future generations have an equal right to use the earth's resources.[71] The paradigm recognizes that developing countries must meet the basic needs of the poor in ways that do not deplete the countries' natural resources, and it also points to a need to reexamine basic attitudes and values in industrialized countries regarding the unnecessary and wasteful aspects of their material abundance.[72]

One of the main anomalies of the classical economic paradigm is its measure of macroeconomic growth, that is, gross national product (GNP). Advocates of sustainable development have noted that GNP fails to reflect the real physical capability of an economy to provide material wealth in the future or to take into account the relative well-being of the society in general. Thus, a country could systematically deplete its natural resources, erode its soils, and pollute its waters without that loss of real wealth ever showing up in its income accounts. Because of the rise of the alternative paradigm, some economists began in the second half of the 1980s to study how to correct this anomaly in conventional accounting and to advocate **environmental accounting** for all governments and international organizations.[73] Critics have proposed alternatives to GNP, such as "real net national product," "sustainable social net national product," or "index of sustainable economic welfare," that include changes in environmental resources as well as other indicators that measure human welfare. Of particular importance is the United Nations Development Programme's (UNDP) annual Human Development Report, which uses "human indicators" to rate the quality of life in all countries by other than economic measures, including literacy, life expectancy, and respect for women's rights.[74] The Himalayan Kingdom of Bhutan has proposed measuring well-being not through GNP but through Gross National Happiness, a concept that encompasses economic development, governance, cultural preservation, and environmental preservation.[75] The "Environmental Sustainability Index" ranks countries on twenty-one elements of sustainability covering natural resource endowments, past and present pollution levels, environmental management efforts, contributions to the protection of the global commons, and a society's capacity to improve its environmental performance over time.[76]

The alternative paradigm points to the failure of markets to encourage the sustainable use of natural resources. Prices should reflect the real costs to society of producing and consuming a given resource, but conventional free-market economic policies systematically underprice or ignore natural resources.[77] Public policies that do not correct for market failure encourage overconsumption and thus the more rapid depletion of renewable resources and the degradation of **environmental services.** (Environmental services are the conserving or restorative functions of nature, for example, the conversion of carbon dioxide to oxygen by plants and the cleansing of water by wetlands.) Raising the prices of resources through taxation to make them reflect real social and environmental costs is the favored means of showing the rates of consumption of energy and tropical timber. **Green taxes** are one tool by which the "polluter pays" principle, endorsed in the Earth Summit's Rio Declaration on Environment and Development, may be implemented. Placing an upper limit on consumption is another method.[78]

The process of paradigm shift began in the early 1990s. The sustainable development paradigm began to displace the exclusionist paradigm in some parts of the multilateral financial institutions, in some state bureaucracies, and in some parliamentary committees dealing with the environment and development. For instance, publications of the Asian Development Bank, the Inter-American Development Bank (IDB), and the Organization of American States (OAS) as early as 1990 impugned mistaken unsustainable development paths of the past and recommended new sustainable development strategies.[79] In 1992, Al Gore, a former U.S. senator and vice president of the United States, published *Earth in the Balance,* in which he declared himself a proponent of a paradigm shift. Gore advocated a new kind of "eco-nomics," one that involves reorienting economic activity toward environmentally sensitive production and investment in future resources. He proposed a global Marshall Plan to stabilize population growth, develop and use "environmentally appropriate technologies," negotiate new international treaties, and increase education about global environmental issues.[80]

The 1992 Earth Summit

The alternative paradigm gained credibility through the United Nations Conference on Environment and Development, also known as the "Earth Summit," held in Rio de Janeiro in June 1992. UNCED was preceded by two years of discussions on domestic environmental and poverty problems and global environment issues, especially questions of North-South inequities and responsibility. The conference, which drew the participation of 110 heads of state, nearly 10,000 official delegates from 150 countries, and thousands of NGO representatives, was a monumental effort by the international community to reach consensus on principles and a long-term work plan for global sustainable development. Conceptually, its explicit focus on integrating environmental and development policies represented a major step forward from the Stockholm Conference on the Human Environment of twenty years earlier.

Earth Pledge

Recognizing that people's actions towards nature and each other are the source of growing damage to the environment and resources needed to meet human needs and to ensure survival and develo

I PLEDGE to act to the best of my ability to help make the Earth a secure and hospitable home for present and future generations.

PHOTO 1.1   UNCED, Rio, 1992. NGO representatives join hundreds of thousands who signed the Earth Pledge leading up to the Earth Summit. Photo by Charles V. Barber, World Resources Institute.

The major output of UNCED was a nonbinding agreement called Agenda 21 (referring to the twenty-first century), which is a global plan of action for more sustainable societies. Negotiations on Agenda 21 were among the broadest and most complex international talks ever held. The 294-page comprehensive Agenda 21 encompassed every sectoral environmental issue as well as international policies affecting environment and development, and the full range of domestic social and economic policies, all adding up to thirty-eight chapters and 115 topics. The conference also produced two nonbinding sets of principles—the Rio Declaration on Environment and Development and the Statement of Forest Principles—that helped create norms and expectations. The climate and biodiversity conventions, which were negotiated independently of the UNCED process on parallel tracks, were opened for signature at the Earth Summit and are often mentioned as UNCED-related agreements.

Negotiations on Agenda 21 registered the state of international consensus on the full range of issues affecting the long-run sustainability of human society, including domestic social and economic policies, international economic relations, and cooperation on global commons issues. On domestic policies, the developing countries accepted the principles of citizen participation in sustainable development. In chapters on poverty, sustainable agriculture, desertification, and land degradation, provisions were adopted calling for the decentralization of natural resources management to the community level, giving rural populations and indigenous peoples land titles or other land rights, and expanding services such as credit and agricultural extension for rural communities. The chapter on major groups called on governments to adopt national strategies for eliminating the obstacles to women's full participation in sustainable development by the year 2000.[81]

Among the more important norms agreed to in the document, despite the reluctance of developing countries and some industrialized countries, are provisions calling for the removal or reduction of subsidies that are inconsistent with sustainable development (such as the sale of U.S. timber from public lands at prices below the full costs of production) and the improvement of price signals through environmental charges or taxes. Implementation of those norms would be a major step toward more sustainable development worldwide.[82]

The issue of inequitable consumption patterns as a cause of global environmental degradation was elevated to a new status in international politics at the insistence of the developing countries. The issue was woven through several chapters of Agenda 21 as well as the Rio Declaration and the Statement of Forest Principles, making it a major theme of the conference. Industrialized countries were asked to accept responsibility to change their "unsustainable lifestyles."

Delegates agreed upon a number of proposals to create new global environmental regimes or strengthen existing ones. Agenda 21 called for negotiations on toxic chemicals, the depletion of the world's fish stocks, land-based sources of marine pollution, desertification, and the unique environmental and development problems faced by Small Island Developing States. Agenda 21 also addressed issues from sustainable human settlements to sustainable agriculture, solid waste and sewage, freshwater resources, air pollution, deforestation, mountains, and radioactive waste.

The questions of financial resources, **technology transfer** (the transfer of scientific and technological knowledge, patents, or equipment, usually from the most industrialized nations to the less-developed ones), education, and capacity building for implementing Agenda 21 and global environmental agreements formed the core of the compact reached at Rio and remain a cen-

CARTOON 1.1   "It's a deal . . . you continue to overpopulate the planet while we squander its natural resources." Copyright 1992 by the *Miami Herald,* reprinted with permission.

tral issue today. The agreement reached in Rio was essentially that developing countries would try to put into practice more environmentally sound development policies if the industrialized countries agreed to provide the necessary support, that is, "new and additional" financial resources, technology transfer on concessional and preferential terms, and assistance with capacity building, education, and training.

Agenda 21 also commits all countries to expand their national statistical accounts by including environmental factors and unpaid work.[83] Yet, more than a decade later, few of these countries have been able to live up to their commitments. National Agenda 21 efforts have led to academic debates, heightened public awareness, and minor adjustments in the system of national accounts and taxation rules, but they have not fundamentally altered the way we manage and measure our national economy.

Paradigm Shift?

Within most of the powerful institutions in the United States and elsewhere in the industrialized world, the assumptions of the exclusionist paradigm still tend to dominate policymaking. Corporations, government ministries deal-ing with trade and finance, the leaders of some political parties, and some of the top officials of the World Bank and other multilateral institutions have been slow to change. National political agendas continue to be determined by interest groups dominated by commerce and industry who are locked on old paradigms, while in the meantime the power of national authorities and national democratic institutions has been gradually eroded by the globaliza-tion of industry, finance, technology, and information.[84]

Has the alternative social paradigm—or sustainable development para-digm—failed? This was one of the questions delegates and observers asked themselves as they gathered in Johannesburg, South Africa, in September 2002 at the World Summit on Sustainable Development (WSSD), to review the implementation of Agenda 21 and the other agreements adopted at the Earth Summit in 1992. Martin Khor of the Malaysian-based Third World Network argues that although the sustainable development paradigm has failed, it is not because it is weak but because it was not given the chance to be implemented. Instead, the 1990s and the beginning of the twenty-first century have been dominated by a variation of the exclusionist paradigm—**"globalization."**[85] Globalization has become identified with a number of trends, including a greater international movement of commodities, money, information, and people; and the development of technology, orga-nizations, legal systems, and infrastructures to allow this movement. Eco-nomic globalization means globe-spanning economic relationships. The interrelationships of markets, finance, goods and services, and the net-works created by transnational corporations are the most important mani-festations of this.

Khor and others see the globalization paradigm as different from the sus-tainable development paradigm; they argue that it advocates the reduction or removal of regulations on the market, lets free market forces reign, and grants a high degree of rights and freedoms to the large corporations that dominate the market. Khor notes that when extended to the international level, the globalization paradigm

advocates liberalization of international markets, breaking down national eco-nomic barriers, and granting rights to corporations to see and invest in any country of their choice without restraints or conditions. Governments should not interfere with the free play of the market, and social or developmental con-cerns (for instance, obtaining grants from developed countries to aid develop-ing countries) should be downgraded.[86]

One of the main factors in the ascendancy of the globalization paradigm and the marginalization of the sustainable development paradigm has been the actions of some of the most powerful developed countries. James Gustave Speth, the former UNDP administrator, argues that many U.S. policymakers have seen the globalization paradigm as supplanting the need for the sustainable development paradigm. "Trade, not aid" has become a Washington mantra. Moreover, even among those U.S. policymakers favorable to environment and development objectives, the priority given to the trade and globalization agenda has tended to occupy the available political space and crowd out sustainable development concerns. In the battle for attention, environment and development objectives have typically lost out.[87]

This said, Speth continues, the eclipse of the UNCED commitments has surely been brought about by more than the ascendancy of the globalization paradigm. The post–cold war period, for example, was supposed to bring a peace dividend of financial and political resources that could have been applied to promoting environmental and development objectives. Instead, the United States and others have been enmeshed in a series of military and peacekeeping engagements, now embracing the war on terrorism, that have consumed much of the available time, energy, and money.[88]

Will the dominant social paradigm retain its dominance or will the alternative social paradigm rise in popularity once again and have a chance at being implemented? A future paradigm shift will have to depend on a "revolution of social consciousness and values." According to Paul Raskin, a new sustainability paradigm is possible, but it will "happen only if key sectors of world society come to understand the nature and the gravity of the challenge, and seize the opportunity to revise their agendas."[89] Governments and, more important, people, do not necessarily change their behavior even when they are aware of the seriousness of a potential threat. With increased public debate and education about the importance of sustainable development in conjunction with changes in economic and political power, it is possible that the paradigm shift will be accelerated.

CONCLUSION

Global environmental politics involve interactions among states and nonstate actors that transcend a given region regarding international decisions that affect the environment and natural resources. The emergence of this issue area in world politics is a reflection of the growing awareness of the cumulative stresses on the earth's resources and life-support systems from economic activities during the past century.

Much of global environmental politics focuses on efforts to negotiate multilateral agreements for cooperation to protect the environment and natural resources. These agreements constitute global environmental regimes of varying effectiveness that govern state behavior in regard to the environmental problem in question.

Legitimate differences in economic, political, and environmental interests make achieving unanimity among states responsible for, and/or directly affected by, an environmental problem a political and diplomatic challenge. The ability of one or more states to block or weaken multilateral agreements is a primary problem in global environmental politics, and how to overcome such blockage is a major concern. For a regime to be formed, veto states and coalitions must be persuaded to abandon their opposition to a proposed regime, or at least to compromise with states supporting it.

Another obstacle has been a dominant social paradigm that justifies essentially unlimited exploitation of nature. Despite the weakening of that paradigm and the apparent widespread recognition of an alternative sustainable development paradigm, especially in conjunction with the 1992 Earth Summit, the shift to this alternative social paradigm has been complicated by the rise of globalization and a resurgence of the traditional paradigm. Subsequent chapters in this book will demonstrate the nature of the actors involved in global environmental politics and how their interests may either promote the alternative paradigm or retain the traditional paradigm of resource exploitation, and just what this entails for the future.

Theoretical approaches that have been advanced to explain the formation of international regimes include the structural, game-theoretic, institutional bargaining, and epistemic community models. These approaches fail to account for most global environmental regimes. To explain why environmental regimes are formed and strengthened, a theoretical approach will have to deal with the central problem of veto coalitions and why they are or are not overcome in regime negotiations. It will have to avoid relying solely on the unitary actor model and encompass domestic political forces, the structure of the negotiating forum, the interplay of economic interests, and the role of other international political concerns.

The subsequent chapters in this book will further explore these issues. Chapter 2 examines the actors who are responsible for the formation of global environmental policies, including the formation of environmental regimes. Although state actors are the final determinants of the outcomes of global environmental issues, since they negotiate the international legal instruments creating global environmental regimes and adopt international trade and financial policies that directly and indirectly affect the environment, nonstate actors have major roles to play as well. Nonstate actors, such as international organizations, nongovernmental organizations, and multinational corporations, help set the global environmental agenda, initiate and influence the process of regime formation, and carry out actions that directly affect the global environment.

Chapter 3 looks at the development of environmental regimes through the presentation of eleven global environmental issues on which there have been multilateral negotiations during the past twenty-five years: **transboundary air pollution,** ozone depletion, climate change, hazardous chemicals and waste, whaling, endangered species, biodiversity loss, desertification, forests, and fisheries. Each issue is analyzed according to the stages of negotiation and the role of veto coalitions in shaping the outcomes of bargaining.

The regime-building process does not end with the signing and ratification of a global environmental treaty. Therefore, chapter 4 looks at obstacles to creating, implementing, and complying with environmental treaties and the means of effective implementation, two issues that contribute to the success of an environmental regime. The first two sections examine factors that make it difficult to create regimes with strong control measures and for states to comply with them. The third section outlines methods to improve compliance and effectiveness. The final section discusses options for increasing the financing available to help implement global environmental regimes. Because the lack of adequate financial and technical resources seriously inhibits the ability of many developing countries to comply with environmental regimes, the question of financial resources has been at the center of global environmental policy for many years and will continue to be for the foreseeable future.

Chapter 5 focuses on the interplay between environmental issues and economic and social development as the three "pillars" of sustainable development. As linkages with economic relations and development have multiplied, the boundaries of global environmental politics have broadened. The first part of the chapter examines North-South economic relations vis-à-vis global environmental politics. Then we analyze the relationship between trade and the environment, a political and economic issue that demonstrates the challenges to achieving a paradigm shift. The chapter concludes with some thoughts on the past, present, and future of global environmental politics.

DISCUSSION QUESTIONS

1. Discuss the ways in which population and environmental factors interact. What is the effect on forests? On energy? Why is per capita consumption an issue?

2. Why are global environmental trends an issue now? Why weren't they an issue before the 1970s? What has changed physically and in people's consciousness?

3. What is a veto state? Why is it so important in global environmental politics?

4. What is an international regime? Describe the different forms it may take and the effectiveness of each type.

5. According to the different theoretical approaches described in this chapter, what factors make it easier or more difficult to achieve strong international agreement on a global environmental issue?

6. What method is currently used to measure macroeconomic growth and why is it an inadequate benchmark? How will alternative methods of measurement overcome the limitations of the present one?

2

◄○►

Actors in the
Environmental Arena

States are the most important actors in global environmental politics. States adopt broad economic, regulatory, trade, and development policies that impact the environment. States decide which issues receive formal consideration by the international community directly (by arguing for international action on an issue) and indirectly (through their membership in the governing councils of international organizations). States negotiate the international legal instruments that create and implement global environmental regimes. Donor states influence the effectiveness of these regimes and other environmental policies through bilateral aid programs and donations to implementation programs and multilateral banks.

But nonstate actors also exert major and increasing influence on global environmental politics. International organizations help to set the global environmental agenda, initiate and mediate the process of regime formation, and cooperate with developing countries on projects and programs directly affecting the environment. Nongovernmental organizations (NGOs) also participate in setting the agenda, influencing negotiations on regime formation, and shaping the environmental policies of donor agencies toward developing countries. Multinational corporations influence the bargaining over regime creation and carry out actions that directly affect the global environment.

NATION-STATE ACTORS: ROLES AND INTERESTS

The most important actions by state actors in global environmental politics are those relating to regime formation. In the negotiations on an environmental

41

regime, a state actor may play one of four roles: **lead state, supporting state, swing state,** or **veto** (or **blocking**) **state.** A lead state has a strong commitment to effective international action on the issue, moves the process of negotiations forward by proposing its own negotiating formula as the basis for an agreement, and attempts to win the support of other state actors.

A supporting state speaks in favor of a lead state's proposal in negotiations. A swing state demands a concession to its interests as the price for going along with an agreement, but not a concession that would significantly weaken the regime, such as a slower timetable for a phaseout. A veto or blocking state either opposes a proposed environmental regime outright or tries to weaken it to the point that it cannot be effective.

States may shift from what appears to be a veto role to a swing role because threatening a veto is sometimes the best means of enhancing bargaining leverage. For example, during the critical second Meeting of the Parties to the Montreal Protocol in London in June 1990, India and China rejected joining an agreement that would bind them to phase out CFCs in 2010 until the industrialized countries agreed to provide significant financial and technical assistance to developing countries to assist them in their transition to less harmful, but equally productive, chemicals and more advanced technology.

There may be more than one lead state on a given issue. Sweden and Norway were allied from the beginning in pushing for a long-range transboundary air pollution agreement, for example. But often one state steps forward to advance a policy that puts it clearly in the lead, as did West Germany on the climate change issue in 1990 and Canada on the fisheries issue in 1992. As issues go through several stages, the role of lead state may shift from one state or combination of states to another. In the negotiation of the Vienna Convention for the Protection of the Ozone Layer in 1985, Finland and Sweden took the lead by submitting their own draft convention and heavily influencing the draft put before the conference. In 1986, the United States stepped into the lead role by proposing an eventual 95 percent reduction in CFCs, and by 1989–1990 several OECD (Organization for Economic Cooperation and Development) states had become the lead states by working for a phaseout before 2000.

Lead states use a wide range of methods for influencing other state actors on a global environmental issue. A lead state may

- fund, produce, and/or call attention to research that defines the problem and demonstrates its urgency, as when Swedish research showed the serious damage done by acid rain, Canadian research re-

vealed long-range dangers posed by chemicals, and U.S.-based research revealed a threat to the earth's protective ozone layer;
- seek to educate public opinion in target states, as did Canada when it supplied U.S. tourists with pamphlets on the acidification of its forests and waters and instructed its Washington embassy to cooperate with like-minded U.S. environmental organizations;
- use its diplomatic clout to encourage an international organization to identify the issues as a priority, as when the United States and Canada persuaded the OECD to take up the ozone layer and CFCs;
- rely on the worldwide network of NGOs to support its position in other countries and at international conferences, as the Alliance of Small Island States (AOSIS) did in its effort to place quantitative limits on greenhouse gas emissions beyond 2000 in the negotiations on the Kyoto Protocol;
- make a diplomatic demarche to a state that is threatening a veto role, as the United States did with Japan on African elephant ivory; or
- pledge to commit financial or technical resources to the problem, such as the positive incentives that developed states accepted in the Montreal Protocol and Stockholm Convention, and so gain significant developing-country participation.

Although scientific-technological capabilities and economic power cannot ensure that a lead state will prevail on an environmental issue, they constitute valuable assets for helping to create a regime. When a big power like the United States has taken a lead role through scientific research, unilateral action, and diplomatic initiative, as it did on the issue of ozone protection in the 1970s and again in the mid-1980s, it helps to sway states that do not otherwise have clearly defined interests on the issue.

States play different roles on different issues. A lead state on one issue may be a potential veto state on another. Whether a state plays a lead, supporting, swing, or veto role in regard to a particular global environmental issue depends primarily on domestic political factors and on the relative costs and benefits of the proposed regime. A third variable, which has been important in some issues, is the anticipation of international political consequences, including increased prestige—or damage—to the country's image worldwide.

Domestic Political Factors

A state's definition of its interests with regard to a particular global environmental issue and its consequential choice of role turns largely on domestic economic and political interests and domestic ideological currents. Whether a government opposes, supports, or leads on an issue depends first on the relative strength and influence of powerful economic and bureaucratic forces and of domestic environmental constituencies. Ideological factors related to broader domestic political themes can also play prominent roles in the definition of interests.

Domestic economic interests are particularly prominent in promoting veto roles. When the Liberal Democratic Party dominated Japanese politics, for example, major trading companies generally received government support for their interests in whaling because of their close ties to the party.[1] Norway's fishery industry, which claims to have suffered declining fish catches because of the international protection of whales, has prevailed on the government of Norway to defend Norwegian whaling before the international community. Norway, Japan, and Greece have all tended to be swing or blocking actors on questions of marine pollution from oil tankers because of the economic importance of their shipping industries. Germany, Italy, the Netherlands, and Sweden, all of which have smaller shipping industries, were more flexible in negotiations on pollution from ships.[2]

A state's position on a global environmental issue sometimes reflects the interests of a dominant socioeconomic elite. Indonesia, for example, allocated control over a large proportion of its forest resources to a relatively small elite of concessionaires. In 1995, twenty Indonesian corporate conglomerates controlled more than 63 percent of the 62 million hectares of the country's timber concessions, and those businesses had close ties with the family of former President Suharto, which allowed them to ignore logging concession regulations. The Suharto regime's forest policy was dominated by a plywood exporters' cartel controlled by a timber baron crony of Suharto's.[3] It is not surprising, therefore, that Indonesia opposed proposals for new international norms on forest management in the early 1990s, or that it supported Canada's 1997 proposal for a forest convention that would allow each major timber-exporting country to create its own eco-labeling system.

Government bureaucracies holding institutional interests that would be negatively impacted by global action on a particular environmental issue often attempt to influence the adoption of swing or blocking roles. During the negotiation of the Montreal Protocol in the mid-1980s, officials in the U.S. Departments of Commerce, the Interior, and Agriculture, together with the Office of Management and Budget, the Office of Science and Technology Policy, and some members of the White House staff, began in early 1987 to reopen basic questions about the scientific evidence and the possible damage

CARTOON 2.1   Anti-Norway feeling increases. Jeff Danziger in the *Christian Science Monitor* © 1993.

to the U.S. economy from imposing additional CFC controls, but they were overruled.[4] The major obstacles to the United Kingdom's agreeing to an acid rain agreement through the mid-1980s were two public bodies, the National Coal Board and the Central Electricity Generating Board, which did everything possible to avoid having to reduce sulfur dioxide emissions.[5]

The ability of powerful economic or bureaucratic interests to resist restrictions on their despoiling of the environment is enhanced by authoritarian political regimes that can simply suppress opposition to their policies. The military regime that ruled Brazil from 1964 to 1985 enjoyed virtually unlimited power in determining how natural resources were exploited, and permitted no opposition to its campaign to open the Amazonian rain forests to agriculture and other large-scale commercial activities. But under an elected government, with NGOs and media freer to criticize it, the government was less hostile toward international agreement to slow deforestation.

When other motives for a lead role on a global environmental issue are present, such a role becomes far more likely if there is little or no domestic opposition. The United States could easily take the lead role on the issue of whaling in the 1970s and 1980s, for example, because the U.S. whaling industry had already been eliminated. Similarly, the absence of significant bureaucratic or business interest in opposing a ban on imports of African elephant ivory products made it easy for the United States to assume a lead role on that issue.

The existence of a strong environmental movement can be a decisive factor in a state's definition of its interest on an issue, especially if it is a potential swing vote in parliamentary elections. The sudden emergence of West German and French bids for leadership roles on environmental issues in 1989 reflected in large part the upsurge of public support for strong environmental protection policies in Western Europe. The West German Greens had already won 8.2 percent of the vote in the 1984 European Parliament elections; and by 1985, the Green Party, backed by popular environmental sentiment, was already a strong force in the German parliament.[6] Before the 1989 European Parliament election, polls indicated a new surge in environmentalist sentiment in West Germany and France. As a result, West Germany and France in early 1989 became part of a lead coalition of states proposing negotiations on a framework convention on climate change to stabilize carbon dioxide emissions not later than 2000. Germany continued to be a lead state on climate change through 2005, in part because of the presence of the Green Party in the coalition government led by the Social Democratic Party and because it has one of the largest and most active environmental movements in Europe.[7] The German environmental movement's clout helped overcome the influence of the powerful German coal industry and contributed to Germany's role as a lead state in the climate change negotiations.

But a strong environmental movement does not guarantee that the state actor will play a lead or supporting role on an issue. The U.S. environmental movement is among the largest and best organized in the world, but it has been unable to sway U.S. policy regarding the Kyoto Protocol or ratification of the Biodiversity, Basel, Rotterdam, or Stockholm Conventions. Powerful interests that oppose U.S. participation in these treaties and an environmental movement that has been unable to influence the outcomes of congressional or presidential elections are responsible for this failure.

Conversely, the absence of a strong environmental movement makes it more likely that a state will play a swing or blocking role on an international environmental issue. For example, Japanese NGOs are relatively underdeveloped in comparison with those in North America and Europe, and the Japanese political system makes it difficult for interest groups without high-level political links to influence policy. The Japanese government therefore felt little or no domestic pressure to support regimes on African elephants, whaling, and drift-net fishing. In contrast, U.S. wildlife NGOs placed a great deal of domestic pressure on the U.S. government to take a strong position on these issues.

A final domestic political factor that has occasionally shaped a country's definition of its interest in an environmental regime is the ideology or belief system of the policymaker. Although the United States has exported very little of its hazardous waste, in the UNCED negotiations the first Bush administration led the veto coalition against a ban on hazardous waste exports to developing countries because of its strong hostility to the intervention of states in national and international markets. The first Bush administration also vetoed a proposal in the UNCED negotiations for targets to be set by industrialized states for per capita energy use because officials saw the proposal as an unwarranted interference by the state in consumer preferences.[8]

Comparative Costs and Benefits of Environmental Regimes

A second group of variables that shape the definition of national interest in a global environmental issue includes the potential costs and risks that an environmental threat poses to a country as well as the costs and benefits associated with the proposed regime.[9] Exceptional vulnerability to the consequences of environmental problems has driven countries to support, or even take the lead, on strong global action. Thirty two small island states that are especially vulnerable to sea-level rise because of global warming formed the Alliance of Small Island States in November 1990 to lobby the climate negotiations for action limiting carbon dioxide emissions from the industrialized countries. States with densely populated coastal plains, such as Bangladesh, Egypt, and the Netherlands, are also likely to face particularly severe disruptions from storm surges, hurricanes, and typhoons as a result of climate change and have generally supported efforts to strengthen the UN Framework Convention on Climate Change.

Sweden and Norway, which led the fight for a Long-Range Transboundary Air Pollution Convention in the 1970s, have been the major recipients of sulfur dioxide from other European countries, and their lakes and soils are also acid-sensitive. The damage from acid rain therefore appeared earlier and was more serious in those Nordic countries than in the United Kingdom or Germany. Similarly, Canada has pushed the United States for stronger action on the issue because it has a higher proportion of soil that is vulnerable to acid deposition than does the United States and receives far more sulfur dioxide from U.S. factories than it sends across the border.

The costs of compliance with a given global environmental regime may differ dramatically from one country to another, and such differences have sometimes shaped the roles played by states in regime negotiations. The ne-gotiation of the Montreal Protocol provides several examples of states whose roles were linked with economic interests. The UNEP executive director, Mostafa Tolba, is reported to have made this observation: "The difficulties in negotiating the Montreal Protocol had nothing to do with whether the envi-ronment was damaged or not. . . . It was all who was going to get the edge over whom."[10] Because of an earlier unilateral ban on aerosols using ozone-depleting chemicals, the United States was ahead of members of the Euro-pean Community and Japan in finding substitutes for CFCs in aerosol cans; it therefore joined Canada and the Nordic states in supporting such a ban. Western Europe and Japan rejected a ban on CFC aerosols in the early 1980s in part because they did not yet have technological alternatives. The Soviet Union, fearful that it would be unable to develop new technologies to replace CFCs, initially resisted the idea of a CFC phaseout in 1986–1987. China and India, who were minor producers at the time but were already gearing up for major production increases, also feared that the transition to ozone-safe chemicals would be too costly without noncommercial access to alternative technologies. Moreover, India's chemical industry planned to export half its projected CFC production to the Middle East and Asia.

The anticipated economic costs of compliance were the underlying issue during the negotiations that resulted in the Kyoto Protocol to the UN Framework Convention on Climate Change. Achieving reductions in greenhouse gas (GHG) emissions is easier and/or cheaper for some coun-tries than others. For example, the European Union (EU) states are gener-ally net importers of fossil fuels and have learned how to reduce energy use without compromising economic growth. Because the EU states saw that their cost of compliance would be relatively low, they were able to play a lead role in the negotiation of the protocol. In March 1997, the EU called for a 15 percent reduction of emissions across the EU by 2010; in doing so, it took into consideration internal burden sharing, which meant that coun-tries able to reduce their GHG emissions at the lowest cost would carry the burden for those countries for which reductions would have a greater eco-nomic burden.

International Political and Diplomatic Considerations

States also consider potential benefits or costs to broader international inter-ests when considering whether to assume a lead or veto role on a particular global environmental issue. A state may hope to gain international prestige by assuming a lead role; or it may decide against a veto role to avoid international opprobrium or damage to its relations with countries for which the environmental issue is of significantly greater concern.

Concern for national prestige—a state's reputation or status in the international community—was once confined to the issue area of international security. But in the early 1990s, a few states began to regard leadership on the global environment as a means of enhancing their international status. The United States and Germany both made bids for leadership on a possible world forest convention in 1990–1991, in large part because both anticipated that such leadership would enhance their environmental image around the world. The European Union had aspirations for a lead role on climate change in the Rio conference to signify its emergence as a global power. In 1994, EU environment commissioner Yannis Paleokrassas hailed the prospect of a regionwide carbon tax, which would give the EU a lead role on climate change and lead to "the resumption of world environmental and fiscal leadership by the European Union," thus suggesting that it would gain a new kind of international prestige.[11]

At the 1992 Earth Summit, the United States tarnished its image because it stood alone in rejecting the Convention on Biological Diversity. Germany and Japan, among other countries, shared the unhappiness of the United States concerning some provisions in the Biodiversity Convention but shunned a veto role for fear of damaging their prestige. A George H. W. Bush administration official later charged that Germany and Japan had departed from the U.S. position in part to demonstrate their new status as emerging, independent world powers.[12]

A state's concern about how a veto role might affect its image sometimes focuses on a particular country or group of countries. For international trade in hazardous wastes, for example, the decision by France and the United Kingdom in 1989 to alter their position and not play a veto role stemmed in part from a broader national interest in maintaining close ties with former colonies in Africa. Japan chose not to block efforts to ban trade in African elephant ivory in 1989 largely because it feared damage to its relations with its most important trading partners, the United States and Europe. Canada ratified the Kyoto Protocol in 2002 in part to protect its "environmentally progressive international image," which would be severely damaged if it rejected the protocol.[13]

Subnational Actors

National governments, despite their assertion of exclusive rights to act in international relations, are no longer the only governmental actors in global environmental politics. In recent years, cities, states, and provinces have shown increased interest in adopting their own environmental and energy policies, and these could have a major impact on global environmental problems, especially global warming.

Large cities are major producers of greenhouse gases in part because of their heavy concentrations of transportation, the biggest source of carbon dioxide emissions. Urban policies, then, if effective, could substantially reduce greenhouse gas emissions. With this in mind, in May 2005, a bipartisan group of 132 U.S. mayors, frustrated by the Bush administration's refusal to ratify the Kyoto Protocol, pledged that their cities would try to meet Kyoto's main target—a 7 percent reduction in emissions of greenhouse gases from 1990 levels in less than ten years. The cities ranged from liberal centers such as Los Angeles, California, to strongholds of conservatism such as Hurst, Texas. Between them, they represent almost 29 million citizens spread across thirty-five states.[14]

In some cities, greenhouse gas reduction policies are already underway. In Seattle, docking cruise ships must turn off their diesel engines while resupplying and rely on electricity provided by the city. The mayor's office believes that by the end of 2005, Seattle's power utility, Seattle City Light, will be the only one in the country able to show no net emissions of greenhouse gases. In Salt Lake City, the city authority has become Utah's largest buyer of wind power. In New York, the administration of Mayor Michael Bloomberg sought to reduce emissions from the municipal motor fleet by buying hybrid-powered vehicles.[15]

There has also been action to reduce GHG emissions at the state level. In November 2004, Colorado acted to ensure that a portion of its electricity is generated from renewable sources when it became the sixteenth state to pass a renewable portfolio standard. Colorado has followed the lead of states such as California, where 20 percent of electricity will come from renewable sources by 2017. The California State Legislature also passed the first GHG caps for the auto industry, the so-called Pavley Bill, calling for 25 percent GHG emissions reductions for cars and light trucks, and 18 percent reductions for larger trucks and sport utility vehicles by 2010. This is significant because California is the sixth largest economy in the world.[16]

In 2003, nine northeast and mid-Atlantic states created the Regional Greenhouse Gas Initiative (RGGI), a cooperative effort to discuss the design of a regional cap-and-trade program initially covering carbon dioxide emissions from power plants in the region. Under the RGGI, industries covered by the schemes will be given allocations in units of one ton of carbon dioxide

produced. Polluters could then either reduce their emissions or buy allocations on a market from others. Along these lines, in April 2000, New Jersey
adopted a statewide goal of reducing greenhouse gas emissions to 3.5 percent
below 1990 levels by 2005. Similarly, in August 2001, the New England gover-
nors and the Eastern Canadian premiers issued a Climate Change Action
Plan calling for the reduction of greenhouse gases to 10 percent below 1990
levels by 2020. New York's State Energy Plan calls for the reduction of the
state's carbon emissions to 5 percent below 1990 levels by 2010 and to 10 percent below those levels by 2020. The regional cap-and-trade program will assist all participating states in reaching these goals. Participating states include
Connecticut, Delaware, Maine, Massachusetts, New Hampshire, New Jersey,
New York, Rhode Island, and Vermont. In addition, Maryland, the District of
Columbia, Pennsylvania, the Eastern Canadian Provinces, and New
Brunswick are observers in the process.[17]

Although municipal and state governments are unlikely to usurp national
government functions in regime strengthening, they may reinforce and supplement efforts by national governments, especially as the world becomes increasingly urbanized.

INTERNATIONAL ORGANIZATIONS AS ACTORS

The influence of international organizations (IOs) on global environmental
politics has greatly increased since 1972. Also referred to as intergovernmental organizations (IGOs), IOs are formed by member states either for multiple purposes—the United Nations and various regional associations such as
the Organization of American States being examples—or for more specific
purposes, such as the Food and Agriculture Organization (FAO) and the
World Health Organization (WHO), both of which are specialized agencies
of the United Nations. IOs range in size and resources from the World Bank,
which has a staff of more than 10,000 and lends billions of dollars annually,
to UNEP, with its annual budget for the biennium 2006–2007 of only $144
million and a professional staff of 325. The multinational officials who staff
these organizations tend to share common approaches to functional problems. Although they are ultimately accountable to governing bodies made up
of the representatives of their member states, staff can take initiatives and influence the outcomes of global issues. The professional skills of these bureaucrats can be an important factor in environmental negotiations. IO
bureaucracies have widely varying degrees of independence. Those at UNEP

and the FAO must take their cues from their governing councils on setting agendas, sponsoring negotiations, and implementing development and environment programs. At the World Bank, which is dependent on major donor countries for its funds, the staff nevertheless has wide discretion in planning and executing projects.

An IO may influence the outcomes of global environmental issues in several ways:

- It may help determine which issues the international community will address through its influence on the agenda for global action.
- It may convene and influence negotiations on global environmental regimes.
- It may develop normative codes of conduct (soft law) on various environmental issues.
- It may influence state policies on issues that are not under international negotiation.[18]

No IO influences global environmental politics by performing all these functions. IOs tend to specialize in one or more political functions, although one may indirectly influence another.

Setting Agendas and Influencing Regime Formation

In the past, the agenda-setting function of global environmental politics was dominated by UNEP because of its unique mandate, growing out of the 1972 Stockholm Conference, to be a catalyst and coordinator of environmental activities and focal point for such activities within the UN system. Through decisions by its Governing Council, composed of fifty-eight UN member governments elected by the General Assembly, UNEP identifies critical global environmental threats requiring international cooperation. In 1976, for example, UNEP's Governing Council chose ozone depletion as one of five priority problems, and consequently UNEP convened a meeting of experts in Washington, D.C., that adopted the World Plan of Action on the Ozone Layer in 1977—five years before negotiations on a global agreement began.

UNEP played a similar role in initiating negotiations on climate change. It cosponsored with the Rockefeller Brothers Fund the Villach and Bellagio workshops that helped create scientific consensus and raised worldwide consciousness about the threat of global warming. Along with the World Meteorological Organization (WMO), UNEP sponsored the Intergovernmental Panel on Climate Change to study scientific and policy issues in preparation for negotiations on a global convention on climate change. UNEP convened international negotiations on many of the major environmental conventions of the past two decades: the Vienna Convention for the Protection of the Ozone Layer (1985), the Montreal Protocol on Substances that Deplete the Ozone Layer (1987), the Basel Convention on the Control of Transboundary Movements of Hazardous Wastes and Their Disposal (1989), the Convention on Biological Diversity (1992), and the Stockholm Convention on Persistent Organic Pollutants (2001). In 1995, the UNEP Governing Council decided that UNEP would convene, together with the FAO, an intergovernmental negotiating committee with a mandate to prepare an international legally binding instrument for the application of the PIC procedure for certain hazardous chemicals in international trade. The PIC Convention was adopted in Rotterdam in September 1998.

UNEP also has sought to shape the global environmental agenda by monitoring and assessing the state of the environment and disseminating the information to governments and NGOs. Since its founding in 1972, UNEP has acted as the secretariat for the UN system-wide Earthwatch and established

- the Global Environmental Monitoring System/Water Programme (1978) to provide authoritative, scientifically-sound information on the state and trends of global inland water quality;
- the Global Resource Information Database (GRID) (1985), a global network of environmental data centers facilitating the generation and dissemination of key environmental information;
- the Intergovernmental Panel on Climate Change, with the World Meteorological Organization (1988), to assess scientific, technical and socioeconomic information relevant for the understanding of climate change, its potential impacts and options for adaptation and mitigation; and
- the UNEP-World Conservation Monitoring Center (UNEP-WCMC) (2000), as the world biodiversity information and assessment center.

UNEP has also undertaken several global assessments, including three Global Environmental Outlook assessments (since 1995), five ozone assessments (since 1998), the Global Biodiversity Assessment (1995), the Cultural and Spiritual Values of Biodiversity Assessment (1999), the Millennium Ecosystem Assessment (since 2001), the Global Marine Assessment (since 2001), the Global International Waters Assessment (2003), and the Global Mercury Assessment (2002).[19]

Mostafa Tolba, the former UNEP executive director, influenced environmental diplomacy through direct participation in the negotiations. In informal talks with the chiefs of EC delegations during the negotiations on the Montreal Protocol, he lobbied hard for a phaseout of CFCs.[20] At the London Conference of the Parties in 1990, he convened informal meetings with twenty-five environmental ministers to work out a compromise on the contentious issue of linking protocol obligations with technology transfer. He also urged a compromise to bridge the gap between U.S. and Western European timetables for a CFC phaseout. At the final session of the negotiations on the Convention on Biological Diversity, Tolba took over when there appeared to be gridlock on key issues regarding the financing mechanism, and he virtually forced the acceptance of a compromise text. (See chapter 3.)

Tolba sometimes openly championed the developing countries against the highly industrialized countries. At Basel in 1989, for instance, he fought for a ban on shipping hazardous wastes to or from noncontracting parties and for a requirement that exporters check disposal sites at their own expense. But Tolba and the developing countries lost on both issues because they were opposed by the waste-exporting states.[21]

In the 1990s, UNEP's role in agenda setting and convening regime negotiations was sharply reduced by several factors. Despite his siding with them on the emotional waste trade issue, the developing countries had begun to lose confidence in Tolba and UNEP by 1990. They thought he was not sufficiently committed to their agenda and that he put too much emphasis on climate change, ozone depletion, and loss of biodiversity, all of which they considered "Northern" issues. When UNCED was being organized in the United Nations General Assembly (UNGA), the **Group of 77** sought emphasis on environmental problems of primary concern to developing nations: drinking water and sanitation, urban pollution, desertification, and so on. It succeeded in naming the twentieth anniversary of the Stockholm environmental conference the 1992 UN Conference on Environment and Development and assigned organizing responsibility to the UN Secretariat rather than to UNEP. At the same time, the UNGA took the climate negotiations out of the hands of UNEP and WMO and gave them to an ad hoc UN body, the Intergovernmental Negotiating Committee (INC), which reported directly to the General Assembly.

And after UNCED in 1992, the UNGA established the United Nations Commission on Sustainable Development (CSD) to monitor and coordinate the implementation of Agenda 21. The creation of the CSD and the replacement of Tolba with a new executive director, Elizabeth Dowdeswell, further reduced UNEP's role in agenda setting for global environmental politics. Among other things, Dowdeswell alienated key donor countries by failing to consult them adequately. There is no doubt that UNEP has had its share of successes; however, there have been dramatic changes in international environmental policymaking in recent years, and UNEP has struggled to keep pace. Chronic financial problems, the absence of a clear focus and mission for the institution, problems of location (Nairobi, Kenya), and management difficulties all contributed to the erosion of UNEP's participation in the international environmental policymaking process during the 1990s.[22]

In February 1998, Dr. Klaus Töpfer was appointed UNEP's executive director. By the 1999 meeting of the UNEP Governing Council, UNEP was trying to adapt itself to new challenges and the full and complex agenda of global environmental concerns. As a result, in a demonstration of renewed faith in the organization, its leadership, and its work program, donor pledges to UNEP's Environment Fund increased. In recent years, UNEP has rebounded, within the confines of budget and location. Among its accomplishments are the development of the Global Earth Observation System of Systems (GEOSS) to achieve comprehensive, coordinated, and sustained Earth observations and so improve integrated environmental assessment; the development of a new Strategic Approach for International Chemicals Management; improving the scientific base of UNEP; and the creation of a Global Ministerial Environment Forum to keep under review the state of the global environment, to assess environmental challenges continuously, to identify new and emerging issues, and to set assessment priorities.[23] Many still argue that UNEP's small budget, small staff, and lack of a strong mandate continue to hinder its effectiveness, but governments have not made serious efforts to strengthen the organization.

Given its position as a highly visible and well-attended UN commission, the fifty-three-member CSD has had an opportunity to play a pivotal role in agenda setting. No other UN institution tries to examine head-on the interlinkages between environmental, social, economic, and political arenas at the global scale. In one sense, the commission has been successful in generating greater concern for some issues on the international sustainable development agenda. By creating the Intergovernmental Panel on Forests and, subsequently, the Intergovernmental Forum on Forests, the CSD was able to focus the forest issue and create more understanding that forests are owned by someone and give livelihood to many people. Freshwater resources and energy are two issues that did not receive much attention in Rio and have gained more prominence under the CSD's agenda and, through that, at the

TABLE 2.1   CSD Achievements

- Recommended a legally binding status for the Prior Informed Consent procedure (1994)
- Called for coordinated consideration of trade and environment issues (1995)
- Established an Intergovernmental Panel on Forests (1995) an Intergovernmental Forum on Forests (1997) and, finally, in the General Assembly a UN Forum of Forests (2000)
- Set a firm date of 2002 for governments to produce their National Sustainable Development Strategies (1997)
- Added, in effect, three new chapters to Agenda 21 on Energy, Transport and Tourism (1997)
- Set up multi-stakeholder dialogues at the UN as part of its official meetings (1998)
- Agreed on changes to the UN Consumer Guidelines to include Sustainable Development (1999)
- Supported the Washington Declaration on the Global Programme of Action for the Protection of the Marine Environment from Land Based Activities (1999)

Source: Felix Dodds, et. al. *Post Johannesburg: The Future of the UN Commission on Sustainable Development*, Stakeholder Forum for Our Common Future, Paper #9 (November 2002).

2002 World Summit on Sustainable Development. Similarly, the CSD's discussions on sustainable production and consumption patterns, sustainability indicators, and the need for technology transfer, education, and capacity building in developing countries have raised the profiles of these issues (see table 2.1).

When it comes to putting new issues on the international agenda, however, the CSD has not been as successful. To its credit, the CSD has put the issues of transport and tourism on the agenda and has advanced discussions on finance, but it has been plagued overall by a focus on the past rather than the future. For example, it has renegotiated principles and past agreements and has failed to progress discussions beyond arguments around fundamental principles and toward a more strategic debate on furthering implementation. Even in the World Summit on Sustainable Development (WSSD) preparations, all governments were in agreement that they did not want to see a renegotiation of Agenda 21, and yet negotiators often moved the debate backwards into the territory of the Rio Principles and core objectives. It seems that for over ten years, negotiators have struggled with making the shift from abstract debate to strategic implementation.[24]

Developing Nonbinding Norms

International organizations also influence global environmental politics by facilitating the negotiation of common norms or rules of conduct that do not have binding legal effect on the participating states. A variety of creative nontreaty measures, often called soft law, have been developed to influence state behavior on environmental issues, including codes of conduct, declarations of principle, global action plans, and other international agreements that create new norms and expectations without the binding status of treaties.[25]

These nonbinding agreements are negotiated by groups of experts representing their governments, usually in negotiating processes convened by international organizations. Most UN agencies have contributed to this process, but UNEP has done the most to promote it. Concerning the management of hazardous waste, for instance, a UNEP ad hoc working group of experts helped draft guidelines in 1984. In 1987, the same process produced guidelines and principles aimed at making the worldwide pesticide trade more responsive regarding threats to environmental health. Other examples include the 1980 International Program on Chemical Safety and the 1985 Action Plan for Biosphere Reserves, each of which has become the recognized standard in the field.

The FAO has drafted guidelines on the environmental criteria for the registration of pesticides (1985) and the International Code of Conduct on the Distribution and Use of Pesticides (1986). Criteria for food regulations, the Codex Alimentarius, also developed under the FAO's aegis, could be used in a trade dispute to declare a national environmental health standard an illegitimate barrier to trade. The FAO Code of Conduct for Responsible Fisheries, adopted in 1995, sets out principles and international standards of behavior for responsible practices with a view to ensuring the effective conservation, management, and development of living aquatic resources.

Soft-law agreements are often a good way to avoid the lengthy process of negotiating, signing, and ratifying binding agreements. They do not require enforcement mechanisms and can sometimes depend on the adherence of networks of bureaucrats who share similar views of the problem. But when soft-law regimes are adopted only because key parties are unwilling to go beyond nonbinding guidelines, the norms agreed upon may be less stringent, and at best, compliance haphazard. The FAO Code of Conduct on pesticide trade, negotiated from 1982 to 1985, and the 1985 Cairo guidelines on international hazardous waste trade are examples of this pattern.

Soft law may be turned into binding international law in two ways: Principles included in a soft-law agreement may become so widely regarded as the appropriate norms for a problem that they are ultimately absorbed into treaty law; or political pressures may arise from those dissatisfied with spotty adherence to soft-law norms to turn a nonbinding agreement into a binding one.

Influencing National Development Policies

A fourth way that IOs affect global environmental politics is to influence the environmental and development policies of individual states outside the context of regime negotiations. National policy decisions on such issues as what goals should be set for population growth rates, how much of the government budget should be allocated to human resource development, how to manage forests, how to generate and use energy supplies, and how to increase agricultural production determine how sustainable the national economies and societies will be. IOs influence such policies, and thus the sustainability of societies, in several ways:

- They provide financing for development projects, as well as advice and technical assistance that help shape the country's development strategy.
- They undertake research aimed at persuading state officials to adopt certain policies.
- They focus normative pressure on states regarding sustainable development policy issues.

The FAO, for example, had a major impact on the policies of the developing world—much of which critics charge has been negative—through its promotion of the commercial exploitation of forests and export crops, large-scale irrigation projects, and heavy use of chemical inputs.[26] More recently, the FAO has used research to promote sustainable alternatives to the conventional agricultural development model. FAO's program on integrated pest control in South and Southeast Asia, launched in the early 1980s, helped spread integrated pest management (IPM) techniques to farmers in several Asian countries. The research done by the FAO showing the superiority of natural pest control strategies over reliance on chemical pesticides helped convince key Indonesian government officials in 1986 to adopt IPM as an alternative to heavy reliance on pesticides and to train Indonesian farmers to make their own informed decisions about pest management.[27]

In the early 1990s, the organization was restructured for the first time for the purpose of integrating sustainability into its programs and activities.[28] In 1993, the FAO received a new mandate from its governing body to focus more on the consequences of the earth's shrinking natural resources, sustainable agricultural and rural development, and food security through the protection of plant, animal, and marine resources. Since 1993, the FAO has focused extensively on the implementation of sustainable agriculture, supported the work of the Commission on Sustainable Development's Intergovernmental Panel on Forests and Intergovernmental Forum on Forests, supported the work of the United Nations Forum on Forests, and cosponsored with UNEP the negotiation of the Rotterdam Treaty for the application of the PIC procedure for certain hazardous chemicals in international trade. The FAO also embarked upon the revision of the 1983 International Undertaking on Plant Genetic Resources to harmonize it with the goals of the Convention on Biological Diversity. The International Undertaking addresses the conservation, exploration, collection, documentation, and sustainable use of plant resources for food and agriculture. Its successor, the International Treaty on Plant Genetic Resources for Food and Agriculture, was adopted in 2001.

The FAO Committee on Fisheries (COFI), consisting of FAO member states, was established in 1965 as a subsidiary body of the FAO Council and has remained the only global forum for the consideration of major issues related to fisheries and aquaculture policy. Until the late 1980s, COFI focused on problems of developing coastal states in the development of their fisheries, especially after they acquired 200-mile coastal fishing zones in the 1970s. But when the pressures of overfishing on global fish stocks became increasingly difficult to ignore, COFI and the FAO Secretariat became more aggressive in pushing for new international norms for sustainable fisheries.

The FAO Secretariat has helped mobilize international support for more sustainable fisheries management by collecting and analyzing data on global fish catch, issuing annual reviews on the state of the world's fisheries, and organizing technical workshops. These efforts have focused government and NGO attention on such issues as excess fishing capacity and fisheries subsidies. In 1991, COFI recommended that the FAO should develop the concept of responsible fisheries in the form of a code of conduct, and the FAO Secretariat convened negotiations on the Code of Conduct for Responsible Fisheries in 1994 and 1995. The Code of Conduct is the most comprehensive set of international norms for sustainable fisheries management that currently exists and, despite its not being legally binding, it has influenced state and producer practices.

UNDP, with a budget of more than $3.2 billion annually, a staff exceeding 5,000 worldwide, and liaison offices in 166 countries, is the largest source of multilateral grant development assistance. Moreover, it has projects in every developing country and allocates its funds for five-year periods according to a formula based primarily on population and per capita GNP; and it is the only UN agency with resident representatives in each member country. In 1994, in direct response to UNCED, James Gustave Speth, a well-known environmentalist who was then the UNDP administrator, made a strategic decision to strengthen UNDP's environment and sustainable development capacity by establishing the Energy and Environment Group (EEG). Since its origin, EEG has worked to support UNDP's overall efforts to help countries successfully design and carry out programs that support the implementation of Agenda 21 and the Rio Conventions. UNDP's Energy and Environment Group works in six areas of high priority:

- frameworks and strategies for sustainable development;
- effective water governance;
- access to sustainable energy services;
- sustainable land management to combat desertification and land degradation;
- conservation and sustainable use of biodiversity; and
- national/sectoral policy and planning to control emissions of ozone-depleting substances and persistent organic pollutants.[29]

UNDP is also one of the three implementing agencies of the Global Environment Facility (GEF) and is the lead UN agency in building the capacity of developing-country governments for sustainable development under its Capacity 21 and Capacity 2015 programs. UNDP also assists in building capacity for good governance, popular participation, private and public sector development, and growth with equity, all of which are necessary in promoting sustainable human development.

In spite of UNDP's intentions, a 1998 study examined UNDP's regular portfolio of projects and determined that many UNDP programs in the 1990s had not been as "pro-environment" as it seemed.[30] For example, UNDP reduced the number of projects and total funding for new and renewable energy from twenty-two projects for a total of $22.6 million in 1993 to only eleven projects for a total of $5.1 million in 1996.[31] Furthermore, in fiscal 1997, UNDP continued to provide four times more grant funding for conventional sources of energy (petroleum, coal, and gas) than it did for "new and renewable sources of energy."[32] To its credit, UNDP has worked to improve its sustainability record. According to UNDP's 2003 *Development Effectiveness Report,* 87 percent of UNDP projects evaluated between 1999 and 2003 were partially or fully sustainable, compared with 74 percent of projects evaluated between 1992 and 1998.[33]

UNDP has also taken key steps toward greater emphasis on new and renewable energy, including the LP Gas Rural Energy Challenge, one of several UNDP initiatives that emerged from the 2002 World Summit on Sustainable Development. The LPG Challenge, as it is known, is a public-private partnership between the World Liquid Petroleum Gas Association and the UNDP. It is designed to create viable and sustainable markets for liquid petroleum gas (LPG) delivery and consumption, thereby contributing to sustainable energy solutions that can improve people's lives in selected developing countries. Specifically, the LPG Challenge aims to address adverse impacts on health, the environment, and economic productivity related to dependence on traditional biomass fuels in rural areas.[34] The Energy Sector Management Assistance Programme (ESMAP) is a joint UNDP-World Bank program that provides global technical assistance and policy advice on sustainable energy development to governments of developing countries and economies in transition. ESMAP also contributes to the transfer of technology and knowledge in energy sector management and the delivery of modern energy services to the poor. Since its creation, ESMAP has operated in one hundred countries through approximately 450 activities covering a broad range of energy issues.[35]

IOs may influence state policy by focusing normative pressures on states regarding the environment and sustainable development even when no formal international agreement exists on the norm.[36] UNDP has gone the farthest of any UN agency in this regard; indeed, it has asserted the allocation of a minimum level of resources for human resource development (health, population, and education) by donor countries and developing-country governments as a norm in the context of what it calls "sustainable human development." Through its annual Human Development Report, which ranks nations according to their provision of these social services, UNDP pressures developing countries into devoting more of their budgets to these social sectors.

Multilateral Financial Institutions as Actors

In terms of direct impact on the development and environmental policies of developing states, the most powerful IOs are the multilateral financial institutions, including the World Bank, the International Monetary Fund, and the regional banks, because of the amount of financial resources that they transfer to developing countries every year in support of particular development strategies and economic policies. Within these IOs, donor countries are the dominant players and voting is weighted according to the size of a country's contributions. The United States has the most power in the World Bank and the Inter-American Development Bank. Japan has the most power in the Asian Development Bank.

The World Bank's influence on the policies of its borrowers has been viewed by environmental activists as contributing to unsustainable development. The Bank has been driven by the need to lend large amounts of money each year; by a bias toward large-scale, capital-intensive, and centralized projects; and by its practice of assessing projects according to a quantifiable rate of return while discounting longer-term, unquantifiable social and environmental costs and benefits. In the 1970s and 1980s, the World Bank supported rain forest colonization schemes in Brazil and Indonesia, cattle-ranching projects in Central and South America, tobacco projects in Africa that contributed to accelerated deforestation, and a cattle development project in Botswana that contributed to desertification.[37]

In response to persistent, well-orchestrated pressure from NGOs and U.S. Congress criticism of such egregious loans, and calls for it to become part of the solution to global environmental problems rather than a contributor, the World Bank began a process of evolution in the mid-1980s toward greater sensitivity to the environmental implications of its lending. It refused to provide new support for some of the worst projects in Brazil and Indonesia, created an environment department, began to build an environmental staff, and financed more explicitly environmental programs.

This process accelerated in the 1990s as the Bank took concrete steps in the area of the environment. In 1990–1991, it became an implementing agency of the nascent Global Environment Facility, the multilateral fund to finance the additional costs to countries of projects that have global environmental benefits, as well as of the Multilateral Fund of the Montreal Protocol. It thus enjoyed the largest portfolio of global environmental projects of all multilateral institutions, albeit funded by other donors.

With regard to forests, the Bank has combined investments in conservation and capacity building in selected tropical forest countries with policy dialogues aimed at eliminating the worst distortions in the sector. It also adopted a new forest policy in 1991 that precluded support for commercial logging in primary tropical forests. The biggest obstacle to success in the Bank's approach was a lack of political will on the part of governments of states that intensively exploit forests.

In Indonesia, the Bank implemented two loans in the late 1980s and early 1990s for the development of a forest database and institution building, but a later project proposing ambitious policy and institutional reforms had to be abandoned during preparation because the Suharto government resisted key policy reforms.[38] In 1998, the Bank negotiated a major structural adjustment loan with Indonesia as part of the economic rescue package, which included pledges to carry out some far-reaching reforms in the logging-concession system. But when Indonesia failed to deliver on its pledges, the Bank was unwilling to suspend payments because its interests in reviving the economy trumped environmental concerns. (See the discussion of adjustment lending below.)

Perhaps reflecting an implicit recognition of its past failure to leverage changes in the forest management policies of clients, in 1998 the Bank tried a different strategy on forests and launched the World Bank-World Wildlife Fund Alliance for Forest Conservation and Sustainable Use. The Forest Alliance represents a sharp shift in the Bank's past approach to one that (a) openly acknowledges the critical problems of commercial logging, the illegal practices in the forest sector, and the frequently corrupt nexus between officials and economic elites; (b) identifies specific measures and ambitious global forest policy goals; and (c) employs a combination of financial resources, technical assistance, and public pressures on government to support sustainable forest management. Since 1998, the Forest Alliance has contributed to the establishment of 50 million hectares (193,000 square miles) of new protected areas, improved management for 70 million hectares (270,000 square miles) of protected areas, and responsible management of some 22 million hectares (85,000 square miles) of commercially harvested forests. These accomplishments have been achieved in pursuit of measurable targets, which the Forest Alliance recently updated and expanded to drive further achievements. In May 2005, the World Bank and the World Wide Fund for Nature announced an ambitious global program aimed at reducing global deforestation rates by 10 percent by 2010.[39]

The Forest Alliance has played a pivotal role in facilitating regional initiatives in the developing world and has been actively working with the private sector to promote responsible forest practices, such as by supporting the Brazilian government's Amazon Regional Protected Area Program (ARPA). This ten-year program will protect 12 percent of the Brazilian Amazon and establish a $220 million trust fund to support the ongoing management of this protected areas network. The scope of ARPA is equivalent to building the entire U.S. national parks system in ten years.[40]

On biodiversity, the Bank adopted a new policy of not supporting projects that would result in significant conversion or degradation of habitats that are

officially designated as critical—a limitation that severely hinders its application. In 1996, the Bank presented its first "biodiversity assistance strategy,"
which emphasized the importance of integrating biodiversity concerns into
country assistance strategies, to the Conference of the Parties to the Convention on Biological Diversity.

As an implementing agency of the GEF, as the principal financial mechanism for the Biodiversity Convention, and in implementing its "biodiversity
assistance strategy," the Bank has pledged publicly to integrate global biodiversity concerns into relevant portions of its lending portfolio. In 1996, it established a program to identify opportunities for promoting development
objectives and global environmental benefits in loan projects when preparing
country lending strategies for each client government. But the Bank devoted
too few budgetary resources and too little staffing to the program, and as a
result its Country Assistance Strategies, written in 1996 and 1997, seldom
made the linkages between renewable resource problems and biodiversity
loss.[41] As a result, in comparison with the six-year period prior to 1994, lending for biodiversity in the Bank's regular loan portfolio did not increase from
1994 through 1997.[42] However, the biodiversity portfolio of the World Bank
has shown steady growth over the past decade. Between 1988 and 2004, the
Bank approved 426 projects that fully or partially supported biodiversity
conservation and sustainable use, and more than a hundred are proposed for
the next three years. These biodiversity initiatives are taking place in 102
countries, and through seventeen regional multi-country efforts. This total
reflects an addition of two hundred projects to the portfolio since 1999.[43]

World Bank support in the area of biodiversity also involves the establishment and strengthening of protected areas (including activities in buffer
zones), the sustainable use of biodiversity outside protected areas, the eradication of alien species, and biodiversity conservation through improved
management and sustainable use of natural resources in the production
landscape. These activities all have important links to poverty alleviation initiatives. In the future, it is expected that the Bank's activities in support of
conservation and sustainable use of biodiversity will further emphasize
mainstreaming of biodiversity in the production landscape, including agriculture, fisheries, and other activities in rural development.

With regard to climate change, the Bank's longtime role as a financier of
large conventional fossil fuel power projects conflicts with the objective of
the UN Framework Convention on Climate Change's to reduce greenhouse
gas emissions. From 1990 through 1997, the Bank approved 170 loans in the
electric power sector totaling more than $24 billion, mostly for governments

that have no obligations to reduce their greenhouse gas emissions, resulting in an additional 10 billion tons of carbon dioxide emissions over the lifetime of the projects.[44] The Bank defended its lending for fossil fuel power plants by arguing that the climate change convention does not require that non-Annex I (developing) countries reduce their emissions and, therefore, does not permit the World Bank to "force" a country to accept a higher-cost energy alternative.[45]

In 1997, the World Bank stated that it would begin to "routinely calculate the potential impact of all its energy projects on climate change and, where there is cause for concern, assist developing country clients to finance more climate-friendly options."[46] According to a 2002 report by the progressive Sustainable Energy and Economy Network (SEEN), however, five years after that commitment, the World Bank still did not "routinely calculate" its projects' potential climate change impact and only rarely did "its project reviews consider carbon dioxide emissions, the truest indicator of the climate change impact of its portfolio."[47] According to SEEN, the World Bank approved over $24 billion in financing for 229 fossil fuel projects from 1992 to 2002 that will produce 46.7 billion tons of carbon dioxide—nearly double the global emissions of carbon dioxide produced from the consumption or flaring of fossil fuels in 2000 (which totaled 23.6 billion tons).[48]

Structural adjustment, which usually involves coordinated lending by the World Bank and the IMF, can strongly influence the policies of heavily indebted developing countries on key issues of sustainability. Structural adjustment programs almost always require that the borrowing country reduce domestic demand by removing subsidies, cutting government budgets, devaluating currencies, and tightening credit; at the same time, the borrowing country must take steps to increase exports in an effort to achieve a positive trade balance and pay off debts. IMF and World Bank officials traditionally argue that economic distortions such as overvalued exchange rates, artificially low agricultural prices, and subsidies only serve to hurt the poorest segments of society and create perverse incentives for activities that degrade the environment.[49] Some analysts argue that the consequences of these programs (greater industrial unemployment and fewer primary health care services) worsen the plight of the poor, cause increased population migration onto marginal lands, and create pressure for more rapid logging or more intensive cultivation of export crops. Others, however, find no clear pattern of adverse environmental impacts of adjustment lending.[50]

In theory, structural adjustment lending can be either bad or good for the environment, depending on the environmental and socioeconomic situation and the conditions for policy reform that are required. If policy reforms are needed to eliminate distortions that result in the unsustainable use of natural resources, their inclusion in a structural adjustment loan agreement could help overcome major political resistance to reform. But as the Indonesian case study below shows, obstacles stemming from the nature of the World Bank and the IMF may constrain the use of structural adjustment lending to achieve major policy reforms not directly related to short-term economic growth and positive trade balances.

The IMF was slower than the World Bank and regional banks to acknowledge the need to take environmental considerations explicitly into account in its lending operations; it defined its role as limited to helping countries achieve a balance of payments and pay off their international debts. Only in 1991 did the IMF executive board consider for the first time the extent to which the IMF should "address environmental issues." It decided that the IMF should avoid policies that might harm the environment but that it should not conduct research or build up its own expertise on the possible environmental consequences of its policies.[51] More recently, the IMF and the World Bank put in place a joint initiative for Heavily Indebted Poor Countries (HIPC Initiative). The Initiative is aimed at reducing the debt-service burden of eligible countries to sustainable levels and helping them exit from the debt-rescheduling process, but they in turn must adopt and pursue strong and sustained programs of adjustment and reform. This Initiative should help eliminate external debt as an impediment to achieving sustainable development.[52]

The IMF has claimed that its mandate and the expertise of its staff limit its ability to address environmental issues. Because the World Bank addresses environmental issues and supports an extensive work program on environmental and other sectoral issues, the Executive Board of the IMF decided early that the IMF should not duplicate the work of the Bank in this area. The IMF's involvement is thus limited to those areas that have a serious and perceptible impact on the macroeconomic outlook of a country or on the effectiveness of macroeconomic policy instruments in achieving domestic and external stability.[53]

Even in these respects, the IMF sometimes runs into obstacles. At times, a member country does not have a National Environmental Action Plan or a stated national strategy to protect the environment. Even where such plans or strategies do exist, they are sometimes not specific enough to allow the IMF staff to consider their macroeconomic implications. Sometimes, the authorities themselves are not fully committed to environmental objectives because of pressure from one or more interest groups or because these objectives conflict with short-run economic growth or with some other objective of the country's policymakers. Thus, the IMF argues, it can integrate environment into its policy dialogue only to the extent that member countries allow it to do so.[54]

When Indonesia's economy collapsed in 1997–1998 and had to be rescued by major loans from the IMF and the World Bank, it presented a unique opportunity to hold the government of Indonesia accountable for reforming its forest exploitation system. The policy reforms negotiated by the IMF with the Suharto regime in early 1998 included pledges to reform the logging concession system and to "reduce land conversion targets to environmentally sustainable levels." The latter pledge referred to the clear-cutting of forests that had already been logged over but were still productive to plant oil palm and timber plantations; indeed, these plantations were rapidly becoming as important a source of logs as commercial logging concessions. Conversion of forests to oil palm plantations was usually accomplished by burning logging refuse after clear-cutting the forests, and was the largest cause of the catastrophic forest fires that raged in Indonesia in 1997–1998.[55]

In July 1998, the World Bank followed the IMF agreement with its own $1-billion structural adjustment loan to post-Suharto Indonesia, which went further on forest policy reform. It required that the Indonesian government prepare an accurate map of the forest areas of key provinces based on recent satellite imagery and identify priority conservation areas. Pending completion of the mapping exercise, the government was required by the loan agreement to "implement and maintain a moratorium on conversion of state forest areas." Future conversion or change in forest land use status was to be reviewed through a transparent and consultative process involving non-governmental stakeholders and interdepartmental dialogue within the government. Finally, the agreement required that the government publish a list of applications received before the date of the agreement and "subject them to public review prior to final approval."[56]

But the government failed to make good on its pledges. The Forestry Ministry argued that it could not turn down applications from companies that had already invested in the conversion process. Some applications were still being approved, despite the pledged moratorium. Moreover, no list of applications was ever published, nor was a public review carried out. The World Bank's Jakarta office was unable to obtain information on approvals or rejections during the first six months of 1999.[57]

Nevertheless, despite this failure to comply with the terms of a critical forest policy reform, the World Bank went ahead with disbursement of the second tranche of $400 million in February 1999. Then it signed a second adjustment loan in May 1999, which was disbursed immediately upon signing. World Bank staff said privately that the Bank could pick only a few policy conditionalities as the basis for deciding whether to go ahead with disbursement and with a new loan.[58]

The World Bank thus let a big opportunity to leverage policy reform in the Indonesian forest sector go by without decisive action. The failure to hold Indonesia accountable for the most elementary forest policy reforms cannot be explained through the Bank staff involved; instead, it reflected the political preferences held by the finance ministries of the major funders of the World Bank and the IMF, starting with the United States, Germany, Japan, and the United Kingdom.

In the 1990s, after twenty years of standard structural adjustment policies and more than forty years of traditional World Bank loans, the international development community recognized that the economic gap between OECD and middle-income countries and some one hundred less-developed countries continued to widen considerably with no sign of abating. As well, the number of poor, particularly the rural poor, has not significantly diminished despite the promise that structural reforms were designed to benefit the world's 2 billion poor.[59] The failure of these policies led to an institutional crisis in the major development institutions in the mid-1990s. In response, the World Bank, the IMF and bilateral development agencies reoriented their investment priorities and agreed that poverty alleviation would, thereafter, be their overarching and unifying goal. From that apparent policy reorientation, a new set of investment guidelines, and conditionalities, has been established, particularly in the case of the World Bank and IMF, in the form of the Poverty Reduction Strategy Papers (PRSPs). PRSPs, meant to be developed primarily by national governments, establish each country's national development strategy against which development assistance is to be charted and assessed. Moreover, the UN Millennium Development Goals (MDGs) embody the commitment to alleviate poverty and to increase country "ownership" of national development strategies.

The MDGs and the PRSPs both fail to recognize that the rural poor, constituting more than 70 percent of the world's poor, have an immediate survival dependence on access to use and sound management of natural resources. Deprived of their natural resource assets, the rural poor either suffer major declines in living standards or migrate to urban areas. This relationship is ignored in the MDGs and PRSPs. The environment is viewed, today as in the past, as a separate sectoral issue and priority rather than as the foundation for attaining all other development goals.[60]

PHOTO 2.1   Jubilee and other NGOs protest World Bank and IMF policies. Photo by Orin Langelle, Global Justice Ecology Project.

Regional and Other Multilateral Organizations as Actors

Regional and other multilateral organizations also play an increasing role in environmental politics. Some, such as the regional fishing organizations, are specific functional groups that have taken on environmental responsibilities out of necessity. Others have broad political and economic agendas that include significant environmental issues. Still others have been specifically established to address environmental concerns.

The European Union (EU) is the only such regional organization whose decisions obligate its members. In the 1950s, six European countries decided to pool their economic resources and set up a system of joint decisionmaking on economic issues. To do so, they formed several organizations, of which the European Economic Community (EEC) was the most important and, eventually, was renamed simply "the European Community."[61] The 1992 Maastricht Treaty introduced new forms of cooperation between the then twelve members on issues such as defense, justice, and home affairs, including the environment. By adding this intergovernmental cooperation to the existing "Community" system, the Maastricht Treaty created the European Union. The EU is unique in that its now twenty-five Member States have set up common institutions to which they delegate some of their sovereignty so that decisions on specific matters, including agriculture, fisheries, and trade, can be made at the European level.

Environmental action by the European Community began in 1972 with four successive action programs based on a vertical and sectoral approach to ecological problems. During this period, the Community adopted some two hundred pieces of legislation, chiefly concerned with limiting pollution by introducing minimum standards, notably for waste management, water pollution, and air pollution. Today, the principle of sustainable development is one of the European Community's aims, and a high degree of environmental protection is one of its absolute priorities.[62]

The sixth and current action program for the environment sets out the priorities for the European Community up to 2010. Four areas are highlighted: climate change, nature and biodiversity, environment and health, and the management of natural resources and waste. Measures to achieve these priorities are outlined: improving the application of environmental legislation, working together with the market and citizens, and ensuring that other Community policies take greater account of environmental considerations. According to the Maastricht Treaty, one of the objectives of Community policy on the environment is to promote measures at the international level to deal with regional or global environmental problems. Accordingly, the Community cooperates with other countries and international organizations. The Community has been a party to international conventions on environmental conservation since the 1970s. At present, it is a party to more than thirty conventions and agreements on the environment and takes an active part in the negotiations leading to the adoption of these instruments. The Community also takes part, normally as an observer, in the activities and negotiations taking place within the context of international bodies or programs and in particular under the auspices of the UN.[63]

The Organization for Economic Cooperation and Development (OECD) is also a player on the international environmental stage. The OECD has played a major role in promoting sustainable consumption and production within its member states and has provided a great deal of background information and support to its members on such issues as climate change, trade- and environment-related issues, and transport and the environment.

The Organization of American States (OAS), one of the oldest regional organizations, was also the first to hold a presidential summit specifically focused on the environment when it convened the Summit of the Americas on Sustainable Development in Bolivia in December 1996. The Office for Sustainable Development and Environment is the principal technical arm of the OAS General Secretariat for responding to the needs of member states on issues relating to sustainable development within an economic development context. With the objective of establishing concrete means to strengthen sustainable development, heads of state and government at the Bolivia Summit conferred responsibility to the OAS for formulating a strategy for the promotion of public participation in decisionmaking for sustainable development.

At the second Summit of the Americas in 1998, governments acknowledged the effort made by the OAS and instructed it, through the Inter-American Commission on Sustainable Development, to continue to fulfill the previous summits' mandates. Leaders also requested that other entities of the inter-American system and the United Nations work to strengthen cooperation in implementing mandates from the Summit on Sustainable Development. By the third Summit of the Americas, the issues to be addressed concerning sustainable development were well established. The third summit therefore focused on the mechanisms for moving these issues forward in hemispheric and international forums. The enactment and enforcement of multilateral environmental agreements (MEAs) and support for the participation in the 2002 World Summit on Sustainable Development were emphasized. Active use of inter-American institutions such as the OAS and the Pan-American Health Organization to implement the sustainable development agenda was also encouraged. The sustainable development agenda is a major element of the Summits of the Americas and now includes specialized ministerial meetings, experts' groups, and interagency task forces to address these issues.

The African Union, which evolved out of the Organization of African Unity in 1999, includes the promotion of sustainable development as one of its official objectives. At its inaugural Summit in mid-2002, the African Union adopted the New Partnership for Africa's Development (NEPAD) as a blueprint for the continent's future development. The primary objective of NEPAD is to eradicate poverty in Africa and to place African countries on a path of sustainable growth and development in an effort to halt the continent's marginalization in the globalization process. NEPAD recognizes the need to protect the environment not only for Africa's benefit but also for the many natural resources of global importance the continent holds, including a wide range of flora and fauna, paleoanthropological resources, and immense forests that act as carbon sinks. These are resources that could be degraded without support from the international community. Implicit in NEPAD's approach is the need for the developed world to support Africa's sustainable development, not only for the sake of Africans but also for the wider global community.

NEPAD has received widespread recognition and expressions of support, including endorsements from the UN General Assembly, the Bretton Woods institutions, the G-8, EU, Japan, the China-Africa Cooperation Forum, and the Non-Aligned Movement. In 2002, the UN General Assembly held a one-day high-level plenary meeting that focused specifically on NEPAD. On the basis of this work, the UN General Assembly adopted a resolution establishing NEPAD as a recurring item on its annual agenda.

Asia-Pacific Economic Cooperation (APEC), which formed in 1989 in response to the growing interdependence among Asia-Pacific economies, includes in its work the consideration of three categories of environmental issues: air, atmospheric, and water pollution, especially those related to energy production and use; resource degradation; and demographic shifts, including rural out-migration, food security, and urbanization. APEC had a major setback in 1998 as a result of the spread of the Asian financial crisis. However, at their November 1998 meeting in Kuala Lumpur, Malaysia, the APEC economic leaders reiterated their "commitment to advance sustainable development across the entire spectrum of [their] workplan including cleaner production, protection of the marine environment and sustainable cities."[64]

The first APEC ocean-related ministerial meeting was held in South Korea on 25–26 April 2002, its theme being "Toward the Sustainability of Marine and Coastal Resources." Sustainable fisheries, ocean science and technology, marine environmental protection, and integrated coastal management were discussed at this meeting. During the meeting, ministers adopted the Seoul Oceans Declaration. The Declaration provided new plans for future implementation in the area of sustainable development, especially on maritime affairs.

Within the United Nations system, the Group of 77 (G-77) functions as the "negotiating arm of the developing countries."[65] The G-77 was established in 1964 by seventy-seven developing countries at the end of the first session of the United Nations Conference on Trade and Development (UNCTAD) in Geneva. Beginning in 1967, a permanent institutional structure gradually developed and led to chapters of the Group of 77 in Rome (FAO), Vienna

(UNIDO), Paris (UNESCO), Nairobi (UNEP) and the Group of 24 in Washington, D.C. (IMF and World Bank). Although the membership of the G-77 has spread to 132 countries, the original name was retained because of its historic significance. China, which has the status of associate member, also plays an influential role in the G-77. As the largest Third World coalition in the United Nations, the G-77 provides the means for the developing world to articulate and promote its collective economic interests, enhance its joint negotiating capacity on all major international economic issues in the United Nations system, and promote economic and technical cooperation among developing countries.[66] As environmental issues have become increasingly intertwined with economic issues and as more developing countries have become involved in the negotiation of multilateral environmental agreements, the G-77 has played an increasing role in these negotiations since the early 1990s.

States have also created regional organizations explicitly to address environmental issues. One such organization is the South Pacific Regional Environment Programme (SPREP). Created in 1982, SPREP has developed a framework for environmentally sound planning and management suited to the South Pacific region. In its efforts to improve and protect the environment, SPREP's action program aims to build national capacity in environmental and resource management. SPREP also provides capacity building, training, and support for member states to improve their ability to represent their interests in international negotiations and United Nations global conferences.[67]

The Central American Commission on Environment and Development (CCAD) was established in 1989 to enable improved regional cooperation on environment and development issues. Since then, CCAD has adopted different regional agreements on the conservation of biological diversity, climate change, transboundary movements of hazardous wastes, the management and conservation of forest ecosystems, sustainable development in oceans and coastal areas, and access to genetic resources.[68]

NONGOVERNMENTAL ORGANIZATIONS AS ACTORS

The emergence of the global environment as a major issue in world politics coincided with the emergence of NGOs as important actors in environmental politics.[69] Although business organizations are often included in the United Nations definition of an NGO, we use the term here to denote an independent, nonprofit organization not beholden to a government or a profit-making organization.

NGO influence on global environmental politics stems from three principal factors. First, NGOs often possess expert knowledge and innovative thinking about global environmental issues acquired from years of focused specialization on the issues under negotiation. Second, NGOs are acknowledged to be dedicated to goals that transcend narrow national or sectoral interests. Third, NGOs often represent substantial constituencies within their own countries and thus can command attention from policymakers because of their potential ability to mobilize these people to influence policies, and even tight elections.

In the industrialized countries, most NGOs active in global environmental politics fall into one of three categories: organizations affiliated with international NGOs (INGOs)—NGOs with branches in more than one country; large national organizations focused primarily on domestic environmental issues; and think tanks, or research institutes, their influence coming primarily from publishing studies and proposals for action.

Some INGOs are a loose federation of national affiliates, others have a more centralized structure. Friends of the Earth International (FOEI), based in Amsterdam, is a confederation of seventy national independent affiliates, half of which are in developing countries. At an annual meeting, delegates democratically set priorities and select five or more campaigns on which they cooperate. Greenpeace is one of the largest INGOs; it has offices in forty-one counties and more than 2.8 million financial supporters/members.[70] Its international activities are tightly organized from a well-staffed headquarters (also in Amsterdam) and guided by issues and strategies determined at an annual meeting.

The Switzerland-based World Wildlife Fund (WWF)—also known in Europe as the World Wide Fund for Nature—is the world's largest and one of the most experienced independent conservation organizations. It has around 5 million supporters and offices in more than ninety countries.

WWF's mission is to stop the degradation of the earth's natural environment and to build a future in which humans live in harmony with nature; the WWF plans to accomplish these goals by conserving the world's biological diversity, ensuring that the use of renewable natural resources is sustainable, and promoting the reduction of pollution and wasteful consumption. WWF focuses on six global issues: climate change, forests, freshwater, marine, species, and toxics. It also works on cross-cutting issues that directly affect programmatic and eco-regional work. These include trade and investment (e.g., World Trade Organization rules), indigenous and traditional peoples (e.g., intellectual property rights), and the impacts of tourism. Particular attention is paid to the root causes of biodiversity loss, such as poverty, migration, macroeconomic policies, and poor enforcement of environmental legislation.

The European Environmental Bureau (EEB), organized in 1974, is now a confederation of 143 national-level environmental organizations in thirty-one countries. The EEB seeks to help improve EU environmental policies and sustainable development policies by effectively integrating environmental objectives in horizontal and sectoral policies of the EU and ensuring compliance with effective strategies to realize these objectives.

The second category of NGOs includes the big U.S. environmental organizations, almost all of which have international programs. Some, such as the Sierra Club, the National Audubon Society, and the National Wildlife Federation (NWF), were formed in the late nineteenth and early twentieth centuries around conservation issues. Others, including Environmental Defense and the Natural Resources Defense Council (NRDC), arose in the early 1970s in an attempt to use legal, economic, and regulatory processes to affect national policy, an initial focus being on air and water pollution. Along with Friends of the Earth USA, they have come to play effective roles on related international issues, particularly in the negotiations on climate and ozone and efforts to reshape the policies of the multilateral development banks. Other organizations with more specific agendas have also become more internationally active on their issues; among these are Defenders of Wildlife and the Humane Society. Total membership in the United States in national environmental organizations increased in the 1980s to an estimated 13 million people and leveled off in the 1990s.

Environmental think tanks, normally funded by private donations or contracts, rely primarily on their technical expertise and research programs to influence global environmental policy. Prominent examples include the World Resources Institute (WRI), which publishes well-respected reports on the global environment and policy studies on specific issues. Publications from the Worldwatch Institute have often identified new problems and suggested alternative approaches to international issues. The International Institute for Environment and Development (IIED) in London drew early attention to the environment/poverty connection in developing countries. In a few countries, government-funded but nevertheless independent institutes seek to influence the policies of their own governments and of international negotiations. The International Institute for Sustainable Development (IISD) of Canada and the Stockholm Environment Institute of Sweden have played such roles. These organizations all collaborate with colleagues in other countries.

Unlike the environmental NGOs of the North, environmentalism in developing countries grew out of a "lopsided, iniquitous and environmentally destructive process of development," and is often interlinked with questions of human rights, ethnicity, and distributive justice.[71] Southern NGOs tend to stress land use, forest management and fishing rights, and the redistribution of power over natural resources rather than ozone depletion and global warming.[72] They also tend to be more critical of consumerism and uncontrolled economic development than their colleagues in the North. But there are many exceptions, such as the Chilean and Argentinean NGOs' interest in the ozone layer and the NGOs in low-lying coastal areas or small islands that are concerned about climate change. Developing-country NGOs have often become involved in international policy issues through opposition to multilateral bank projects and government policies that displace villages or threaten rain forests, and they tend to regard transnational corporations as enemies of the environment. Inherently critical of their governments on most domestic policies, NGO members who are committed to environmental protection have often been harassed, subjected to political repression, and jailed. In some countries, however, they have acquired political legitimacy and a measure of influence on national environmental policy issues.

India, which is symbolic of a number of developing countries, has an environmental movement the origins of which can be dated back to the Chipko movement, which started in the Garhwal Himalaya in April 1973. Between 1973 and 1980, more than a dozen instances were recorded in which men, women, and children threatened to hug forest trees rather than allow them to be logged for export. Unlike environmentalists in the North, however, the peasants were not interested in saving the trees but in using the forest for agricultural and household requirements.[73]

The Chipko movement was the forerunner of and the direct inspiration for a series of popular movements in defense of community rights to natural resources. Sometimes these struggles revolved around forests; in other instances, around the control and use of pasture lands, minerals, or fisheries. Most of these conflicts have pitted rich against poor: logging companies against hill villagers, dam builders against forest tribal communities, multinational corporations deploying trawlers against traditional fisherfolk in small boats.[74]

In the 1980s, rubber tappers organized to resist the destruction of the forests that had supported them and that they had tended for decades. In 1989, after a cattle rancher murdered Chico Mendes, a key leader of the rubber tappers, the Brazilian government took action. The country set aside "extractive reserves" to protect forests where tapping and other sustainable extraction could continue. In Sarawak, Malaysia, loggers cleared 2.8 million hectares, or 30 percent of the forest, between 1963 and 1985. Many of the timber licenses issued by the Sarawak government covered the customary land of the natives who depend on the forests for food and shelter; indeed, for their very survival. Beginning in early 1987, natives started erecting blockades across timber roads in a desperate attempt to stop the logging.[75] The conflict continues to this day.

The Green Belt Movement, based in Kenya, is a grassroots NGO that focuses on environmental conservation, community development, and capacity building. Professor Wangari Maathai established the Green Belt Movement in 1977 under the auspices of the National Council of Women of Kenya. Its vision is to create a society of people who consciously work for the continued improvement of their environment and for a greener, cleaner Kenya. Programs include tree planting, biodiversity conservation, civic and environmental education, advocacy and networking, food security, and capacity building for women and girls. In 2004, Professor Maathai received the Nobel Peace Prize for her efforts with the Green Belt Movement—the first Nobel Peace Prize given to an environmentalist.[76]

Many environmental and development battles continue to be fought at the community level in developing countries, but some NGOs and coalitions in developing countries also tackle a broader range of environmental and development issues. The Third World Network, for example, is an independent nonprofit international network of organizations and individuals involved in issues relating to development, the Third World, and North-South issues. Its objectives are to conduct research on economic, social and environmental issues pertaining to the South; to publish books and magazines; to organize and participate in seminars; and to represent Southern interests and perspectives at international fora such as the UN conferences and processes. Headquartered in Penang, Malaysia, the Third World Network also has regional offices in Delhi, India; Montevideo, Uruguay; Accra, Ghana; and Geneva, Switzerland. It also has affiliated organizations in several Third World countries, including India, the Philippines, Thailand, Brazil, Bangladesh, Malaysia, Peru, Ethiopia, Uruguay, Mexico, Ghana, South Africa, and Senegal.[77]

The Center for Science and Environment (CSE) in India seeks to increase public awareness on science, technology, environment, and development issues and search for solutions that people and communities can implement themselves. Founded in 1980, it has worked on a wide range of issues in India, including air and water pollution, human health, and monitoring the

PHOTO 2.2   Nobel Laureate Wangari Maathai at a tree-planting ceremony at the United Nations in New York in May 2005. Courtesy IISD/*Earth Negotiations Bulletin.*

environmental performance of Indian industry. Like the Third World Network, it is also involved at the global level and has a large project on global environmental governance.[78]

Developing-country NGOs often form national-level coalitions, such as the Indonesian Forum for Environment (WALHI), which unites hundreds of environmental organizations countrywide. Indigenous minorities in the five Amazon Basin countries have also organized their own national-level coalitions, which, in turn, have formed a coordinating body (called COICA, for its Spanish name) to lobby for a voice in all Amazon development projects affecting them. Indeed, UNCED recognition of indigenous groups in Chapter 26 of Agenda 21 with their highly visible participation in subsequent global conferences and the work of the Convention on Biological Diversity have given a boost to the rights of indigenous peoples and provided them with a way to influence international environmental negotiations.

International coalitions of NGOs working on a specific environmental issue have also become a means of increasing NGO influence. The Antarctic and Southern Oceans Coalition is a consortium of two hundred environmental organizations in thirty-three countries that lobbied against the Antarctic minerals treaty and for an Antarctic environmental protocol. The Climate Action Network, formed in 1989, has more than 340 member organizations around the world that work to promote government and individual action to limit human-induced climate change.

North-South NGO alliances have sometimes been effective in influencing international events. An alliance between U.S. NGOs and indigenous opponents of rain forest destruction brought worldwide attention to Brazilian policy in 1986. Together, they helped stop the World Bank's Polonoreste project, an Amazonian road building and colonization scheme, persuaded President José Sarney to halt the tax incentives for agriculture and ranching that had stimulated the Amazon land boom, and persuaded members of the U.S. Congress and officials of the Inter-American Development Bank to support extractive reserves.[79]

The Internet has facilitated North-South NGO cooperation on various issues. For example, in 1997, a coalition of Northern and Southern NGOs, ranging from the Third World Network to the Council of Canadians, used the World Wide Web, electronic mail, and electronic conferencing to organize swift opposition to the Multilateral Agreement on Investment (MAI). The prospective treaty to liberalize international investment rules was being negotiated behind the closed doors of the OECD.[80] In December 1998, the

OECD canceled negotiations, acknowledging that the NGOs had aroused enough opposition in many countries to derail the process.

But relations between Northern and Southern NGOs are not always smooth. At climate-change negotiations in February 1991, developing-country NGOs charged that they had not been consulted by Northern NGOs advocating steeper curtailment of CO_2 emissions, the burden of which they thought would fall on developing countries. There was a similar division in the pre-UNCED discussions of a forest treaty. In this matter, also, the Southern NGOs' position tended to parallel that of their governments. A Southern resentment of Northern NGOs sometimes persists, especially at the big international conferences where the better-prepared, better-financed U.S. and European NGOs are heavily represented.

Despite potential tensions, however, there have been many instances of close North-South cooperation in lobbying. One example is the Pesticide Action Network, a network of more than six hundred participating nongovernmental organizations, institutions, and individuals in more than ninety countries working to replace hazardous pesticides with ecologically sound alternatives. Its projects and campaigns are coordinated by five autonomous regional centers. The Pesticide Action Network and partner groups from around the world have been working together to lobby for the phaseouts of **persistent organic pollutants** (POPs) during the negotiation and implementation of the Stockholm Convention on Persistent Organic Pollutants, an international treaty that sets mandatory timetables for POPs phaseouts and provides technical and financial assistance to help developing countries eliminate POPs.

Another successful coalition of North-South NGOs has been the International POPs Elimination Network (IPEN), which works for the global elimination of POPs on an expedited yet socially equitable basis. Founded in early 1998 by a small number of NGOs, IPEN was formally launched with a public forum during the first session of the POPs INC in Montreal in June 1998— the start of formal negotiations on creating a global treaty to control and/or eliminate POPs. Throughout the five negotiating sessions, IPEN grew to include more than 350 public health, environmental, consumer, and other nongovernmental organizations in sixty-five countries. The network worked to mobilize grassroots support for a global treaty to eliminate POPs. It also leveraged the resources and created a forum for NGOs and activists from around the world to participate in the negotiations. IPEN coordinated NGO conferences and workshops at each of the five negotiating sessions.[81]

One of the most important organizations through which NGOs influence environmental politics is the World Conservation Union (IUCN), which brings together eighty-two states, 111 government agencies, more than eight hundred NGOs, and some 10,000 scientists and experts from 181 countries in a unique worldwide partnership Governed by a general assembly of delegates from its member organizations that meets every three years, the IUCN has had a major influence on global agreements on wildlife conservation. Although IUCN actions tend to be limited by state member agencies and often embrace only broad consensus positions, IUCN has been successful in drafting environmental treaties and assisting in monitoring their implementation.

Influencing Environmental Regime Formation

NGOs can attempt to influence the development, expansion, and implementation of international regimes in various ways. These include

- influencing the global environmental agenda by defining a new issue or redefining an old one;
- lobbying governments to accept a more advanced position toward an issue, by advancing new proposals, carrying out consumer boycotts and educational campaigns, or bringing lawsuits;
- proposing draft texts for including in conventions in advance of conferences;
- lobbying and participating in international negotiations;
- supporting ratification and implementation of the regime by the government in their host country;
- providing reporting services;
- assisting implementation of the regime, particularly in developing countries; and
- monitoring the implementation of conventions and reporting to the secretariat and/or the parties.

One example of an NGO influencing the global environmental agenda is the role that WWF and Conservation International played in 1988–1989 in creating a new issue of banning commerce in African elephant ivory by publishing a report on the problem and circulating it to the CITES parties.

Pressing for changes in the policy of a major actor is sometimes the best way for NGOs to influence an international regime. In efforts to protect the ozone layer, in the late 1970s the U.S. Clean Air Coalition, a group of national environmental organizations, successfully lobbied for a domestic ban on aerosols and the regulation of CFCs. Because they lobbied for a total phase-out of CFCs before negotiations on the Montreal Protocol began, they contributed to U.S. international leadership on this issue. Similarly, three U.S. NGOs working with pro-treaty biotechnology firms were a major influence on the Clinton administration's decision to reverse the Bush administration's position and sign the biodiversity convention in 1993.[82] Although effective consumer boycotts are rare, an NGO-organized boycott affected the whaling issue in 1988 when a hundred school districts and several fast-food and supermarket chains boycotted Icelandic fish because of Iceland's pro-whaling stand and brought a temporary halt to that country's whaling.[83]

Greenpeace's monitoring and reporting on the toxic waste trade was a key factor in encouraging a coalition of countries to push for a complete ban on North-South waste trade under the Basel Convention.

NGOs can influence international regimes in a more specialized way by writing a potential text for inclusion in a convention or amendment and circulating it in advance of the negotiations in the hope that it will be formally supported and submitted by a national delegation. In exceptional cases, this strategy can even include developing an entire draft convention. Few NGOs have the staff resources to devote to such a task, and only IUCN has succeeded in having draft conventions used as the basis for negotiations. The Convention Concerning the Protection of the World Cultural and Natural Heritage, signed in 1972 in Paris, was based on a draft produced by IUCN. CITES, signed in 1973, was the result of an IUCN initiative that went through three drafts over nearly a decade.[84]

NGOs have become especially active and well organized in lobbying at international negotiating conferences. The conferences of the parties to most environmental conventions permit NGO observers, enabling NGOs to be actively involved in the proceedings. Certain NGOs specialize in the meetings of particular conventions and over the years have acquired a high level of technical and legal expertise. The Humane Society of the United States has been lobbying at meetings of the International Whaling Commission (IWC) since 1973, and Greenpeace has been active in the Conference of the Parties to the London Convention since the early 1980s. The Climate Action Network was extremely active in the negotiation of the Framework Convention on Climate Change and the Kyoto Protocol, and it continues to participate in the meetings of the Conference of the Parties to the convention. The Climate Action Network lobbied extensively for greater commitments toward the reduction of greenhouse gas emissions beyond the year 2000 during the Kyoto Protocol negotiations. The Pesticide Action Network and the International POPs Elimination Network have been active in lobbying at negotiations for the Stockholm Convention on POPs.

NGOs also influence international conferences primarily by providing scientific and technical information and new arguments to delegations that are already sympathetic to their objectives. In the process leading up to the whaling moratorium, NGOs supplied factual information on violations of the whaling convention as well as scientific information not otherwise available to the delegations.[85] In some circumstances, NGOs have a particularly strong influence on a key delegation's positions, an example being the biodiversity negotiations in 1991–1992 when WWF/Australia and other NGOs represented on the Australian delegation were consulted on all major issues in the convention before the delegation adopted positions.[86] The Foundation for International Environmental Law and Development (FIELD) has assisted the Alliance of Small Island States within the context of the climate change negotiations. FIELD has been instrumental in providing AOSIS with advice and legal expertise, which in turn has enabled the Alliance to wield unexpected influence in the climate negotiations.[87] Greenpeace provided a great deal of technical support to African and other developing countries, which were supporting a ban on the dumping of hazardous wastes in developing countries during the negotiation of the Basel Convention.

NGOs can also provide useful reporting services during these conferences. *ECO* has been published by NGOs at numerous UN-sponsored environmental conferences since 1972 and provides a combination of news stories and commentary. The *Earth Negotiations Bulletin,* published by IISD, has provided objective reports of United Nations environment and development negotiations since 1992.[88] The reporting of ongoing negotiations is something countries cannot do easily or effectively on their own. If a government attempted to provide such reporting, the reports would be derided as biased. If the UN or a formal secretariat published daily reports, they would have the status of official documents; member governments would have difficulty agreeing on content, style, tone, and so forth. However, because the NGO community is already providing the information in a fair manner and free of charge, governments have little incentive to step in.[89]

NGOs can sometimes assist governments in implementing the provisions of environmental regimes. This can include offering assistance in drafting national legislation, providing technical and scientific assistance on relevant issues, and brokering the provision of essential financial support.

NGOs can also influence regime formation by monitoring compliance with an agreement once it goes into effect. Investigation and reporting by NGOs can bring pressure on parties that are violating provisions of an agreement. They can demonstrate the need for a more effective enforcement mechanism (or for creation of a mechanism where none exists) or help build support for the further elaboration or strengthening of the existing regime rules.

This NGO function has been especially important with regard to the CITES and whaling regimes. The international Trade Records Analysis of Flora and Fauna in Commerce (TRAFFIC), a joint wildlife trade monitoring program of WWF and IUCN, has played a vital role in supplementing the CITES Secretariat in monitoring the compliance of various countries with CITES bans on trade in endangered species.[90] Climate networks in the United States and the EU produced specific critical reviews of countries' national climate action plans even before the climate treaty came into effect. Greenpeace's aggressive reporting of hazardous wastes dumped in violation of the Basel and Bamako agreements helped create a climate in which a full ban on international shipping of such wastes to non-OECD countries was accomplished in 1994.

NGOs and International Institutions

Influencing the structure and policies of major international institutions active in global environmental politics poses a different set of challenges to NGOs. The international NGO community has taken on a wide range of global institutions, from the World Bank and the GEF to the International Tropical Timber Organization (ITTO) and the WTO. These institutions have different characteristics that help to explain the success of NGO efforts to influence the policies and structures of each.

The most successful such NGO effort was influencing the restructuring of the Global Environment Facility, on which Southern and Northern NGOs were in full agreement. NGOs were highly critical of the GEF as administered by the World Bank during its 1991–1993 pilot phase. They supported the developing-country position for the creation of a GEF Secretariat independent of the World Bank and for a transparent and more democratic project approval process.[91]

U.S. NGOs were also effective in forcing changes in the lending of multilateral development banks (MDBs)—primarily because of the importance of the U.S. Congress in approving funding for the MDBs.[92] Between 1983 and 1987, U.S. environmental NGOs in alliance with congressional fiscal conservatives persuaded congressional appropriations subcommittees to sponsor legislation directing the U.S. executive directors of the MDBs to press for environmental reforms. As a result, by 1986, the United States began voting against particularly egregious World Bank loans, actions that in 1987 helped prompt a commitment from Barber Conable, the former World Bank president, to pay greater attention to the environment.

In the late 1980s, NGO campaigning for bank reform began to focus on issues of public participation and accountability. About 150 NGOs worldwide participated in some fashion in a campaign to spur greater openness and accountability and to encourage debt reduction and development strategies that were more equitable and less destructive to the environment. Today, partly as a result of this high-profile pressure, about half of the Bank's lending projects have provisions for NGO involvement, up from an average of only 6 percent between 1973 and 1988. The Bank has even included NGOs such as Oxfam International in multilateral debt relief discussions.

Much more difficult still for NGOs is the trade and environment issue, to which they turned their attention only in 1990. The goal of the General Agreement on Tariffs and Trade (GATT), determined half a century ago, is to reduce tariffs and other trade barriers. The GATT has never had provisions for NGO observers. Environmental activists have been campaigning for increased transparency, participation, and accountability in the WTO, portraying it as a secretive organization lacking in accountability. They argue that NGOs can play a crucial role in making the world trading system more transparent and accountable.[93] Before the third WTO ministerial talks, which took place in Seattle in December 1999, many believed that although NGO demands for participation were unlikely to be met in the near future, governments were attempting to engage in a more open manner with development and environmental organizations.[94] In the aftermath of the violent street protests during the Seattle meeting, however, the WTO decided to hold its next ministerial meeting in Doha, Qatar, where, through visa requirements, restrictive security, and the higher cost of travel, they could easily enforce limits on the number of NGOs and street protesters that could attend (see table 2.2).

CORPORATIONS AS ACTORS

Private business firms, especially multinational corporations, are important actors in global environmental politics. Their core activities, although often essential, consume resources and produce pollution; furthermore, environmental regulations often directly affect their economic interests. Corporations also have significant assets for influencing global environmental politics. They have good access to decisionmakers in most governments

TABLE 2.2   NGO Participation at WTO Ministerial Conferences

	# of eligible NGOs	NGOs represented	# of registered participants
Singapore 1996	159	108	235
Geneva 1998	153	128	362
Seattle 1999	776	686	approx. 1,500
Doha 2001	651	370	370
Cancún 2003	961	795	1,578

Source: World Trade Organization, "NGO participation in Ministerial Conference was largest ever," Press Release (October 6, 2003) [Internet: http://www.wto.org/english/news_e/news03_e/ngo_minconf_6oct03_e.htm]

and international organizations and can deploy impressive technical expertise on the issues in which they are interested. They have national and international industrial associations that represent their interests in policy issues, as well as significant financial and technical resources important to developing solutions.

Corporations often oppose national and international policies that they believe would impose significant new costs on them or otherwise reduce expected profits. Indeed, at times, corporations have worked to weaken several global environmental regimes, including ozone protection, climate change, whaling, the international toxic waste trade, and fisheries. Corporations sometimes support an international agreement if it would create weaker regulations on their activities than those that they would expect to be imposed domestically.

At the same time, however, corporate interests vary across companies and sectors and, at times, some corporations support national and international policy. When faced with existing strong domestic regulations on an activity with a global environmental dimension, corporations are likely to support international agreements that would impose similar standards on competitors abroad. For example, on fisheries management issues, U.S. and Japanese fishing industries are more strictly regulated on various issues of high seas fishing, particularly quotas on bluefin tuna and other highly migratory species, than those of other Asian fishing states (Republic of Korea, China, Taiwan, and Indonesia); their respective fishing industries therefore pushed the United States and Japan to take strong positions on regulation of high seas fishing capacity in FAO negotiations in 1998.

The interests of a particular industry in regard to a proposed global environmental regime are often far from monolithic. On ozone, climate change, biodiversity, and fisheries, industries have been divided either along national lines or between sectors or subsectors of industry. On climate, European-based energy firms have been more willing to see such an agreement as a business opportunity because they have had experience in using greater energy efficiency to become more profitable, whereas U.S.-based firms, which have little or no such experience, have been much more resistant to such plans.

But even the U.S.-based energy industry is not united on the issue of climate change. Three major energy companies (Shell, Sunoco, and BP Amoco) have decided to seek a seat at the table rather than remain in opposition to the Kyoto Protocol, joining the Pew Center on Global Climate Change. BP Amoco and Royal Dutch Shell have already voluntarily reduced their greenhouse gas emissions by 10 percent from 1990 levels.[95] U.S. automobile manufacturers, who were once central players in the anti-protocol Global Climate Coalition, have also noted opportunities for future markets under the Kyoto Protocol. For example, major automakers signed an agreement in April 2005 with the government of Canada to reduce greenhouse gas emissions from new cars and trucks. The Canadian agreement calls for annual greenhouse gas emissions from tailpipes to drop by 5.3 million tons by 2010, nearly a 6 percent reduction in the total amount of greenhouse gas emissions projected from all vehicles in Canada, according to government figures.[96]

When companies see a positive stake in a global environmental agreement, they can dilute the influence of other companies that seek to weaken it. In 1992, the Industrial Biotechnology Association (IBA) opposed the biodiversity convention because it feared the provisions on intellectual property rights would legally condone existing violations of those rights.[97] But the issue was not a high priority for most of the industry, and two of its leading member corporations, Merck and Genentech, believed the convention would benefit them by encouraging developing countries to negotiate agreements with companies for access to genetic resources. After those companies joined environmentalists in calling for the United States to sign the convention in 1993, the IBA came out in favor of signing it.[98]

Similarly, when U.S. industries interested in promoting alternatives to fossil fuels began lobbying at meetings of the Intergovernmental Negotiating Committee for the climate convention in August 1994, they succeeded in reducing the influence of pro-fossil-fuel industries, which had previously monopolized industry views on the issue. Similarly, insurance companies have become more concerned about the increased hurricane and storm damage that may be caused by global warming. As a result, they have become proactive in supporting targets and timetables for greenhouse gas emissions reductions. The insurance industry has tried to raise awareness on the issue of climate change and its implications through applied research projects looking into the impacts of windstorms and floods. The Insurance Industry Initiative, which was set up by UNEP in 1996, is increasing its political efforts to create a wider and more responsive lobby group with which it can steer the debate within the UN Framework Convention on Climate Change.[99] At the tenth Conference of the Parties to the UNFCCC, Munich Re, one of the world's biggest reinsurance companies, announced that during the first ten months of 2004 natural disasters cost the insurance industry more than \$35 billion, up from \$16 billion in 2003. When releasing their report on weather or climate-related disasters, Munich Re urged governments to make a strong commitment to a post-Kyoto agenda, otherwise "the industry's appetite to finance and insure projects . . . will be blunted."[100]

Corporate Influence on Regime Formation

Corporations may influence global environmental regimes either indirectly by influencing regime formation or directly by undertaking business activities that weaken a regime or contribute to its effectiveness. To influence the formation of regimes, they may

- shape the definition of the issue under negotiation in a way that is favorable to their interests;
- persuade an individual government to adopt a particular position on a regime being negotiated by lobbying it in its capital; or
- lobby delegations to the negotiating conference on the regime.

The greatest success of corporations in defining an issue to shape regime formation in their favor was the International Convention for the Prevention of Pollution of the Sea by Oil (1954). The seven major oil companies and global shipping interests (most of which were owned directly or indirectly by the oil companies) were the only actors with the technical expertise to make detailed proposals on maritime oil pollution. The technical papers submitted by the International Chamber of Shipping, composed of thirty national associations of shipowners, and the Oil Companies International Marine Forum, representing the interests of major oil companies, defined the terms of the discussion of the convention.[101] That ensured that the convention would be compatible with oil and shipping interests—and quite ineffective in preventing oil pollution of the oceans. That degree of success in defining an issue is unlikely to recur in the future because governments and NGOs now have more expertise on issues being negotiated; furthermore, NGOs are better organized and more aggressive.

In most global environmental issues, corporations have relied on their domestic political clout to ensure that governments do not adopt strong policies adversely affecting their interests. The domestic U.S. industry most strongly opposed to a ban on hazardous waste trade, the secondary-metals industry, helped persuade U.S. officials to block such a ban in the negotiation of the Basel Convention. And on ozone depletion, Japan agreed to a phaseout of ozone-depleting chemicals only after some of its largest electronic firms agreed to phase out their use by 2000.

In regard to the climate change regime, industry lobbying in the United States succeeded in reducing the flexibility of the executive branch in the negotiations. Some of the most powerful trade associations launched the Global Climate Information Project (GCIP) in 1997. Through a multimillion-dollar print and television advertising campaign, the GCIP cast doubt upon the desirability of emissions controls in the Kyoto Protocol, which was entering the final stages of negotiation, by arguing that emissions controls would raise taxes on gasoline, heating oil, and consumer goods and reduce the competitiveness of American businesses. An alliance of business and labor succeeded in persuading the U.S. Senate to vote 95–0 for a resolution stating that the president should not sign a protocol that requires greenhouse gas reductions without commitments from developing countries, or that would result in serious harm to the economy of the United States.[102]

Industry associations have been actively involved in influencing the negotiation of several global environmental regimes. When the industry enjoyed particular technical expertise or relatively unchallenged influence over the issue, it was represented on one or more key countries' delegations; for example, the Japanese commissioner to the International Whaling Commission has generally been the president of the Japanese Whaling Association.[103] U.S. and Canadian food manufacturers have participated on U.S. delegations to the FAO's Codex Alimentarius Commission, which sets international food standards.[104] Other active industry coalitions include the Global Climate Coalition, which worked closely with the delegations from the United States and Saudi Arabia during the negotiation of the UN Framework Convention on Climate Change.

EMISSION CONTROLS
NECESSARY TO HALT
GLOBAL WARMING

*In conclusion, Mr President, we at Exxon feel that
human survival may simply not be economic.*

CARTOON 2.2   "In conclusion, Mr. President,
we at Exxon feel that human survival may simply
not be economic." Copyright Richard D. Willson,
reprinted with permission.

Like NGOs, representatives of corporate interests lobby negotiations on
environmental regimes primarily by providing information and analysis to
the delegations that are most sympathetic to their cause. During the climate
change negotiations, for example, coal interests were active in advising the
U.S., Russian, and Saudi delegations on how to weaken the regime.[105] Industry groups had a particularly strong presence at the negotiating sessions for
the Cartagena Protocol on Biosafety. Their interest in participating in the negotiations grew during the talks: Eight industry groups were represented at
the first round of negotiations in Aarhus, Denmark, in 1996, but twenty such
groups were present at the 1999 meeting in Cartagena. Individual corporations, among them Monsanto, DuPont and Syngenta (formerly Novartis and
Zeneca), having a strong interest sent their own representatives to many of
the meetings. Industry lobby groups enjoying wide memberships present at
the negotiations included Biotechnology Industry Organization (BIO) (a
U.S.-based biotechnology lobby group), BioteCanada, Japan Bioindustry Association, the International Chamber of Commerce, and the International
Association of Plant Breeders for the Protection of Plant Varieties.[106]

Corporations also may facilitate or delay, strengthen or weaken global environmental regimes by direct actions that have an impact on the environment. These actions may be taken unilaterally or may be the result of agreements reached with their respective governments. Such actions can be crucial to the ability of a government to commit itself to a regime-strengthening policy. The climate-change and ozone-protection regimes are particularly sensitive to the willingness of corporations in key countries to take actions that would allow the international community to go beyond the existing agreement.

In the ozone-protection issue, the U.S. chemical industry delayed movement toward any regime for regulating ozone-depleting CFCs in the early 1980s, in part by reducing their own research efforts on CFC substitutes.[107] Subsequently, CFC producers gave impetus to an accelerated timetable for a CFC phaseout by unilaterally pledging to phase out their own uses of CFCs ahead of the schedule already agreed to by the Montreal Protocol parties. In 1989, Nissan and Toyota pledged to eliminate CFCs from their cars and manufacturing processes as early as the mid-1990s. In 1992, Ford Motor Company pledged to eliminate 90 percent of CFC use from its manufacturing processes worldwide by the end of that year and to eliminate all CFCs from its air conditioners and manufacturing by the end of 1994.

Early in the climate-change negotiations, the Japanese auto industry, which accounts for 20 percent of Japan's overall carbon emissions, adopted a goal of improving fuel efficiency by 8.5 percent above its 1990 level by 2000, thus encouraging a Japanese government commitment to the national goal of stabilization of carbon emissions at 1990 levels by 2000.[108] More recently, numerous corporations around the world have pledged to reduce their greenhouse gas emissions and to improve their environmental accounting.[109]

Industry and Nonregime Issues

Corporations have their greatest political influence on a global environmental issue when there are no negotiations on a formal, binding international regime governing the issue. Under those circumstances, they are able to use their economic and political clout with individual governments and international organizations to protect particular economic activities that damage the environment.

For example, in the past, the agrochemical industry enjoyed strong influence on the FAO's Plant Protection Service, which was responsible for the organization's pesticide activities. The industry's international trade association even had a joint program with the FAO to promote pesticide use worldwide until the 1970s.[110] This influence was instrumental in carrying out the industry's main strategy for avoiding binding international restrictions on its sales of pesticides in developing countries. Instead of binding rules, a voluntary "code of conduct" on pesticide distribution and use was drafted by the FAO between 1982 and 1985 in close consultation with the industry.

The logging of tropical rain forests for timber exports is another example of a global environmental issue on which multinational corporations have had a major influence. Major Japanese trading companies, such as Mitsubishi Corporation, have been heavily involved in logging operations in the Philippines, Indonesia, Malaysia, Papua New Guinea, Brazil, and Siberia. U.S. companies have also been involved in Southeast Asia. These companies have provided much of the financing for logging in those countries and then imported the raw logs—sometimes illegally harvested—or wood chips to Japan. They have also purchased timber from Myanmar, Thailand, Vietnam, Cambodia, and Laos. And they have had the cooperation of the Japanese government, which subsidized the construction of roads to be used by the Japanese-financed logging in Malaysia and Papua New Guinea.[111] Close ties between state leaders—such as former President Suharto of Indonesia and Chief Minister Taib Mahmud of Sarawak, Malaysia—and corporate executives have shielded destructive loggers throughout the Asia-Pacific. These ties have distorted state policies, including reforestation and conservation guidelines, sustainable management plans, tax and royalty rates, processing incentives, and foreign investment regulations. In this context, state implementers, in exchange for gifts, money, and security, often ignored or assisted illegal loggers, smugglers, and tax evaders.[112] The governments of some of the tropical forest countries have been the main actors in fending off moves to establish an international regime for managing forests, but multinational corporations have played a critical role in establishing and maintaining the international system of exploitation of those forests.

Although corporations usually resist strong international environmental agreements when they are not in their interest, in recent years certain corporations have been positioning themselves as advocates of global sustainable development, including DuPont, BP Amoco, General Electric, and Royal Dutch Shell. Under greater public scrutiny of their environmental behavior and pressure from consumers for environmentally friendly products, these corporations have discovered that preventing pollution is good for profitability. The result is the emergence of a group of corporate leaders who support some of the main aspects of the new paradigm of sustainable development as well as the development of certain environmental regimes.

In 1991, at the request of UNCED Secretary-General Maurice Strong, Swiss industrialist Stephan Schmidheiny enlisted a group of forty-eight chief executive officers of corporations from all over the world to set up the Business Council on Sustainable Development (BCSD) to support the objectives of the Earth Summit. The BCSD issued a declaration calling for the prices of goods to reflect environmental costs of production, use, recycling, and disposal and for changes in consumption patterns.[113] In January 1995, the BCSD and the World Industry Council for the Environment, an initiative of the International Chamber of Commerce, merged into what is today a coalition of 175 international companies united by a shared commitment to sustainable development via the three pillars of economic growth, ecological balance, and social progress. Drawing members from thirty-five countries and more than twenty major industrial sectors, the resulting World Business Council on Sustainable Development addresses a range of issues, including corporate social responsibility, access to clean water, capacity building, sustainable livelihoods, harmonizing international trade law with multilateral environmental agreements, and developing public-private partnerships in key areas of sustainable development, including support for the Kyoto Protocol.[114]

CONCLUSION

State and nonstate actors play key roles in the creation and implementation of national and international environmental policy. State actors have the primary roles in determining the outcomes of issues at stake in global environmental politics, but nonstate actors—IOs, NGOs, and corporations—influence the policies of individual state actors toward global environmental issues as well as the international negotiation process itself. Whether a state adopts the role of lead state, supporting state, swing state, or veto state on a particular issue depends primarily on domestic political factors and on the relative costs and benefits of the proposed regime. But international political-diplomatic consequences can also affect the choice of role.

International organizations, especially UNEP, WMO, and FAO, have played important roles in regime formation by setting the international agenda and by sponsoring and shaping negotiations on global environmental regimes and soft-law norms. The CSD has called attention to issues that should be on the international agenda as well as areas where there has been a failure to implement recommendations contained in Agenda 21. The Bretton Woods institutions and certain UN agencies, particularly UNDP and FAO, influence state development strategies through financing and technical assistance. IOs also seek to exert influence on state policy through research and advocacy of specific norms at the global level.

NGOs influence the environmental regimes by defining issues, swaying the policy of a key government, lobbying negotiating conferences, providing information and reporting services, drafting entire convention texts, and monitoring the implementation of agreements. They have also sought to change the policies and structure of major international institutions, such as the World Bank and the WTO, with varying degrees of success. They have been more successful when the institution in question is dependent on a key state for funding and less successful when the institution is not so dependent or has no tradition of permitting NGO participation in its processes.

Corporations have been active in international relations longer than NGOs and have influenced regime creation. They can sometimes employ special political assets—including particular technical expertise, privileged access to certain government ministries, and political clout with legislative bodies—to veto or weaken a regime. They can also directly affect the ability of the international community to meet regime goals by their own actions. They are able to maximize their political effectiveness in shaping the outcome of a global environmental issue when they can avert negotiations on a binding regime altogether.

DISCUSSION QUESTIONS

1. In what ways do the domestic politics of various states influence their policies toward global environmental issues?
2. Why might some states feel that there are "winners" and "losers" in a particular proposal for international cooperation on the environment, even though it may be in the interest of all states?
3. Discuss different ways that international organizations can affect global environmental politics. To what extent have IOs contributed to regime formation?
4. What role do multilateral banks, commercial banks and bilateral development assistance programs play in global environmental politics?

5. How have NGOs contributed to the development of international environmental policies and regimes?
6. What NGOs would you expect in a coalition on ozone depletion? Climate change? Biodiversity? Why? What governments would they be likely to befriend or criticize?
7. How do particular U.S. industries affect the position of the U.S. government on international environmental issues?
8. Develop a profile of any of the states frequently mentioned in this chapter—the U.S., the EU, China, India, Indonesia, Mexico, Brazil, and Malaysia—and describe how active they are in lead or blocking roles. Could you do the same for Russia? What other countries are conspicuously absent?

3

The Development of Environmental Regimes: Eleven Case Studies

The development of global environmental regimes often involves four processes or stages: issue definition, fact-finding, bargaining on regime creation, and regime strengthening. Within each environmental issue, the sequencing of these stages and the length of time that each takes vary greatly. The stages are not always distinct; the definition stage may overlap the fact-finding stage, which may, in turn, overlap the bargaining stage. Nevertheless, examining negotiations through stages or phases can provide a framework that reduces some of the complexities of multilateral negotiation to a more manageable level for understanding and analysis. It essentially divides the negotiation process into successive, often overlapping, phases; in each one, the negotiators present a particular focus of attention and concern.

Issue definition involves bringing the issue to the attention of the international community and identifying the scope and magnitude of the environmental threat, its primary causes, and the type of international action required to address the issue. An issue may be placed on the global environmental agenda by one or more state actors, by an international organization (usually at the suggestion of one or more members), or by a nongovernmental organization. The actors who introduce and define the issue often publicize new scientific evidence or theories, as they did for ozone depletion, **transboundary air pollution,** fisheries, toxic chemicals, and climate change. But issue definition may also involve identifying a radically different approach to international action on a problem, as it did for whaling, desertification, the hazardous waste trade, toxic chemicals, and endangered species.

Fact-finding involves efforts to build consensus on the nature of the problem and the most appropriate international actions to address it through an international process of studying the science, ecology, and economics surrounding the issue. In practice, fact-finding may vary from well developed to nonexistent; a mediating international organization that has brought key policymakers together in an attempt to establish a baseline of facts on which they can agree can be considered a successful example. When there is no such mediated process of fact-finding and consensus building, the facts may be openly challenged by states opposed to international action. The fact-finding stage often shades into the bargaining stage. Meetings ostensibly devoted to establishing the scope and seriousness of the problem may also try to spell out policy options. During this stage, a lead state may begin to advance a proposal for international action and try to build a consensus behind it. International cleavages and coalitions begin to form.

The nature of global environmental politics raises fundamental questions concerning the bargaining process. To be truly effective, a regime to mitigate a global danger such as ozone depletion or climate change must have the participation of virtually all the states contributing to the problem. However, at some point, negotiators must determine whether to go ahead with a less than optimal number of signatories or to accommodate veto state demands. Can a regime successfully address the problem without the participation of key nations? On the other hand, can an agreement be considered a success if it has universal support but has been weakened by compromises with veto states?[1] The outcome of the bargaining process depends in part on the bargaining leverage and cohesion of the veto coalition. The veto states can prevent the creation of a strong international regime by refusing to participate in it, or they can weaken it by insisting upon a toothless regime. However, one or more key members of the veto coalition usually make major concessions to make regime creation or regime strengthening possible. In certain cases, a regime may be created without the consent of key members of the veto coalition and thus remain a relatively ineffective regime, as in the case of transboundary air pollution. In other cases, as happened with forests, a regime cannot be created.

Regime building does not end with the signing and ratification of a global environmental convention. Once established, a regime can be strengthened, its central provisions made clearer or more stringent through further bargaining. The strengthening of a regime may occur either because new scientific evidence becomes available on the problem, because there are political shifts in one or more major states, or because the existing regime is shown to be ineffective in bringing about meaningful actions to reduce the threat.

The process of regime strengthening is encouraged by the review process that takes place at the periodic meetings of the Conference of the Parties mandated by most global environmental conventions. Regime strengthening may take one of three forms:

1. The Conference of the Parties can formally amend the treaty, as has been done in the case of uplisting the African elephant and big-leaf mahogany in CITES and the moratorium on commercial whaling adopted by the International Whaling Commission.
2. The Conference of the Parties can adopt a protocol that establishes concrete commitments or targets, as in the cases of the parties to the Vienna Convention negotiating the Montreal Protocol, the parties to the UN Framework Convention on Climate Change negotiating the Kyoto Protocol, and the parties to the Convention on Long Range Transboundary Air Pollution negotiating protocols on sulfur dioxide, nitrogen oxide, and volatile organic compounds.
3. In some treaties, the Conference of the Parties can make decisions requiring important new actions by the parties without either amending the convention or creating a new protocol, as in the cases of the tightening of phase-out schedules in the Montreal Protocol, the ban on hazardous waste exports to developing countries in the Basel Convention, and the adoption of conservation measures by regional fisheries commissions.

The adoption of protocols has been used successfully to strengthen regimes that began as a framework convention. A framework convention does not establish detailed, binding commitments, such as targets or timetables for national actions, usually because the negotiators have not been able to reach agreement on such measures. Rather, the framework convention requires sharing of information, study of the problem, and perhaps national plans or strategies aimed at reducing the threat. Creating a conference of the parties allows further negotiations on more concrete, binding actions that take the form of one or more protocols.

This two-stage approach has allowed the international community to establish the institutional and legal framework for regime strengthening even when there was no agreement on the specific actions to be taken. However, the framework convention-protocol approach has been criticized for taking too much time. For example, it took more than six years to negotiate the Climate Change Convention and the Kyoto Protocol, and it took more than seven years for the protocol to enter into force. But it would not have been possible to reach earlier agreement on targets and timetables because domestic political forces in veto states dictated the pace of progress toward stronger regimes, not the choice of approach.

Regime strengthening by formal amendment normally requires either consensus of the parties or, if that is not possible, a "supermajority" (either two-thirds or three-fourths of those present and voting).[2] But most treaties also allow parties to opt out of the amendment if they do not support it. CITES and the International Whaling Commission allow amendment by two-thirds and three-fourths majorities, respectively, but both have opt-out provisions for amendments. These opt-out provisions applied to the decisions on uplisting of African elephants and the moratorium on commercial whaling, respectively. The Basel Convention requires specific steps to "opt in" by all parties willing to be bound by the amendment. These arrangements allow changes to take effect without long ratification delays but also risk the blocking of effective action by key states that do not support it. Protocols to a framework convention are treated as an entirely new agreement and must be ratified by a certain number of signatories, as specified in the protocol itself, thus requiring that each party "opt in."

Some environmental regimes allow new or stronger actions to be mandated without a formal amendment or protocol procedure. The Montreal Protocol allows a supermajority to "adjust" technical appendices or annexes that are binding on all the parties. Thus the Conference of the Parties can amend the technical annexes by a supermajority without either "opt-out" or "opt-in" requirements. The London, Copenhagen, and Montreal Amendments, which changed the chemicals covered by the Montreal Protocol as well as the targets and timetables for their phaseout, applied to all parties, regardless of whether they supported them. The Basel Convention allows "substantive decisions" to be made by a two-thirds majority of those present and voting, without any opt-out provision for those who oppose it, which is how the ban on the trade in hazardous wastes was adopted.

In this chapter, we analyze eleven global environmental issues on which there have been multilateral negotiations during the past thirty years. Each issue is analyzed according to the stages of negotiation and the role of veto coalitions in shaping the outcomes of bargaining. This sample of issues represents a wide range of environmental and political circumstances. It shows the similarities and differences in the political processes and provides a basis for addressing the question of why states agree to cooperate on global environmental issues despite divergent interests. The cases are presented chronologically and by issue area. The first five regimes address toxic chemical and atmospheric issues (transboundary air pollution, ozone depletion, climate change, the hazardous waste trade, and toxic chemicals). The next four address species-related issues (whaling, trade in endangered species, biodiversity loss, and fisheries depletion). The final section addresses land resources (desertification and forests).

TRANSBOUNDARY AIR POLLUTION

Transboundary air pollution is an issue on which a veto coalition has been divided and weakened over time by defections, permitting a strengthening of a regime that was initially considered weak. New scientific evidence was a significant force for change in the position of key states, which switched from being part of the veto coalition to advocating a strong international regime for the reduction of transboundary air pollution. But the evidence has had limited impact on the policies of the states remaining in the veto coalition.

In the 1960s, emissions of sulfur dioxide and nitrogen oxide became an international problem after developed countries raised the heights of their industrial chimneys by as much as six times so that pollutants could be dispersed into the atmosphere. Previously, industries had polluted only the area immediately surrounding them, but now they exported their pollution to other countries downwind of the sites.

The definition of transboundary air pollution as an issue in global environmental politics began in the late 1960s with Sweden as the lead actor. In 1968, Swedish scientist Svante Oden presented scientific evidence showing that the long-range transport of sulfur dioxide emissions was the source of Swedish aquatic acidification, and he accused the rest of Europe of launching an "insidious chemical war" on Scandinavia. Sweden's efforts to put the issue of long-range transboundary air pollution on the international agenda were advanced by Sweden's offer to host the first UN environmental conference in 1972 in Stockholm.

There was still relatively little or no interest on the part of other European states. But Sweden and other Nordic states succeeded in persuading the OECD to monitor transboundary air pollution in Europe in 1972, thus successfully completing the definition process. The OECD monitoring program from 1972 to 1977 was an international fact-finding mission that confirmed pollution was being exported across boundaries and that the problem required international cooperation. Interest started to build following the 1975 Helsinki Conference on Security and Cooperation in Europe when the Soviet Union proposed a high-level East-West meeting to discuss the environment, energy, and transport. The Soviet Union's primary motivation was apparently to continue the process of détente in a policy realm other than human rights or arms control. The task of considering specific options fell to the UN Economic Commission for Europe (ECE), which included the states of Eastern and Western Europe as well as the United States and Canada.[3]

Within the ECE, states that had been the victims of this export of acid rain—notably Sweden, Finland, and Norway—took the initiative to negotiate for stringent and binding regulations on emissions of sulfur dioxide and nitrogen oxide.[4] But the industrialized states that were net exporters of acid rain formed a veto coalition, mostly because of their reliance on coal-fired power stations, which accounted for two-thirds of all sulfur dioxide emissions. Its members were the United States, the United Kingdom, the Federal Republic of Germany (FRG), Belgium, and Denmark, the United Kingdom and the FRG taking the lead role.[5] The veto coalition rejected agreements that included specific commitments to reduce emissions. Only after pressures from France, Norway, and Sweden did the FRG and United Kingdom accept vague obligations to reduce transboundary air pollution "as far as possible." The Convention on Long-Range Transboundary Air Pollution (LRTAP), concluded in Geneva in 1979 with thirty-five signatories, can fairly be described as a "least common denominator" compromise. No country accepted an explicit commitment if it was going to be significantly costly. The convention establishes the principle that transboundary air pollution should be reduced as much as is economically feasible, and creates a mechanism for collecting and disseminating information on air pollution flows, national reduction strategies, and abatement technologies. LRTAP did represent two important advances, however. First, it marked acceptance by Eastern Europe and the Soviet Union of Western norms concerning transboundary air pollution as well as their participation in ongoing Western monitoring and reporting programs. Second, it was a framework convention that created an institutional apparatus for performing the information functions and for facilitating regime strengthening.[6]

That process was impelled by new and more convincing scientific evidence of damage to European forests and historic buildings from acid rain.[7] Some major exporters of acid rain—especially the FRG—began to change their stance in the early 1980s because of domestic concerns about forest death, or

Waldsterben, which was especially pronounced in the Black Forest. At the first meeting of the assembly of signatory parties in 1983, Norway and Sweden proposed a program to reduce emissions of sulfur dioxide by 30 percent of 1980 levels by 1993 and were supported by three defectors from the veto coalition: the FRG, which was seeing forest damage, and France and Italy, which had less reason to hold out because they relied heavily on nuclear and hydroelectric power.[8] The United States and the United Kingdom continued to oppose formal pledges of emissions reductions.

In an unusual departure from diplomatic tradition, some states committed themselves formally to larger unilateral reductions, thus setting the standard by which other states would be judged. At a conference in Ottawa in March 1984, ten states pledged to reduce sulfur dioxide emissions by 30 percent and to substantially reduce other pollutants, especially nitrous oxide, thus forming the "Thirty-Percent Club." The club propelled agreement on the Protocol on the Reduction of Sulfur Emissions or Their Transboundary Fluxes by at Least 30 Percent (also known as the Helsinki Protocol), signed by twenty-one states in 1985. The protocol came into force in September 1987, but it lacked the adherence of three major exporters of acid rain: the United States, the United Kingdom, and Poland, which together represented more than 30 percent of total world emissions of sulfur dioxide.[9]

The second sulfur protocol was signed in Oslo, in June 1994, by twenty-eight parties to the convention. Different requirements were set for each country, the aim being to attain the greatest possible effect for the environment at the least overall cost. It also contained some specific requirements, not very rigorous, for large combustion plants. The text for basic obligations said that parties would control and reduce their sulfur emissions to protect human health and the environment from adverse effects, and that they would ensure that sulfur depositions did not, in the long term, exceed critical loads. The concept of critical loads denotes an attempt to establish a critical environmental level below which no harmful effects occur. Emissions reductions are divided among countries on a regional basis in an attempt to minimize the costs for the region as a whole. Retaining 1980 levels as a baseline, and using an "effects-based" approach setting "target loads" based on calculated critical loads, states agreed to different emissions reductions by 2000, 2005, and 2010; this represented a 60 percent reduction in the difference between existing emissions levels and critical loads.[10] This protocol came into force in August 1998.

In negotiations on reducing nitrogen oxide emissions, three dramatically different positions were advanced by states and NGOs. Austria, the Netherlands,

Sweden, Switzerland, and West Germany advocated a 30 percent reduction in emissions by 1994; but the United States demurred, arguing that it should be credited with previous abatement measures. The Protocol Concerning the Control of Emissions of Nitrogen Oxides or Their Transboundary Fluxes (better known as the Sofia Protocol), signed by twenty-three European countries, the United States, and Canada in 1988, also reflected compromise between the lead states and the veto coalition. It required only a freeze of nitrogen oxide emissions or transboundary flows at 1987 levels while allowing most countries to postpone compliance until 1994 by providing credits for reductions in previous years—a concession to U.S. demands.

In November 1991, the parties adopted a protocol on volatile organic compounds (VOCs, i.e., hydrocarbons), which is the second major air pollutant responsible for the formation of ground-level ozone. The VOC negotiations elicited three broad sets of national positions. The majority of countries were willing to sign an across-the-board 30 percent reduction protocol. Countries that have low ozone problems as a result of meteorological and geographical conditions, including the USSR, Norway, and Canada, however, wanted to commit only to reducing VOCs in regions responsible for transborder fluxes. Most Eastern European countries wanted to commit only to a freeze. Eventually, twenty-one parties signed a protocol that merely listed three forms of regulation (based on the three sets of national positions).[11] Most of the signatories committed themselves to reducing their emissions by at least 30 percent by 1999, with five different base years between 1984 and 1990 because countries were permitted to select their own base year. Because ratification was drawn out, the protocol did not enter into force until September 1997.

The Protocol on Heavy Metals was adopted in June 1998 in Aarhus, Denmark. It targets three particularly harmful metals: cadmium, lead, and mercury. The protocol aims to cut emissions from industrial sources, combustion processes, and waste incineration. The protocol also requires that parties phase out leaded gasoline. It introduces measures to lower heavy-metal emissions from other products, such as mercury in batteries, and proposes the introduction of management measures for other mercury-containing products, such as thermometers, fluorescent lamps, dental amalgam, pesticides, and paint. The protocol entered into force in December 2003.

The Protocol on Persistent Organic Pollutants was also adopted in June 1998. Canada and Sweden were the lead states on POPs, because POPs tend to bioaccumulate in the Arctic and have had an impact on Arctic populations in both countries.[12] The fact-finding process took place in a special task force established to investigate POPs, which met from 1991 to 1994. Assessments continued in 1995 and 1996 in the preparatory working group, and formal negotiations began in 1997. A major part of negotiating the protocol was deciding which substances the protocol would cover. Most of the European countries, led by Sweden, advocated a large list of POPs, whereas the United States, as a veto state, favored a more limited list. Negotiators resolved most of the disagreements over the POPs to be included by setting up a set of criteria and then screening the POPs and ranking them according to their toxicity and bioaccumulation potential and then assessing long-range transport risk. The United States did succeed in blocking the inclusion of pentachlorophenol under the protocol. The United States argued that this wood preservative, which is widely regulated in Europe, should not be considered a POP and threatened not to sign the protocol if pentachlorophenol was included. The United States was successful in its efforts, primarily because Sweden and other countries thought that it was crucial for the United States to be a party to the protocol; they were willing to leave off pentachlorophenol at this stage because there are provisions for placing additional POPs under the protocol.[13] The protocol covers eleven pesticides, two industrial chemicals, and three by-products/contaminants. The ultimate objective is to control, reduce, or eliminate POPs. The protocol bans the production and use of some products outright and schedules others for elimination at a later stage. The protocol includes provisions for dealing with the wastes of products that will be banned. It entered into force in October 2003.

Meanwhile, by the mid-1990s, acidification problems were still severe. Urban air quality was deteriorating; about 70 percent of the population of European cities equipped with monitoring stations was being exposed to pollution levels above EU air quality standards.[14] As a result, the need to adopt stronger regulatory measures was recognized; and, in 1995, Sweden, which had recently joined the EU, began to press for the development of a more comprehensive EU Acidification Strategy. Within the LRTAP and EU contexts, there followed a couple of years of producing the scientific groundwork for a new "multi-pollutant approach." The idea was to address multiple effects (acidification, tropospheric ozone formation, and **eutrophication**) and multiple pollutants (nitrogen oxides, volatile organic compounds, sulfur dioxide, and ammonia).[15]

In early 1999, at the beginning of the negotiations of the eighth LRTAP protocol, the European Commission, Austria, Denmark, Finland, the Netherlands, and Sweden supported fairly substantial reductions in emissions of the four pollutants. Although this reflects essentially the same group of lead states as in earlier negotiations, there were a few differences. Partly related to increasing domestic concern about air pollution, an earlier laggard and big emitter, the United Kingdom, joined the lead states and showed the greatest negotiating flexibility.[16] The role of the Eastern European countries, including Russia, was not much more constructive in these negotiations than in the earlier ones. Although the general East-West atmosphere was more relaxed in the post–cold war 1990s, this did not lead to greater flexibility. Similarly, the high emitters—Germany, France and Italy—were concerned about the cost of high emissions reductions.[17]

The result of the negotiations was the Protocol to Abate Acidification, Eutrophication and Ground-Level Ozone, which was adopted in Gothenberg, Sweden, in December 1999. The protocol aims to cut emissions of sulfur, nitrogen oxides, volatile organic compounds, and ammonia from energy generation, industrial sources, motor vehicles, agriculture, and products. The protocol sets reduction targets for all four pollutants. By 2010, Europe's sulfur emissions should be cut by 63 percent, its NOx emissions by 41 percent, its VOC emissions by 40 percent, and its ammonia emissions by 17 percent compared to their 1990 levels. Each country's individual ceilings depend on the impact that its emissions have on public health and on the vulnerability of the environment that they pollute. Countries producing emissions that have the most severe health or environmental impact, and whose emissions are the cheapest to reduce, will have to make the biggest cuts. The Gothenberg Protocol entered into force in May 2005 (see table 3.1).[18]

In summary, a small group of blocking states, usually led by the United Kingdom, Germany and/or the United States, has either refused to join the air pollution agreements or demanded that they be watered down. Like other regimes negotiated in the 1970s and 1980s, the international regime for transboundary air pollution has lent itself to strengthening through regular review and action that depends on increasing scientific evidence, an understanding of the health effects of continued transboundary air pollution, and the negotiation of protocols, although the protocol negotiations themselves involved some of the same challenges by the same blocking states as the original treaty.

OZONE DEPLETION

Ozone is a pungent, slightly bluish gas composed of three oxygen atoms (O_3). Ninety percent of naturally occurring ozone resides in the **stratosphere**.[19] This "ozone layer" helps to shield the earth from ultraviolet radiation produced by the sun and plays a critical role in absorbing UV-B

TABLE 3.1   Percentage Change in Emissions of Acidifying Substances: 1990–2001

Country	Change 1990-2001 (%)
Austria	-13%
Belgium	-27%
Bulgaria	-57%
Cyprus	2%
Czech Rep.	-77%
Denmark	-42%
Estonia	-62%
Finland	-45%
France	-26%
Germany	-66%
Greece	1%
Hungary	54%
Iceland	11%
Ireland	-6%
Italy	-34%
Latvia	-72%
Liechtenstein	-31%
Lithuania	-63%
Luxembourg	-37%
Malta	NA
Netherlands	-37%
Norway	-10%
Poland	-48%
Portugal	12%
Romania	-32%
Slovak Rep	-69%
Slovenia	-51%
Spain	-15%
Sweden	-25%
Turkey	35%
United Kingdom	-55%

Source: European Environment Agency, *Emissions of Acidifying Substances*, Factsheet, 2003. [Internet: http://themes.eea.eu.int/Specific media/air/indicators/ acidification%2C2003/acidification2003.pdf]

radiation. Because large increases in UV-B radiation would seriously harm nearly all plants and animals, the ozone layer is considered an essential component of the natural systems that make life on earth possible.

In the 1970s, scientists discovered that certain man-made chemicals, called chlorofluorocarbons (CFCs), posed a serious threat to stratospheric ozone.[20] CFCs release chlorine atoms into the stratosphere that act as a catalyst in the destruction of ozone molecules. Created in the 1920s to replace flammable and noxious refrigerants, CFCs are inert, nonflammable, nontoxic, colorless, odorless, and wonderfully adaptable to a wide variety of profitable uses. By the mid-1970s, CFCs had become the chemical of choice for coolants in air conditioning and refrigerating systems, propellants in aerosol sprays, solvents in the cleaning of electronic components, and the blowing agent for the manufacture of flexible and rigid foam. Scientists later discovered other ozone-depleting compounds, including halons, a tremendous and otherwise safe fire suppressant, carbon tetrachloride, methyl chloroform, and methyl bromide. Each can release ozone-destroying chlorine or bromine atoms into the stratosphere.

The economic importance of these chemicals, especially CFCs, made international controls extremely difficult to establish.[21] The absence of firm scientific consensus on the nature and seriousness of the problem, a strenuous anti-regulatory campaign by corporations producing or using CFCs, concerns for the cost of unilateral regulation, worries by developing countries that restricting access to CFCs would slow economic development, and opposition by the European Community prevented effective action for many years.

The political definition of the ozone depletion issue began in 1977. The fact-finding process lasted many years, however, because scientific estimates of potential depletion fluctuated widely during the late 1970s and early 1980s, and no evidence emerged in nature to confirm the theory. Indeed, when the bargaining process formally began in 1982, the exact nature of the threat was unclear even to proponents of international action.[22]

The United States, which at that time accounted for more than 40 percent of worldwide CFC production, took a lead role in the negotiations in part because it had already banned CFC use in aerosol spray cans, a large percentage of total use at that time, and wanted other states to follow suit. However, for an ozone-protection policy to succeed, it was essential that all states producing and consuming CFCs be part of the regime. Thus, the European Community, which also accounted for more than 40 percent of global CFC production and exported a third of that to developing countries, opposed controls and constituted a potential veto coalition. Germany supported CFC controls, but the EC position was effectively controlled by the other large producing countries—France, Italy, and the United Kingdom—which doubted the science, wanted to preserve their industries' overseas markets, and wished to avoid the costs of adopting substitutes. Japan, a major user of CFCs, supported this position.

Large developing countries, including Brazil, China, India, and Indonesia, formed another veto coalition. Their bargaining leverage stemmed from their potential to produce very large quantities of CFCs in the future—a situation that would eventually eviscerate the effectiveness of any regime.[23] Although most developing countries did not play an active role early in the regime's development, they eventually used this leverage to secure a delayed control schedule and precedent-setting financial and technical assistance.

Although negotiations began with an explicit understanding that only a possible framework convention would be discussed, in 1983, the lead states (the U.S., Canada and the Nordic states) proposed the adoption of binding restrictions on CFC production. The veto coalition, led by the EC, steadfastly rejected negotiations for regulatory protocols. Thus, the regime's first agreement, the 1985 Vienna Convention for the Protection of the Ozone Layer, affirmed the importance of protecting the ozone layer and included provisions on monitoring, research, and data exchanges, but imposed no specific obligations to reduce the production or use of CFCs. Indeed, it did not even mention CFCs. However, because of a last-minute U.S. initiative, states did agree to resume formal negotiations on a binding protocol if further evidence emerged supporting the potential threat.

Only weeks after nations signed the Vienna Convention, British scientists published the first reports about the Antarctic ozone hole.[24] Although the hole had been forming annually for several years, the possibility of its existence fell so far outside the bounds of existing theory that computers monitoring satellite data on ozone had ignored its presence as a data error. Publication of its existence galvanized proponents of CFC controls, who argued that the hole justified negotiations to strengthen the nascent regime (despite the lack of firm evidence linking the hole to CFCs until 1989).[25] Thus, faced with domestic and international pressure, the veto states returned to the bargaining table in December 1986.

The lead states—a coalition that now included Canada, Finland, Norway, Sweden, Switzerland, and the United States—initially advocated a freeze followed by a 95 percent reduction in production of CFCs over a period of ten to fourteen years. The industrialized-country veto coalition—the EC, Japan, and the Soviet Union—eventually proposed placing a cap on production capacity at current levels. Lead states argued that the capacity cap could lead to actual increases in CFC production (and involve few adjustment costs for veto states) because Europe already possessed significant excess production capacity. Lead states then offered a 50 percent cut as a compromise. As late as April 1987, the EC would not accept more than a 20 percent reduction, but relented in the final days of negotiations. The ten-year evolution of the EC position from rejecting all discussion of control measures to proposing a production cap to accepting a compromise reduction target reflected several factors: disunity within the European Community (West Germany, Denmark, Belgium, and the Netherlands all supported strong regulations); the personal role played by UNEP Executive Director Tolba; diplomatic pressures by the United States; pressure from domestic NGOs; and reluctance by the EC to be seen as the culprit should negotiations fail to produce an agreement.

The 1987 Montreal Protocol on Substances That Deplete the Ozone Layer mandated that industrialized countries reduce their production and use of the five most widely used CFCs by 50 percent. Halon production would be frozen. The expanded regime also included scientific and technological assessment panels, reporting requirements, potential trade sanctions for countries that did not ratify the agreement, and a robust procedure for reviewing the effectiveness of the regime and strengthening controls through amendment and adjustments.[26] To gain the acceptance of the developing country veto coalition, delegates agreed to give developing countries a ten-year grace period, allowing them to increase their use of CFCs before taking on commitments.

Within months of the Montreal accord, there emerged new scientific evidence supporting strengthening the regime. In late 1987, scientists announced that initial studies suggested that CFCs probably were responsible for the ozone hole, which continued to grow larger every year, although natural processes peculiar to Antarctica contributed to its severity. Studies during the next two years confirmed these findings. In March 1988, satellite data revealed that stratospheric ozone above the heavily populated Northern Hemisphere had begun to thin.[27] Finally, the 1989 report of the regime's own Scientific Assessment Panel signaled conclusively that the world's scientific community had reached broad agreement that CFCs had indeed begun to deplete stratospheric ozone.[28]

This period also saw changes in the pattern of economic interests. In 1988, Du Pont announced that they would soon be able to produce CFC substitutes. They were followed the next year by other large chemical manufacturers, including several in Europe. The major producers no longer opposed a CFC phaseout but lobbied instead for extended transition periods and against controls on potential substitutes, particularly hydrochlorofluorocarbons (HCFCs)—a class of CFC substitutes that deplete ozone but at a significantly reduced rate. In response to these scientific and economic changes, and to increased pressure from domestic environmental lobbies, the EC abruptly shifted roles.[29]

At the second Meeting of the Parties to the Montreal Protocol (MOP-2), in London in June 1990, EC states assumed a lead role during difficult negotiations that eventually produced amendments and adjustments that significantly strengthened the regime.[30] Production of the CFCs and halons controlled in 1987, and of carbon tetrachloride and all other CFCs and halons, would now be phased out by 2000, and methyl chloroform by 2005. MOP-2 also created the Multilateral Fund for the Implementation of the Montreal Protocol, the first such fund established under an environmental agreement. Its creation addressed demands by large developing countries that had refused to join the regime without it. The Fund meets the incremental costs to developing countries of implementing the control measures of the protocol and finances clearinghouse functions, country studies, technical assistance, information, training, and costs of the Fund secretariat. The Fund is replenished every three years and administered by an executive committee made up of seven donor and seven recipient countries. Since its establishment, the Fund has disbursed over $1.59 billion to more than 4,600 projects in 134 countries.[31]

In response to evidence of increasing ozone-layer depletion, parties again strengthened the regime at MOP-4 in Copenhagen in 1992. Delegates accelerated the existing phaseouts and added controls on additional chemicals, including methyl bromide, a toxic fumigant used in agriculture and the second most widely used insecticide in the world by volume, and HCFCs, which parties agreed to phase out by 2030, all but 0.5 percent being eliminated by 2020. MOP-4 also established an Implementation Committee that examines cases of possible noncompliance and makes recommendations to the MOP aimed at securing compliance.

During this period, the EC and United States completed a near reversal of their respective roles during the regime's development in the 1970s and 1980s. In 1993, the EC argued for the importance of eliminating all threats to the ozone layer as soon as possible when it began the first in a series of attempts to accelerate HCFC controls.[32] Meanwhile, a veto coalition led by the United States and Australia argued that further restrictions on HCFCs would not reduce enough total damage to the ozone layer to justify the extra costs; it would prevent firms that had made significant, and good-faith, investments in HCFC technologies (as substitutes for CFCs) from recouping their investment; a significant proportion of the substitutes for HCFCs would be hydrofluorocarbons (HFCs), which are potent greenhouse gases manufactured almost exclusively by European companies; and other available measures would have a greater impact on the ozone layer.

A similar division developed with respect to methyl bromide. Since the early 1990s, NGOs had called for a rapid phaseout of methyl bromide because of its threat to human health and the ozone layer. Many industrialized countries, including the United States and EC, had taken steps domestically to limit or even phase out methyl bromide and supported regulating it under the protocol and providing corresponding financial and technical assistance to developing countries. However, the United States had also successfully championed a significant loophole that allows parties to continue using methyl bromide for "critical" uses even after the phaseout date.

At MOP-9, held in Montreal in 1997, parties moved the phaseout of methyl bromide for industrialized countries up to 2005. Developing countries, previously committed only to a freeze by 2002, would eliminate it by 2015 and received assistance specifically earmarked for methyl bromide projects from the Multilateral Fund. MOP-9 also addressed the issue of illegal trade in CFCs, creating a new licensing system for CFC imports and exports of CFCs and a system of regular information exchanges between parties.

At MOP-11, held in Beijing in 1999, the EC finally secured U.S. agreement to strengthen controls on HCFCs, albeit modestly. MOP-11 also agreed to phase out the production of bromochloromethane (a recently developed ozone-depleting chemical), and to require that parties report on their use of methyl bromide for quarantine and pre-shipment applications (a relatively noncontroversial exempted use of methyl bromide to clean shipping containers). The Beijing amendment also bans trade in HCFCs with countries that do not ratify the 1992 Copenhagen amendment, which introduced the HCFC phaseout.

Like its predecessors, MOP-15 in 2003 produced decisions on a range of issues relating to regime implementation. However, parties could not resolve significant disagreements concerning the allowable size and time period for the critical-use exemptions (CUEs) that allow for continued use of methyl bromide beyond the phaseout date. Some delegates argued that the exemptions sought by the United States, Spain, Italy, and several other countries, were unjustifiably large. The EC also argued that exemptions should be limited to one year, requiring countries to re-apply annually. The United States favored multiyear exemptions. With no compromise in sight, delegates took the unprecedented step of calling an "extraordinary" MOP in their attempts to resolve these and other issues.

The first Extraordinary Meeting of the Parties to the Montreal Protocol convened in March 2004. Parties reached compromises on various methyl bromide-related issues, including CUEs for 2005, conditions for granting and reporting on CUEs, and working procedures for the Methyl Bromide Technical Options Committee. However, delegates could not reach agreement on a permanent structure for the size and duration of exemptions beyond 2005.

MOP-16, which took place in Prague in November 2004, continued the process of strengthening the ozone regime with regard to data reporting,

PHOTO 3.1   Anti–methyl bromide picket signs outside the first Extraordinary Meeting of the Parties to the Montreal Protocol in Montreal in March 2004. Courtesy IISD/*Earth Negotiations Bulletin*.

compliance, and illegal trade in ozone depleting substances. However, in spite of lengthy discussions, parties still could not reach agreement regarding methyl bromide exemptions for 2006 and beyond. Indeed, the talks did nothing to mend the deep divisions on the issue between European-lead states and U.S.-led veto states. Moreover, the meeting appeared to confirm that certain pesticide and agricultural producers, working in concert with powerful agricultural and pesticide lobbies, had been able to push their governments to pursue large, ongoing use of methyl bromide in their sectors.[33]

The second Extraordinary Meeting of the Parties met in Montreal on July 1, 2005, and reached agreement on CUEs for 2006, but larger issues remained on the table and have produced several concerns. Some worry that it might erode the commitment of developing countries to phase out methyl bromide in light of the poor example set by some OECD parties. Some developing countries that have reduced their use of methyl bromide wonder whether they will suffer negative competitive impacts on their agricultural exports if certain industrialized countries continue to request and receive large CUEs. Similarly, the producers and users of alternative pesticides now find their incentives to continue have been reduced because their promised markets may not materialize. Finally, environmentalists worry about the impact on the ozone layer if large CUEs receive systematic and long-term approval.

These and other issues will be on the agenda at future meetings. Indeed, the regime still faces significant challenges, including the transition away from HCFCs, fully implementing the phaseout schedules in developing countries, and addressing the large requests for critical-use exemptions for methyl bromide. How the parties address these issues will determine the continued growth and ultimate success of the ozone regime.

The history of global ozone policy illustrates the role that veto coalitions play in weakening a regime as well as how veto states sometimes shift roles as a result of increasing scientific evidence, domestic political pressures, and changing economic interests. It is also the best example of a global environmental regime that has been continually strengthened in response to new scientific evidence and technological innovations.

Indeed, when one combines all the amendments and adjustments to the Montreal Protocol, the current set of binding controls is impressive. Industrialized countries were required to phase out halons by 1994; CFCs, carbon tetrachloride, methyl chloroform, and HBFCs by 1996; bromochloromethane by 2002, and methyl bromide by 2005—although various exceptions exist. These parties must still phase out HCFCs by 2030 as well as meet important interim targets. Developing country parties were required to phase out hydrobromofluorocarbons by 1996 and bromochloromethane by 2002. These parties must still phase out CFCs, halons, and carbon tetrachloride by 2010; methyl chloroform and methyl bromide by 2015; and the consumption of HCFCs by 2040.

The ozone regime stands as perhaps the strongest and most effective global environmental regime. The worldwide consumption of CFCs, which was about 1.1 million tons in 1986, was approximately 100,000 tons in 2003.[34] The Ozone Secretariat calculates that without the Montreal Protocol, global CFC consumption would have reached about 3 million tons in 2010 and 8 million tons in 2060, resulting in a 50 percent depletion of the ozone layer by 2035.[35] (See fig. 3.1.) Most parties continue to meet their commitments to reduce or eliminate production and consumption of ozone depleting chemicals; as a result, atmospheric concentrations of these chemicals are declining and, if all the mandated phaseouts are fully achieved (still a big "if"), the ozone layer could fully recover during the twenty-first century.

FIGURE 3.1   **Worldwide Production of CFCs, HCFCs, and HFCs**

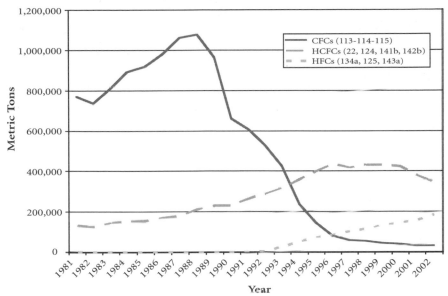

Data source: Alternative Fluorocarbons Environmental Acceptability Study (AFEAS), "Production and Sales of Fluorocarbons," (Arlington, VA: RAND Environmental Science & Policy Center, 2004). http://www.afeas.org/2002/production_2002.html.

CLIMATE CHANGE

Climate change is the prototype of the global commons issue. All nations are affected by the earth's climate system, and broad international cooperation is required to mitigate the threat of global warming. The negotiation of a regime to mitigate global climate change has been complicated by the multiple sources of emissions that contribute to global warming; by scientific uncertainties, especially the chemistry of the atmosphere; and by dependence on global climate modeling, far from an exact science.[36] Even more important, however, is that energy is central to every nation's economy, and the policy changes required to reduce greenhouse gas emissions raise politically difficult political questions of who should bear the immediate costs. Even to stabilize the global concentrations of carbon dioxide (which would not reduce the warming caused by emissions already in the atmosphere) would require reducing current emissions by roughly one-half. That would necessitate major gains in conservation and a switch from coal and oil to natural gas and renewable sources, all of which would affect

FIGURE 3.2   Atmospheric Concentration of Carbon Dioxide, 1744–2000

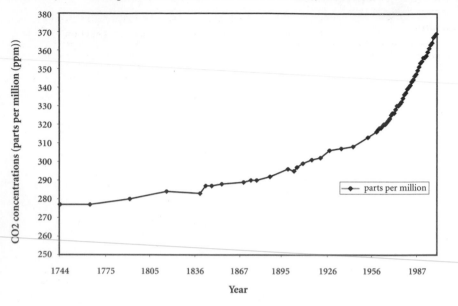

Data Source: Carbon Dioxide Information Analysis Center, http://cdiac.esd.ornl.gov.

powerful economic and political interests in some of the most important emitters of greenhouse gases.

Greenhouse gas emissions from the burning of fossil fuels account for roughly 80 percent of total world emissions, and deforestation and natural sources of methane contribute most of the rest. Fossil fuel burning has increased atmospheric concentrations of carbon dioxide by 30 percent since pre-industrial times (see fig. 3.2). The top twenty emitters of carbon dioxide, led by the United States (21 percent) account for about 70 percent of the world's emissions (see table 3.2).

The way in which key participants in the negotiations on climate change have defined their interests has been more closely correlated with their perceptions of the costs of the regime than their perceptions of vulnerability to the threat. The perceived costs of climate change, moreover, are related primarily to the country's "energy culture," that is, its historical experience with fossil fuels in relation to its economic growth. Because governments cannot estimate the eventual costs of mitigation measures in overall economic growth without far more information, perceptions of costs are usually shaped by their overall biases regarding energy policy.[37] Thus three groups of states were initially distinguished:[38]

TABLE 3.2   Twenty Countries with the Highest CO_2 Emissions

Country	2000 Total CO_2 Emissions* (1000 metric tons of carbon)	National Per Capita estimates (metric tons of carbon)
United States	1,528,796	5.40
China	761,586	0.60
Russian Federation	391,664	2.69
Japan	323,281	2.55
India	292,265	0.29
Germany	214,386	2.61
United Kingdom	154,979	2.59
Canada	118,957	3.87
Italy	116,859	2.02
Republic of Korea	116,543	2.47
Mexico	115,713	1.19
Saudi Arabia	102,168	4.77
France	98,917	1.68
Australia	94,094	4.91
Ukraine	93,551	1.89
South Africa	89,323	2.04
Iran	84,689	1.33
Brazil	83,930	0.50
Poland	82,245	2.13
Spain	77,220	1.95
Global Total	**6,975,000**	

* Total CO_2 emissions are from fossil-fuel burning, cement production and gas flaring.

Source: Gregg Marland, Tom Boden, and Bob Andres, *Global, Regional and National CO_2 Emissions. In Online Trends: A compendium of Data on Global Change* (Carbon Dioxide Information Analysis Center, Oak Ridge National Laboratory, U.S. Department of Energy, Oak Ridge, Tenn., U.S.A.) [Internet: http://cdiac.esd.ornl.gov/trends/emis/em_cont.htm]

- Those states that are relatively dependent on imported energy and thus have learned to maintain high living standards while reducing their use of fossil fuel. This group includes Japan and most European Union states, including Germany, Italy, France, the Netherlands, Denmark, Finland, and Sweden.

- Those states with large supplies of cheap energy resources and a culture of highly inefficient energy use. This group includes the United States, Russia, China, India, Brazil, and Mexico.
- Those states highly dependent on fossil fuel exports for income, such as the Arab oil states, Australia, Norway, and, initially, the United Kingdom.

The "energy culture" of states generally determined whether a state would join a lead state coalition or a veto state coalition with regard to commitments to greenhouse gas emissions targets and timetables. The EU was the leader in pushing for targets and timetables during the 1990s, and the United States was the main veto state. Russia, China, India, and Brazil have consistently played veto roles.

There have also been some exceptions: Norway and Australia were early lead states, mainly because domestic political pressures and an initial focus on vulnerability drove their positions, but they later retreated to veto roles in negotiations over targets and timetables. The United Kingdom now supports a strong climate regime, despite being a fossil fuel exporter, because its overall energy and industry policies have been transitioning to a greater emphasis on energy efficiency and natural gas and less on coal. Japan was initially part of a veto coalition, but has shifted its position over time; it now gives more support to the regime to fight climate change, although it still appears to be questioning the practicality of future emissions commitments.

Scientists have long known that the buildup of carbon dioxide in the atmosphere can cause climate change. But the process of issue definition began to accelerate in 1985–1986. The WMO and UNEP took the first major step with a 1985 conference in Villach, Austria, that produced a new scientific consensus that global warming was a serious possibility.[39] And in 1986, WMO, the National Aeronautics and Space Administration (NASA), and several other agencies issued a three-volume report concluding that climate change was already taking place at a relatively rapid rate. The unusually hot summer of 1988 accelerated media and congressional attention, and it even thrust the climate issue into the presidential campaign. The testimony of prominent U.S. scientists suggesting that the climate was already changing irreversibly, primarily because of carbon dioxide emissions, further contributed to the definition of the climate change issue.[40]

The fact-finding process coincided with the issue definition stage. In 1988, the WMO and UNEP organized the Intergovernmental Panel on Climate Change (IPCC) in an attempt to establish a common factual basis for negotiations that would focus on policy options.[41] The First Assessment Report of the IPCC—approved by the participating states after long, grueling negotiations in August 1990—reaffirmed that global warming is a serious threat. The report predicted that if states continue to pursue "business as usual," the global average surface temperature will rise during the next century by an average of 0.3 degrees C per decade, a rate of change unprecedented in human history. However, despite the success of the IPCC in establishing a strong scientific consensus on climate change, it failed to establish a consensus on the economics of the problem, which was one of the key points of contention during subsequent negotiations.

Once the scientific certainty of climate change had been acknowledged, some states and NGOs pressed for the international discussion of necessary actions to confront it. In calling for specific targets and timetables for emissions, they seized the attention of those states with energy cultures highly dependent on fossil fuels. To adhere to such targets and timetables, these energy cultures would have to transform, affecting economic and political interests more drastically than many were ready for. Thus, during the negotiations that followed distinct conditions emerged—lead state coalitions favoring a climate convention and veto state coalitions.

The initial coalition of lead states (Norway, Sweden, Finland, and the Netherlands) squared off with the United States, as leader of the veto coalition, on whether the negotiations should produce a protocol containing specific obligations on emissions. The lead states wanted to negotiate a framework convention in parallel with negotiations for a protocol limiting emissions, to be completed no later than a year after the convention. When the United States insisted on a framework convention that had no parallel negotiations on protocols, it argued that regulating carbon releases would require major changes in lifestyle and the industrial structure. But in October 1990, Japan broke ranks with the United States on the issue by committing itself to stabilizing its greenhouse gas emissions at 1990 levels by 2000. That left the United States and the Soviet Union alone among industrialized countries rejecting a target and timetable for controlling emissions in a climate regime.[42]

Formal negotiations for a climate convention began officially in February 1991 under the auspices of the Intergovernmental Negotiating Committee for a Framework Convention on Climate Change, which was created by the UN General Assembly. The European Community led the negotiations by virtue of its commitment to lowering its joint carbon dioxide emissions to 1990 levels by the year 2000. Germany, Denmark, Austria, Australia, the

Netherlands, and New Zealand committed themselves to reducing their emissions by 2000 or 2005.

Had binding commitments for controlling greenhouse emissions been included in the text, developing countries' agreement would have been crucial to the regime. The biggest rapidly industrializing countries (China, India, and Brazil) already accounted for 21 percent of global emissions from all sources in 1989 (about the same as the United States), and, as their economies grew, their emissions levels would certainly rise. Because they viewed fossil fuels as a vital component of their success as potential industrial powers, they formed a potential veto coalition.[43]

The negotiations in February 1992 ended without resolution of the issue of a stabilization target and timetable. German, British, Dutch, and other EC member governments sent officials to Washington before one more session in April in an unsuccessful effort to persuade the United States to go along with a commitment to stabilize emissions at 1990 levels by 2000. But during the April session, President George Bush personally called Prime Minister Helmut Kohl of Germany and asked him to drop his government's demand for the stabilization commitment in return for Bush's participation in the upcoming Earth Summit. Bush announced his decision to attend the Rio conference only after the final text of the climate change convention was adopted without reference to binding commitments to controlling greenhouse gases.[44]

In June 1992, 154 countries gathered in Rio and signed the United Nations Framework Convention on Climate Change (UNFCCC). At this point, forty industrialized countries, including the United States, Russia, Australia, Japan, and Ukraine, as well as the EEC, agreed to take the leading roles in reducing greenhouse gas emissions, defined as Annex I Parties.[45] It declares as its goal the restoration of greenhouse gas emissions in 2000 to "earlier levels"—a phrase interpreted by the EC to mean 1990 levels—but does not commit governments to hold emissions to a specific level by a certain date. Nor does it address emissions reduction targets after the year 2000. But the text does provide for regular review of the "adequacy" of the commitments.

The UNFCCC entered into force in March 1994 after ratification by the minimum necessary fifty states.[46] The climate regime resulting from the exercise of veto power by the United States was generally regarded as weak. However, Germany joined with an international network of NGOs and Small Island Developing States to press for a significant strengthening of the regime. The EU issued a statement upon signing the convention calling for an early start on negotiation of a protocol with binding targets and timetables.

The first Conference of the Parties (COP) of the UNFCCC in March–April 1995 agreed to negotiate by the end of 1997 quantitative limits on emissions beyond the year 2000; but it could not agree about whether those limits would be reductions or which countries would be subject to the new commitments. The EU supported a commitment of substantial reductions, but the JUSCANZ, group (Japan, U.S., Canada, Australia, and New Zealand) which constituted a new veto coalition, opposed negotiations for reduced emissions. To reduce emissions beyond 2000, the industrialized countries would have to adopt new economic measures that would facilitate fundamental changes in energy use. So COP-1 created the Ad Hoc Group on the Berlin Mandate (AGBM) to negotiate a binding agreement on actions to be taken after the year 2000.

The AGBM met eight times between August 1995 and December 1997. Halfway through the process, the second COP met in July 1996 and adopted the IPCC's Second Assessment Report of December 1995. That report concluded that the earth's temperature had increased by 0.3 to 0.6 percent—nearly 1 degree Fahrenheit over the previous one hundred years—and that there was a "discernible human influence" on climate. The report predicted an increase of another 2 to 6 degrees over the next century if the trend in concentration of carbon dioxide in the atmosphere was not reversed.

By mid-1997, the EU had maintained its lead state role by tabling a proposal for reductions of the three main greenhouse gases (carbon dioxide, methane, and nitrous oxide) from 1990 levels of at least 7.5 percent by 2005 and of 15 percent by 2010. The EU proposal included all EU member countries, but allowed some states, such as Germany, to undertake deeper emissions reductions and poorer EU states to accept lower targets. In sharp contrast, the United States proposed the stabilization of all six greenhouse gases (including three the impacts of which were less quantifiable) at 1990 levels by the years 2008 to 2010 for all Annex I parties.

The United States also proposed the trading of emissions among parties, beginning at once without specified conditions for its application, and assigning the emissions reductions to Russia and former Soviet bloc states in Central and Eastern Europe. These emissions were called "hot air" because these countries were already more than 30 percent below their 1990s level after shutting down so many obsolescent plants. Although the EU did not oppose carbon trading, it did strongly object to trading without adequate guidelines, and especially trading in "hot air" because it would allow the parties to meet targets on paper without taking direct action.

Meanwhile, Australia had opened up yet another front in the diplomatic struggle: It argued that because its economy was far more heavily dependent on exports of fossil fuels than the average Annex I party, it should not have to reduce as deeply as most such parties. This demand for differentiation represented another way for the veto coalition to weaken the targets and timetables agreement, by allowing some states to justify lower targets.

At the third COP in Kyoto the differences between lead and veto states widened rather than narrowed. The United States, which had previously supported equal reductions for all industrialized country parties, also endorsed the concept of differentiation to take into account the greater economic burdens that equal reductions would impose on certain states. The U.S. delegation also took the position that it could not accept any emissions reductions unless developing countries also agreed formally to control their emissions— a condition that had been mandated by a unanimous vote in the U.S. Senate but was clearly unacceptable to developing countries. New Zealand similarly demanded that developing countries specify by the year 2002 how much they would slow their emissions over the next twelve years. Japan called for only a 2.5 percent cut in emissions by 2010.

Following a week and a half of intense negotiations, the parties finally adopted the Kyoto Protocol.[47] The protocol states that industrialized-country parties should reduce overall emissions of six greenhouse gases by at least 5.2 percent below their 1990 levels between 2008 and 2012. Although no formula for differentiation based on objective characteristics of the party was adopted, the protocol does differentiate national targets, based on bargaining between and among veto states and the EU. The national targets vary from a 10 percent increase for Iceland and an 8 percent increase for Australia to 8 percent reductions for the EU and most of Eastern Europe. The United States agreed to accept the target of a 7 percent reduction but won a concession on the three newer greenhouse gases, which are to be calculated from a 1995 baseline rather than 1990 (see table 3.3). This not only made the target much less demanding but also revealed the first of a number of limitations of the protocol's potential success.

The U.S. proposal for a formal commitment by developing countries to control and eventually reduce their emissions was dropped after China, India, and other developing-country parties attacked it. Even an "opt-in" position that would have provided for voluntary adoption of an emissions target by non-Annex I states was vetoed by their delegations.

To alleviate the costs of achieving its emissions targets, the Kyoto Protocol recommends that countries use three "flexibility mechanisms": the **Clean Development Mechanism** (CDM), **Joint Implementation** (JI), and **emissions trading**.[48] Although many argued that the environmental integrity of

TABLE 3.3   Target Greenhouse Gas Emissions Reductions by
2012, Kyoto Protocol.

Country	Kyoto Target (percent change from 1990 emissions)
Australia	+8
Bulgaria	-8
Canada	-6
Croatia	-5
Estonia	-8
European Union	-8
Hungary	-6
Iceland	+10
Japan	-6
Latvia	-8
Liechtenstein	-8
Lithuania	-8
Monaco	-8
New Zealand	0
Norway	+1
Poland	-6
Romania	-8
Russian Federation	0
Slovakia	-8
Slovenia	-8
Switzerland	-8
Ukraine	0
United States	-7

Source: United Nations Kyoto Protocol to the United Nations
Framework Convention on Climate Change, Article 3, Annex B.
Reprinted with permission from the World Resources Institute,
World Resources 1998–99 (New York: Oxford University Press, 1998).

the protocol and inequity among member states represent potential weaknesses in the flexibility mechanisms, the goals of the creators were to achieve widespread consensus in the international community to lower emissions to below 1990 levels. The CDM is a procedure under the Kyoto Protocol under which developed countries may finance or invest in projects that avoid greenhouse-gas emissions in developing countries, and receive credits for doing so that they may apply towards meeting mandatory limits on their own emissions.

Joint implementation is similar to the CDM, but instead of involving cooperation between developed and developing countries, it involves industrialized countries and countries with economies in transition (the former Soviet bloc). For example, a JI project could involve German support for replacing a coal-fired plant in Romania with a more efficient energy source. JI projects must be approved by all parties involved and must result in emissions reductions or removals that are greater than any that would have otherwise occurred.

The third Kyoto Mechanism is emissions trading, whereby an Annex I party with excess emissions credits sells its credits to another Annex I party unable to meet its commitments. However, some expressed concern that this could allow the United States and others to accomplish many of their reductions by acquiring emissions credits from Russia, which, along with Ukraine, was not required to reduce emissions below 1990 levels.[49] The developing countries had initially opposed that provision, but finally agreed to avoid a complete collapse of the negotiations.

Despite the adoption of the Kyoto Protocol, many challenges remained on the horizon. The Kyoto Protocol could enter into force only after ratification by fifty-five parties to the convention, accounting for at least 55 percent of the carbon dioxide emissions in 1990. Although most developing countries and small island states ratified immediately, other countries waited; Annex I parties planned to use subsequent COP meetings as forums to address remaining concerns and negotiate more favorable terms for ratification.

The fourth meeting of the Conference of the Parties in 1998 ended with the adoption of the Buenos Aires Plan of Action, which set a two-year deadline to strengthen UNFCCC implementation and prepare for the entry into force of the Kyoto Protocol. Among other things, the meeting also set the stage for future discussions on supplementarity, the requirement that the three mechanisms can be used only *in addition* to significant domestic action to meet a country's targets, ceilings, long-term convergence, and emissions equity among parties to Kyoto. When that deadline approached two years later in The Hague, carbon sinks within the CDM proved to be of greatest contention. The EU opposed the United States and a new veto coalition, the Umbrella Group (Russia, Japan, Australia, Canada, New Zealand, Norway, Iceland, and Ukraine). The EU proposed a "concrete ceiling" on the use of carbon sinks.[50] The United States pushed for liberal use of the mechanisms, especially the CDM, and would not agree to ceilings on carbon sinks.

It was not until the seventh Conference of the Parties in Marrakesh, Morocco, in November 2001, that delegates finally reached agreement on ways to operationalize the Kyoto Protocol and complete the mandate set forth in Buenos Aires three years before. The EU and the Group of 77 and China remained steadfast in their goals of achieving full ratification of the Kyoto Protocol, even though it required concessions to some of the demands of Umbrella Group countries. First, the group compromised on the issue of carbon sinks; and Russia, Canada, Japan, and Australia were able to use the ratification card (their ratification was necessary for the protocol to enter into force once the United States announced it was pulling out) to push for a weaker compliance system, lower eligibility requirements for mechanisms, greater state sovereignty, and minimized requirements for providing information on carbon sinks.[51]

Despite progress during the meetings of the Conference of the Parties between 1997 and 2003, one question remained: Would the protocol ever enter into force? Many thought that the Kyoto Protocol had received a death sentence when President George W. Bush rejected the protocol in March 2001: "I oppose the Kyoto Protocol because it exempts 80 percent of the world, including major population centers such as China and India, from compliance, and would cause serious harm to the U.S. economy," he wrote. Bush furthermore referred to "the incomplete state of scientific knowledge of the causes of, and solutions to, global warming."[52] Although Kyoto could enter into force without the United States, its decision not to ratify played a large role in delaying the decisions of other economically powerful countries. Furthermore, under most scenarios, the protocol would need the ratification of at least all of the members of the European Union, Canada, Japan, and the Russian Federation to enter into force without the United States. By mid-2004, Russia had become the focus of attention. With more than 120 countries having ratified already—including more than thirty Annex I parties—representing 44 percent of that group's 1990 emissions, the 55 percent threshold required for Kyoto's entry into force as a legally binding international treaty was now tantalizingly close, even without U.S. involvement. If

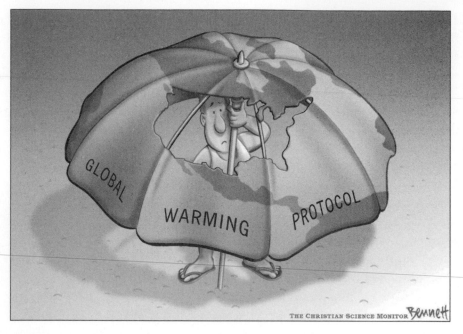

CARTOON 3.1   Kyoto Protocol. Clay Bennett/©2001. *The Christian Science Monitor* (www.csmonitor.com). All rights reserved.

Russia, which represented 17.4 percent of 1990 emissions, signed up, the treaty would have more than enough support to bring it over the top.[53]

Russia stood to gain economically from ratifying the protocol because emissions trading enables it to sell the emissions that remained after the fall of communism left its smokestack industry in ruins. Also, as an economy in transition, such opportunities to attract foreign investment make the emissions trading mechanism particularly appealing to Russia. It would also receive substantial financial aid for preserving and expanding its Siberian forests via the CDM's use of carbon sinks. Russia's desire for accession into the WTO, which the European Commission affirmed would be conditional only upon Russia's ratification of Kyoto, provided the final incentive. On November 18, 2004, the Duma finally approved ratification. The Kyoto Protocol entered into force on February 16, 2005.

Now that the protocol has entered into force, the lead countries are attempting to progress beyond Kyoto and consider more stringent future commitments. At the tenth Conference of the Parties in Buenos Aires in December 2004, the United States continued its veto role and actively obstructed discussion of more stringent commitments. Despite their differences in opposition to greenhouse gas reductions, the United States formed a reformulated veto coalition with Australia, China, India, and the OPEC countries. In accordance with their energy cultures, they also reaffirmed staunch opposition to all proposals. On the other hand, some developing countries shifted their roles: The entire Group of 77 and China (G-77/China) negotiating group has traditionally opposed binding commitments, but this time they appeared willing to negotiate.

The effective implementation of the Kyoto Protocol and progress on reducing greenhouse gas emissions and developing new adaptation and mitigation strategies beyond Kyoto (post-2012) depends on a number of factors. The first factor is the engagement of the veto coalitions—non-parties and developing countries. To engage developing countries, it is important to ensure that issues of impacts and adaptation are addressed in such a way that they give developing countries confidence in a post-2012 regime. Adaptation to climate change will require further research to predict the impacts to enable the public and private sector to develop adaptation options. These impacts differ from region to region and include flood protection measures, appropriate land use methods, adjusted building codes and urban plans, and insurance coverage. Adaptation will also entail the early prediction of more frequent and more damaging natural disasters. Developing countries are the most vulnerable given their high dependence on climate-sensitive economic sectors and their low capacity to adapt. Strengthening their adaptive capacity would contribute to their development. Developing countries can also become more engaged by addressing their emissions without imposing additional economic burdens, for example, by giving the Clean Development Mechanism and other funds much needed support.[54]

Engaging veto states such as the United States and Australia will require a little more creativity. One option would be to make provisions for "as-if-parties" (including subnational actors) who are willing and able to play by the rules of the treaty but have not managed to (or cannot) obtain formal ratification. Likewise, it will be important to retain the flexibility enshrined in the Kyoto Protocol in future treaties (i.e., differentiated mandatory emissions caps) to try to bring these countries into the regime.[55]

The future of the climate change regime still hangs in the balance. Nevertheless, what was once criticized by many to be void of any real potential for success has shown the world that progress indeed remains possible. In gaining entry into force without the United States, the Kyoto Protocol has become a symbol of hope for the lead coalition favoring a regime to mitigate climate change. Although major issues remain, the continued injection of science into the policymaking process, along with necessary financial and technical assistance to developing countries, may help the various veto coalitions to make the necessary compromises for a stronger climate change regime in the future.

INTERNATIONAL TOXIC WASTE TRADE

The United Nations Environment Programme has estimated that between 300 and 500 million tons of hazardous waste are generated each year.[56] Industrialized countries generate the vast majority of this waste. It is generally accepted that about 10 percent of generated hazardous wastes are shipped across international boundaries, primarily between OECD countries.

As laws regulating hazardous waste disposal grew in OECD countries, individual firms sought cheaper sites for their disposal. As a consequence, North-South hazardous waste shipments increased significantly in the 1970s and 1980s, including several notorious cases of illegal dumping.[57] Developing countries, particularly the poorer states in Africa, Central America, and the Caribbean, were tempted by offers of substantial revenues for accepting wastes but lacked the technology or administrative capacity to dispose of them safely. The trade was often illegal, the wastes entering the countries covertly as a result of bribes to corrupt officials.

The issue definition stage began in 1984–1985 when a UNEP working group of legal and technical experts elaborated a set of voluntary guidelines (the Cairo Guidelines) on the management and disposal of hazardous wastes. The guidelines specified prior notification of the receiving state of an export, consent by the receiving state prior to export, and verification by the exporting state that the receiving state has requirements for disposal at least as stringent as those of the exporting state.

Soft law did not satisfy key actors, notably African states that received the bulk of illegal hazardous waste exports. The issue of banning international hazardous waste trade, as opposed to regulating it, was defined primarily by African states: They characterized the trade as a form of exploitation of poor and weak states by advanced countries and businesses. This characterization drew support from some officials in the industrialized states, particularly in Europe.[58]

In 1988, parliamentarians from the European Community joined with representatives from sixty-eight developing states from Africa, the Caribbean, and the Pacific in demanding arrangements banning interna-

CARTOON 3.2   "Looks like they've heard of us." Copyright the Los Angeles Times News Syndicate, reprinted with permission.

tional trade in wastes. The Nonaligned Movement also called for industrialized countries to prohibit waste exports to developing countries.

The bargaining stage began in 1987 when UNEP organized a working group to negotiate a global convention to control international trade in hazardous wastes. During the next eighteen months, major differences emerged between African and industrialized countries. African states wanted a total ban on such waste exports and export-state liability in the event of illegal traffic in wastes, in part because developing countries had neither the administrative, technical, nor financial ability to enforce a ban on their own. Waste-exporting states wanted a convention that would permit the trade, providing that importing countries were notified and agreed to accept it—known as an informed-consent regime.

The final bargaining stage took place in Basel, Switzerland, in March 1989, where the veto coalition, led by the United States, took advantage of the fact that the waste-exporting states could continue to find poor countries willing to accept wastes. The United States exported only 1 percent of its hazardous wastes, mostly to Canada and Mexico, but led the veto coalition largely because of an ideological position that rejected limitations on its right to export. The veto coalition gave the waste-importing states a choice: Accept an informed-consent regime or get none at all. The Organization of African Unity (OAU) proposed amendments to prevent the export of wastes to countries that lack the same level of facilities and technology as the exporting nations and to require inspection of disposal sites by UN inspectors; but the industrialized countries rejected the amendments.[59]

The Basel Convention on Control of Transboundary Movements of Hazardous Wastes and Their Disposal banned exports of hazardous wastes to countries with less advanced storage and disposal facilities unless the importing state had detailed information on the waste shipment and gave prior written consent.[60] Agreements between signatory states and nonsignatory states were permitted, although they needed to conform to the terms of the convention. Critics charged that the convention did not go further than the existing regulations in most industrialized countries that had already failed to curb legal or illegal waste traffic. Moreover, the convention suffered from a lack of precision on key definitions, such as "environmentally sound" and "hazardous wastes," and contained no liability provisions.[61]

As in other global environmental issues, the signing of the Basel Convention began a new phase of maneuvering and bargaining for a stronger regime. Surprisingly, however, this process did not take place in the Basel Convention Conference of the Parties alone.

In April 1989, thirty states (not including the United States) and the EC pledged to dispose of wastes at home and to ban the export of hazardous wastes to countries that lacked the legal and technological capacity to handle them.[62] Later in 1989, the EC reached agreement, after extended negotiations, to ban waste shipments to sixty-eight former European colonies in Africa, the Caribbean, and the Pacific (ACP), after ACP negotiators had rejected a proposed EC exception for countries with "adequate technical capacity."[63] This concession by the EC appears to have reflected particular conditions affecting member states, such as a French decision to give priority to cultural and economic ties with France's former colonies, heavy pressure on the United Kingdom from its former colonies, and West Germany's lack of interest in exporting to developing countries. In January 1991, twelve African states signed the Bamako Convention, which banned all imports of hazardous wastes into their countries. The convention underlined African determination to end the international hazardous waste trade. Combined with the other unilateral and multilateral bans on hazardous waste trade, the Bamako Convention created a stronger waste trade regime outside the Basel Convention than within it, although it did largely exclude Latin American and Asian states.[64]

The Basel Convention came into effect in May 1992 as a weak regime, without ratification by any of the major exporting states that composed the victorious veto coalition during the negotiations.[65] In less than two years, however, growing demands for a complete ban on hazardous waste trade would transform the Basel Convention into a stronger regime. By early 1994, more than one hundred countries had banned the import of hazardous wastes, although not all of them had the administrative capacity to do so unilaterally.[66] Some of the credit must go to Greenpeace, which published an exposé volume documenting 1,000 cases of illegal toxic waste exports.[67] Even the United States, although not a party to the regime, signaled it would support a ban on hazardous waste exports if it exempted scrap metal, glass, textiles, and paper, which are widely traded for recycling.[68]

At COP-2, a broad coalition pressed for a complete ban on hazardous waste exports from OECD countries to non-OECD countries, including those exported for recycling.[69] They argued that shipments of recyclables often were not recycled but just dumped in a developing country and that the OECD countries would never reduce their waste as long as they could ship it out.

The G-77, the lead state coalition, called for the ban to go into effect immediately. Denmark was only a step behind, calling for the ban to begin in 1995. The United Kingdom, Australia, Germany, the Netherlands, Japan, Canada, and the United States wanted to exempt recyclables. China and the former socialist states of Central and Eastern Europe came out in favor of the G-77 proposal. Greenpeace also made an important contribution to the G-77 position. Reporting on a seven year study that closely examined more than fifty recycling operations in non-OECD countries, Greenpeace produced concrete evidence of widespread dumping of hazardous wastes that had been falsely labeled and shipped as "recyclables"[70] as well as many shipments of recyclables that had not been recycled at all but just dumped in developing countries.[71]

Despite intensive lobbying by exporting countries, particularly in support of allowing bilateral agreements on hazardous waste exports for recycling, the G-77 remained firm, agreeing to negotiate only on the timetable for implementing the ban. Confronted with non-OECD unity, the veto coalition began to divide. Now that it had this new-found support, COP-2 approved the ban. The remaining veto states obtained nothing more than a delay in its full implementation of a total export ban. Because several veto states, including the United States, had not ratified the convention, they were all severely hampered; as non-parties, they were technically outside the decisionmaking process.

COP-3 significantly strengthened the ban by adopting it as a formal amendment to the convention (it had been approved in a less legally binding form at COP-2). The ban amendment (also known as Decision III/1) prohibits export of hazardous wastes for final disposal or recycling from countries listed in Annex VII of the convention (currently EU, OECD, and Liechtenstein) to non–Annex VII countries. The ban amendment does not use an OECD/non-OECD distinction and thus is not in itself a barrier for developing countries to retain the option of receiving OECD hazardous wastes because they can do so by joining Annex VII.

The most controversial aspect of the ban amendment is the prohibition on exports of wastes intended for recovery and recycling, such as scrap metal. Because of the veto coalition's economic interests, and, increasingly, those of some developing countries, in the maintenance of a lucrative trade in wastes for recycling, in mid-2005 the ban still had not become law. The amendment needs to be ratified by three-fourths of the parties present at COP-3 in 1995 to enter into force. The debate had centered on the question of which wastes were defined as "hazardous" for the purposes of recycling and recovery and thus covered within the scope of the convention. To remedy this situation, a COP-authorized Technical Working Group drew up lists of banned and exempted wastes. COP-4 approved these lists; in doing so, it diffused the industry argument that nobody knew what the ban was banning. It was hoped that the new lists would speed up the ratification and implementation of the ban amendment.

Parties have also worked to strengthen the Basel Convention by addressing questions of liability, and in December 1999, COP-5 adopted the Basel Protocol on Liability and Compensation. The protocol addresses concerns by developing countries that they lack sufficient funds and technologies to prevent or cope with the consequences of illegal dumping or accidental spills. The protocol seeks to deter such actions by establishing provisions for determining liability and compensation for damage resulting from the legal or illegal transnational movement of hazardous wastes. The protocol requires twenty ratifications to enter into force.[72]

COP-6, held in Geneva in December 2002, agreed upon a prioritized plan for implementing the Basel Convention over the next decade. The plan emphasizes the need to tackle priority waste streams such lead-acid batteries, PCBs, used oil, electronics, and obsolete pesticides. Parties also streamlined the institutional architecture of the convention, created a compliance mechanism to review and assist implementation, and confirmed the role of the

Basel Convention Regional Centers (BCRCs) to facilitate implementation in developing countries through capacity-building, public education, data collection, reporting, promoting environmentally sound waste management, facilitating the transfer of cleaner production technologies, and helping to train customs officials. There are now fourteen BCRCs located in different parts of Latin America, Africa, Asia, and Eastern Europe. Additional centers may be created in the future.

COP-7 convened in Geneva in October 2004. As at previous COPs, parties adopted a variety of decisions on expanding or implementing the regime, including new technical guidelines to assist industry and government officials in managing hazardous waste in an environmentally sound manner. Guidelines are now in place for nearly twenty different types of hazardous wastes, including organic solvents, waste oil, biomedical and health-care wastes, POPs, and obsolete ships. Although the meeting achieved significant results in some areas, financial issues remain a serious concern. Indeed, given the limited availability of resources to implement the convention, financial resources will likely remain a contentious matter.

Nevertheless, several major issues hinder effective implementation of the Basel Convention. The Ban Amendment is now ten years old, yet has still not entered into force. Likewise, the Liability Protocol has a long way to go before its entry into force. The United States remains the only OECD country that has not ratified the convention and remains one of the largest exporters of hazardous wastes. Existing issues, such as the export of hazardous wastes for recycling, and new issues, including electronic waste and the dismantling of toxic ships, are all likely to dominate debate at COP-8 and beyond.

The relatively strong regime on the international hazardous waste trade that emerged from the 1995 COP represented a complete reversal of the original Basel Convention regime. The convention has been central to the elimination of some of the worst forms of toxic waste dumping by industrialized countries in developing countries. The evolution of the Basel Convention shows how veto power can dissipate under pressure from a strong coalition, including all the developing countries, along with the added support of various key OECD countries. The pressure and publicity generated by the activities of several key NGOs, especially Greenpeace, also had an impact on overriding the veto coalition. Once the hazardous waste trade issue had become a matter of political symbolism uniting developing countries behind the demand for a complete ban, it overcame the leverage of waste exporters that had weakened the regime in 1989.

TOXIC CHEMICALS

The systematic development and use of chemicals for commercial purposes began after World War II. Today, approximately 100,000 chemicals are in regular commercial production worldwide. Not all chemicals are hazardous, of course, but toxic chemicals are produced or used in virtually every country in the world. Toxics are released into the environment through the normal use of certain products (e.g., pesticides and fertilizers), industrial and manufacturing practices that involve or produce hazardous chemicals, leakage from wastes, mismanagement, accidents, and intentional dumping. Once dispersed into the environment, the complete cleanup of toxic chemicals is difficult, sometimes impossible, and their harmful effects can continue for many years.

A number of international treaties, international organizations, and soft-law mechanisms address the threats that toxic chemicals pose to human health and the environment. These include the 1998 Rotterdam Convention on the Prior Informed Consent Procedure for Certain Hazardous Chemicals and Pesticides in International Trade (PIC), the regional 1998 Aarhus Protocol on Persistent Organic Pollutants (a protocol to LRTAP), the Inter-Organization Programme on the Sound Management of Chemicals (IOMC), the Intergovernmental Forum on Chemical Safety (IFCS), the nascent Strategic Approach to International Chemicals Management initiative (SAICM), UNEP Chemicals, FAO's work on hazardous pesticides, and elements of the Basel Convention. But the most important part of the global chemicals regime, and the focus of this section, is the 2001 Stockholm Convention on Persistent Organic Pollutants (POPs)—the only chemicals treaty that establishes binding global controls on the production, use, and emissions of specific toxic chemicals.

The issue definition phase for toxic chemicals began in the 1960s when concern started to grow about potentially negative impacts from pesticides and other chemicals. Instrumental in this process were groundbreaking publications, such as Rachel Carson's *Silent Spring,* and high-profile accidents, such as the 1968 tragedy in Yosho, Japan, where many people were poisoned after eating rice contaminated with high levels of **PCBs** (polychlorinated biphenyls). In the late 1960s and early 1970s, new risk assessments led many industrialized countries to adopt domestic regulations on a relatively small set of hazardous chemicals. The United States, for example, banned DDT in 1972 and initiated controls on PCBs in 1976.[73] During this period, the OECD became one of the first international organizations to address toxic chemicals. The focus of its initial efforts was on information exchange and improving scientific and policy measures in the industrialized countries.

Stimulated in part by work done on hazardous chemicals at the 1972 United Nations Conference on the Human Environment,[74] governments adopted several multilateral agreements in the 1970s and early 1980s to help protect oceans, regional seas, and rivers from dumping and pollution.[75] In 1976, UNEP created the International Register of Potentially Toxic Chemicals (IRPTC) to gather, process, and distribute information on hazardous chemicals. The FAO and UNEP led the development of the 1985 International Code of Conduct for the Distribution and Use of Pesticides and the 1987 London Guidelines for the Exchange of Information on Chemicals in International Trade. Unfortunately, many developing countries lacked the regulatory infrastructure that would enable them to use the information made available through these initiatives.[76]

In 1989, amendments to the FAO Code of Conduct and the UNEP London Guidelines created a voluntary **Prior Informed Consent** (PIC) **procedure** to help countries, especially developing countries, learn about chemicals that had been banned or severely restricted in other countries so that they could make informed decisions before they allowed them as imports. Although the voluntary PIC system was seen as a victory for NGOs, which had long called for its adoption, and for developing countries, because they hoped it would allow them to regulate such imports, many believed that a voluntary system would prove insufficient.[77]

The fact-finding process coincided with the Earth Summit in Rio when delegates agreed to devote an entire chapter in Agenda 21 to chemicals, which, among other things, called on states to create a mandatory PIC procedure and to improve coordination among the many national agencies and international organizations working on chemicals or related issues. To this end, governments created the Intergovernmental Forum on Chemical Safety (IFCS) in 1994 to address coordination among governments, and the Inter-Organization Programme for the Sound Management of Chemicals (IOMC) in 1995 to address coordination among international organizations.[78] The fact-finding process continued in these two bodies.

Responding to UNCED's call, UNEP and FAO jointly convened formal intergovernmental negotiations in 1995 with the goal of adopting a binding PIC procedure. The result was the 1998 Rotterdam Convention on the Prior Informed Consent Procedure for Certain Hazardous Chemicals and Pesticides in International Trade, which mandates that parties export certain toxic chemicals only with the informed consent of the importing party.[79]

During this period, concern had also grown regarding a particular set of toxic chemicals known as POPs. Some believed that international action might be warranted to limit their production and use. POPs are among the most toxic pollutants released into the environment.[80] Observed or suspected impacts of POPs on wildlife and humans include reproductive disorders, birth defects, cancers, developmental impairment, damage to central and peripheral nervous systems, impairment of the immune system, and endocrine disruption.[81] POPs are also stable and persistent compounds that resist photolytic, chemical, and biological degradation. This means that once released into the environment, most POPs remain toxic for years before breaking down.

POPs also bio-accumulate. Once ingested, POPs are readily absorbed by, and remain in, the fatty tissue of living organisms. Over time, POPs concentrations can build up in animals and people, potentially reaching 10,000 times the background levels found in the surrounding environment. Fish, birds, mammals, and humans can absorb high concentrations of POPs quickly if they eat multiple organisms in which POPs have already accumulated. Mammals and people can then pass these chemicals to their offspring through breast milk.

Finally, POPs engage in long-range transport across national borders and can be found in ecosystems, waterways, animals, and people thousands of kilometers from the nearest location of their production, use, or release. POPs travel through air currents, waterways, migrating animals, food chains, and a process known as the "grasshopper effect," in which POPs released in one part of the world can, through a repeated process of evaporation and deposit, be transported through the atmosphere to regions far away from the original source.

In the 1980s and 1990s, Canada and Sweden played lead roles in the issue definition and fact-finding phases by supporting POPs research and putting POPs on the agenda of several international forums. Much of this work had been initiated after an unrelated study had found very high levels of certain POPs in wildlife and even the breast milk of Inuit women in northern Canada, thousands of miles from the nearest source of emissions. These findings and subsequent studies added a normative component to the issue definition phase because POPs were now seen as a threat to the food chain, and hence the cultural survival, of the Inuit.[82]

The issue definition phase reached a turning point in May 1995 when UNEP's Governing Council called for an international assessment of twelve POPs known as the "dirty dozen": aldrin, chlordane, dieldrin, dioxins, DDT, endrin, furans, heptachlor, mirex, and toxaphene; and the industrial chemicals, PCBs, and hexachlorobenzene. UNEP acted in response to growing scientific data regarding the transnational movement and toxicity of POPs as well as the cumulative political efforts of the lead states, NGOs, and, increasingly, representatives of the Inuit and other indigenous peoples whose traditional food sources were becoming contaminated by POPs.[83]

In response to UNEP's call, the IOMC established a UNEP/IFCS ad hoc working group on POPs to proceed with fact finding. In June 1996, the working group concluded that scientific evidence supported international action to reduce the risks posed by POPs. In February 1997, the UNEP Governing Council endorsed this conclusion and authorized formal negotiations aimed at creating a global POPs treaty.

The fact-finding process continued in eight regional workshops on POPs, which were convened by UNEP and the IFCS in preparation for the negotiations. More than 138 countries participated in the workshops, which increased awareness of POPs issues, particularly in developing countries and countries that have economies in transition.[84] Preparations also include studying specific aspects of previous negotiating processes on chemicals and the actual content of the Rotterdam PIC Convention and the POPs Protocol to the Convention on Long-Range Transboundary Air Pollution.[85]

The bargaining process began in June 1998 and lasted three years. Individual sessions included five official week-long meetings of the Intergovernmental Negotiating Committee (INC), the main negotiating body; two meetings of the Criteria Expert Group, which focused on developing procedures for identifying and adding new chemicals to the treaty; a formal intersessional consultation on issues related to financial and technical assistance; numerous formal contact groups; and countless informal consultations.[86]

During the negotiations, the EU, Canada, NGOs, and representatives of northern indigenous peoples played the lead role in support of a strong regime. Indeed, the POPs negotiations were notable for the prominent role given to the Inuit and other northern indigenous peoples, who were given ample opportunity to speak of the threat that POPs posed not only to their health but to their cultural heritage of subsistence hunting and fishing.

Countries playing veto roles shifted according to the issue in question. Interestingly, no governments opposed the creation of strong controls on the dirty dozen. The issue definition and fact-finding phases, combined with efforts that took place before the negotiations, produced a ringing endorsement at INC-1 of the need for global regulations. This reflected a general acceptance not only of the science regarding POPs but also of the relatively modest adjustment costs. Indeed, most industrialized countries already had significant controls on the dirty dozen.

With regard to specific issues, NGOs and the EU supported creating controls on chemicals beyond the dirty dozen, but these efforts were successfully opposed by a broad coalition that included most developing countries, the United States, Australia, Japan, and companies that made the chemicals in question. African countries and health-related NGOs strongly opposed the elimination of DDT because its use was essential for battling malaria. This position quickly gained near universal support. Although there was general agreement on the need to grant exemptions to a complete phaseout of the dirty dozen, a variety of views existed on which chemicals or uses deserved such exemptions and how they should be administered. As they had in previous negotiations on biodiversity, climate, and desertification, industrialized and developing countries strongly disagreed on the mechanism for providing financial assistance. Resolving these and other issues required difficult and detailed negotiations.

The resulting 2001 Stockholm Convention on Persistent Organic Pollutants seeks to protect human health and the environment by eliminating or reducing the production, use, trade, and emissions into the environment of twelve POPs.[87] In particular, all parties must eliminate the production and use of aldrin, chlordane, dieldrin, endrin, heptachlor, mirex, toxaphene, PCBs, and hexachlorobenzene. Parties must restrict the production and use of DDT except for that needed for disease-vector control, especially against malaria mosquitoes, and when there are no suitable and affordable alternatives.[88] Parties must minimize the creation and release of dioxins and furans in the environment. To complete the loop, parties must ban the import or export of POPs controlled under the convention, except for narrowly defined purposes or environmentally sound disposal; promote the use of the best available technologies and practices for replacing existing POPs, reducing emissions of POPs, and managing POP wastes; and take steps to prevent the development and commercial introduction of new POPs.

Although there was no debate on the need to control the dirty dozen, several prominent countries supported the continued but limited use of certain POPs for selected purposes if economic, safety, or other conditions made an immediate phaseout too difficult. For example, Russia, the United States, and many other countries noted that PCBs were once widely used in electrical transformers and other equipment, and although equipment using new PCBs is no longer produced, hundreds of thousands of tons of PCBs were still in use in existing equipment. Australia and China supported using mirex to control

PHOTO 3.2   WWF protesters outside POPs INC-4 negotiations in Bonn, Germany, in March 2002. Courtesy IISD/*Earth Negotiations Bulletin.*

certain termites in certain areas. Botswana and China supported continued use of chlordane to protect wooden dams and certain other structures from termites. Other parties argued they would need small amounts of aldrin for use as an insecticide during the transition to alternatives.

Therefore, in addition to the broad health-related exemption granted for DDT, a specific exemption for PCBs allows countries to maintain existing equipment containing PCBs until 2025. Parties are also allowed to exercise "country-specific exemptions" that permit the continued use of small amounts of specific POPs for essential applications for five years (for such things as termite control), after which an extension must be granted by the COP.

The Stockholm Convention also establishes scientifically based criteria and a specific step-by-step procedure for identifying, evaluating, and adding chemicals to the convention. This critical feature of the regime, which ensures its continued relevance beyond the dirty dozen, took a long time to develop. The EU and its Member States had advocated a process that would emphasize the precautionary principle and allow the addition of chemicals relatively easily and quickly. The United States, Japan, and Australia, among others, wanted a more regimented mechanism that required explicit risk analyses and clear evidence of existing harm before the COP could add a chemical.

The resulting fifteen-step process represents a working compromise between these views that incorporates precaution, risk analysis according to set criteria, use of experts, flexibility, and sovereign control by the parties.[89] (See fig. 3.3.) Under the treaty, any party may nominate a chemical for evaluation. A POPs Review Committee (POPROC) made up of technical experts will then work on behalf (and under the oversight) of the parties and consider the nominated chemical in detail; then it will develop risk profiles and risk management evaluations. In doing so, the POPROC will use specific scientific criteria for identifying candidate POPs (as set out in Annex D of the convention), specific information requirements for developing a risk profile for candidate POPs (Annex E), consideration of socioeconomic impacts of controlling a POP (Annex F), and a strong perspective of precaution. Indeed, as demanded by the EU, precaution informs the process in such a way that the absence of strict scientific certainty will not prevent parties from controlling a potentially hazardous substance.[90]

At the same time, sovereign control is preserved, as demanded by the United States. Safeguards exist to ensure that all parties have opportunities for a full hearing on any candidate POP, that parties (not the POPROC) hold final decisionmaking authority, and that each party, if it chooses, could refuse to ratify a particular amendment adding a chemical.

Another critical feature of the convention is the financial mechanism that assists developing countries and countries with economies in transition in meeting their treaty obligations. Under the convention, industrialized countries must provide new financial resources, albeit at unspecified levels, and promote the transfer of technical assistance. Although nearly all negotiators acknowledged the importance of providing financial and technical assistance (FTA), there were diverse views regarding the proper level and delivery mechanisms. Developing countries strongly supported creating a new standalone financial institution patterned after the one developed under the Montreal Protocol. They opposed designating the GEF as the financial mechanism because of concerns about the GEF's willingness to address POPs and the Stockholm Convention as priority areas and to receive direction on POPs-related issues from the COP. The G-77 also insisted that all FTA be new and additional to current programs so that POPs-related activities did not mean less FTA in other areas. Donor countries countered that the GEF could provide important efficiencies and expertise, and that new FTA programs

FIGURE 3.3   Process for Adding New Chemicals to the Stockholm Convention

Process for Adding New Chemicals to the Stockholm Convention

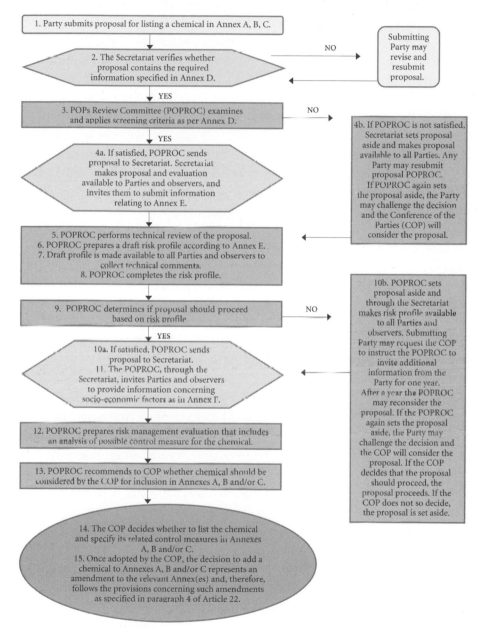

could be bundled and augmented with existing programs in other forums, such as the Rotterdam and Basel Conventions.

In the final compromise, the GEF was designated as the main financing mechanism, but only on an interim basis.[91] Industrialized countries agreed to provide new and additional financial resources for POPs and the COP will give instructions to, and regularly review the performance of, the GEF with regard to its role as the Convention's financial mechanism. In response to the concerns expressed during the negotiations, the GEF has created a dedicated POPs program and funded a fairly large number of POPs projects, particularly in the areas of capacity building and preparation of national implementation plans for the convention. Thus, although future COPs will decide whether the GEF remains the principal entity of the financial mechanism for the POPs Convention, the combination of donor support and GEF lobbying makes it unlikely that an existing or new institution will supplant the GEF.

The regime-strengthening process began almost as soon as the convention was adopted. In particular, a series of negotiating sessions were convened before the first Conference of the Parties (COP-1) in May 2005 in Punta del Este, Uruguay. Because of the preparatory work, COP-1 succeeded in adopting several decisions essential to making the convention operational. These included approving rules of procedure and financial rules; adopting the budget for the secretariat; formally establishing the POPs Review Committee; adopting guidance for the GEF as the financial mechanism; approving a memorandum of understanding with the GEF; beginning preparations for a review of the financial mechanism; establishing a review process for specific exemptions; and delineating schedules for the reporting requirements.

The chemical regime faces several challenges. One is to increase the number of parties to its constituent treaties. The United States and other key countries in Latin America and Asia, for example, remain non-parties to the POPs convention. Although the United States signed and publicly praised the Rotterdam and Stockholm Conventions, and the Bush administration has stated that it supports their ratification, concerns by the chemical industry regarding future expansion of these treaties have blocked their ratification by the U.S. Senate. For the global chemical regime to be successful, the United States and many other key countries need to participate fully.

Another important challenge is to improve coordination among the Stockholm, Rotterdam, and Basel Conventions, as well as related regional treaties. This would allow for more effective use of limited resources, help avoid unnecessary duplication of tasks, and help prevent unintended and counterproductive conflicts between the chemicals treaties. Parties recognize the need for this work; indeed, it has been called for by several international forums, including the 2002 World Summit on Sustainable Development and the UNEP Governing Council, but much effort needs to be put forth. Current efforts by the COPs, such as co-locating and combining elements of the Rotterdam and Stockholm Secretariats, are important steps in this direction.

Another challenge, common to all environmental regimes, is the need for more financial and technical resources to assist developing countries' transition away from the use of as many toxic chemicals as possible and to better manage those that remain. Regime compliance and regime strengthening will require the availability and proper application of sufficient financial and technical assistance.

Finally, many observers believe that the content of the Rotterdam and Stockholm Conventions represents only a first step toward global chemical safety. Many chemicals known to be extremely hazardous are subject to neither national nor international regulations. Thus, the ultimate success of global chemical policy may be its ability to grow stronger by adding additional substances to its control regime.

WHALING

The development and expansion of global policy to safeguard whales illustrates the transformation of an international regime from one that allowed virtually unregulated exploitation of an endangered species to a framework for global conservation, despite the continued resistance of a strong veto coalition. At present, the international whaling regime is at a crossroads. The balance of power in the global decisionmaking body, the International Whaling Commission (IWC), rests narrowly with the states favoring a whaling ban; however, the veto coalition, growing in support and empowered by the ability to exit the relevant international agreement at any time, is gaining ground. Although recent advances in population monitoring and technology offer the prospect of developing a biologically sound system of management, strong emotions on both sides of the issue threaten an impasse that, if left unresolved, could endanger the regime.

Indeed, to a significant degree, emotions and concerns for national sovereignty influence the global debate on whaling more than detailed scientific analysis and debate or economic interests (whaling no longer represents a significant economic enterprise on a global or even national basis). For some governments and many environmental NGOs in the United States and Western

Europe, whaling represents an example of unnecessary human cruelty to an intelligent species and a powerful symbol of environmental overexploitation. To whaling states, however, harvesting whales represents the right to preserve cultural traditions and maintain coastal livelihoods, thus constituting an important matter of national sovereignty.

In 1946, the long history of overexploitation of whales, which had threatened many species with extinction, led to the establishment of the International Whaling Commission by the International Convention for the Regulation of Whaling. The convention prohibited killing certain species that were nearly extinct, set quotas and minimum sizes for whales caught commercially, and regulated whaling seasons. The convention was not, however, a prohibition regime but a club of whaling nations designed to manage the catch. The regime's designated decisionmaking body, the IWC, met in secret each year to haggle over quotas that were set so high that far more whales were being killed annually under the new regime than before the regulations had gone into effect. Indeed, the number of whales killed more than doubled between 1951 and 1962. And the IWC had no power to enforce its regulations on the size of catch or even its bans on the killing of endangered species. Although the major whaling nations that were responsible for most of the catch were members of the IWC, many developing countries, including China, South Korea, Brazil, Chile, Ecuador, and Peru, refused to join or to abide by its restrictions. They allowed "pirate" whalers, often financed by selling to the Japanese, to operate freely.

The process of fact-finding and consensus building played virtually no role in relations among the members of the IWC. Scientific knowledge was usually subordinated to political and economic interests. The IWC's scientific committee routinely produced data and analyses supporting continued commercial exploitation, and no outside international organization existed that could facilitate a different framework for decisions based on the scientific facts on whaling. Given this situation, it is not surprising that by the 1960s, the survival of the largest species, the blue whale, was in doubt, finback stocks were dwindling, and the filling of quotas for other species with younger and smaller whales had produced overall population declines.

When increasing public awareness of the diminishing stocks, including the potential extinction of the blue whales, combined with the emerging environmental movement, the tide against commercial whaling began to turn. In the United States, the plight of the whales seized the imagination of many Americans, who were beginning to learn more about the intelligence of cetaceans, and the new awareness led to broad popular support for meaningful protections. Responding to the 1969 Endangered Species Act, the United States declared eight whale species endangered in 1970 and began to take the lead in defining the whaling issue internationally.[92]

Placing the issue of whaling in the context of the broader international environmental agenda, the United States first proposed an immediate moratorium on commercial whaling at the 1972 United Nations Conference on the Human Environment. Adopted unanimously by fifty-two nations, the proposal signaled strong international support for a moratorium. However, because it had not been generated through the IWC, it carried no force of law within the whaling regime itself. In the IWC, the whaling states (Norway, Japan, the Soviet Union, Iceland, Chile, and Peru) constituted a veto coalition that could not only remove themselves from the IWC but also held a majority, and a similar moratorium proposal there was defeated by a vote of 6 to 4, with 4 abstentions.

Seeing the need to seek change within the whaling regime itself, and taking advantage of the fact that the IWC does not limit membership to whaling nations, the United States, Sweden, and other conservationist states sought to overcome the veto coalition by recruiting non-whaling states into the Commission. Thus, rather than pursue regime transformation through a process of fact-finding and consensus building within the IWC, this group sought to assemble the three-fourths majority required to institute a whaling ban. Between 1979 and 1982, the anti-whaling coalition recruited the Seychelles and seven other developing states, most of which viewed the whaling issue from the perspective that the oceans and their natural resources are the "common heritage of humankind."[93]

The United States, as the lead state, also sought to weaken the veto coalition through the threat of economic sanctions. It used domestic legislation to ban imports of fish products and to deny fishing permits within the U.S. 200-mile **exclusive economic zone** to countries violating international whale-conservation programs. This action put pressure on Chile and Peru, both heavily dependent on U.S. fishing permits and markets, to comply with the moratorium.

By 1982, enough developing-country non-whaling nations had joined the IWC to tilt the balance decisively. A five-year moratorium on all commercial whaling, to take effect in 1985, was passed 25 to 7, with 5 abstentions. Four of the veto coalition states (Japan, Norway, Peru, and the Soviet Union), which accounted for 75 percent of the killing of whales and almost all the consumption of whale meat and other whale products, filed formal reservations to the moratorium but chose not to defy it openly when it went into effect.

Japan, Norway, and the Soviet Union all formally ended commercial whaling activity by the 1987–1988 whaling season. Soon after, however, Japan, Iceland, and Norway unilaterally began the practice of what they called "scientific" whaling, which is permitted in the whaling convention. Most IWC members found no scientific merit in this whaling, which was conducted by commercial ships, because it killed hundreds of minke whales annually. However, the ability of the United States and other countries to pressure whaling states to end this practice was weakened by other economic and political interests. For example, to avoid a probable Japanese retaliation on U.S. fish exports, the United States decided not to ban imports of $1 billion in Japanese seafood annually, instead choosing the lesser sanction of denying the Japanese permission to fish in U.S. waters. The United States also reached successive bilateral agreements in 1987 and 1988 with Iceland condoning its "scientific" whaling in part because Washington feared that otherwise it could have been denied use of its Air Force base in Reykjavik. Only a boycott of Icelandic fish products organized by conservationists, who were unburdened with such broader concerns, persuaded Iceland to pledge a halt in whaling, at least until 1991.[94] The Soviet Union, meanwhile, continued whaling in spite of the moratorium, bringing in the world's second-largest catch in the 1980s.[95] Underreporting of the Soviet catch during that decade may very well have distorted the estimates of surviving stocks.

Although the adoption of "scientific" whaling programs and a request for a change in the status of the Northeast Atlantic minke whales from "protection stock" to "sustainable stock" represented interim attempts to allowing whaling to continue, the whaling states had their sights set on the larger target of repealing the whaling moratorium. At the 1990 IWC meeting, however, with the five-year moratorium ending, the United States led a majority of IWC members in blocking a proposal allowing limited commercial whaling in the Atlantic, and instead extended the moratorium for another year. In response, Iceland, Japan, and Norway resorted to the ultimate weapon of threatening to leave the IWC if the moratorium was not overturned at the next meeting. Only Iceland followed through with the threat, however, leaving the Commission in 1992.

Before the 1993 IWC meeting in Kyoto, Japan and Norway prepared for another attempt to end the whaling ban. Norway announced its intention to resume modest commercial whaling (160 minke whales from the North Atlantic) in the 1993 season, reportedly because Prime Minister Gro Harlem Brundtland needed the Arctic whaling communities' votes in a tight upcoming election. Japan planned to request authority to resume the commercial whaling of a limited number of Antarctic minkes and for the harvest of fifty more by village fishermen off the Japanese coast. Meanwhile, both governments spent large amounts of money and effort on public relations in non-whaling countries to promote the position that minke whales were no longer endangered and that whaling villages, severely impoverished by the moratorium, were being denied the right to pursue a cultural tradition.[96] In addition, Japan induced six Caribbean IWC members to support its position by providing funds for new fishing vessels and paying their annual IWC membership fees.[97] However, at Kyoto, the IWC again extended the whaling moratorium for another year, rejecting Japan's requests. Norway resumed limited whaling in 1993 in spite of the moratorium, but came under increased international pressure when the Clinton administration certified that Norway was eligible for U.S. trade sanctions and the U.S. House of Representatives called unanimously for the application of such sanctions. President Clinton delayed the application of sanctions pending efforts to convince Norway to end its defiance of the moratorium.

The whale protection regime was further strengthened at the 1994 IWC meeting in Mexico by the adoption of a long-term no-catch area for all whales inhabiting waters below 40 degrees south latitude. The action created an Antarctic whale sanctuary that could protect up to 90 percent of the estimated 3.5 million remaining great whales. The whaling nation most affected by the vote was Japan, which was taking three hundred minkes from the Antarctic annually, ostensibly for "scientific" purposes. Nevertheless, Japan and Norway continued to defy both the whaling moratorium and the no-catch area. In 1997, Norway hunted five times as many whales as it did in 1992, and Japan continued to hunt whales in the Antarctic whale sanctuary.[98]

Responding to the standoff over the whaling moratorium, and broad consensus among anti-whaling nations that "scientific whaling" simply provided a front for commercial harvest, Ireland made a proposal at the 1997 IWC meeting in Monaco that would end the moratorium on commercial whaling, terminate the practice of "scientific whaling," and bring commercial whaling back under the control of the Commission. Central to the Irish proposal was that the Commission should formally adopt the Revised Management Scheme (RMS), a regulatory mechanism that includes scientific guidelines for setting catch limits and incorporating population uncertainty levels (the Revised Management Procedure, or RMP), guidelines and methods for monitoring and inspection, area restrictions (such as permitting coastal whaling within 200 miles of countries having a long whaling tradition and designating a global whale sanctuary), prohibiting international trade in whale products, and ending the practice of "scientific whaling."

Despite attempts to consider the Irish proposal to lift the whaling moratorium with the above conditions at the fifty-first meeting in May 1999 in Grenada, the IWC voted to defer the decision until 2000, even though the majority of the thirty-four governments present appeared to support the proposal.[99] Many of the nations that had spoken up in support of whale protection did not openly support the Irish proposal. Nervous about being criticized by environmental and animal welfare organizations, they were reluctant to endorse a plan that would officially allow commercial whaling, even though the present strategy of a simple moratorium on whaling is allowing more and more whales to be killed each year.[100] (See fig. 3.4.)

The RMS relies on scientific data for developing sustainable harvest quotas. The scientific aspects of the RMS are assembled under the banner of the RMP, which comprises methods of setting harvest quotas based on computer simulations of future population trends.[101] Although the Commission has accepted and endorsed the RMP for commercial whaling, it has noted that work on the RMS on various issues, including specification of an inspection and observer system, must be completed before the Commission will consider establishing catch limits other than zero. Despite resolutions each year during the period 2000–2004 establishing working groups and intersessional meetings to move the RMS forward, the scheme has not been adopted and catch limits remain at zero. A proposal by Japan at the 2004 meeting in Sorrento, Italy, to mandate a vote on the RMS at the 2005 IWC meeting was defeated by a simple majority vote. Japan has threatened to leave the IWC (as it has at several past meetings) in 2006 if the RMS and lifting of the moratorium have not been enacted by the commission.[102]

The bitter stalemate over the moratorium on commercial whaling has raised concern about the IWC's role in the future. The ability of the regime to control whaling activities faces several major challenges: the build-up of a pro-whaling coalition within the IWC, outright defiance of international whaling rules, misuse of scientific whaling, the potential for weakened support for the moratorium, and the use of other processes, including CITES, to attempt "end-runs" around IWC prohibitions.

In a development reminiscent of the building of the anti-whaling coalition in the late 1970s and early 1980s, an alliance to reverse the whaling ban has been steadily growing since the early 1990s. This coalition has been built largely by Japan, which has engaged in "vote buying," that is, building support for its position on whaling through foreign aid and paying IWC membership fees for small-nation coalition members. The head of Japan's Fisheries Agency confirmed this practice, but government officials subse-

FIGURE 3.4   Total Whales Killed in Whaling Operations: 1987–2003

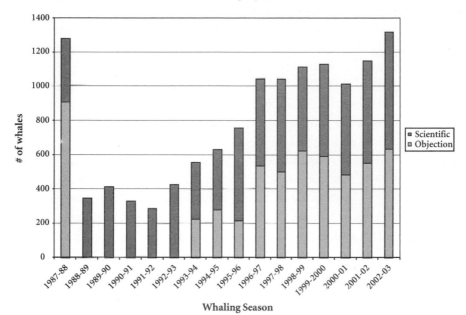

Note: In 1987–1988, Iceland had a scientific permit and Japan and Norway caught whales in objection to the moratorium. Beginning in 1993-94, Japan did all of the scientific whaling and Norway continued to catch whales in objection to the moratorium. Iceland did not kill any whales after the 1989–1990 season.

Source: World Wide Fund for Nature, "Total Whales Killed in Whaling Operations since the IWC Whaling Moratorium Went into Effect," Factsheet (June 2005).

quently denied it.[103] By 2005, the IWC had grown to sixty members, the anti-whaling bloc holding only a slight simple majority. Although gaining a simple majority would be insufficient to overturn the moratorium, it would allow the veto coalition to affect other aspects of the regime, including the abolishment of the conservation committee.[104] Japan proposed overturning the moratorium once again at the 2005 IWC meetings in Ulsan, South Korea, but the proposal was defeated by a vote of twenty-nine countries in favor of retaining the moratorium, twenty-three countries supporting Japan, and five abstentions.[105] Another Japanese proposal would have allowed the use of secret ballots for IWC proposals, lessening the transparency of decision-making within the Commission and attempting to further strengthen the veto coalition. This proposal was also defeated.

Although the whaling moratorium suggests a strong degree of protection for whales, it is severely weakened by outright defiance of the whaling moratorium and the whale sanctuaries (both in the southern ocean and the Indian Ocean) and the use of loopholes in the regime such as scientific whaling. Norway registered a formal reservation to the moratorium at the time of its passage, and, in spite of significant international pressure for it not to do so, has since conducted commercial whaling outside the control of the IWC. Japan, on the other hand, has conducted its whaling operations mostly under the banner of "scientific whaling" while also seeking to weaken the controls over sanctuary areas and the moratorium itself. Nations engaged in "scientific whaling" defend the practice by pointing to the large amount of scientific data it has generated. Some of these data, including stomach contents and reliable estimates of age, cannot be collected without taking whales. However, many scientists contend that, although the data are collected by using a high degree of scientific rigor, the resulting information does not provide new and important information relevant to the management of stocks but instead largely supports previous knowledge.[106]

Changes in position by anti-whaling members, such as that of the United States in 2002 in regard to Japanese coastal whaling (criticized by some observers as a concession to win Japanese support for allowances of harvests of bowhead whales by Native Alaskans) also threaten to weaken the regime.[107] The acceptance of reduced protection for whales by the United States, the architect and lead state of the anti-whaling coalition, not only represents a demoralizing blow to the NGOs that oppose whaling under any circumstances but may further empower the veto coalition in seeking a rapid resumption of commercial whaling.

Finally, pro-whaling nations have also attempted an "end-run" around the IWC by seeking to reduce species protections for whales in CITES. During the thirteenth CITES Conference of the Parties in 2004, Japan entered a proposal to down-list three populations of minke whales from Appendix I to Appendix II; this proposal was rejected, however, as were similar proposals in 1997, 2000, and 2002.[108] Beginning in 1979, and affirmed by resolution 11.4 at the twelfth CITES Conference of the Parties in 2000, the position of CITES has been to assure that no conflict exists between two treaties and to support the IWC moratorium by maintaining Appendix I listings for all whale species.[109] Down-listing in CITES may not affect the measures imposed by the IWC on its member states, but it would remove barriers to international trade in whale species, thus opening international markets if commercial whaling resumes, and would provide an important negotiating argument for the veto coalition.

The building of coalitions in support of the commercial whaling moratorium and in opposition to it have been characterized more by political maneuvering than by a process of fact-finding and consensus building. Science appears to have played a marginal role in decisionmaking, with its credibility diminished by the practice of commercial whaling being carried out under the banner of "scientific whaling." However, recent advances in the ability to monitor whale populations and the development of the RMP may lead to more scientifically-based management in the future.

INTERNATIONAL TRADE
IN ENDANGERED SPECIES

The regime governing trade in endangered species, the Convention on International Trade in Endangered Species of Flora and Fauna, is really an "umbrella regime" containing a multitude of smaller "regimes-within-regimes" that address specific species. Under this umbrella, proponent and veto coalitions vary across the specific agreements on individual species (or groups of species) and often cross traditional North South divisions.[110] In contrast to the broader biodiversity regime, CITES focuses on a single cause of species loss, contains generally clearer, stronger, and more straightforward protection targets and corresponding regulations, and lacks the North-South struggle over intellectual property rights issues.

International trade in exotic wildlife is an enormous and lucrative business. Approximately 350 million individual plants and animals, and their parts and derivatives, are bought and sold each year.[111] Much of this multibillion dollar trade is illegal. Indeed, illegal trade in wildlife is the third largest international market in illicit goods, behind drugs and weapons.[112] The worldwide market for animals, parts, and derivatives plays an important role in species loss by producing significant incentives to overexploit particular natural resources legally and illegally.[113] Moreover, many "range" states, the nations in which traded species naturally reside, lack the monitoring or enforcement capacity needed to regulate legal harvests and prevent illegal ones.

To address species loss resulting from international trade, in 1973 governments adopted the Convention on International Trade in Endangered Species, commonly known as CITES. CITES combats commercial overexploitation of wild animals and plants by delineating threatened species, establishing rules regarding trade, and imposing trade sanctions against violators.[114] CITES currently protects more than 33,000 species against illegal trade. There are currently 167 parties to the convention. A COP meets every two years to decide how to regulate trade in species in different degrees of danger. UNEP provides the secretariat that administers the regime on behalf of the parties.

CITES creates three categories of species according to the threat to their existence, and for each one various levels of controls are in place. Those in Appendix I are threatened with extinction and are not to be traded unless for scientific or cultural endeavors. Species listed in Appendix II, although not yet endangered, are considered to be affected by international trade which, if left unregulated, would endanger them. Thus, to allow exports of an Appendix II species, a scientific authority must determine that the proposed export will not be detrimental to the survival of the species. Those in Appendix III are listed voluntarily by range states seeking cooperation in the control of international trade and do not require a vote. Currently, Appendix I lists more than 800 species; Appendix II, more than 32,500; and Appendix III, more than 290.[115]

In the negotiations to create CITES, countries expressed strong support for the overall goal of protecting endangered species. Nations where the traded species lived also supported (and continue to support) CITES because it would help protect their valuable wildlife resources from poachers and illegal traders. Importing countries supported (and continue to support) the regime because it protected the interests of their legitimate dealers.

Differences arose, however, concerning how to list specific species that would be restricted from trade. Many countries wanted a system that would require all parties to protect a species if a majority voted to list the species. Others insisted on a system that would protect economic interests and the principle of sovereign control. In the end, a potential veto coalition forced the convention's strongest proponents to allow a party to enter a reservation to (i.e., "opt out" of) the listing of a species as controlled or banned if the party claimed an overriding economic interest in continuing to exploit the species. A reservation such as this makes that party in effect a non-party with regard to that particular species. Because listing decisions are made on a two-thirds super majority voting system, negotiations are constrained by the option of member states to enter a reservation to a specific Appendix I or II listing. In certain circumstances, this can give some states de facto veto power over a listing. If one or a few states control the great majority of trade in a species, they can essentially veto a listing by entering a reservation to it. It takes two countries to overcome a CITES listing efficiently, however, and in cases where reservations exist by range states, it is not unusual for importing countries to pass national laws that are stricter than CITES in an effort to prevent loopholes. But the effects of the so-called veto power are more evident when dealing with marine species because species are introduced directly from the sea and the two-party relationship does not take place.

Because of the number and different geographical distributions of species endangered by international trade, as well as variation in the countries where market demand for a given species exists, the proponent and veto coalitions and the comparative difficulty of obtaining a listing differ between species. Two examples, African elephants and big-leaf mahogany, illustrate some of these differences.

African Elephants

The African elephant was first listed under CITES Appendix II in 1977. Beginning in the early 1980s, African elephant populations began to decline precipitously, falling from 1.3 million in 1979 to 625,000 in 1989.[116] Most of this decline, which triggered calls for more serious action, was caused by the illegal poaching of ivory for international markets. To control the international traffic, CITES in 1985 established a system of ivory export quotas for countries supporting elephant herds. Declines continued, however, and a study sponsored by the World Wildlife Fund and Conservation International concluded that African elephants were being harvested at a rate far exceeding that considered to be sustainable. This rate of loss, driven primarily by the international trade in ivory, led to increasing calls for placing African elephants in Appendix I of CITES and establishing a worldwide ban on trade in African elephant ivory.

The bargaining stage began at the seventh CITES Conference of the Parties in October 1989 when an odd international coalition consisting of Kenya, Tanzania, Austria, the Gambia, Somalia, Hungary, and the United States initiated an effort to list the African elephant in Appendix I and ban trade in ivory products entirely. Another unlikely coalition, uniting foes in southern Africa's struggle over apartheid (Botswana, Malawi, Mozambique, Zambia, South Africa, and Zimbabwe), opposed the listing. The reason for their resistance was that in the 1980s several southern African herds had grown as a result of conservation efforts financed through the limited hunting of elephants and commercial trade of elephant parts. Despite this resistance, a two-thirds majority of all CITES Parties voted to place all African elephant herds in Appendix I.[117] The southern African states lodged reservations against the ban and announced plans to sell their ivory through a cartel, the proceeds to be used to finance conservation.[118]

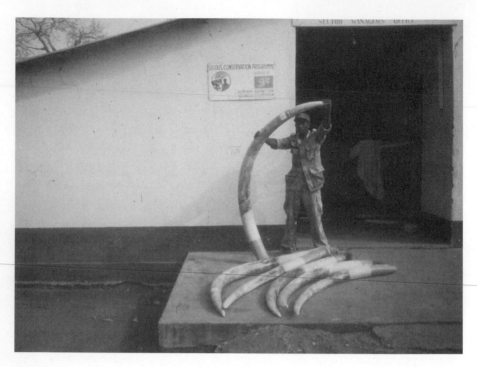

PHOTO 3.3   Examining poached elephant tusks. Photo by Rob Barnett/TRAFFIC.

It was Japan, however, not the African states, that determined the viability of the regime. In 1989, the worldwide ivory market was worth an estimated $50-60 million annually. Japan dominated this market and made it the potential leader of a veto coalition by importing more than 80 percent of all African ivory products.[119] As the major consumer nation, Japan had been expected to enter a reservation, allowing a significant portion of the market to remain viable and effectively vetoing the ban. But facing heavy pressure from NGOs, the United States, and the EC, Japan eventually decided not to oppose the ban. World prices for raw ivory soon plunged by 90 percent.[120]

In the 1990s, three southern African countries (Zimbabwe, Namibia, and Botswana) called for an end to the ivory trade ban, proposing that the African elephant be "down-listed" from CITES Appendix I to Appendix II. Efforts to this effect were initiated unsuccessfully at CITES meetings in 1992 and 1994.[121]

At the tenth Conference of the Parties in June 1997 in Harare, Zimbabwe, the debate over the proposal by the three southern African range states and

Japan for a "split" down-listing of the elephant populations in their countries was long and acrimonious. The three range states argued that their herds had grown to a combined total of about 150,000, and that continued inability to exploit the herds commercially was costing them revenues that could be used to increase their conservation budgets. The United States and other parties feared that even a partial easing of the trade ban would result in a new flood of illegal trade in ivory. They cited deficiencies in enforcement and control measures that had been identified by the CITES panel of experts in the three African countries and Japan. They pointed out that, without adequate controls in place, it would be extremely difficult to discover where elephant tusks originated.

In the end, a committee of nineteen CITES members worked out a compromise under which each of the three states could get permission to sell a strictly limited "experimental quota" of ivory under a stringent set of conditions.[122] A heavily regulated one-time sale of ivory from these countries was also approved after monitoring deficiencies were adequately addressed. All experimental sales went to Japan, all funds obtained by the sale to be invested in elephant conservation efforts.[123] The split down-listing was maintained at the eleventh Conference of the Parties in 2000, but no further ivory sales were authorized.

At the twelfth Conference of the Parties in 2002, Botswana, South Africa, and Namibia once again advanced a proposal for the limited sale of ivory. This proposal was accepted after the removal of an annual quota, and under strict monitoring and verification conditions. It was agreed that 20,000 kg, 30,000 kg, and 10,000 kg from Botswana, South Africa, and Namibia, respectively, would be traded in one shipment once the secretariat had verified the prospective importing countries, and the MIKE (Monitoring of Illegal Killing of Elephants) program had reported to the secretariat on the baseline information (e.g., elephant population numbers, incidence of illegal killing).[124]

Again in 2004, at the thirteenth COP, Namibia proposed a 2,000 kg annual quota of raw ivory in addition to the trade of worked ivory, leather, and hair products. The proposal involving raw ivory was rejected, but Namibia was allowed to participate in trade in leather and hair products and noncommercial trade in worked ivory amulets, known as *ekipas*.[125]

Big-Leaf Mahogany

Trade in mahogany is a lucrative business. With an average price of $1,700 per cubic meter of wood, global sales approached $200 million in 2004.[126]

High international demand has put incredible pressure on mahogany populations. Honduran mahogany and Caribbean mahogany were once staples of the timber market, but overexploitation has now made them commercially extinct. With these species unavailable for large-scale profitable harvest, the market shifted its focus to big-leaf mahogany, with predictable results. In Central America alone, big-leaf mahogany coverage fell from 45 million hectares in the 1940s to 13 million hectares in the 1990s.[127] Although not as dramatic as that of the African elephants, this decline was still considered an alarming trend.

Despite the notable population decline in the 1980s, mahogany did not immediately emerge as a candidate for a CITES Appendix listing. In 1992, at the eighth Conference of the Parties, the United States and Costa Rica put forth a proposal for an Appendix II listing for big-leaf mahogany. In response, a subset of Latin American range states argued that insufficient information regarding the population declines and inadequate national infrastructures could not effectively support trade restrictions. As a result, the proposal failed to garner the required votes.

Negotiations continued over the next several years. At the ninth Conference of the Parties in 1994, the Netherlands and El Salvador proposed an Appendix II listing. This proposal failed by only six votes. Taking what unilateral action it could, in 1995 Costa Rica voluntarily listed big-leaf mahogany as a CITES Appendix III species. In 1997, at the tenth Conference of the Parties, the United States and Bolivia made a third attempt to list mahogany in Appendix II, a proposal that was once again narrowly rejected. However, that same year, Bolivia, Brazil, Colombia, Mexico, and Peru voluntarily listed big-leaf mahogany under Appendix III.

Some range states that opposed further action hoped that placing big-leaf mahogany in Appendix III would retard the progression of an Appendix II listing. Proponents of an Appendix II listing maintained that the voluntary Appendix III listings did not offer sufficient guarantees that trade would consist only of legally obtained timber or that the harvest did not threaten the survival of the species. For example, illegal trade in Brazil continues because border authorities often do not require CITES certificates of origin from timber imports from Bolivia and Peru.[128]

Although the proposal for an Appendix II listing did not succeed, the Conference of the Parties did create a working group, supported by both import and export countries, to examine the population status, management, and trade in big-leaf mahogany throughout its entire range. In 2000, at the eleventh Conference of the Parties, delegates established additional working groups to continue the collection of scientific information and help frame the negotiations.

As information began to accumulate, Nicaragua and Guatemala tried again to list big-leaf mahogany in CITES Appendix II in 2002. Their proposal pointed to evidence that the status of the species had not changed in the five years since being listed on Appendix III because of weak implementation and lack of political will.[129] Brazil continued to oppose the proposal, emphasizing that Appendix II listing would not only produce trade barriers and prevent access to markets but also place a restriction on national sovereignty over natural resources. Despite this opposition, the fourth attempt to list big-leaf mahogany on Appendix II was successful, and the listing entered into force in November 2003.

The cases concerning African elephant ivory and big-leaf mahogany help to illustrate several distinctive features of the CITES regime. First, and as noted above, CITES is an umbrella regime enveloping a multitude of "mini-regimes" across which states' political and economic interests vary from species to species. These "mini-regimes," although sharing a common organizational structure, are each characterized by an individual set of developmental stages, proponents, and coalitions. The coalitions often consist of unusual alliances that cross traditional North-South lines. Veto coalitions can be led by producer nations, which happened with big-leaf mahogany, or by producer and consumer nations, which happened with elephant ivory. In both instances, range states split over listing. With ivory, the split largely reflected differences in the viability of central versus southern African elephant populations. Central African states with rapid elephant population declines and high levels of poaching supported an Appendix I listing. Southern African states with growing elephant populations opposed the ban. For big-leaf mahogany, range states with commercially extinct populations tended to favor an Appendix II listing. States with active legal trade (despite also having a high level of illegal trade) tended to oppose listing out of concern that it would promote a perception that mahogany was an "endangered species" and harm the image of legally-traded products.[130] The United States, the largest consumer of big-leaf mahogany, supported listing as a means to assure that any imports were legally obtained. The largest consumer of elephant ivory, Japan, opposed that listing due to commercial concerns but did not register a reservation to the listing because of broader political concerns.[131]

Second, the role of science in the listing of species can also vary by species. Although logically associated with the stages of issue definition and fact finding, scientific knowledge can also play an important role in bargaining and regime strengthening. In the case of African elephants, an important scientific role is indicated in issue definition and fact finding via the documentation of the initial population crashes, as well as in the bargaining and regime-strengthening stages via the documentation of different population trajectories for southern and eastern African elephant populations. Documentation of population declines was also important in raising the profile of big-leaf mahogany.

Third, the development of modern techniques for genetic analysis of living plants or animals, as well as plant and animal parts or extracts, has transformed the monitoring of trade in endangered species and can lead to the ability to produce Appendix listings that work at a finer population scale. Fourth, the elephant and mahogany cases show that, although scientific knowledge can inform debates, specific courses of action are often determined by economic and political factors that science cannot inform. Strong commercial interests on the part of consumer nations or issues such as national sovereignty may lead nations to oppose listings despite strong evidence of declining populations.

Finally, the success of CITES listings in controlling population declines also varies by species. CITES listings can be ineffective in stopping overexploitation, particularly if important trading countries file a reservation to the listing, trade is predominantly domestic rather than international (e.g., trade in Chinese tigers and tiger parts), factors other than trade are more important in driving loss (e.g., habitat loss), or monitoring is difficult because of the type of product traded (e.g., sawn wood or plant extracts). CITES listings may also be ineffective when improperly obtained export permits place a veneer of legality over trade in an endangered species, which, it has been suggested, is true of mahogany.[132] An argument exists that CITES listing could even be detrimental to a species by driving trade in the black market, although little empirical evidence exists to support this view.[133] Nevertheless, no species listed in a CITES Appendix has become extinct.

CITES is widely considered to be among the most effective global environmental regimes, despite the powerful commercial interests involved and the ability of parties to "opt out" of regulation by entering reservations on particular species. This case, like those of whaling and ozone depletion, illustrates the importance of bans or prohibitions as an effective mechanism for regulating activities that threaten the environment, natural resources, and wildlife.

BIODIVERSITY LOSS

Over the past 50 years, humans have changed ecosystems more rapidly and extensively than in any comparable period of time in human history, largely to meet rapidly growing demands for food, fresh water, timber, fiber and fuel. This has resulted in a substantial and largely irreversible loss in the diversity of life on Earth.

This was one of the key findings of the second Millennium Ecosystem Assessment report, *Biodiversity and Human Well-being*, released in May 2005.[134] Biological diversity—or biodiversity—is most often associated with the earth's vast variety of plants, animals, and microorganisms, but the term encompasses diversity at all levels, from genes to species to ecosystems to landscapes. Approximately 1.75 million species have been identified, mostly small creatures such as insects. Many scientists believe that there could be as many as 13 million species, although individual estimates range from 3 to 100 million. Ecosystems are another aspect of biodiversity. In each ecosystem, including those that occur within or between forests, wetlands, mountains, deserts, and rivers, living creatures interact with each other as well as with the air, water, and soil around them; in this way, they form an interconnected community. Biodiversity also includes genetic differences within species, such as different breeds and varieties, as well as the chromosomes, genes, and genetic sequences (DNA).

According to the Millennium Ecosystem Assessment, humans have increased species extinction rates by as much as 1,000 times over background rates of extinction. Some 12 percent of birds; 23 percent of mammals; 25 percent of conifers, and 32 percent of amphibians are threatened with extinction. The world's fish stocks have been reduced by an astonishing 90 percent since the start of industrial fishing. Although the loss of species is seen as a threat to the well being of future generations of humans, the formation of a regime for conserving biodiversity has suffered from differences concerning the definition of the problem, the application of the principles of national sovereignty versus that of the common heritage of mankind,[135] and resistance to strong legal obligations by a veto coalition of developing states holding most of the world's biodiversity, as well as inconsistent commitment from the United States and several other key industrialized states.

By the early 1980s, scientific consensus emerged that the rate of species extinction had increased alarmingly. In response, the IUCN General Assembly initiated a process aimed at producing a preliminary draft of a global agreement on conserving the world's genetic resources.[136] The United States also helped put the issue of biodiversity loss on the international agenda, encouraging the UNEP Governing Council in 1987 to create an ad hoc working group of experts to study an "umbrella convention" to rationalize activities in biodiversity conservation.[137] But it quickly became apparent to the experts that an umbrella convention would be an unworkable approach to the problem.

As the UNEP *ad hoc* working group continued its work and began the process of issue definition in 1990, the idea of a biodiversity convention became entangled in North-South struggles over plant genetic resources, and **intellectual property rights** (IPR). The debate took shape around the "ownership" of genetic resources, with Southern states arguing for explicit state sovereignty over the genetic resources within their borders and Northern states arguing the view, previously accepted under international law, of these resources as part of the "common heritage of mankind." However, in 1983, when the nonbinding International Undertaking on Plant Genetic Resources for Food and Agriculture was adopted by the FAO Conference, eight developed countries where major seed companies were located (Canada, France, West Germany, Japan, the United Kingdom, and the United States) were reluctant to apply the principle of common heritage to their modern varieties because of possible implications for IPRs. The FAO International Undertaking, the first comprehensive international agreement dealing with plant genetic resources for food and agriculture, was based on the principle that plant genetic resources are a heritage of mankind and consequently should be available without restriction. As a result of the novelty requirement of intellectual property protection, traditional and farmers' varieties have been regarded as "prior art" within the public domain and have been effectively part of the common heritage of humanity, but modern varieties have been considered private property. This asymmetry between improved and traditional **germplasm** has led to a sense of unfairness among developing countries: Their germplasm could be acquired, shared freely, and used in the development of modern varieties, which would then be protected by exclusive property rights. They consequently used the principle of national sovereignty over genetic resources to correct this asymmetry.

Some developing countries began to insist that genetic resources belong to the states in which they are located and that access should be based on a "mutual agreement between countries." They also argued for the inclusion of provisions for noncommercial access to biotechnologies based on plant genetic resources found in the South as a central element in any biodiversity convention. Most industrialized countries initially opposed the inclusion of biotechnology in the convention and attempted to define the scope of the regime to include only the conservation of biodiversity in the wild and mechanisms to finance such efforts.[138]

Formal negotiations on what would become the Convention on Biological Diversity (CBD) were completed in five sessions over nine months from July 1991 to May 1992. The bargaining stage, polarized largely along North-South lines, was shaped by four factors: the veto power of developing countries over biodiversity conservation provisions, the veto power of industrialized countries over **technology transfer** and financing provisions, the aggressive role played by UNEP executive director Mostafa Tolba, and the implicit deadline imposed by the Earth Summit in Rio in June 1992.

Under the objectives of biodiversity conservation, sustainable use of its components and the fair and equitable sharing of the benefits arising out of the utilization of genetic resources, the resulting regime obligates parties to inventory and monitor biodiversity, incorporate the concepts of conservation and sustainable development into national strategies and economic development, and preserve indigenous conservation practices. The scope of the conservation provisions in the CBD was narrowed by the unwillingness of key actors to consider quantitative targets for the percentage of land that should be set aside for biodiversity conservation. Germany informally raised the idea early in the negotiations, but a veto coalition led by developing countries holding a large proportion of the world's biodiversity (Mexico, Brazil, and Indonesia) vociferously opposed such stringent provisions. Interestingly, most European countries also opposed such targets because they thought they could embarrass developed countries that had already cut down most of their forests in past centuries.[139]

The regime relies more on economic incentives than on legal obligations for biodiversity conservation, putting access to genetic resources under the authority of the state in which they are found, and calls for access to be granted on "mutually agreed terms." Thus, companies interested in prospecting for genetic resources in a particular country have to negotiate with government entities over the terms of that access, including royalties from any biotechnologies transferred from the genetic resources included within the agreement. Such deals are intended to provide a new economic incentive for developing countries to conserve biological resources.

The most contentious issues—transfer of technology and financing— resulted in compromises that left most of the major actors unsatisfied. On technology transfer, a struggle developed between India, on behalf of the Group of 77, and the United States concerning language governing obligations of biotechnology companies in industrialized countries to disseminate knowledge and access to patented technology. The United States succeeded in guaranteeing that technology transfers would protect IPR. India insisted that this guarantee be linked to an ambiguous compromise paragraph ensuring that IPR are "supportive of and do not run counter to" the convention's objectives, a paragraph opposed by the United States as hostile to IPR.[140]

Debate concerning the convention's financial mechanism proved equally divisive. Donor countries and most Latin American states supported mandating the GEF to serve as the funding mechanism for the convention. Asian and African states, led by India and Malaysia, argued for creating a freestanding biodiversity fund independent of the GEF, which, they believed, donor countries controlled.

During the final negotiating session in May 1992, UNEP Executive Director Mostafa Tolba, confronted with the possibility that countries might fail to reach an agreement in time for the Rio conference, took over the negotiations personally. This included replacing the designated Chair and drafting and submitting compromise texts to the delegations. He proposed that the convention designate the GEF as the interim funding mechanism, but would call for greater GEF transparency and democracy with respect to this role. The CBD COP would exercise authority over the GEF in its capacity as the financial mechanism, a proposition that appeared to leave open the possibility that the COP could determine levels of financial resources to be contributed by donor countries. Tolba submitted the text to the delegations as a fait accompli to be accepted or rejected shortly before the diplomatic conference that would formally adopt the convention.[141] Although the industrialized countries had concerns, particularly regarding the financial mechanism, they believed the proposed text offered the best agreement that could be reached in time for the treaty to be opened for signature at the Earth Summit only ten days later. They chose to issue their own interpretations of the text on financing and to sign the convention in Rio.

One hundred and fifty-three countries signed the convention at the Earth Summit in June 1992. In fact, only the United States refused to do so, citing the provisions on financing and intellectual property rights. The United States reversed its position after the Clinton administration came into office and signed the convention in June 1993.[142] The United States has not ratified the convention, however, and is not yet a party. The convention entered into force on December 29, 1993. By June 2005, 188 countries had ratified the convention.[143]

The process of regime strengthening for the Convention on Biological Diversity has been less focused than in some of the other major global environmental regimes. The ambiguity of the process reflects the more diffuse nature of the regime's rules and norms, the absence of a strong lead state coalition, the absence of an enforcement mechanism, and a general lack of political will to strengthen the regime. The key challenges for strengthening the regime include identifying global conservation priority areas and developing protocols or work programs on conservation and/or sustainable use in particular sectors; avoiding distractions that divert attention away from key issue areas; and addressing several controversial issues, such as access to genetic resources and benefit sharing.

One major task facing the parties has been identifying global conservation priority areas and developing protocols for clarifying conservation strategies and obligations, two areas that were not explicitly addressed in the original convention text. Over the past decade, the Conference of the Parties has made some progress in this process by developing seven work programs that address the conservation of several areas of special concern in sustaining biodiversity and providing critical ecosystem services: mountain regions, dry and sub-humid lands, marine and coastal areas, islands, inland waters, agricultural systems, and forests.[144]

Drafting the work programs proved a long and arduous process. Discussions began at the first COP in 1994, but parties did not adopt the first until 1998. The programs' current conservation measures are largely ineffective because they lack precise binding language. Further inhibiting effective policymaking has been the formation of various veto coalitions based on common economic or political interests arising around a particular issue. For example, major forest-product exporting countries, including Brazil, Canada, and Malaysia, ensured that the convention would not take the lead on forests by blocking the development of a strong work program in this issue area.

Progress in drafting and implementing ecosystem-focused work programs was further hindered by the COP's decision to negotiate a protocol on **biosafety** on the basis of Article 19.3 of the convention. These negotiations took much of the time and energy of the parties between 1996 and 2000. Biosafety refers to a set of precautionary practices to ensure the safe transfer, handling, use, and disposal of living modified organisms derived from modern

biotechnology. Many countries with biotechnology industries had domestic biosafety legislation in place, but there were no binding international agreements on the problem of genetically modified organisms (GMOs) that cross national borders. Biotechnology, particularly its applications in agriculture, remains a highly controversial issue. Policy responses vary widely in different legal orders, the most well-known example being the contrasting approach between the United States and the European Union, the latter calling for a precautionary approach towards modern biotechnology. In 1999, several European governments joined European environmental NGOs in calling for a moratorium on the import of genetically modified foods. Although the moratorium ended in 2004, it has provoked a WTO dispute between the United States and the EU.

The biosafety protocol was negotiated during a series of six meetings from 1996 to 1999. In February 1999, delegates convened in Cartagena, Colombia, intending to complete negotiations on the protocol. But a veto coalition, called the Miami Group, consisting of the world's major grain exporters outside of the EU (Argentina, Australia, Canada, Chile, the United States, and Uruguay), successfully thwarted efforts to complete the protocol on schedule. The veto coalition argued that the trade restrictions would harm the multibillion-dollar agricultural export industry, that uncertainty regarding the precise meaning of key provisions created important weaknesses in the protocol, that countries would be able to block importation for reasons based on their own criteria rather than on sound scientific knowledge, and that the increased documentation required under the protocol would create unnecessary and excessive procedures and financial costs.[145] Informal consultations continued over the next year to address outstanding issues and to facilitate discussions between the major coalitions, including the Central and Eastern European Group; the Compromise Group (Japan, Mexico, Norway, Republic of Korea, and Switzerland, joined later by New Zealand and Singapore); the EU; the Like-minded Group (the majority of developing countries); and the Miami Group. Finally, after a week of formal negotiations in Montreal in January 2000, the major coalitions reached an agreement and adopted the Cartagena Protocol on Biosafety.[146] The protocol entered into force in September 2003.

The viability of the Cartagena Protocol hinges on the interplay of economic interests. This has played out in various ways, including the difficulties the parties have had in reaching agreement on documentation requirements for bulk shipments of living modified organisms intended for food, feed, and for processing. According to the protocol (Article 18.2 (a)), parties were required to make a decision on the detailed requirements for such documentation within two years of the entry into force of the protocol. At the second Meeting of the Parties in May 2005, delegates attempted to resolve this issue. Exporting countries expressed concern that labeling shipments that might include living modified organisms (LMOs) as including them could interfere with trade. Apart from fears that many commodity producers do not have the capability to account for small amounts of LMOs that might be contained in a shipment, there is widespread concern that stricter documentation requirements could prove costly, restrict market access, and have a negative impact on countries that rely heavily on agricultural exports. Importing countries fear that lax documentation requirements will give too much flexibility to exporters and that all shipments they receive could include a long list of LMOs the shipment may or may not contain.[147]

Another challenge to regime strengthening is the continuing divisive debate over issues such as access to genetic resources and benefit sharing. Throughout the process of regime strengthening, developing countries have advocated an increased focus on the convention's third official objective: fair and equitable sharing of benefits arising from the use of genetic resources.[148] This issue relates to the way foreign companies, collectors, researchers, and other users gain access to valuable genetic resources in return for sharing the benefits with the countries of origin and with local and indigenous communities. The discussion addresses three main arguments: state sovereignty and the mandatory disclosure of country of origin in patent applications, the relationship of the original genetic resources and their derivatives, and the protection of traditional knowledge.

Tension within these issues continues to fall along North-South lines. Access and benefit-sharing issues are inextricably linked to the issue of state sovereignty, especially with regard to the country of origin of genetic resources. In general, developing countries want the convention to mandate the disclosure of the country of origin for genetic resources in patent applications, but developed states such as Norway and the EU support voluntary disclosure. Furthermore, developing countries want the principle of sovereignty, therefore national legislation, to determine levels of access to resources found within their borders, and they also push for the development of a specific international regime or protocol on access and benefit sharing to include genetic resources and their derivatives. Industrialized countries argue that such actions would interfere with intellectual property rights and that the matter is best resolved through "mutually agreed terms," or private-law bilateral contracts.

The one thread of consensus on this issue among developing and industrialized parties appears to be the protection of indigenous and local communities and their traditional knowledge. Article 8(j) of the convention calls on parties to "respect, preserve and maintain knowledge, innovations and practices of indigenous and local communities embodying traditional lifestyles relevant for the conservation and sustainable use of biological diversity; and promote their wider application." Intimate knowledge of genetic resources and land-use types results from many generations of experience and is adapted to the local culture and environment. The Like-minded Group of Megadiverse Countries,[149] Canada, and the EU have all promoted the protection of traditional knowledge and agree that the convention must guarantee the rights of indigenous communities to this knowledge and prevent its misappropriation through IPR, and they encourage the indigenous communities' participation before initiating further negotiations on access and benefit sharing.

Resolving the debate over these controversial issues has not been an expeditious process. As called for in the convention, an ad hoc working group was set up to draft voluntary guidelines to assist stakeholders when negotiating contractual agreements over genetic resources. The Bonn Guidelines resulted from the first meeting of this group in Bonn, Germany, in 2001, and were adopted at the sixth COP in 2002. At its seventh meeting in 2004, the COP decided to mandate the working group to begin official negotiations on an international access and benefit sharing regime and so follow the call of the 2002 World Summit on Sustainable Development.

Although parties have made progress on important issues, the convention remains surprisingly weak. The complexity of the biodiversity crisis, the multiple levels at which it can be addressed (e.g., ecosystem, species, genes), the North-South contrasts in the distribution of biodiversity resources, and the many ways that biodiversity protection can conflict with important economic, social, and political interests make drafting of action-forcing language a contentious and intractable process. Numerous work programs, working groups, and subsidiary bodies have served to increase the number of meetings each year and decrease the amount of focus that parties have on any one aspect of the convention, its strengthening, and its implementation. Action to strengthen the biodiversity regime will depend, in part, on greater commitment by lead states with significant economic, political, or biodiversity resources. Some European states have been active in trying to strengthen the regime, but without greater clout—and the support of developing countries as well as the United States, which remains a non-party to the regime— the convention will remain unfocused and ineffective.

FIGURE 3.5   State of the World's Fish Stocks (2004)

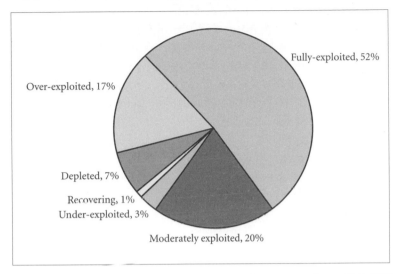

Data Source: FAO, *Review of the State of World Marine Fishery Resources* (Rome: FAO, 2005).

FISHERIES DEPLETION

For many centuries, the ocean's bounties have been viewed as limitless. But for the past three decades, the world's marine fisheries have been in crisis, as they have been overexploited to the point that the most valuable fish stocks have been depleted and sometimes virtually eliminated. By 2004, about 77 percent of the world's marine fish stocks were already depleted, slowly recovering from depletion, overexploited, or fully exploited (see fig. 3.5).[150] Because fishing fleets could overexploit one fishery and then move on to another, and because fleets continued to catch high levels of lower-value fish even after depleting the most desirable stocks, the fisheries crisis was disguised by a constant increase in global catch figures from 16.7 million tons annually in 1950 to 80 million tons in the late 1980s, where it has leveled off and fluctuated between 77 and 86 million tons ever since.[151]

The primary reason for the worsening depletion of fishery resources is the uncontrolled escalation of fishing vessels and the introduction of increasingly effective fishing technologies, such as electronic fish-finding equipment, bigger nets, larger storage capacity, more powerful engines, and mechanized hauling gear, all of which give fleets far more catching power than fisheries could support. By the early 1990s, the global fishing fleet had as much as two and a half times more capacity than could be used sustainably.[152]

Inadequate regulations on catch and enforcement and illegal, unreported, and unregulated fishing also contributed to the crisis.

Fishery resources are found under national jurisdiction and in international waters, and often in some combination of the two, a situation that complicates the politics of forming a regime governing the global overfishing problem. The seven biggest fishing states (China, Peru, United States, Japan, Chile, Indonesia, and the Russian Federation) account for 51 percent of the global catch.[153] The countries with "distant-water" fishing fleets (Russia, Japan, Spain, Poland, the Republic of Korea, and Taiwan) are responsible for the majority of the catch in international waters. These countries had the greatest potential for vetoing an international agreement to address the overfishing problem.

Ninety-five percent of the fish catch worldwide is taken within the 200-mile **exclusive economic zones** (EEZs) under national jurisdiction. But some important fish stocks, such as cod and pollack, occur within the EEZs of coastal states and in the adjacent high seas. And some highly migratory stocks, especially tuna and swordfish, move long distances through the high seas and through the EEZs of coastal states. Straddling and highly migratory fish stocks are particularly important on the Challenger Plateau off the coast of New Zealand, off Argentina's Patagonian Shelf, off the coasts of Chile and Peru, in the Barents Sea, off the coast of Norway, in the Bering Sea, the Sea of Okhotsk, and the South Pacific Ocean, and on the Grand Banks of Newfoundland outside Canada's 200-mile nautical zone. As straddling stocks and highly migratory fish stocks have dwindled and been depleted, coastal and distant-water states have each blamed overfishing on the other.

The first binding global agreement to address overfishing, the United Nations Agreement for the Implementation of the Provisions of the United Nations Convention on the **Law of the Sea** of 10 December 1982 Relating to the Conservation and Management of Straddling Fish Stocks and Highly Migratory Fish Stocks (UN Fish Stocks Agreement), came about mainly because of these conflicts over straddling stocks and highly migratory stocks. Canada was the lead actor in putting the issue of a new global management regime for these stocks on the political agenda for action; but, although it tried to define the issue, it did not put forward a definition that could be the foundation of a successful conservation regime.

Canada was motivated to push for formal agreement limiting the freedom of distant-water fishing fleets to exploit these stocks because of a dispute with the EU, and especially Spain, about the Spanish fleet's overfishing of the stocks on the Grand Banks outside Canada's EEZ. The regional fisheries management organization responsible for regulating fishing in the Grand Banks area, both within Canada's EEZ and on the high seas, is the Northwest Atlantic Fisheries Organization (NAFO), founded in 1979. From 1986 to 1990, the NAFO failed to enforce high-seas catch limits agreed to by the organization on most of the straddling stocks because the EC had exercised its right to opt out of the regional quotas; Canada, therefore, appealed to the broader international community to adopt a global policy governing the problem.

During the UNCED negotiations in 1991, a paper from coastal states proposed that new conservation rules should be established for high-seas fisheries, but not for fisheries under national jurisdiction. Canada proposed language calling for recognition of the special interests of coastal states in highly migratory stocks and stocks that straddle national EEZs and international waters. The EC disagreed, producing a diplomatic deadlock on the issue. The issue remained unresolved until the Rio Conference, when UNCED Main Committee Chairman Tommy Koh asked the United States to broker a compromise between Canada and the EC. The result was an agreement to hold an intergovernmental conference under UN auspices "with a view to promoting effective implementation of the provisions of the Law of the Sea on straddling and highly migratory fish stocks." The EC agreed to that formula because its diplomats believed the Convention on the Law of the Sea guaranteed the sovereign right of states to fish on the high seas. Canada, however, hoped that the need for conservation would trump that traditional sovereign right.

The UN Conference on Straddling Fish Stocks and Highly Migratory Fish Stocks opened in July 1993 under the authority of the UN General Assembly. The main conflict of interest in the negotiations was between the seventy coastal fishing states and the ten distant-water fishing states. The coastal states, led by the "like-minded" caucus (Argentina, Canada, Chile, Iceland, New Zealand, Norway, and Peru) accused the distant-water fishing states of abusing their right to fish to the detriment of straddling stocks. The distant-water fishing states, led by the EC (on behalf of its distant-water fishing states),[154] Japan, and the Republic of Korea, pointed out that mismanagement of national fisheries by coastal fishing states was just as much to blame for the most serious problems of stock depletion.[155] Both sides were only half right, a conclusion based on the Canadian-EU case: The evidence is clear that there was gross mismanagement and overfishing within the Canadian EEZ, and that from 1986 to 1989 the Spanish and Portuguese fleets were consistently catching several times the EU's NAFO allocation of groundfish catch.[156]

CARTOON 3.3   "Ocean into Desert." Steve Greenberg, *Ventura County Star*, Calif., 2003.

As they had during the UNCED negotiations, the "like-minded" caucus proposed a legally binding agreement that would prescribe conservation rules for high-seas fishing that affected straddling stocks and highly migratory stocks. But the coastal states resisted international rules that would limit their freedom to manage their EEZs. Distant-water states called for nonbinding conservation guidelines that would apply equally to coastal state fisheries and the high seas. They had long argued that the regulation of fishing practices on the high seas should be left to regional or subregional organizations. While the UN conference was going on, consultations were also being held on a non-binding FAO Code of Conduct for Responsible Fisheries, and the two groups of fishing states took opposite positions about that process: Coastal states insisted that the entire text be bracketed until the UN agreement on straddling stocks and highly migratory stocks was adopted, whereas the distant-water fishing states favored the FAO process because it was voluntary.

Both groups of states were thus separate veto coalitions who were prepared, at least initially, to block agreement on needed measures to conserve stocks effectively. The United States, which is a coastal fishing state and a distant-water fishing state, was in a pivotal position to play the role of lead state in negotiating the regime. Initially, however, the United States was ready to join with the distant-water states to oppose a binding convention because of its close historic ties with the EU and Japan on Law of the Sea issues. The United States had clashed with Canada and other coastal states during the negotiations on the Law of the Sea Treaty. But in 1994, officials in the White House and the National Oceanic and Atmospheric Administration who had a strong commitment to conservation intervened in the issue after being lobbied by NGOs. As a result, the United States decided to come out for a binding agreement and began playing the role of lead state.

One of the U.S. contributions to the text was a proposal that the "precautionary approach" to fishing be applied by requiring the adoption of "reference points" (target levels of fishing effort aimed at conserving fish stocks) and measures for rebuilding the stocks, including reduced fishing effort, if the reference points are exceeded. Canada resisted the application of precautionary reference points within fisheries under national jurisdiction, along with other conservation requirements, as a violation of national sovereignty. The United States pushed Canada and the like-minded caucus to accept certain basic conservation principles and guidelines for their application to straddling stocks on the high seas and within areas under national jurisdiction, but the issue remained unresolved even after the fourth session in April 1995.

Another issue pressed by the "like-minded" caucus was the right of a coastal state to board and inspect fishing vessels in international waters. It argued that such a right was necessary to ensure compliance with international conservation measures. Traditionally, the enforcement of legal obligations on the high seas was in the hands of the "flag state" (the state in which the vessel was registered), and distant-water fishing states wanted to maintain the status quo. The United States again sided with the like-minded caucus in supporting wider latitude for high-seas inspection by states other than the flag state under certain circumstances, but the distant-water states continued to resist until the last session.

Before the negotiations could be completed, tensions between Canada and the EU escalated to the use of force over Spanish fishing for turbot, allegedly in violation of NAFO quotas. In September 1994, the thirteen members of NAFO voted to reduce the annual total allowable catch of rapidly declining stocks of turbot by 38 percent and reallocated much of the EU share of the quota to Canada. The EU again used its right to opt out of the quota and set its own, much higher, unilateral quota. In response, in February 1995, the Canadian fisheries minister warned that Canada would not let EU vessels "devastate turbot the way it devastated other ground fish stocks."[157] In March

1995, Canadian ships aggressively pursued and seized or cut the nets of Spanish trawlers outside the Canadian EEZ.

The Canadian actions angered the EU and temporarily polarized the conference. The March-April 1995 round of negotiations was still deadlocked on the issue of the right of coastal states to board ships on the high seas when they are suspected of having violated a regional fisheries conservation measure. The chairman's draft allowed wider latitude for such high-seas boarding and inspection than the distant-water states were prepared to accept.

But a new Canadian-EU agreement reached immediately after that round may have contributed to a successful conclusion of the negotiations. Canada compromised on the 1995 quota and agreed to give the EU the same amount as Canada instead of the one-fifth of the Canadian quota that had been authorized by NAFO. Canada also dropped charges against the Spanish trawler it had seized and repealed legislation authorizing such actions in international waters. In return, the EU agreed to a new regime of independent inspectors onboard every EU ship in the NAFO area to ensure that conservation rules were being followed.[158]

In the fifth and final negotiating session in August 1995, high-seas boarding and the "precautionary approach" to fisheries management were still being resisted by distant-water states. On the issue of boarding and inspecting on the high seas, the distant-water states had agreed to boarding and inspecting in principle, but there were still differences about whether the regional fisheries organization had to reach agreement on procedures governing such boarding and inspecting: Canada insisted that it would not require prior agreement on procedures by the organization, whereas Japan and South Korea both insisted on regional agreement as a precondition for such boarding and inspection. A compromise that was ultimately adopted, namely, states that are parties to regional fishing organizations could board and inspect vessels on the high seas of parties to the Fish Stocks Agreement suspected of violating regional conservation measures without prior regional agreement, but only if the regional organization had failed to adopt procedures for such boarding and inspection for two years prior to the boarding.

The precautionary approach requires that scientific uncertainty not be used as a reason for postponing or failing to take effective conservation and management measures.[159] Japan was concerned that the coastal states would use the precautionary approach as an open license to adopt moratoria on fishing as a new management norm and was reluctant to see it enter into a binding international agreement. But Japan finally accepted the precautionary approach, perhaps because it did not want to be blamed for the collapse of the negotiations and considered nonratification as an option.

Once it was ratified by thirty signatories, the UN Fish Stocks Agreement entered into force in December 2001. But in mid-2005, only five of the top twenty fishing states (Norway, Russia, the United States, Iceland, and India) and the EU had ratified the treaty. And many of the most important fishing states, including Peru, Chile, Thailand, Mexico, Malaysia, and Vietnam, had not even signed the agreement. Although these countries' support was not needed for the UN Fish Stocks Agreement to enter into force, their compliance is essential if the treaty is to be effective.

Although the agreement represents a major step forward in global cooperation for conservation of fish stocks, it did not effectively address three primary global management issues. The first is that regional fisheries organizations that make decisions on management measures such as catch quotas normally allow member states simply to opt out of the decision if they don't like it—the weakness that prompted Canada's original push for a new regime. The second problem is overcapacity in the global fishing fleet. Although the agreement calls for states to take measures to "prevent or eliminate excess fishing capacity," it does not spell out this obligation or set up a mechanism for implementation. Finally, the agreement does not apply to all fish stocks under national jurisdiction but only to those referred to in the title—approximately 20 percent of the global fish catch.

Although these weaknesses remain in the Fish Stocks Agreement, several other nonbinding agreements have been adopted since then to supplement the regime. In October 1995, governments adopted an international Code of Conduct for Responsible Fishing. The Code of Conduct provides principles and standards applicable to the conservation and management and development of all aspects of fisheries, such as the capture, processing and trade of fishery products, fishing operations, aquaculture, fisheries research, and the integration of fisheries into coastal area management. To support implementation of the Code of Conduct, the FAO Technical Guidelines for Responsible Fisheries were elaborated.[160]

The FAO also developed International Plans of Action addressing specific issues in implementing the Code of Conduct. The 1999 International Plan of Action for the Management of Fishing Capacity aims to reduce excess fishing capacity in world fisheries. This is to be achieved through assessment plans to reduce capacity and the strengthening of national and regional organizations to better manage capacity issues. Priority is to be given to those fisheries and fleets that show the effects of overcapacity and overfishing. The 2001 International Plan of Action to Prevent, Deter and Eliminate Illegal, Unreported and Unregulated (IUU) Fishing recommends good practice and calls upon states to adopt national plans of action to combat IUU fishing. It describes highly detailed measures to halt IUU fishing, including improved control of nationals to ensure they do not engage in IUU fishing, tougher requirements for vessel authorizations and registers, port state controls to restrict IUU landings, and market-related measures to prevent IUU catch from being traded or imported.[161]

Although voluntary instruments such as these can be useful, a key problem is their nonbinding nature, which significantly impedes their effectiveness. Thus far, efforts to achieve the fine balance between encouraging widespread and international participation and the effective implementation of the guidelines and measures outlined in these voluntary instruments have largely failed. Key contributing factors to this problem, aside from the lack of legal weight, are the vagueness of some of the concepts and the lack of legal reporting requirements.[162]

The regime formation process for the Fish Stocks Agreement is one in which not one veto coalition but two—the "like-minded" caucus of coastal states and the major distant-water states—initially opposed key provisions of the regime. The original impetus for the agreement does not appear to have been a broad demand for conservation of straddling and highly migratory fish stocks as much as Canada's desire to overcome the EU's ability to determine its own catch levels in the Grand Banks fishery.

The shift of the United States from veto state to lead state was undoubtedly a major factor in overcoming the resistance of the two veto coalitions and gave greater impetus to the adoption of innovative conservation measures in the convention. And the willingness of Canada to use physical force on the high seas in its dispute with the EU, with the result that the EU agreed to onboard inspectors on the high seas, probably helped put the issue of boarding and inspecting in a different light for a key veto state; however, the continued presence of these veto states and their refusal to ratify the agreement continue to impede its effectiveness.

Although state parties have incorporated provisions of the agreement into their national legislation and established new regional fisheries management organizations, it remains that the majority of the major fishing countries have not ratified the agreement. As a result, many problems and challenges remain in the management of straddling fish stocks and highly migratory fish stocks. These include overcapacity and overfishing; IUU fishing; the effects of fishing on ecosystems (e.g., by-catch and the impacts of fishing gear); the continued use of flags of convenience (when a ship flies the flag of a country other than the country of ownership because the flag state has cheap registration fees, low or no taxes, and freedom to employ cheap labor); and a lack of capacity in developing countries to implement the agreement.[163] As long as the veto states remain such, the depletion of the world's fish stocks will continue.

DESERTIFICATION

The Convention to Combat Desertification is one of only two international regimes established on the initiative of developing countries despite the resistance of industrialized countries. Desertification, which affects the lives of 1 billion people in more than 110 countries around the world, had been the subject of international cooperation for nearly three decades, since the first major drought in sub–Saharan Africa, but was put on the UNCED agenda in 1992 only because African countries persisted. As the first treaty to be negotiated after UNCED, it was looked upon by some as a test of whether governments had the political will to follow up on Agenda 21 commitments.

The issue definition stage was plagued by complexity, vagueness, and disagreement on whether desertification was indeed a "global" problem. Desertification was defined by UNEP and by most specialists as sustained land degradation in arid, semiarid, and dry subhumid areas resulting mainly from adverse human impact.[164] But the term *desertification* evokes images of deserts advancing and destroying productive land, whereas scientists have found no evidence to support claims that the Sahara is expanding at an alarming rate. Foes of a convention exploited that fact: At one point in the UNCED negotiations, the United States dismissed the term *desertification* and suggested substituting *land degradation*.[165] Some donor countries objected to the designation *global* because it might imply that treaty implementation efforts would be eligible for funding from the Global Environment Facility.[166]

African countries encountered other problems in defining desertification. First, desertification does not involve resources or life support systems of global interest, as do other environmental issues on which regimes have been negotiated. It affects countries not suffering from desertification only because it threatens the economies and societies of many other countries. Second, a bewildering array of natural and social factors appears to affect land

PHOTO 3.4   Eucalyptus saplings planted to prevent soil erosion.
Lompoul, Senegal, 1984. Photo by J. Issac, UN/DPI.

degradation in drylands, including overpopulation, climatic cycles, social
and economic structures, poor pastoral or agricultural practices, bad policies
on the part of governments and donors, and North-South economic relations. It was difficult, therefore, to articulate simply and clearly either the nature of the problem or the international actions needed to address it.

Indeed, for many African countries, there is a strong link between poverty alleviation and desertification control. The African countries' definition of the problem emphasized the need for additional funding for as yet unidentified activities. These countries hoped that a desertification convention would help them gain access to additional funding through the Global Environment Facility, which had rejected desertification as one of the global environmental problems it could finance.[167]

Finally, the African countries' attempt to define the desertification issue was hampered because the earlier Plan of Action to Combat Desertification (PACD), launched in 1977, was generally acknowledged as a failure. A UNEP evaluation of the plan had blamed the failure on African governments and the donor community for not giving the issue priority. UNEP had also found that only $1 billion of the $9 billion provided by donor agencies from 1978 to 1983 was spent on direct field projects.[168]

So when the issue of a desertification convention was first raised during the UNCED process, only France, with its special ties with Africa, expressed support for the idea. Most industrialized countries and the World Bank argued that the primary problems were with the structure and macroeconomic policies of African governments (such as excessive taxes on agriculture and failing to grant enforceable property rights) and that policy reforms, better planning, and more popular participation would achieve better results than a new international program or formal agreement.[169] Moreover, the G-77 failed to endorse the African call for a desertification convention in the communiqué of the 1992 Kuala Lumpur ministerial meeting, which was dominated by host government Malaysia.

Despite these problems in the definition of the issue of desertification, UNCED put it on the global agenda because of African persistence and because the United States unexpectedly supported the African position. At the Earth Summit in Rio, the United States, after opposing a desertification convention throughout the negotiations, shifted to backing such a convention in the hope of winning African support on forests and on the remaining issues in the Rio Declaration.[170] Other industrialized countries then followed suit, but the EC initially resisted the U.S. proposal. Finally, the EC relented, and the call for a desertification convention became part of Agenda 21.[171]

Negotiations by the Intergovernmental Negotiating Committee on the International Convention to Combat Desertification (INCD) began in May 1993 and were completed in fifteen months. The formal fact-finding process, carried out in an "information sharing segment" at the first session of the INCD, focused primarily on socioeconomic strategies for slowing and reversing desertification and on reports from individual countries rather than on scientific understanding of the problem. That process produced general agreement on the importance of such strategies as integrating arid and semiarid areas into national economies, popular participation in antidesertification efforts, and land tenure reform.[172] As a result, the convention would be the first to call for affected countries to provide for effective participation by grassroots organizations, NGOs, and local populations—men and women—in the preparation of national action programs.[173]

The bargaining stage revolved not around commitments to environmental conservation actions but around financial, trade, institutional, and symbolic issues. The African countries were the lead states. The OAU had detailed draft sections for every section of the convention, some of which were accepted as the basis for negotiation.

Whether debt and trade issues should be included within the scope of the convention was a central issue that affected the obligations, action programs, and regional annexes, as well as sections on scope, objectives, and principles. The OAU and other developing countries asserted that external debt burdens and commodity prices, among other international economic policy issues, affected their ability to combat desertification. The industrialized countries argued that those North-South economic issues could be negotiated only in other international forums. They did agree to general obligations to "give due attention" to the trade and debt problems of affected countries and so create an "enabling international economic environment" for those countries.

Differences over financial resources and the financial mechanism nearly caused the negotiations to collapse. Some members of the G-77 and China demanded commitments to "new and additional" financial resources and creation of a special fund for desertification as the centerpiece of the convention. Industrialized countries acted as a united veto coalition in rejecting provisions for new and additional financing, agreeing only to ensure "adequate" financial resources for antidesertification programs. The developed countries felt they bore no responsibility for the problem of desertification worldwide, a position unlike that for the issues of ozone depletion and climate change, and were therefore unwilling to incur obligations to increase their financial assistance to affected countries.[174] They insisted that the overhead associated with a special fund would reduce the resources needed in the field and that existing resources could be used more effectively. They also vetoed the use of GEF funds unless the project contributed either to the prevention of climate change or to the conservation of biodiversity.

The deadlock on a funding mechanism was broken only after the United States proposed a "global mechanism" under the authority of the conference of the parties, to be housed within an existing organization, which would improve monitoring and assessment of existing aid flows and increase coordination among donors. Developing countries remained dissatisfied because such a mechanism would not increase development assistance to African and other countries suffering from desertification. But they ultimately accepted it as the only compromise acceptable to the donor countries.[175]

The problem of how to reflect the priority to be given to Africa, called for in the UN General Assembly resolution on the convention, while meeting demands from other regions for equitable treatment, arose in negotiating regional annexes to the convention. The original intention of African and industrialized countries' delegations was to negotiate a regional implementation annex only for Africa by the deadline of July 1994, but other developing-country delegations demanded that implementation annexes for their own regions be negotiated simultaneously with the one for Africa. In the end, each regional grouping received its own annex, but the priority for Africa was ensured by a special resolution that encouraged donor countries to provide financial support for national action programs in Africa without waiting for the convention to come into force.

The Convention to Combat Desertification was opened for signature in October 1994 and entered into force on December 26, 1996. In May 2005, 191 countries had ratified or acceded to the convention. The convention recognizes the physical, biological, and socioeconomic aspects of desertification, the importance of redirecting technology transfer so that it is demand-driven, and the importance of local populations in efforts to combat desertification. The core of the convention is the development of national and subregional/regional action programs by national governments in cooperation with donors, local populations, and NGOs.

The regime-strengthening stage began at the first meeting of the Conference of the Parties in Rome in October 1997, and has been shaky at best. Challenges during this period included the definition, establishment, and operationalization of the "Global Mechanism," a financial mechanism created by and loosely defined in the convention. Another challenge has been reconciling the convention's emphasis on "bottom-up" approaches and involvement at all levels by all relevant actors while remaining an international coordinating body. At the national level, the challenge has been for affected countries to develop effective action programs in conjunction with donor countries and organizations as well as local communities and NGOs.[176]

Between 1997 and 2003, the Conference of the Parties set up institutional mechanisms to enable effective implementation of the convention. This work and the lack of a dedicated financing mechanism in the convention meant that the first five Conferences of the Parties spent time on procedures and institutions rather than on substance. During this period, they established two subsidiary bodies—a Committee on Science and Technology and a Committee for the Review of the Implementation of the Convention. After a long-fought battle, the convention designated the Global Environment Facility as the financial mechanism for the convention, once the GEF agreed to establish a program to fund projects to combat desertification. A fifth regional implementation annex for Central and Eastern Europe was adopted and numerous education and awareness-raising programs were conducted. The sixth Conference of the Parties, in Havana in 2003, officially marked the transition from issues of process, institutions, and budgets to concrete action such as support for stronger efforts and implementation on the ground. This transition has not been easy.

Unlike other regimes, the UNCCD's implementation has not been hindered by a strong veto coalition or scientific uncertainty. In fact, the knowledge and technical skills exist to halt desertification, but political and economic factors will determine whether the expertise is ever put into practice. Implementation has proven difficult because of the nature of the problem, lack of political commitment, and bureaucratic mistrust. Desertification is a worldwide problem, but solutions are essentially local or regional, not global. The idea of addressing a global "public good" through a global convention, which happens with the other Rio conventions (climate change and biodiversity), does not function as well in the UNCCD case.[177] A question that the CCD will have to consider is which issues in the desertification battles ahead need to be addressed in the far removed and bureaucratic "virtual world" of the international level, and which are best decided in the "real world," nationally or locally. The disconnectedness between these two worlds is illustrated by the fact that many concrete projects to combat desertification are being implemented by NGOs working on the ground, yet less than half a dozen parties were able to submit reports on projects they were undertaking at COP-6. Moreover, despite the COP's repeated decisions, less than a third of the parties have submitted their national action programs.

The new focus on implementation, rather than on raising awareness, also places a great responsibility on the secretariat, which has not been able to gain the trust of the donor countries. The secretariat has repeatedly come under fire for questionable management practices and lack of transparency. At COP-6, the general discontent over the budget, elections of officers and financing the participation of only NGOs known to be supportive of the secretariat came to the fore. These concerns, strongly articulated by Canada during the closing session, provided food for thought for the secretariat. In her statement, the Canadian delegate expressed regret that the budget negotiations put accountability, transparency, and effectiveness into doubt. She warned that her country would not hesitate to redirect its funds into processes that combat desertification more efficiently if these three principles remain neglected at COP-7.[178] Unless the secretariat can effectively address these issues and the UNCCD can refocus itself on implementation, within the context of reduced financial contributions and wavering political commitment from some donor parties, the future of the first "sustainable development" convention may be bleak indeed.

FORESTS

The issue of forests is unique among these case studies in that it continues to defy the creation of a comprehensive regime because of its complexity and the successful efforts of a veto coalition. As demonstrated in several other cases, the make-up of a veto coalition can change over time, but none of the other cases illustrates just how much a veto coalition can change in membership and rationale, yet still block the negotiation of a treaty.

Forests cover 3.8 million hectares, or about 30 percent of the total land area of the world (not including Greenland and Antarctica). However, only about 40 percent of the earth's forests are in relatively undisturbed tracts ("frontier forests") that are large enough to provide habitats for large species of mammals. Half of those undisturbed forest tracts are **boreal forests** (slow-growing forests lying between arctic tundra to the north and warmer temperate forests to the south) in Canada, Russia, and Alaska. Forty-four percent of the remaining frontier forests are tropical forests, those located in warm regions within 30 degrees of the equator, whereas only about 3 percent of the remaining "frontier forests" are temperate forests, which extend through Europe, the United States, parts of Canada, Australia, New Zealand, Chile, and Argentina.[179]

Even as public awareness of the impact of global deforestation has increased over the last twenty-five years, and actual forested land has increased in some

FIGURE 3.6   Annual Forest Cover Change, 1990–2000

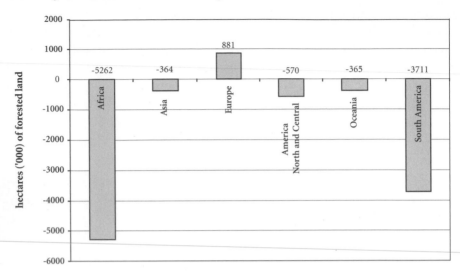

Data Source: FAO, *State of the World's Forests, 2005* (Rome: FAO, 2005).

regions as a result of new **plantation forests**, deforestation continues. Although the rate of deforestation (forests converted permanently to non-forest uses such as agriculture, highways, or urban settlement) slowed slightly in the 1990s, deforestation and forest degradation rates remain high in many countries. Between 1990 and 2000, the extent of the world's forests decreased by some 9.391 million hectares annually, the largest annual rates of change being in Africa and South America (see fig. 3.6).[180] The many causes of forest degradation include overharvesting of industrial wood and fuelwood, overgrazing, fire, insect pests and diseases, storms, and air pollution. Most forests are being cleared to provide land for food and cash crops. Fuelwood is also the main cooking fuel of nearly half the world's people, the poorest of them. Wood is essential for building construction and a host of other uses. Timber exports are a source of foreign exchange for many countries. Although cutting trees and clearing forests make perfect sense to those who are doing it, as the trees disappear there are also losers: Forest dwellers, often the poorest and most vulnerable members of society, are deprived of their homes and livelihoods. Fuelwood and other forest products become harder to obtain. Flooding results, land is eroded, and lakes and dams are filled with silt. With fewer trees to soak up carbon dioxide from the atmosphere, the risk of global warming is increased. As plant and wildlife species become extinct, biological diversity is reduced.[181]

Countries have been discussing international forest policy issues within the United Nations system since the end of World War II.[182] The FAO Conference, which first met in 1945, was the principal global forum for the discussion of international forestry issues from the mid-1940s until 1971, when the FAO established the Committee on Forestry (COFO). Since its first session in 1972, COFO has met regularly at two-year intervals to review forestry problems of "an international character."[183] Forest industries and the restoration of timber supplies were prominent topics of early conferences, and they, together with logging and the marketing and utilization of forest products, have remained on COFO's agenda.

Other milestones in the global forest policy dialogue include the adoption of the International Tropical Timber Agreement (ITTA) in 1983 and the establishment of the International Tropical Timber Organization (ITTO) in 1986 to promote international trade in tropical timber, the sustainable management of tropical forests, and the development of forest industries. The ITTO's membership represents 90 percent of world trade in tropical timber and 80 percent of the world's tropical forests. Regional initiatives to protect forests and promote their sustainable management have also been developed, including the 1978 Amazon Cooperation Treaty and the 1990 Ministerial Conference on the Protection of Forests in Europe.

The 1992 UN Conference on Environment and Development marked a turning point in the international forest policy dialogue and started a new process of issue definition when forests were examined within the context of sustainable development. Negotiations on forests during the UNCED Preparatory Committee quickly became polarized. Three competing public claims to the world's forests were made during the negotiations. The developed countries, which had called for a forest convention in 1990 in the European Parliament and at the G-7 Houston summit, ventured that forests could be seen as a global common because all humanity has a stake in forest conservation. On the other side, the Group of 77, led by Malaysia and India, claimed that forests are a sovereign national resource to be used in line with national development objectives. NGOs and indigenous peoples' groups made a third claim that contested the negotiations: Forests should be seen as local commons, and the best chance for a forest conservation was for secure land tenure rights to be granted to local communities the livelihoods of which depend directly on the conservation of forest resources.[184] With the rejection of a treaty by the Group of 77, delegates instead negotiated two non-legally binding agreements on forests: the "Forest Principles,"[185] and Chapter 11 of Agenda 21 on Combating Deforestation.[186]

During the UNCED negotiations, the United States and Canada tried to link the principle of the sovereignty of countries over their own forest resources with the principles of national responsibility and global concern for forests. Canada, with huge forest resources under rapid development, proposed to establish the principle that forests are of interest to the international community, that international standards should be implemented in forest management, and that targets and time frames should be included in national forestry plans. But Malaysia and India saw these formulations as an effort to establish the legal principle that forests are "global commons," or part of the "common heritage of mankind," giving industrialized countries the right to interfere in the management of the tropical forest countries' resources.[187] Malaysia, as the world's largest exporter of tropical timber, had a particularly intense interest in the issue. It was determined to become a "fully developed country" by 2020, using export earnings from timber and other export crops grown on land converted from forests.[188]

The final version of the Forest Principles only hints that forests are a global environmental issue and drops not only the idea of international guidelines for forest management but also all references to trade in "sustainably managed" forest products. It also gives blanket approval to the conversion of natural forests to other uses. The agreement was widely regarded by developed countries as worse than no declaration at all because it appeared to legitimize unsustainable forest management policies.[189] The Forest Principles and Chapter 11 of Agenda 21 both reaffirmed the rights of sovereign nations to use their forests in accordance with their national priorities and policy objectives. The Rio agreements also stress the cross-sectoral nature of forests and point out that forests simultaneously provide a wide range of socioeconomic benefits as well as environmental values and services.

The Forest Principles agreement and the North-South confrontation over the issue seemed to shut the door on global negotiations on forests. Between 1992 and 1995, however, a series of international meetings and ongoing initiatives, including several joint North-South collaborations, began a new process of maneuvering over **sustainable forest management.**[190] These initiatives, which contributed to the review of the Forest Principles and Chapter 11 of Agenda 21 by the UN Commission on Sustainable Development (CSD) in 1995, helped some key forest countries identify areas of common interest and develop a common international agenda on forests.[191] The result was agreement to begin the next phase of fact finding and bargaining within a new forum, the Intergovernmental Panel on Forests (IPF).

CARTOON 3.4   "And see this ring right here, Jimmy? . . . That's another time when the old fellow miraculously survived some big forest fire." The Far Side © Far Works Inc. Dist. by Universal Press Syndicate, reprinted with permission. All rights reserved.

Intergovernmental Panel on Forests

The IPF was possible, in part, because of a shift of position by the Malaysians. After UNCED, responsibility for international forest negotiations in Malaysia was moved from the Ministry of Foreign Affairs to the Ministry of Primary Industries.[192] Malaysia subsequently shifted to support a convention. A factor here appears to have been the position of the Malaysian Timber Council. Malaysia is one of the few developing countries in which timber corporations conduct substantial logging operations in other countries. Malaysian forest industry businesses are active in Africa and South America and the Malaysian Timber Council has openly acknowledged that it supports a convention to enable "access to markets."[193]

With Canada and Malaysia in the lead, the CSD established the IPF with a two-year mandate to build consensus on eleven priority issues under five interrelated categories of issues: implementation of UNCED decisions related to forests at the national and international level; international cooperation in financial assistance and technology transfer; scientific research, forest assessment, and development of criteria and indicators for sustainable forest management; trade and environment relating to forest products and services; and international organizations and instruments, including the possibility of a forests convention.[194]

By the time the IPF had completed its work in February 1997, it had developed more than one hundred proposals for action on issues related to sustainable forest management, including national forest programs; forest assessment; criteria and indicators; traditional forest-related knowledge; and underlying causes of deforestation.[195] These recommendations, most of which related to national forest programs, did not effectively leverage changes in forest management policies and practices. Many involved lengthy texts that did not identify key issues and actions to be taken; others did not clearly indicate whether action should be taken at the national or international level. Relatively few suggested regulatory measures. And implementation was left to the discretion of the country. No mechanism for reporting or follow-up on the recommendations was created by the IPF, further limiting the recommendations' impact on policy. An intergovernmental paper on the implementation of the IPF proposals in 1999 concluded that it was "difficult to single out the impacts of IPF from those induced by macroeconomic changes and other policy processes."[196]

The debate about a global forest convention was just as polarized as it was in 1992; by 1997, however, there was a new alignment of countries. Malaysia and Canada, the lead states, apparently believed that a global agreement on sustainable forestry could be the basis for an officially sponsored international eco-label for wood products and that their timber industries could use the label to fend off pressures for certification by the Forest Stewardship Council (FSC). The former Canadian natural resources minister, Anne McLellan, said in a 1997 speech to the Canadian pulp and paper industry that Canada was leading a push for a forest convention to secure an internationally recognized eco-label for wood-based products. She linked the project to the threat to Canada's forestry industry, the country's largest export sector, from environmental protests and boycotts over clear-cutting of old-growth forests.[197]

The European Union still officially supported the negotiation of a binding treaty. Some of its key member states (Germany, France, and Italy) had long been the staunchest supporters of a global forest treaty. But by 1996, some environmental groups and aid agencies in EU member states had begun to oppose a binding agreement, in part because they saw that no new money would be forthcoming to support it. Germany had started to view it as a potentially dangerous agreement, pushed by some of the very states that had opposed meaningful norms of forest management at UNCED.[198]

Some developing countries, including Indonesia, Costa Rica, the Philippines, and Papua New Guinea, also changed their position to support a convention in the hope that it would generate new sources of development assistance for forests. There was also some movement from the African countries in favor of a convention. At UNCED, the African countries had supported the Group of 77 position against a convention despite an attempt by the Europeans to split the Group of 77 by promising the sub–Saharan African countries a convention on desertification if they would support a forest convention. By 1997, many African countries were prepared to support a convention. However, with the major South American countries remaining firmly opposed, the position of the Group of 77, which sought to speak with one voice, was that it was too early to start negotiations for a convention; however, the desirability of a convention would be reassessed at a later stage.[199]

The United States, which had supported a convention in Rio, now opposed it and so became one of the leaders of the veto coalition. The influence of the corporate sector, which opposes a convention on the grounds that it would be interventionist and regulatory, was largely responsible for this shift.[200] Japan, which had also formally endorsed a convention at UNCED without actively supporting it, now opposed the idea, as did Australia and New Zealand, along with the major South American countries, led by Brazil. As another leader of the veto coalition, Brazil's strong resistance to a binding treaty on forests reflected similar fears about environmental requirements finding their way into the agreement. The forest convention issue thus shows how different states — and the timber industry in different countries—can share the same political and economic interests (in this instance freedom from third-party certification by a system that the industry didn't trust) but come out on opposite sides of the issue because of differing assessments of the situation.

There was also a major shift in the NGO community. In Rio, many international NGOs tended to favor a convention if it contained strong conservation commitments and firm provisions respecting the rights and traditions of indigenous forest peoples. But at the IPF, a declaration was issued by NGOs against a convention. NGOs had noticed the shift by major tropical timber producers such as Malaysia and Indonesia in favor of a convention. Coupled with the long-term support from the Canadian government and the Canadian forest industry, along with support from Finland and Russia, this led NGO campaigners to query the underlying interests supporting a convention and the values it would promote.[201]

In the end, the IPF was unable to agree on recommendations for a global forest convention. The panel proposed the following three options to the CSD: to continue the policy dialogue within existing forums; to continue the dialogue through another intergovernmental forum under the CSD; or to establish under the authority of the UN General Assembly an intergovernmental negotiating committee on a legally binding instrument. The commission declined to take a decision and passed it to the UN General Assembly Special Session to review implementation of Agenda 21, which in June 1997 agreed to establish an Intergovernmental Forum on Forests (IFF) under the auspices of the CSD.[202] In other words, governments supported the need for dialogue but could advance matters no further than the status quo.

Intergovernmental Forum on Forests

The Intergovernmental Forum on Forests, which held its first meeting in October 1997 and concluded its work in February 2000, was charged with promoting and facilitating implementation of the IPF's proposals for action; reviewing, monitoring, and reporting on progress in the management, conservation, and sustainable development of all types of forests; and considering matters left pending by the panel, in particular trade, finance, and technology transfer, and a possible forest convention.

The same issues that stymied the IPF continued to prove difficult for the IFF. Trade and sustainable forest management issues continued to provide some of the most intense debates. Long-held differences between developed and developing countries on the financial resources and the provision of new technology also remained unresolved. Canada did not give up its aim of securing agreement on a global forest convention. But the veto coalition of industrialized and developing states opposed to negotiating a forest treaty doomed the Canadian effort. After round-the-clock negotiations, delegates agreed to recommend to the CSD that the UN establish an intergovernmental body called the UN Forum on Forests and, within five years, "consider with a view to recommending the parameters of a mandate for developing a legal framework on all types of forests." The language is sufficiently obscure that the lead and veto coalitions both felt they had achieved a successful outcome to the negotiations.

United Nations Forum on Forests

The UN Forum on Forests (UNFF) was established by ECOSOC in 2000 as a "central intergovernmental forum to deliberate international policy."[203] A Collaborative Partnership on Forests (CPF) was also established to support the work of the UNFF and its member countries and to foster increased co-operation and coordination on forests.[204] The UNFF held five sessions be-tween 2001 and 2005. During these sessions, the dialogue on forests continued through a work program that focused on issues affecting the im-plementation of the IPF/IFF proposals for action. At its third session in 2003, the UNFF decided to establish three expert groups to support its work. The expert groups focused on (1) approaches and mechanisms for monitoring, assessment and reporting; (2) finance and transfer of environmentally sound technologies; and (3) consideration of the parameters of a mandate for de-veloping a legal framework on all types of forests.[205]

The discussion on a forests convention or other "international arrange-ment on forests" resumed in September 2004 at the meeting of the Ad Hoc Expert Group for the Consideration of the parameters of a mandate for de-veloping a legal framework on all types of forests and continued at UNFF-5 in May 2005. The coalitions that emerged in 1997 were largely unchanged by 2005 and the debate appeared to be as polarized as ever. There was wide agreement that the global forest agenda had made some progress under the UNFF but that deforestation and forest degradation continued at an unsus-tainable high rate; however, there was no consensus on how to proceed.

The developing countries, although divided on the need for a treaty, were united in their call to implement commitments related to financial resources, capacity-building, and technology transfer, which they saw as critical to advancing the management, conservation, and sustainable devel-opment of all types of forests.[206] Canada, Malaysia, Switzerland, and the Eu-ropeans continued to call for a treaty, although they recognized that a treaty might not be possible and started to look for alternative proposals. The veto coalition continued to oppose a treaty and called instead for the continua-tion and strengthening of the UNFF and the CPF. Several compromise pro-posals began to emerge. Some countries called for a non-legally binding voluntary "code of conduct" with clear overarching goals and a limited number of targets. The United States, Switzerland, and Canada, among oth-ers, supported this proposal, but Brazil and others rejected quantifiable goals and argued that the Forest Principles was a code of conduct. Negotia-tion for targets and timetables began, but although there was tentative agreement about goals and the possibility of negotiating a voluntary code, there was no consensus on the details. NGOs argued that members had en-gaged in policy talks for too long; meanwhile, deforestation had continued unabated and unchallenged. They argued that governments must adopt clear, measurable targets, provide the necessary resources to implement actions to achieve them, and ensure broad participation of NGOs and indigenous people.

In the end, countries recognized that without the support of two key players in the veto coalition—the country with the largest timber industry (the United States) and the country with the world's largest tropical forest (Brazil)—no treaty would be possible. Other options were put on the table, but there was still no consensus on the adoption of targets, a voluntary code of conduct, or the consideration of a treaty in the future. With no agreement possible, delegates agreed to reconvene at UNFF-6 in early 2006 to try, yet again, to reach consensus on a future international arrangement on forests— an agreement that has succeeded in eluding international forest policymakers since 1992.

Although it may appear that the international forest policy debate is at a complete stand-still, the dialogue is in full swing in other fora. The rapid emergence of illegal logging as an issue of concern for the international forest policy community, coupled with the stalled UNFF process, suggests that the international community might be moving away from the issue of sustainable forest management towards illegal logging as its main area of concern.[207] That the issue of illegal logging is being addressed for the most part through the various Forest Law Enforcement and Governance ministerial processes (Africa, East Asia, Europe, and North Asia) also suggests a regionalization of the global forest discourse.[208] Illegal forest activities may contribute to increased poverty and conflict; foster a vicious cycle of bad governance; pose a significant threat to the sustainability of forest ecosystems; and, according to the World Bank, cause significant losses of tax revenues to the order of $10–15 billion a year. If captured by governments, these losses could support expenditures in education and health that will exceed current development assistance to these sectors.[209] As illegal forest activities move to the center of international forest dialogue, the evolution of an international forest regime may shift directions yet again.

CONCLUSION

These cases of environmental regime formation show that the negotiation of a strong global environmental regime almost always depends on inducing one or more key states in a veto coalition to go along with one or more of the core proposed provisions of the regime. By a strong or effective regime, we mean an agreement that includes obligations or norms that make it sufficiently clear that parties can be held accountable for implementing them, and that calls for actions reasonably expected to have an impact on the problem if they are implemented. Whether a regime succeeds in addressing an environmental threat depends, of course, on how strong the regime is in the above sense and on the degree to which parties comply with its core provisions. When veto power has been successfully overcome, and when vital norms or actions have been agreed to, it has been for one of four possible reasons:

- A veto state changed its own understanding of the problem because of new scientific evidence.
- A veto state had a change of government, and the new government had a different policy toward the issue.
- A veto state came under effective domestic political pressure to change its policy.
- A veto state feared negative reactions from other governments or adverse international opinion, which it regarded as more important than its interest in vetoing a specific provision of the regime.

As table 3.4 shows, in some of these cases one or more veto states either agreed to the central obligation proposed by the lead state coalition or accepted the regime in general despite earlier rejection.

New scientific evidence has helped move veto states on some issues (acid rain, ozone depletion, and climate change) but has been secondary or irrelevant in other issues (whaling, hazardous waste trade, desertification and African elephants). International considerations were primary in several cases: Japan's concern with economic and diplomatic ties with other major trading nations and its international image helped tilt its stand on the ivory ban. French and British desires to maintain close relations with former colonies were a factor conditioning their views on the hazardous waste trade issue. The leading distant-water fishing states dropped their resistance to key provisions in the Fish Stocks Agreement at least in part because they did not want to appear to be blocking the first major global agreement on sustainable fishing. The lack of an agreement on a forest treaty demonstrates how economic and political concerns can also prevent states from reaching an agreement.

In most of these cases, domestic political developments played a key role in facilitating agreement. Business and industrial concerns have affected the U.S. response to climate change as well as the dispute over methyl bromide in

TABLE 3.4   Veto States and Regime Creation or Strengthening

Issue*	Key Veto States	Basis of Veto Power	Veto State Concession
Acid rain (sulfur dioxide)	Germany, Belgium, and Denmark	Export of sulfur dioxide	Joining the "30-Percent Club"
Ozone depletion	European Commission	Percent of CFC production	Agreeing to 50-percent cut; agreeing to phase-out
Climate change	United States	Percent of CO_2 emissions	Agreeing to stabilization goal**
Toxic waste trade	United States, EU, Japan	Percent of exports	Agreeing to ban exports
Toxic chemicals	Developing countries who use DDT for malaria control	Percent of use of DDT; global support for increased malaria control	Acceptance of elimination of DDT but with blanket exception for disease control; acceptance of regular reviews on continued need for DDT
Whaling	Japan and Norway	Percent of catch	Acceptance of ban on whaling against depleted populations
African elephant ivory	Japan, southern African states	Percent of imports (Japan); elephant herds (southern African states)	No reservation to CITES uplist
Big-leaf mahogany	Bolivia, Brazil and other exporters	Source of Big-leaf mahogany	No reservation to CITES uplist
Biodiversity loss	United States	Percentage of financing of GEF; biotechnology	Signing the agreement**
Fisheries depletion	European Commission, Japan and the Like-Minded caucus	Percentage of global catch of straddling and highly migratory stocks	Agreement to precautionary reference points and new enforcement measures
Desertification	EC, United States	Percentage of ODA	Agreeing to negotiate regime
Forests	Brazil and Latin American countries, United States	Percentage of the world's forests; largest timber industry	No agreement

* This chart outlines one aspect of the veto coalition situation for each case as a point of comparison.
**In both of these cases veto state power has not totally been overcome because although the U.S. in each case made certain concessions in the negotiations, the result was a much weaker treaty.

the Montreal Protocol. Concern about POPs in the Inuit communities of northern Canada pushed Canada to the forefront of the negotiations to ban certain types of POPs.

Regime formation also requires leadership by one or more states committed to defining the issue and proposing a detailed policy approach as the basis for the regime. Sometimes, that lead role is played by states that are motivated by particular vulnerability (Sweden, Finland, and Norway on acid rain; the African countries on hazardous waste trade and desertification; the small island states on climate change) and sometimes by a state that has an advantageous legal or economic status (the original U.S. call for a phaseout of CFCs).

But as these cases show, the United States has greater diplomatic influence on other state actors and IOs than any other state. When the United States has taken the lead, as it did on the Montreal Protocol on ozone depletion, whaling, or the African elephant, the result has been a much stronger regime than would otherwise have been established. In the case of the fishing regime, the leadership role of the United States was crucial to agreement on conservation norms applying on the high seas and within EEZs. But when the United States has been a veto state, as in the sulfur dioxide protocol to the acid rain convention, the hazardous waste trade convention, the biodiversity convention, and the climate convention, the result is a significantly weaker regime.

In the cases of the climate change and biodiversity regimes, veto power wielded by key states has not yet been overcome either in the initial negotiations on regime formation or in subsequent negotiations on regime strengthening. The result is regimes that are notably weak in the expected impact of the norms and regulations adopted on the threats in question. In the negotiations on strengthening the climate-change regime, the key veto states have been the United States, China, India, and Brazil, which together account for much more than half of global greenhouse gas emissions. The United States, hobbled by strong domestic political opposition to a meaningful commitment for emissions reduction, has consistently opposed ambitious targets for reducing greenhouse gas emissions and has the greatest impact on the effectiveness of the resulting targets (although the resistance of other countries has also contributed to the result). But the insistence of major developing countries, whose emissions already account for a large proportion of global emissions, that no obligations for controlling emissions be placed on them threatens the effectiveness of the existing regime.

The absence of an effective lead state coalition, however, can also contribute to a regime's ineffectiveness, as is true of the biodiversity regime. The fact that the language of the main conservation provisions of the biodiversity treaty remains for the most part more advisory than binding is not the result of a few veto states but of the absence of a lead state coalition effort to strengthen the regime. For several reasons (greater complexity, lack of high levels of media interest, less domestic lobbying by environmental NGOs, and the proliferation of working groups), the biodiversity convention has not received as much high-level political attention in major states as the climate change convention. In the case of desertification, although the African countries have formed an active lead state coalition, their weak political and economic influence has contributed to the ineffectiveness of the regime.

As these cases of environmental regimes indicate, the international community has been able to reach an impressively large number of agreements to reduce environmental threats. This could be interpreted as an indicator of the paradigm shift toward sustainable development. Many of these agreements were believed impossible to achieve only a few months before they were successfully completed. Moreover, many were negotiated more rapidly than previous treaties dealing with environment and natural resources, indicating a process of international learning about how to reach agreement on complex and contentious environmental issues.

Global environmental regimes also have evolved into conventions that have achieved nearly universal adherence. Almost every country in the world is a party to the climate change, biodiversity, ozone, and desertification conventions. Finally, some of these regimes (climate, biodiversity, hazardous waste trade, toxic chemicals, and desertification) have the potential for affecting fundamental economic development strategies, production technologies, and even domestic political processes.

DISCUSSION QUESTIONS

1. In which cases did countries change roles from veto states to lead state or the reverse? Why did these changes occur?
2. On which global environmental issues has new scientific evidence altered the positions of government negotiators? On what other issues might it be relevant? To which has it been irrelevant? Why?

3. Consider the veto coalitions opposing strong action on the issues in this chapter. What are the primary motives of each individual member? What are the reasons for those coalitions weakening?
4. Trace the role of a particular state on a variety of issues and try to assess the extent of its involvement in leadership or blocking roles.
5. What might be the effect of growing economic prosperity or recession in the United States or other countries on the specific global environmental issues discussed in this chapter?
6. Compare and contrast two conventions or protocols and the political, economic and environmental factors that influenced their evolution.

4

◄◦►

Effective Environmental Regimes: Obstacles and Opportunities

The last thirty years have seen an unprecedented explosion of international negotiations and cooperation on global environmental issues. In 2002, when countries gathered in Johannesburg for the World Summit on Sustainable Development, more than nine hundred international legal instruments (binding and nonbinding) were focused on environmental protection or contained one or more important provisions addressing the issue.[1] Yet, despite the successful negotiation of so many important agreements, including those outlined in chapter 3, international environmental regimes are only as effective as the parties make them.

The *effectiveness* of an environmental regime, the extent to which it produces measurable improvements in the environment, is a function of three factors. First is *regime design,* particularly the strength of the key control provisions aimed at addressing the environmental threat, but also the provisions on reporting, monitoring, regime strengthening, noncompliance, and financial and technical assistance. Second is the level of *implementation,* the extent to which countries (and to a lesser extent international organizations) adopt formal legislation and other regulations to enact the agreement. Third is *compliance,* the degree to which countries and other actors actually observe these regulations and the extent to which their actions conform to the explicit rules, norms, and procedures contained in the regime.[2]

This chapter examines some of the factors that inhibit or promote effective environmental agreements. The first section outlines obstacles that can make it difficult to create and implement regimes with strong, binding control measures. The second section looks at variables that negatively influence

197

compliance with environmental agreements. The third section outlines potential avenues to improve compliance. The final section discusses options for increasing the financing available to implement global environmental regimes. For some countries, the major obstacle to compliance, and therefore to regime effectiveness, is the lack of adequate financial and technical resources to fulfill treaty obligations. The question of financial resources has been at the center of global environmental policy for many years and will continue to be for the foreseeable future.

OBSTACLES TO CREATING
STRONG ENVIRONMENTAL REGIMES

This section examines four types of obstacles to creating strong environmental regimes: (1) systemic or structural obstacles that stem from the structure of the international system, the structure of international law, and the structure of the global economic system; (2) a lack of necessary and sufficient conditions, in particular, public and/or official concern, a hospitable contractual environmental, and capacity; (3) procedural obstacles inherent in international environmental negotiations; and (4) obstacles that stem from common characteristics of global environment issues.[3] Of course, when thinking about these categories of obstacles, it is important to see them as indicative and heuristic rather than exhaustive and exclusive. In the real world, these factors are interrelated and their individual and relative impact varies significantly across countries and issue areas.

Systemic Obstacles

Some impediments to creating strong global environmental regimes result from inherent elements of the global political, ecological, legal, and economic systems. Anarchy, defined in this usage as the absence of a world government with recognized authority, is a structural characteristic of the international system. Political scientists have long argued that aspects of this structure have broad consequences for international relations.[4] In particular, states tend to believe they can rely only on self-help to ensure their safety; states usually attempt to balance the power of others through alliances and armaments; states prefer independence over interdependence; and states can find it difficult to achieve effective cooperation.

The last consequence is perhaps the most relevant to environmental regimes. Just as in security or economic issues, the pressures that system structure places on state actors can make it difficult to create strong environmental regimes (although to a lesser extent). Strong states attempt to dictate terms to weaker states. States worry that other countries might gain relative economic or political advantages[5] (such as the United States in the climate change negotiations) or fear that others will not fulfill regime obligations.[6] States sometimes try to avoid paying a fair share of the costs (free-riding);[7] have incentives to pursue policies that appear rational but help destroy a common-pool resource (such as fisheries);[8] fail to locate mutually advantageous policies because of market failure;[9] misperceive the motives, intentions, or actions of other governments;[10] and compromise environmental negotiations by linking them to unrelated political, security, and economic issues.

Another systemic or structural obstacle is the lack of congruence between the global political and ecological systems. The causes, consequences, and geographic scope of environmental problems do not respect national boundaries. Pollution released into the air or water spreads easily to other countries. CFCs deplete the ozone layer without respect to which country released them. High-seas fisheries and atmospheric chemistry are outside the political control of any one state. Ecological systems operate independently of national and international political and legal systems. Simply put, "The structure of the global political system, composed of independent sovereign states, is not well suited to address complex, interdependent, international environmental problems whose causes, impacts, and solutions transcend unrelated political boundaries."[11] This structural conflict has impacted negotiations on global commons issues—the atmosphere (ozone depletion and climate change) and the high seas (fisheries and whales)—as well as negotiations on problems where air and water pollution cross national borders. For example, upwind and downwind states sometimes hold different views on the need for strong regimes to control air pollution, as was apparent in negotiations to create particular protocols to LRTAP and the U.S.-Canada acid rain agreement.

A similar conflict exists between the foundations of international law and the requirements for effective international environmental policy. Perhaps the most fundamental principle of international law is sovereignty. States have nearly unassailable control over activities within their borders, including the use of natural resources. At the same time, however, legitimate actions within one country can create environmental problems for another. Usually, then, effective international policy requires limiting what a state does within its own borders. This conflict is embodied in Principle 21 from the 1972 Stockholm Conference, often cited as one of the most important foundations of modern international environmental law. It reads:

> States have, in accordance with the Charter of the United Nations and the principles of international law, the sovereign right to exploit their own resources pursuant to their own environmental policies, and the responsibility to ensure that activities within their jurisdiction or control do not cause damage to the environment of other states or of areas beyond the limits of national jurisdiction.[12]

Overcoming the inherent tension captured in this sentence is one of the most fundamental challenges of global environmental politics. Many states strongly resist regime provisions that, although beneficial to the environment, involve compromises to national sovereignty. For example, many of the most controversial proposals during negotiation of the Biodiversity Convention involved potential restrictions on state control over genetic resources within their borders.[13] The debate over a forest convention has been strongly affected by states wanting to ensure that they maintain clear sovereignty over their forest resources. And concerns about potential infringements on national sovereignty led to the inclusion of veto clauses that allow each party to block third-party adjudication under the Basel Convention.[14]

Some argue that elements of the international economic system also present a structural impediment to creating and implementing strong and effective global environmental regimes. Different discussions along these lines point to the system's emphasis on resource extraction, globalization, free trade, lowest-cost production, high levels of consumption and consumerism, and, especially, the failure to cost-in environmental degradation. Certainly the emphasis on resource extraction, the need to pay off large debts, and the desire to industrialize as quickly as possible has produced serious environmental problems in some developing countries. There is also increasing consensus among a variety of theorists and politicians from both the right and the left regarding the need to include the costs of environmental degradation into the larger economic system, although they often reach different conclusions about how to accomplish this. Debate also continues on the ultimate impact of free trade and economic integration on the environment,[15] although some domestic environmental laws have been overruled by free-trade rules (see chapter 5). For example, the GATT determined that the U.S. embargo on Mexican-caught tuna without a dolphin-safe net was illegal. Under WTO rules, the United States succeeded in forcing the EU to accept imports of U.S.

beef that contained growth (and other) hormones, and Canada forced the EU to back down from banning fur imports from animals caught in legholds.

Yet it is probably too simplistic to assert that the global economic system inhibits strong environmental regimes. Indeed, when properly harnessed, these same forces can support environmental regimes. For example, in the expansion of the ozone regime, the global economic system supported the introduction of more environmentally friendly technology into developing countries much faster than many had expected. The financial power amassed by the global insurance industry supports stronger action on climate change. Free trade rules and economic integration has likely improved overall energy efficiency in Europe. Thus, the key may be to examine, case by case, how dominant economic interests and systems run counter to the goals or operation of a particular environmental regime, and how this relationship might be reversed—rather than reflexively accepting that such economic interests and systems necessarily inhibit stronger policy.

The Absence of Necessary Conditions: Concern, Contractual Environment, and Capacity

As discussed by Peter Haas, Robert Keohane, and Marc Levy, effective environmental regimes require three necessary, but not sufficient, conditions.[16] First, there must be *sufficient concern* within the government, and perhaps the public at large, so that states decide to devote resources to examining and addressing the problem and implementing potential solutions. Environmental problems compete with many economic, security, and social issues for space on national and international agendas. Sufficient concern must exist for the issue-definition, fact-finding, bargaining, and regime strengthening phases to occur and be completed successfully.

Second, there must be a *hospitable contractual environment* so that states can gather to negotiate, negotiate with reasonable ease and costs, make credible commitments to each other, reach agreement on policies, and monitor each other's behavior in implementing those policies. In other words, if too many of the negative consequences of system structure—such as misperceptions or fears of cheating or free riding—are present or transaction costs are too high (meaning the time, money, and effort involved in negotiating a treaty), then creating strong agreements is difficult.

Third, states must possess the scientific, political, economic, and administrative *capacity* to understand the threat; participate in creating the global regime; and then implement and ensure compliance with the regime's principles, norms, and rules. Although concern, contractual environment, and capacity are not obstacles themselves (and it is easy to oversimplify the concepts), their absence significantly inhibits, if not prevents, the creation and implementation of strong environmental regimes.

Procedural Obstacles

Once states begin the bargaining or negotiation phase, procedural problems can arise. Two stand out: the *time lag* and *lowest common denominator* problems.[17] Each is a product of how international negotiations work, the structural obstacles outlined above, and varying levels of national concern for particular environmental issues.

It is neither an easy nor a speedy process to create and implement strong global environmental policy. The international agenda must be set, negotiations convened, appropriate policies identified and adopted, implementation strategies agreed to, treaties ratified, national and international policies implemented and reported upon, environmental problems monitored, and international policies revised in light of lessons learned. The common practice of starting with a framework convention and adopting subsequent protocols adds even more time. Enough governments must ratify the convention and protocols so that they can enter into force and be effective. To have an impact on the environmental problem, the implementation and revision phase must occur over a sufficient length of time.

Each step in this series can be time-consuming. Problems posed by hazardous waste shipments were identified in the 1970s, but the Basel Convention did not come into effect until 1992, and the Ban Amendment still requires additional ratifications to take effect. The UN Convention on Law of the Sea, a complex treaty that contains provisions on most aspects of maritime law, took nearly ten years to negotiate and another twelve to receive enough ratifications to enter into force. The International Convention for the Prevention of Pollution from Ships (MARPOL) experienced a ten-year time lag from its negotiation to its entry into force, in spite of the decades of collaborative efforts on oil pollution leading up to it. In 1859, John Tyndal, an Irish physicist, became one of the first scientists to identify the greenhouse effect as well as the relative radiative forcing of gases in the atmosphere. However, formal negotiations on a framework convention for climate change did not begin until 1991; and today, nearly 150 years later, only modest controls exist for greenhouse gas emissions. Scientists discovered the threat to ozone layer in 1974, but negotiations did not begin until 1982, the first binding controls did not come into force until 1988, and large developing countries still have not phased out all CFCs.

PHOTO 4.1   The first Meeting of the Parties of the Cartagena Protocol on Biosafety in February 2004. Courtesy IISD/*Earth Negotiations Bulletin*.

Yet, environmental issues do not wait for the policy process—species become extinct and biodiversity declines, greenhouse gases accumulate in the atmosphere, toxic chemicals are released, and hazardous wastes are not disposed of properly. As the process of regime creation and expansion drags on, environmental problems become worse, not better, making it even more difficult to create and implement effective regimes.

The second procedural obstacle, the lowest common denominator problem, is created by veto states. Because all states are sovereign entities, they can choose to join or not to join a global environmental agreement. However, because active participation by many countries is required to address a global environmental problem, the countries most interested in addressing a particular issue often need support from countries showing far less interest. Thus, an environmental treaty can be only as strong as its least cooperative state allows it to be. The regime's overall effectiveness is undermined by the compromises made in persuading these states, the veto states, to participate.

For example, during negotiations of the Stockholm Convention, countries critical to its long-term success insisted on specific exemptions so that they could continue using small amounts of certain POPs. During negotiation of the 1991 Protocol on Environmental Protection, which protects the Antarctic from possible mineral exploitation, opposition from the United States resulted in a fifty-year moratorium rather than the initially proposed permanent protection.[18] As discussed in chapter 3, from 1977 to 1989, the EC acted as a veto state and set the lowest common denominator for global ozone policy, forcing the lead states to accept much weaker regime rules in the 1985 Vienna Convention and 1987 Montreal Protocol.

The least common denominator problem also severely limited the strength of the MARPOL agreement, even though the oil pollution regime had a long history. Laggard states pushed for the cheapest methods of accommodating pollution complaints. Jurisdictional issues brought stronger proposals for the rejection of port state inspection rights: States were relentless in their protection of exclusive flag-state sovereignty over ships, particularly Liberia for economic reasons and the USSR for security.[19] Furthermore, the proposal that states provide on-shore reception facilities for waste was agreed to only in its weakest form as states kept the rule legally non-binding.[20]

Characteristics of Global Environmental Issues

A final set of obstacles to creating strong regimes stems from common characteristics inherent in global environmental problems. Although certainly not unique to environmental issues, and with impacts that vary across countries and issue areas, these characteristics are important elements of global environmental politics and have the capacity to exacerbate many of the other obstacles outlined above.[21]

One of the most critical characteristics is that *environmental issues are inextricably linked to important economic and political interests.* Environmental issues, and therefore environmental negotiations, are not independent of other economic and political activities and interests; environmental issues exist because of these activities and interests. Environmental problems are produced as externalities of individuals, corporations, and nations pursuing other interests. They result from such important local, corporate, national, and international economic and political activities as energy production, mining, manufacturing, farming, fishing, transportation, resource consumption, livestock husbandry, urbanization, weapons production, territorial expansion, and military conflict. That many of these activities could be pursued successfully while doing less harm to the environment does not erase the links between the issues.[22]

Creating strong international environmental regimes, therefore, often requires addressing important economic, social, and even security interests; but, justified or not, this is obviously a very difficult proposition. The presence of important economic interests can lower relative concern, make veto states more determined, and bring powerful domestic economic actors to lobby for their views. They can enhance fears of free riding, create more opportunities for positional bargaining, and otherwise harm the contractual environment. Examples of the obstacles posed by the links between environmental problems and economic interest are common. Protecting the earth's remaining biodiversity requires addressing the economic and political pressures that cause habitat destruction, something that has proved almost impossible to date. A strong regime to address climate change will likely require significant changes in fossil-fuel consumption, which currently remain out of reach, especially in the United States. Complete protection of the ozone layer requires a near total phaseout of methyl bromide emissions, but major agricultural interests, particularly in the United States, are hesitant to agree to this. Combating deforestation in some developing countries would have a major impact on the timber industry and the national economy. Addressing the serious decline in fisheries will impact the economies of both distant-water fishing states and coastal states. The total elimination of DDT would prevent its use as an inexpensive tool in the battle against malaria in Africa.

A second characteristic, and one closely linked to the first, is *unequal adjustment costs*. Addressing a global environmental problem means changing the economic, political, and/or cultural activities that ultimately cause the problem. Making these changes, or "adjustments," carries different economic and political costs in different countries. Countries face different adjustment costs depending on the environmental issue, its impact, their contribution to the cause of the problem, existing regulation, level of economic development, enforcement capability, resource base, trade profile, method of energy production, transportation policy, and a host of other factors.

Large variations in adjustment costs in countries essential to a regime act as obstacles to creating a strong regime. Large and unequal adjustment costs "accentuate the difficulties inherent in international cooperation and significantly impact the contractual environment. Because states can be concerned with relative or positional advantages, they may reject solutions that ask them to bear a relatively larger burden than other states. Alternatively they may demand special compensation for joining the regime,"[23] which, in turn, can weaken the regime.

Unequal adjustment costs exist in all the regimes outlined in chapter 3. Indeed, they are part of the reason veto coalitions form. During negotiation of the Kyoto Protocol, many governments argued that their different levels of industrialization, energy profile, transportation infrastructure, core industries, and even local temperatures made adhering to one set of mandatory reductions in CO_2 emissions inherently unfair. As a result, the Kyoto Protocol contains not only a relative modest set of controls but no mandatory reductions of CO_2 emissions for developing countries, and different targets for most developed countries. More broadly, unequal adjustment costs pose a huge long-term problem for the climate regime. Strong controls would likely mean enormous adjustment for oil-exporting states and countries that depend on cheap coal for energy, but not for countries such as France, which relies on nuclear power for most of its electricity, or Iceland, which uses geothermal energy. Reconciling these positions is a huge challenge. Similar problems exist in other regimes. Examples include demands for special exemptions in the chemicals regime, continuing support for whaling by Iceland, Japan, and Norway, and fear among some tropical countries that future efforts to protect biodiversity, or a future forest convention, will include attempts to prevent their use of large forested areas for traditional types of economic development.

A third obstacle is that environmental issues often involve significant *scientific complexity and uncertainty*. Uncertainty regarding the scope, severity, impact, or time frame of a problem can make it difficult to attribute responsibility, design possible solutions, and create strong regimes. Lack of knowledge about an environmental problem can undermine concern. Large degrees of scientific uncertainty can allow other, more certain economic or political interests to be prioritized in the policy hierarchy. The scientific complexity of environmental issues can challenge the capacity of government bureaucracies to understand the problem or implement proper solutions. Uncertainty and complexity can lead different states to perceive the payoff differently, perhaps reducing incentives to risk cooperation and increasing incentives either to free-ride or to ignore the problem altogether, thereby harming the contractual environment.[24]

For example, opponents of a strong regime for climate change have succeeded to date by emphasizing not only the costs of such an agreement (the links to economic interests) but also what they argue are important uncertainties regarding the severity and perhaps even the existence of a problem (most scientists and the IPCC do not share this view). Lack of certainty regarding the long-term impacts of low exposure to, and slow accumulation of, toxic chemicals inhibits the chemicals regime from expanding quickly, despite evidence that causes many to express concern. Biodiversity loss, biosafety, ozone depletion, and acid rain are some of the other issues where scientific complexity and uncertainty slowed or prevented the creation of strong regimes.

A fourth characteristic that can act as an obstacle to creating and implementing strong regimes is the *time horizon conflict*. Because the most serious consequences of many environmental problems will not occur for many years, policymakers sometimes find it difficult to create strong regimes with significant short-term costs, even if such action would be less expensive and more successful in the long run. That some environmental issues do not develop in a linear, predictable pattern complicates matters. The time-horizon obstacle is enhanced if concern for the problem is low, the nature of the threat is not well defined, or the costs of acting are very high. Ozone depletion, biodiversity loss, and climate change are obvious examples of issues impacted by time-horizon conflicts. Efforts to add additional toxic chemicals to the PIC and POPs regimes also face this problem. Outside of relatively rare incidents of large, short-term exposure from accidents, such as the 1984 gas leak in Bhopal, India, the greatest long-term and most widespread threats posed by many of these chemicals, including potential impacts on reproductive health, could occur in the future as a result of long-term exposure from their slow accumulation in humans and the environment. Preventing these impacts requires preventing the buildup, and this means accepting certain current costs for likely but future benefits.

Fifth, states and groups within states sometimes possess *different core religious, cultural, or political beliefs and values* relevant to environmental issues. For example, some groups in Iceland and Norway have strong cultural links to whaling. Some individuals in Asia believe products from endangered animal species, such as rhino horn, have important medicinal, physical, or sexual properties. This creates a market for these animals and undercuts international controls designed to protect them. Many Catholics and Muslims oppose policies designed to control human population growth. Some political ideologies treat economic development and freedom from government regulations as higher priorities than environmental protection. Some NGOs, such as Earth First!, believe the opposite. Conflicting core beliefs and values can play important roles in environmental negotiations: They can limit transnational concern, block potential policies, cause some actors not to participate or comply, and necessitate compromises that weaken the resulting regime.

A sixth obstacle is that *large numbers* of actors must cooperate to create and implement an effective global environmental regime. Social science has long acknowledged the difficulties that large numbers pose for cooperation. An increase in the number of actors often causes more heterogeneity of interests and perceptions as well as more uncertainty within each actor as to the preferences of others. Thus, the search for solutions to an environmental problem becomes more difficult as the number of parties increases. The larger the number of actors, the more likely it is that an agreement, if concluded at all, will be "partial" in at least one of three ways: (a) covering only some of the agenda topics; (b) leaving some disagreement latent in an ambiguous text; or (c) being signed and accepted only by some states. Second, the risk of suboptimal outcomes, or least common denominator agreements, seems to increase as the number of actors increases.[25]

Large numbers can also increase incentives for noncompliance (because of reduced fears of detection), particularly if the benefits of cooperation are suspect or the adjustment costs are high or uneven. Large numbers can be particularly dangerous to the success of a regime that seeks to protect the commons, such as the oceans or atmosphere, which all can use but no one controls. If some states fear that others will cheat, they may believe they face a "use it or lose it" scenario that compels them to use the resource, leading to its more rapid degradation.[26]

OBSTACLES TO COMPLYING WITH GLOBAL ENVIRONMENTAL CONVENTIONS

Treaties contain many different types of obligations. The most important are sometimes referred to as substantive obligations, particularly obligations to cease or control a specific activity such as CFC production or whaling. Also important are a variety of procedural obligations, such as reporting requirements. Compliance refers to whether countries adhere to the mandatory provisions of an environmental convention and the extent to which they follow through on the steps they have taken to implement these provisions.[27]

Global environmental regimes and national governments employ a variety of mechanisms to promote compliance. These include regular reporting by the parties; independent evaluation and public availability of such reports; review of implementation at regular meetings of the parties; the readiness of some parties to call noncomplying parties to account publicly; the monitoring of compliance by NGOs; and technical and financial assistance for building capacity, and otherwise assisting certain parties to fulfill their obligations under the regime.[28] Of course, not all regimes or countries employ each measure, and their success varies significantly across regimes and among parties.

Most countries that sign and ratify an international convention do so with the intention of complying with its provisions, and most comply to the best of their ability.[29] However, compliance sometimes turns out to be politically, technically, administratively, or financially impossible, even if a government remains committed to the regime. Sometimes compliance becomes sufficiently difficult that a state decides to focus time, effort, and resources in other areas; that is, compliance is still possible, but a state chooses not to comply because of other priorities. Only rarely does a state deliberately set out to sign and ratify a treaty with no intention of complying.

As attention turns from creating new global environmental regimes to implementing and strengthening existing ones, compliance has become an even more important issue in global environmental politics. In addition to the general obstacles outlined above, the growing literature on implementation and compliance with international environmental agreements suggests that noncompliance can be traced to several different types of factors; these include the inadequate translation of regime rules into domestic law; insufficient capacity to implement, enforce, or administer relevant domestic law; a lack of respect for rule of law; the high relative costs of compliance; inadequate financial and technical assistance; the inability to monitor compliance; poorly designed regimes; and the large number of environmental conventions and the confusing and uncoordinated web of requirements they have produced.[30]

Inadequate Translation of Regime Rules into Domestic Law

Some states fail to adopt the domestic legislation necessary to implement and fully comply with an international agreement. This can include failing to adopt any or all of the needed regulations, or adopting poorly crafted regulations. For instance, Peter Sand has noted that "the main constraint on the implementation of CITES in each Party has been the need to create national legislation. Although this is an obligation under [CITES], several countries have not complied. . . . Others have only incomplete legislation, lacking . . . means for sanctions against offenders."[31]

The failure to enact domestic law can stem from a variety of factors. Sometimes, domestic economic or political opposition that was unable to block a country from negotiating or signing a particular treaty can nevertheless prevent the country from ratifying the treaty. If national ratification depends on approval by a legislative branch, as it is in the United States, treaty ratification can be prevented by interest groups or lawmakers opposed to its goals or means, by politicians seeking leverage to achieve other political ends, by an overburdened legislative agenda, or by conflicts about resource allocations. For example, since the early 1990s, opposition from powerful interest groups and key senators has prevented the United States Senate even from holding formal ratification votes on several key treaties, including the Kyoto Protocol and the Biodiversity, Basel, Rotterdam, and Stockholm Conventions.

Even when a treaty is ratified, interest groups or political opposition might still be able prevent or significantly weaken the necessary implementing legislation. Weak legislative and bureaucratic infrastructures or a lack of expertise on the issue can also prevent the most effective regulations from becoming law. Some of the chemical treaties, for example, require relatively high levels of knowledge regarding toxic chemicals and their management to enact all their provisions effectively into domestic law. Inefficient legislative procedures or political or economic instability also can keep states from fully or accurately enacting necessary domestic legislation. Finally, in democracies with nonintegrated federal structures, the federal government simply may not have the jurisdiction to implement international environmental agreements at the state or provincial level. For example, in Belgium, each of the autonomous regions must separately adopt environmental legislation. In Canada, the provinces, not the federal government, control most aspects of environmental policy.[32]

Insufficient Capacity to Implement, Administer, or Enforce Domestic Legislation.

It is not enough simply to enact laws and regulations. They must also be effectively implemented, administered, and enforced. Doing so requires sufficient and issue-specific skills, knowledge, technical know-how, legal authority, financial resources, and enforcement capacity at the individual and institutional levels. Therefore, a second reason for inadequate compliance is insufficient state capacity to implement, administer, or enforce the relevant domestic policies and regulations. Insufficient capacity is a particular problem for developing countries, but it exists in all parts of the world and varies from issue to issue and country to county.

Examples of capacity problems inhibiting compliance are unfortunately common. CITES has provisions for trade measures to enforce its controls on wildlife trade, but many countries, including industrialized countries, lack the budgets or trained personnel needed to comply fully and effectively.[33] Compliance with the Convention on Biological Diversity has been hindered by a lack of national capacity to manage protected-area systems and to analyze the impacts of development projects on biodiversity. Russia did not comply with its obligations under the ozone regime for several years because its government temporarily lacked the capacity to stop black market production and the export of CFCs. Full compliance (and effective implementation) of the Stockholm Convention includes locating, identifying, and destroying stockpiles of obsolete pesticides in an environmentally sound manner, something beyond the technical and financial ability of many countries. The Basel Convention contains no provision for international monitoring of the accuracy of hazardous waste labels or spot-checking shipments in the ports of receiving countries. Developing countries, of which their inability to monitor and regulate the trade led them to call for a ban on international waste shipments in the first place, often do not have the capacity to monitor this shipping themselves.[34]

Lack of Respect for the Rule of Law

A related obstacle is a lack of respect for the rule of law within some countries. Merely passing implementing legislation has no practical effect if the government, companies, or the public then simply ignore it; or if the government cannot enforce it or chooses not to. This problem tends to arise more often in developing countries in situations where severe economic pressures, political instability, and patterns of corruption lead particular groups, government officials, or the general public to ignore elements of the legal system.

For example, in Kenya during the rule of Daniel arap Moi, from 1978–2002, systematic corruption, extreme poverty, and the absence of a meaningful democratic process caused many people to feel alienated from the lawmaking apparatus; as a result, their respect for the law, including regulations on wildlife conservation, was undermined.[35] Similarly, the epidemic of illegal logging in national parks in Indonesia following the 1998 financial crisis resulted, at least in part, in a breakdown of law and order combined with economic pressures in the affected areas.[36]

High Relative Costs of Compliance

Domestic compliance with international environmental agreements is also affected by the costs of such compliance relative to the country's level of economic development, current economic situation, resource base, and budgetary preferences.[37] Affluent countries experiencing relatively high economic growth rates are historically far more willing to comply with environmental regulations than poorer states or states with economies that are growing slowly or not at all. States with low per capita incomes are generally reluctant to commit significant funds to comply with commitments to reduce global threats, even if it is in the country's long-term interest, because such compliance would likely come at the expense of spending for economic development or social goals. Other competing budgetary preferences, such as military spending, can also inhibit compliance. On the other hand, if the costs of compliance are relatively modest, or if compliance produces a net economic gain, a state's level of economic well-being may be less critical.

Countries experiencing economic and financial crisis often refuse or become unable to comply fully with global environmental agreements. The Russian Federation, for example, could not immediately comply with the 1996 phaseout of CFCs because of its critical economic situation. At different times, other countries also have failed to comply with particular aspects of the ozone regime because of what they perceived to be the relatively high costs of implementation relative to other immediate needs.[38] Structural adjustment programs can also negatively impact the relative cost of compliance because they usually involve budget cuts in the debtor countries and favor programs designed to promote exports that limit pollution, conserve resources, or protect biologically important areas.

Inadequate Financial and Technical Assistance

Many global environmental regimes—including those for ozone, climate, biodiversity, desertification, and toxic chemicals—contain specific measures for providing technical and financial assistance to developing countries and so help them fulfill their obligations. For some developing countries, such measures are critical to their ability to comply with the regime; for others, they provide an important boost. Outside the ozone regime, however, one can argue that the provision of financial and technical assistance has not reached levels that ensure compliance by many developing countries. Indeed, many negotiators believe it is the most important obstacle to improved compliance.[39] Areas of need highlighted in regime negotiations (which vary significantly issue to issue and country to country) include environmental assessments, monitoring, reporting, capacity building, drafting appropriate legislation, equipment, regulatory and administrative infrastructure, customs control, technology transfer, and affordable access to alternative products and processes and other environmentally friendly technology.

Inability to Monitor Compliance and Report on Implementation

States unable to monitor their own relevant activities can easily overlook violations of the national laws that implement an environmental regime. Therefore, even states that want to comply can end up not complying because they do not know what is happening domestically. Two principal sets of factors impact the ability of states to monitor domestic compliance with environmental laws: (1) whether states have adequate feedback mechanisms, such as on-site monitoring by inspectors, reporting requirements, complaint mechanisms, or close working relationships with NGOs; and (2) the number and size of the potential violators whose conduct the government must monitor.[40] For example, the relatively high level of compliance with the Montreal Protocol results not only from the widely accepted science regarding the cause and potential impact of the problem but also from the manageable limits the regime places on the number of sources or sites that require monitoring. Monitoring compliance with the Kyoto Protocol may prove far more difficult, however, because of the large number of sources of greenhouse gas emissions. Similarly, monitoring compliance with CITES remains difficult in part because the number of potential violators is so large.

Poorly Designed Regimes

A party's failure to comply with a regime sometimes reflects problems with the regime itself. As Ron Mitchell puts it, "Regime design matters."[41] Control measures and reporting requirements that are too complex or extremely vague allow states to make honest or intentional errors when translating them to domestic law. Rules inappropriate to the issue area are unlikely to be implemented. Regimes without flexibility or that cannot be adjusted in response to new information leave states without recourse when domestic circumstances change significantly. Regimes that do not pay attention to the ability of states to enact necessary domestic legislation, to the relative costs of compliance, to the importance of reporting and monitoring, or to the need to provide sufficient financial and technical assistance are vulnerable to the problems discussed earlier in this section. Compliance, to some extent, is also a function of regime design.

Many Regimes, Little Coordination

Another obstacle to compliance is the sheer number of environmental conventions and the confusing and uncoordinated web of requirements they now include. Since all state parties, particularly developing countries, have only a limited amount of financial, technical and political resources available to implement environmental treaties, the more complex and confusing the total set of obligations are, the more likely that compliance is going to suffer.

Each environmental regime has its own set of core control measures, reporting requirements, monitoring systems, assessment mechanisms, implementation procedures, meeting schedules, financing requirements, and review procedures. In addition, nearly all of these regimes exist independently of each other. As such, they sometimes place uncoordinated and confusing obligations on states that are difficult to fulfill. For example, mandatory reporting requirements often conflict, or at least remain uncoordinated, in their schedules, procedures, units of analysis, and required methods and formats. This is true even among the suite of treaties that address toxic chemicals (LRTAP, Basel, Rotterdam, and Stockholm) and the institutions involved in the ozone regime (Ozone Secretariat, Multilateral Fund, and GEF).

In addition, some regime rules establish contrary rules or incentives. For example, HFCs are considered a replacement for CFCs under the ozone regime but are a greenhouse gas subject to mandatory controls under the climate regime. Some closely related regimes have uncoordinated membership and regulatory gaps that potentially impede effectiveness. For example, different ratification patterns in the Basel, Rotterdam, and Stockholm Conventions and related regional treaties, especially the Aarhus POPs Protocol under LRTAP, mean that certain countries have pledged to fulfill obligations under some chemicals agreements but not others. This threatens the effective implementation of the agreements, individually and as a package, because each treaty focuses on different aspects of the chemical life cycle (production, use, emissions, trade, destruction, and disposal), and a slightly different set of chemicals and wastes. Parties that implement one convention but not another allow certain chemicals or certain parts of their life-cycles to escape global control.

OPPORTUNITIES TO IMPROVE COMPLIANCE

Several options are available to strengthen compliance with global environmental agreements. None of these options can address all the obstacles discussed in the previous two sections. Furthermore, whether these options or incentives can actually lead a government to comply also depends on the willingness of states and other actors to take action. However, existing experience with global environmental regimes, academic research, and deductive logic indicate that regime compliance and effectiveness can be improved.

Build Domestic Capacity

Improved compliance requires increased funding from donor countries and multilateral agencies for programs that strengthen the capacity of developing countries to implement environmental conventions. Governments and international organizations recognize this need. The GEF and UNDP's Capacity 21 and Capacity 2015 programs strengthen developing-country capacity largely through funding for the implementation of projects for which individuals and institutions gain critical technical, financial/business, and regulatory skills. All GEF projects on biodiversity and climate change focus on capacity building or integrate capacity-building components into investment projects. Capacity-building activities also exist within particular regimes. The CITES training strategy, for example, "trains the trainers" in-country by holding seminars and providing training materials.[42] The ozone regime supports significant capacity building through its Multilateral Fund. The Basel Convention Regional Centers act as nodes for capacity-building programs on issues relating to hazardous wastes and, increasingly, toxic chemicals.

Despite these efforts, many of which are important and productive, results to date in most regimes indicate that more training and technical and financial assistance are needed to make long-term and permanent differences in the capacity of some recipient countries. Areas of particular need include environmental assessment and analysis, monitoring, reporting, regulatory infrastructure, enforcement, science education, public education and communication, and the use and maintenance of a wide variety of environmentally friendly technologies.

Increase and More Effectively Target
Technical and Financial Assistance

In addition to building capacity, technical and financial assistance are needed to augment compliance in many other areas. The line between capacity building and other types of technical and financial assistance is largely an artificial one; but, in general, "capacity building" refers to permanent improvements in the ability and self-sufficiency of a country to comply, whereas "technical and financial assistance" refers to help regarding specific instances or types of compliance. As noted above, the provision of effectively targeted financial and technical assistance is one of the most important avenues toward improved compliance and regime effectiveness. The most important areas include obtaining access to new products and processes; technology transfer; developing new or expanded legislation and regulations; purchasing scientific, monitoring, administrative, and communications equipment; helping to develop and carry out national implementation plans; financing individual implementation projects; properly disposing of hazardous wastes and toxic chemicals; and introducing substitute technologies.

However, the mere availability of increased financial and technical assistance should not be seen as a panacea. Increased compliance also requires more effective assistance. That is, assistance targeted toward the most important needs; monitored to avoid waste; provided conditionally in stages to promote real action; continually assessed and reviewed so that procedures can be improved; and coordinated within and across regimes to achieve potential synergies and to avoid duplication and unintended negative consequences.

Build Secretariat Capacity and Responsibility

Environmental regimes require treaty secretariats to fulfill a variety of key functions. Secretariats coordinate and facilitate day-to-day regime operations, organize meetings of the parties and subsidiary bodies, draft background documents on relevant policy issues, facilitate communication among parties, manage regime reporting, gather and disseminate information on treaty implementation, maintain clearinghouse mechanisms and Web sites, and support public education on the issue. Yet, secretariats' staffs tend to be small and their budgets minuscule in comparison with formal international organizations and most national bureaucracies. Combined with problems caused by late or nonpayment of financial pledges by some parties, the small staffs and limited budgets decrease the ability of many secretariats to perform these functions. For example, the widespread use of short-term contracts (one to six months) for staff positions in secretariats, a practice caused by budget uncertainties and funding constraints, negatively impacts secretariat productivity, reduces institutional memory, and limits the development of long-term working relationships with national officials so important to effective implementation.[43]

However, secretariats have significant potential to do far more to support and monitor regime compliance. Their staffs concentrate solely on the relevant environmental issue, possess comprehensive knowledge of the regime, know which states and other actors do not comply with a treaty, and are thus in a unique position to understand and potentially respond to compliance problems that arise at the national level.[44] Thus, a modest and affordable step toward enhanced compliance would be for donor countries to negotiate new joint commitments to increase funding for secretariats of global environmental conventions and to end the practices of late payment and nonpayment of pledges to them. This would provide secretariats with the capacity and resources they need to enhance reporting, monitoring, and compliance, and, with a slight expansion in the scope of secretariat functions, work more closely with countries that request assistance in complying with the specific aspects of a convention.

A more ambitious strategy would be to give regime secretariats new compliance monitoring, assessment, and assistance powers by amending environmental conventions. This would create a small, full-time group of experts focused on monitoring regime compliance, analyzing national reports, augmenting agreed upon enforcement mechanisms, assessing obstacles to compliance, and working with parties to help remove those obstacles. The United States is one of the countries that has resisted such proposals on the grounds that monitoring authority should not be given to international civil servants.[45] Although protective of sovereign authority, this position also appears to provide greater opportunities for noncomplying parties to "free ride" without detection or consequence and, in doing so, to harm regime effectiveness.

In certain regimes, additional monitoring and enforcement duties might even be appropriate. For example, enforcement officials having links to Interpol or other law enforcement agencies could be included in secretariats for regimes in which smuggling or other illegal activity is a principal problem. This might include CITES, other wildlife-related treaties, the Basel Convention (with regard to illegal dumping), and even the Montreal Protocol (with regard to CFC smuggling). Precedent exists for such procedures. In the early 1990s, CITES formally attached an enforcement officer to its secretariat who could conduct onsite investigations. And under the CITES Lusaka Agreement, CITES enforcement officers in member countries could link directly with Interpol.

Emphasize and Support National Reporting and Monitoring

Reporting is an essential component of monitoring and an important tool for improving compliance and regime effectiveness. Without regular and accurate reporting, it is difficult to assess the baseline, trend, and current status of an environmental problem, to assess current levels of regime implementation, to identify specific instances or patterns of noncompliance, and to develop potential solutions. Studies on institutional effectiveness indicate that regimes employing systems of regular reporting and monitoring of the relevant actions of parties have better levels of domestic implementation and compliance than those that do not.[46] Thus, regardless of the role of secretariat officials, efforts to emphasize and improve national reporting and associated monitoring will help to increase regime compliance and effectiveness.

At present, most environmental regimes require parties to submit data and reports on issues related to the environmental problem as well as on their implementation of the regime. Secretariats often compile this information and make it available to other parties and the public. Unfortunately, not all countries submit the required data and reports, and, among those that do, significant variations exist in their quality and timeliness. In addition, because most countries rely on existing national systems to gather information for regime reporting, the reports often define, estimate, and aggregate the required data in different ways, making comparisons and analysis difficult.

As a result of these problems, some regimes have large information gaps. For example, reporting from parties under the Basel Convention has often been incomplete, late, and sometimes based on different standards of measuring (or estimating) the generation, management, and disposal of hazardous wastes.[47] Analysts believe that differences in national reporting systems under the Long-Range Transboundary Air Pollution regime in Europe has undercut the effectiveness of the data-reporting requirements and the secretariat's ability to analyze the relevant data.[48] Large data gaps exist regarding the production, use, trade, management, and potential environmental and human health consequences of many known toxic chemicals and perhaps the majority of commercial chemicals.[49] Less than a third of the parties to the Desertification Convention had submitted their national action programs as of COP–6 in 2003, despite repeated decisions of the COP urging parties to do so.

Emphasizing and providing support for regular and harmonized reporting from all parties represents an effective and financially efficient opportunity to enhance regime compliance and effectiveness. For example, CITES requires that countries provide annual reports, which include export and import permit data, as well as biennial reports on legislative, regulative, and administrative measures undertaken to improve implementation and enforcement. For many years, the secretariat repeatedly expressed frustration with the quality and quantity of reports it received from parties. In 1991, parties adopted a resolution that failure to file the required annual report on time is an infraction of the treaty. A list of countries committing infractions was compiled and circulated publicly. In April 1993, the secretariat sent a letter to countries telling them that if they did not file reports, that failure would be considered a "major implementation problem" under the convention. The letter further offered the assistance of the secretariat in preparing and filing the reports. As a result of these measures, the number of the reports increased and their timeliness and quality improved.[50] Observers believe that regular and harmonized reporting from parties to the Basel, Rotterdam, and Stockholm Conventions would allow for far more accurate assessments of global levels and trends in the production, use, generation, transport, management, and disposal of hazardous chemicals. It would also make it easier to monitor progress in implementing these conventions and improve the ability to direct international policies toward areas where they would have the most impact.[51]

However, even when parties submit reports on time and with the required information, some conventions fail to give the secretariat or another body the necessary authority or resources to evaluate and verify information properly. This limits the value that regular reporting can have, for example, in revealing areas in need of technical or financial assistance or in producing information relevant to placing public pressure on governments to comply with an agreement.

In the absence of formal mechanisms, some regimes, secretariats, and governments depend on cooperation with NGOs, IOs, academics, and industry to help monitor and enhance different aspects of compliance. For example, governments, the major industries in the private sector, and NGOs monitor compliance with the Montreal Protocol. International NGOs also work closely with the CITES secretariat to monitor wildlife trade. TRAFFIC—the wildlife trade monitoring program of the WWF and IUCN—helps ensure that wildlife trade is at sustainable levels and in accordance with domestic and international laws and agreements. Established in 1976, TRAFFIC is now a network of twenty-one offices organized in seven regional programs. TRAFFIC assists in official investigations and enforcement actions; provides expertise for formulation, review, and amendment of wildlife trade legislation; and liaises with key wildlife consumers, producers, and managers to determine how best to dissuade unsustainable and illegal trade and to advocate to stakeholders solutions to problems identified.[52] Despite such examples, however, meaningful improvements in compliance will require increased emphasis and support for reporting and monitoring accompanied by greater authority and resources for secretariats to review, publicize, and act on the information.

PHOTO 4.2   Rifles and ivory tusks taken from poachers in Kenya, with the assistance of the NGO, TRAFFIC. Photo by Rob Barnett/TRAFFIC.

Augment Coordination Between Regimes and Conventions

The broadest issue-areas in global environment politics now involve multiple and overlapping global and regional regimes, international organizations, and soft-law guidelines and procedures. Indicative examples include the atmosphere (ozone, climate and LRTAP regimes), chemicals and wastes (the Basel, Rotterdam, and Stockholm Conventions; the Montreal Protocol and various regional treaties), biodiversity, wildlife and habitat protection (CBD, CITES, Ramsar Convention, the Convention on Migratory Species, and a host of wildlife-specific treaties), oceans (the Law of the Sea, the London Convention, and MARPOL), and fisheries (the Fish Stocks Agreement, the FAO Code of Conduct for Responsible Fisheries, and numerous regional fisheries agreements). The Desertification Convention contains provisions that address biodiversity, climate change, forests, and freshwater resources, as well as other issues that overlap with other regimes. Improved coordination among treaties and organizations with overlapping concerns would improve compliance with environmental regimes by (a) helping to remove the obstacles produced by the lack of such coordination (outlined above); (b) allowing for more effective use of limited resources; (c) avoiding unnecessary duplication of tasks; and (d) potentially creating unforeseen opportunities where efforts for joint initiatives could improve reporting, monitoring, environmental assessments, financing, and implementation.

The potential for such activity is broadly recognized. UNEP has repeatedly addressed the issue, and environmental ministers have discussed it in a variety of fora.[53] UNCED and the WSSD both endorsed the concept. A variety of secretariats consult regularly. A formal initiative to address issues relating to increasing coordination in the chemicals sector is under way[54] and the Basel, PIC, and POPs secretariats are co-located in Geneva. These are only first steps, however, and far more significant work remains to be done. Opportunities for enhanced coordination that have received particular attention and exhibit promise include examining and eliminating regulatory gaps or conflicts; coordinating reporting schedules and formats; co-locating more secretariats and relevant international organizations; coordinating the scheduling of COPs of related regimes; supporting ratification to remove membership gaps; integrating appropriately related implementation activities; and establishing common regional centers and other programs for capacity building and the provision of financial and technical assistance.

Trade Sanctions

Improving compliance may require additional sticks as well as more carrots. In some cases, trade sanctions against parties found in willful noncompliance could be employed. Although little support exists for trade sanctions as a remedy for treaty violations, they would make sense in situations such as illegal, unreported, and unregulated fishing, where sanctions (in this example, curbs on fishing rights or imports) could be directly related to the failure to comply with the treaty. To be effective, trade sanctions must be credible and potent. States that are consciously violating a treaty or measures adopted by a multilateral environmental agreement must be convinced not only that they will face penalties for the violation but also that the costs of the violation will exceed the gains expected from it.[55] Trade sanctions could represent such a cost in some cases, but the larger the economy of the violating country, the less likely it is that sanctions will bite hard enough.

The use of trade sanctions in situations of noncompliance, however, is controversial. Although some treaties, such as the Montreal Protocol and CITES, already embody sanctions as a potential punishment for noncompliance, this is a subject of much debate within MEAs and the WTO. The key question is within the economic framework of multilateral trade: Under what conditions should national governments have policy space to pursue ecological goals by restricting international trade in certain goods to promote the conservation of environmental resources harmed by production of those goods?[56] (See chapter 5 for more about this debate.) Furthermore, developing countries do not support the use of sanctions; they cite the UN Charter and the Rio Declaration's claims that sanctions may violate national sovereignty and could be used as a disguised form of trade protectionism.[57]

Negative Publicity

Fear of negative publicity has proven to be a meaningful deterrent to treaty violations. Therefore, environmental conventions could create mechanisms by which secretariats or COPs would publicly consider complaints brought by states, IOs, NGOs, or other actors regarding noncompliance by a particular party.[58] The Internet, global television networks, and improved telecommunications make it easier, cheaper, and faster than ever to collect and distribute information, and evidence exists that such campaigns can work. Norway lost money and public support when the European Union boycotted Norwegian fish products because of Norway's position on whaling. The U.S. agricultural industry was forced to respond to European boycotts and negative publicity with regard to genetically modified crops. Negative publicity can also be used to expose and deter corporate noncompliance with national laws. In the United States, for example, environmental groups have been an important complement to the government's enforcement efforts, in particular, when they serve as watchdogs reporting violations to the appropriate authorities.

INCREASING FINANCIAL RESOURCES FOR IMPLEMENTING GLOBAL ENVIRONMENTAL REGIMES

The issue of financing the implementation of environmental regimes has been and will continue to be a central issue in global environmental politics. Providing developing countries with financial and technical assistance to help them comply with their obligations under environmental treaties and soft-law regimes such as Agenda 21 remains a crucial challenge.[59]

External assistance for developing countries declined in the last decade of the twentieth century. Despite the call in Rio for increased **official development assistance** (ODA), levels fell from $58.3 billion in 1992 to $53.1 billion in 2000. Most of the least-developed countries suffered a decline in ODA of at least 25 percent, and seven countries, all in Africa, saw ODA reduced by more than 50 percent.[60] (See fig. 4.1.) At the UN Conference on Financing for Development, held in Monterrey, Mexico, in March 2002, major donors, including the United States and the European Union, announced increases in ODA levels that were expected to generate an additional $12 billion per year by 2006. As a result, net ODA levels have risen again over the past few years as governments have fulfilled their pledges and contributed additional funds for emergency relief, debt relief, and aid to Afghanistan and Iraq.[61] Nevertheless, slower growth worldwide and deeper indebtedness in the poorest developing countries has put greater pressure on national budgets for the environment in general, not to mention compliance with environmental treaties.

Each of the opportunities outlined in the previous section for improving compliance would also require additional financial and technical resources. More broadly, successfully expanding and implementing the newest generation of global environmental regimes, including those for climate, biodiversity, desertification, fisheries, and chemicals, will require transitions to environmentally sound technologies and new strategies for natural resource management. Such transitions will be expensive and require significant investments both to implement and ease the transition as well as to overcome

FIGURE 4.1   Net ODA Flows, 1972–2003

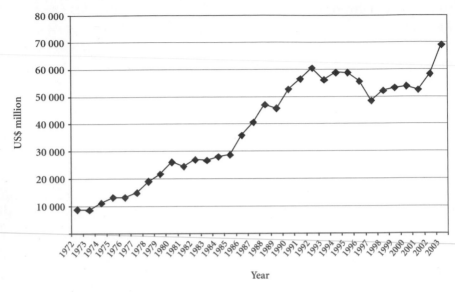

ODA flows include both bilateral and multilateral assistance. Multilateral assistance includes contributions to UN-related funds, EU funds, the World Bank, IMF, and other organizations and funds, including conventions and the GEF.
Data Source: OECD/DAC, *Statistical Annex of the 2004 Development Cooperation Report* (Paris: OECD, 2005).

likely resistance from powerful economic and political interests in developing and industrialized countries alike.

Most treaties have no separate funding mechanism; the ozone regime is the exception. The Montreal Protocol is the first regime in which the financing mechanism was a central issue in the negotiations; it demonstrated that donor and recipient countries participating in a global environmental regime can devise a financial mechanism that equitably distributes power and that effectively links financial assistance with compliance. The Global Environment Facility (GEF), which the biodiversity, climate, desertification, and chemicals regimes use as their financing mechanism, has a somewhat similar governance structure but faces more difficult issues in trying to link assistance with global environmental benefits. The GEF was created in 1991 essentially as an arm of the World Bank, with UNEP and UNDP providing technical and scientific advice. The grants and concessional funds disbursed complement traditional development assistance by covering the additional costs (also known as *agreed incremental costs*) incurred when a national, regional, or global development project also targets global environmental objectives; for example, not for local pollution clean-up but for climate, oceans, biodiversity, and ozone depletion, from which other countries would benefit as well. Initially, the GEF provided funding only for four global environmental issues: ozone depletion, international waters, climate change, and biological diversity. Subsequently, land degradation/desertification and POPs were added to the GEF's portfolio. Since 1991, the GEF has provided $4.5 billion in grants and generated $14.5 billion in co-financing from other partners for projects in developing countries and countries with economies in transition. At its last replenishment in 2002, thirty-two donor countries pledged $3 billion to fund operations between 2002 and 2006.

However, given the immense challenges ahead, the Global Environment Facility is very unlikely to receive sufficient funds from donor countries to enable it to assist developing countries achieve full compliance with the biodiversity, climate change, desertification, and POPs conventions, particularly if their controls expand. And even with the significant expansion of assistance pledged for Africa agreed to at the G-8 meeting in 2005,[62] donor countries do not yet seem to have the political will to provide adequate bilateral funding in support of global environmental objectives.

So what potential sources exist that could provide significant increases in financial resources for implementing global environmental regimes and sustainable development goals? This section outlines several possibilities, some possible in the near term, others farther down the road. They include refocusing existing bilateral and multilateral assistance toward projects supportive of environmental regimes; developing revenue from emissions trading; creating new revenue streams from coordinated taxes on air travel, energy, currency transactions, the arms trade, or pollutant emissions; canceling developing-country debt; and eliminating subsidies for natural resource extraction and shifting the money to conservation. Each of these options has been proposed by governments, NGOs, or other experts in different international fora, and each is theoretically possible. Yet, each faces significant obstacles before it could become international policy.

Refocus Multilateral and Bilateral Assistance Toward Projects That Will Be Supportive of Environmental and Sustainable Development Goals.   Existing ODA programs, which dwarf environmental funding in size, could apply more resources to programs that also enhance environmental goals. Overall ODA flows would not be reduced. Instead, governments would funnel greater levels of aid to programs with shared environment and development goals. Thus, ODA programs focused on industrialization or energy production would support only projects that produce or use high levels of "green" energy, employ significant energy conservation measures, and emit low levels of air or water pollution. Cleaning and redeveloping "brownfields"—former industrial properties containing hazardous substances, pollutants, or contaminants—would enjoy priority over clearing forest land for construction or agriculture. Projects that use or produce toxic chemicals would not be funded. Reuse and recycling projects would be emphasized over mining projects or production processes that require large amounts of raw materials. Funding would be increased to countries that followed these types of guidelines in their own policies and decreased to countries that continued "business as usual."

Donors or recipients wishing to focus all or part of their ODA programs on health and social issues could effectively pursue these goals while also promoting the social bases of sustainable development, including basic health and nutrition, vaccinations, family planning, land preservation, and education—especially for women and girls. Indeed, better health and education are widely shown to contribute to smaller, healthier families, more productive agriculture, higher incomes, and less stress on the environment and natural resources.

Develop Revenue from Emissions Trading. A potential source of financing for greater energy efficiency, zero-emission energy sources, technological innovation, and technological diffusion is emissions trading, such as the mechanism under the Kyoto Protocol (see chapter 3). Under the Kyoto Protocol emissions trading programs, countries or private corporations that significantly reduce their emissions through conservation or by using wind, solar, geothermal, co-generation, or zero-CO_2 emission coal, oil, or gas power plants (currently under development) can sell their excess rights to emit CO_2. By making emission reductions a potential profit source, the competitive nature of market capitalism could be employed to combat climate change.

Title IV of the U.S. Clean Air Act of 1990 established one of the first national systems for emissions trading for meeting sulfur dioxide emissions targets in the electric power sector as a means to reduce acid rain in the United States. In Europe, the European Union Greenhouse Gas Emission Trading Scheme (EU ETS) commenced operation in January 2005 as the largest multicountry, multisector greenhouse gas-emission trading scheme worldwide.

The difficulty is to create and then continually improve such systems so that they work both at the business and the environmental level. It is still too early to tell whether the Kyoto or EU system will work; however, the success of emissions trading programs in the United States for other pollutants, such as SO_x, means that it is at least theoretically possible, although maintaining an effective and efficient trading system for CO_2 represents a more difficult challenge.

Create New Revenue Stream From Coordinated Taxes on Air Travel, Energy, Currency Transactions, the Arms Trade, or Pollutant Emissions. Many ideas exist for global or coordinated national taxes to raise new revenue for sustainable development and protection of the environment.[63] In each, countries would enact similar taxes or user fees and then pool or use the money individually to finance sustainable development and environmental regimes. Taxes would be levied on activities harmful in their own right, and thus reasonable to discourage through taxes, or so small that they would not meaningfully impact individual consumers.

The European Union has called for an air fuel tax to raise funds for environmental projects. The revenue from such a tax, which could generate more than $1 billion in Europe alone,[64] would have the added benefit of encouraging even more fuel economy. A global energy tax of $1 per barrel of oil or its coal equivalent could raise $66 billion annually while acting as a further incentive for conservation. Another well-known proposal is to tax large-scale speculative currency trading. A levy of just 0.005 percent could generate $15 billion a year for environmental projects if enacted in countries through which most of such trading takes place. Larger levies, which have been proposed, would raise even more and also act as a small brake on such speculation, which some argue presents an unnecessary threat to the stability of national currencies.[65] Taxes on arms sales could raise similar sums with appropriate ancillary benefits. Other possibilities include taxes on emissions of toxic chemicals, heavy metals, or other types of air or water pollution. In addition to raising funds for implementing globally agreed-upon environmental goals, the taxes would create additional economic deterrents to unnecessary pollution. An analogous and successful domestic example is the excise tax on CFCs enacted by the United States to help implement its obligations under the ozone regime. The tax has raised several billion dollars for the U.S. Treasury and acted as a significant incentive for companies to speed their transition to alternatives.[66]

Many practical issues exist concerning the administration of such taxes, and the system would be subject to significant concerns about free riders. In addition, some national governments fear losing revenue, some that the money would be wasted, and some that the taxes would be used to create slush funds for international organizations. The U.S. Congress, for example, passed legislation making it illegal for the United States to participate in global taxes. Although a national tax, albeit one enacted in concert with other governments, administered domestically by the United States and with proceeds distributed only by the United States might pass muster against this legislation and meet at least some of the concern expressed by other countries, it would still face formidable political obstacles.

Forgiving Debt Obligations of Developing Countries in Return for Sustainable Development Policy Reforms and Investments.   Debt obligations can place huge burdens on developing countries; sometimes they are forced to mine their natural resources for export and use up budgetary resources at the expense of implementing environmental conventions or sustainable development programs. Implementing aggressive debt-relief programs in concert with agreements by the debtor country to use a specific amount of the savings for environmental programs offers potential to tap an additional source of funds for areas largely neglected by most assistance programs, such as programs needed to combat desertification in Africa.

Several initiatives in this direction have occurred in the past decade. Under pressure from poor countries and NGOs in September 1996, the World Bank and the IMF launched the Initiative for Heavily Indebted Poor Countries (HIPC).[67] The HIPC initiative is an agreement among official creditors designed to help the poorest and most heavily indebted countries escape from unsustainable debt. It enables poor countries to focus their energies on building the policy and institutional foundation for sustainable development and poverty reduction. The initiative is designed to reduce debts to sustainable levels for poor countries that pursue economic and social policy reforms and is used specifically where traditional debt-relief mechanisms will not be enough to help countries exit from the rescheduling process. Unlike earlier debt-relief mechanisms, it deals with debt in a comprehensive way and involves all creditors, including multilateral financial institutions.

Under current rules, thirty-eight countries can potentially receive debt relief under the enhanced HIPC Initiative. By April 2005, twenty-seven countries had received debt relief. Eighteen of these countries had reached the final point in the process and were receiving irrevocable debt relief. Nine countries were in an interim stage and receiving debt service relief. The remaining eleven suffer from persistent governance challenges, civil strife, cross-border armed conflict, substantial arrears, and other problems that prevent them from establishing the track record of government and macroeconomic performance required for participating in the program.[68]

Perhaps the most substantive action occurred at the 2005 G–8 summit, where leaders of the world's eight leading industrialized countries agreed to cancel the debt of eighteen of the world's poorest nations and to increase overall aid to Africa to $50 billion by 2010.[69] This debt cancellation addresses some of the countries that were eligible for HIPC but could not participate because of the exigencies of their domestic situation and the structural adjustments required by the program. Several broad alliances of various religious, charitable, environmental, and labor groups (of which the best known is the Jubilee network) continue to advocate debt cancellation.[70] Although the HIPC and G–8 initiatives represented significant steps, debt levels and related structural adjustment programs remain an impediment to successful environmental protection and sustainable development in many developing countries.

Eliminating Subsidies in Industrialized Countries for Use of Natural Resources (Water and Energy) and for Environmentally Harmful Activities (Use of Pesticides and Fertilizers) and Shifting Resources to Conservation. One direct method for increasing the sustainability of agriculture, forestry, and fisheries is to eliminate subsidies that contribute to the unsustainable use and long-term degradation of the affected land, forests, and fish. The period from the 1960s through the 1980s saw a rapid expansion of subsidies to natural resource production worldwide. Although some reductions occurred in subsidies to agriculture and fisheries in the 1990s, the scale of environmentally harmful subsidies remains staggering.[71] For example, estimates of subsidies in the energy, road transport, water use, and agricultural sectors in the mid–1990s ranged from approximately $700 billion to $870 billion annually.[72] (See chapter 5.)

Despite the overall financial and environmental advantages of ending such subsidies, governments tend to keep such policies in place in response to political pressures and powerful economic elites. The WTO Agreement on Subsidies and Countervailing Measures attempts to discipline the use of subsidies, but it concentrates only on subsidized imports that hurt domestic producers. It will take a concerted effort to fashion the necessary national and international consensus needed to end or even severely limit subsidies impeding conservation. Doing so, however, would release billions of dollars that currently subsidize environmental degradation, perhaps allowing some to be used for environmental protection.

CONCLUSION

Regime building does not end with the signing and ratification of a global environmental convention but continues through the implementation of the convention. Usually, this period involves efforts to strengthen the regime and increase its effectiveness, considered by many to be the most important parts of the regime life cycle. The effectiveness of an environmental regime, the extent to which it produces measurable improvements in the environment, is a function of regime design, particularly the strength of the key control provisions aimed at addressing the environmental threat; the level of implementation, the extent to which countries adopt domestic regulations to enact the agreement; and compliance, the degree to which countries conform to these regulations and other regime rules and procedures.

Many factors can inhibit or promote the effectiveness of an environmental regime. Among the most fundamental are four sets of obstacles that can make it difficult to create regimes with strong and binding control measures: (1) structural or systemic obstacles that arise from the structure of the international system, the structure of international law, and the structure of the global economic system; (2) a lack of sufficient concern, a hospitable contractual environment, or necessary capacity; (3) the time lag and the lowest-common-denominator procedural obstacles; and (4) obstacles that stem from the characteristics of global environmental issues themselves. These include the inherent links between environmental issues and important economic and political issues, unequal adjustment costs, scientific complexity and uncertainty, time-horizon conflicts, the presence of different core values and beliefs, and the large numbers of actors that need to cooperate when addressing a global environmental problem.

Once regimes are created, certain factors can then negatively influence national compliance with their requirements. These include inadequate translation of regime rules into domestic law; insufficient capacity to enact, administer, or enforce the domestic regulations; a lack of respect for rule of law; the relative costs of compliance; inadequate financial and technical assistance; an inability to monitor compliance; poorly designed regimes; and the lack of coordination among the increasingly large number of environmental conventions.

Despite these obstacles, options exist to strengthen compliance with environmental agreements. Among the most important: augmenting domestic capacity; increasing and more effectively targeting technical and financial assistance; enhancing secretariat capacity and responsibility; emphasizing and supporting improved national reporting and monitoring; enhancing coordination between regimes and conventions; applying trade sanctions; and utilizing negative publicity.

Lack of financial resources is often cited as the primary reason why many countries do not effectively implement and comply with global environmental regimes. External financing for environmental agreements is closely linked to the economic and political interests and resources of industrialized countries. Given the current reluctance among donor countries to increase financing for environmental regimes, and the potentially large amounts needed to assure their effectiveness, it appears necessary for regimes to seek alternative sources for such resources. This chapter has outlined several ways to increase funding for global environmental regimes, including refocusing existing bilateral and multilateral assistance toward projects directly supportive of environmental regimes and sustainable development; utilizing incentives from emissions trading; creating new revenue streams from coordinated taxes on energy, currency transactions, arms trading, or pollutant emissions; canceling debts owed by poor countries; and eliminating subsidies for natural resource extraction and shifting some of the savings to conservation.

In spite of daunting obstacles that prevent the creation and effective implementation of international environmental agreements, successful conventions and protocols do exist. It is also important to examine the obstacles to creating strong agreements and options for increasing compliance and significantly augmenting the financial resources available for implementing environmental regimes so that we can gain insight into additional tools for creating effective global environmental policy. Although we have outlined what leading experts see as policy prescriptions that could help solve these problems, the most important factor needed to meet the challenge is political will. Political will often hinges on domestic economic policies or interests that still subscribe to the social paradigm that justifies nearly unlimited exploitation of nature and places certain economic and political interests above the environment.

DISCUSSION QUESTIONS

1. What are some of the obstacles encountered in creating strong environmental regimes? What examples of these obstacles can you see in the cases discussed in chapter 3?

2. What is a least-common-denominator agreement? Can you give an example of a provision in a treaty that is the result of such an agreement?

3. What are some of the problems regarding implementation and compliance by parties to a convention? How might some of these problems be overcome?

4. What options for strengthening compliance with an agreement do you think may be the most effective in the short term? Why?

5. Why has the proliferation of environmental conventions possibly had a negative impact on implementation? How do you think this might be overcome?

6. Which of the options available for generating additional financial support for the implementation of environmental conventions do you think would be the most effective? How would you overcome political resistance to this option?

5

·····<O>·····

Economics, Development, and the Future of Global Environmental Politics

In recent years, global environmental politics have become increasingly intertwined with the politics and the concept of sustainable development as environmental issues have impinged on core economic and social development concerns of countries. Trade and environment, the financing of sustainable development, HIV/AIDS, and unsustainable consumption patterns were not on the international political agenda twenty years ago. But several developments converged to change all that: the emergence of environmental problems and regimes that require social and economic transitions in all societies, the recognition of these issues during the first global negotiations encompassing environmental and economic policies—the 1992 United Nations Conference on Environment and Development; the subsequent United Nations global conferences in the 1990s covering issues including women, population, social development and human settlements; the UN Millennium Summit; and the growing influence of the World Trade Organization.

North-South economic issues have become a crucial element of the political context of global environmental politics. The perception of many developing countries of global economic relations as fundamentally inequitable often shapes their policy responses to global environmental issues and their strategies for negotiating on issues as different as elephants and climate. Moreover, unfavorable trends in North-South economic relations since the mid-1970s not only have sharpened the inequalities between North and

South but also have affected the bargaining position of the South on issues involving North-South economic relations, including environmental issues.

As linkages with economic and social development have multiplied, the boundaries of global environmental politics have broadened and, sometimes, have been lost within the larger context of sustainable development. This chapter looks at three elements in this broadening debate: North-South economic relations and the environment; the clash between the drive for free trade and the drive to protect the environment; and the role of environmental politics in the evolution of global economic and social development policies.

NORTH-SOUTH INEQUALITIES AND THE ENVIRONMENT

In 1974, encouraged by a surge in commodity prices and the Organization of Petroleum Exporting Countries' (OPEC) successful manipulation of oil supplies in the early 1970s, developing countries attempted to restructure the global economic system. The South called for a bold but largely unrealistic plan, the **New International Economic Order** (NIEO); a list of demands for redistribution of wealth, which would include a new system of international commodity agreements; a unilateral reduction of barriers to imports from developing states in industrialized countries; the enhancement of developing countries' capabilities in science and technology; increased Northern financing of technology transfer; and changes in patent laws to lower the cost of such transfers.[1] It was a strong bid for equality.

From the late 1970s onward, however, the NIEO faded from the global political agenda as economic trends turned against the South; the North consequently felt even more strongly that it could disregard such Southern demands for change. Yet, although some Northern observers might have considered the South's NIEO agenda "discredited,"[2] it remained unfinished business for much of the South and was still considered a goal "very much worth pursuing."[3] By the beginning of the 1990s, a sense of new vulnerabilities, the persisting pangs of an unfinished agenda, and the opportunity of renewing a North-South dialogue under environmental auspices began to serve as a new rallying point and translated into a renewed assertiveness by the South, especially around the broad issue of sustainable development.[4]

Economic Realities

Commodity prices, debt, and barriers to free trade have all shaped the economic picture in developing countries since the 1980s. Falling commodity prices devastated the economies of countries that were heavily dependent on commodity exports. Between 1980 and 1991, the weighted index for thirty-three primary commodities exported by developing countries, not including energy, declined by 46 percent.[5] Meanwhile heavy debt burdens, taken on at a time when commodity prices were high and Northern banks were freely lending dollars from Arab oil revenues, siphoned off much of the foreign exchange of many developing countries. By 1995, the total external debt of the least-developed countries was $136 billion, a sum that represented 112.7 percent of their GNP that year.[6]

During the early 1990s, trade barriers erected by industrialized countries against imports of manufactured and processed goods from the developing countries continued to increase even as most developing countries (under pressure from international financial institutions) were lowering their own barriers to imports.[7] Tariffs on textiles and clothing and other products of particular importance to developing countries' exports tended to be the highest tariff rates in industrialized countries, which often increase tariff rates on goods in proportion to the degree of processing involved, a process called "tariff escalation." New kinds of **nontariff barriers** to trade (such as antidumping and countervailing duty actions), export-restraint agreements (such as the Multi-Fibre Arrangement), and direct subsidies have been used to protect industries in the industrialized countries against imports from developing countries. To this day, developing countries are suspicious of anything called a nontariff barrier.

The negotiations on liberalization of world trade, known as the **Uruguay Round,** began in 1985 under the auspices of the Global Agreement on Tariffs and Trade (GATT) and concluded in April 1994. The Uruguay Round was supposed to reduce some of these barriers, but the overall impact appears to have been slight. Although the average level of protection in the industrial countries is relatively low, there are serious barriers to entry in certain sectors of particular interest to developing countries, including agriculture, textiles, clothing, and fish and fish products. Developing countries continue to express concern about preference erosion, tariff escalation, and the risks in being left out of the proliferating free trade areas and customs unions.[8]

There has also been growing discontent among developing countries toward developed countries' agricultural policies. Several developing countries have complained that they have liberalized their agricultural markets only to face domestic competition from subsidized agricultural imports from developed economies. At the same time, they charge that developed countries' markets remain relatively closed to agricultural exports from developing countries through such nontariff barriers to trade as sanitary measures and country-of-origin labeling. Exacerbating the situation, developing countries' attempts to modernize their agriculture infrastructure have been hampered by depressed commodity prices and a subsequent decline in investment in agriculture.

Despite the rapid growth in East Asian economies in the 1980s, the income gap between the industrialized world and the developing world continued to grow. Whereas in 1960 the richest 20 percent of the world controlled 70 percent of global gross domestic product (GDP), by 2000 the richest 20 percent controlled 80 percent of global GDP.[9]

Existing patterns of North-South economic relations have also contributed to the degradation and depletion of natural resources. Sudden increased demand in the North for certain commodities has increased their price and stimulated exploitation of the resource. When Japan began major imports of tropical timber in the 1960s and 1970s, for example, it raised tropical timber prices and encouraged the Philippines and Indonesia to step up their exports of raw logs and processed timber products, regardless of long-range environmental and development implications.[10]

But the pressure on natural resources also increases when falling commodity prices are combined with debt burdens and protectionism. Countries that are indebted and heavily dependent on commodity exports often have adjusted to falling prices by increasing the volume of commodity exports, thus depleting agricultural land, forests, and other natural resources. For example, several of the Sahelian countries in sub–Saharan Africa increased their cotton production by 20 percent in the 1980s, even as world cotton prices fell by 30 percent. The expansion of cotton production forced grain farmers off their land, encouraged the heavy use of pesticides, and exacerbated the problem of soil depletion and desertification.[11]

Northern protectionism may also force developing countries to exploit their natural resources more heavily. Subsidies to agricultural exporters in the United States and other OECD countries exacerbate trade imbalances and developing-country indebtedness because they deprive developing-country producers of markets and depress world prices for those goods. European beef exporters undercut African producers by massive subsidies, for example, and thus dominated African markets.[12] Subsidized European sugar exports have decreased world prices and reduced export opportunities for other exporters. Oxfam estimated that EU sugar subsidies translated into economic losses in the region of $494 million for Brazil, $151 million for Thailand, and $60 million each for South Africa and India in 2002.[13] Depressed food prices discourage farmers in food-exporting countries from making the investments in soil conservation and water management necessary for sustainable agricultural development. Meanwhile, subsidized prices for exportable agricultural commodities provide powerful incentives for the agricultural sector in developed countries to use more fertilizers, pesticides, and water; thus, groundwater supplies are polluted and underground aquifers depleted.[14]

Northern and Southern Perspectives on the Global Environment

Historically, developing countries have perceived global environmental issues as a distinctively North-South issue and, sometimes, as an effort to sabotage their development aspirations. This was exemplified in the 1971 "Founex Report," which was produced by a group of Southern intellectuals as part of the preparatory process for the Stockholm Conference on the Human Environment.[15] The tone and substance of the report foreshadowed, nearly exactly, what was soon to become the rhetoric of the South not only during the NIEO debates in the early 1970s but also during UNCED and subsequent global environmental conferences. The Founex Report provides critical testimony that (a) these interests have remained unchanged over time; (b) they are the same interests that informed the NIEO ideology; and (c) these same interests lie at the heart of today's global politics of sustainable development.[16] As the Founex Report puts it:

> The developing countries would clearly wish to avoid, as far as feasible, the [environmental] mistakes and distortions that have characterized the patterns of development of the industrialized societies. However, the major environmental problems of the developing countries are essentially of a different kind. They are predominantly problems that reflect the poverty and very lack of development in their societies. . . . These are problems, no less than those of industrial pollution, that clamor for attention in the context of the concern with human environment. They are problems which affect the greater mass of mankind. . . . In [industrialized] countries, it is appropriate to view development as a cause of environmental problems. . . . In [the Southern] context, development becomes essentially a cure for their major environmental problems.[17]

Within this context, although many officials of developing countries, particularly in environment ministries, recognize the seriousness of local and global environmental degradation for their own economic future, many of them regard environmental regimes as a means by which industrialized countries will maintain their control over resources and technology, or even gain control over resources now located in the South. One developing-country delegate to the second meeting of the parties to the Montreal Protocol in 1990 declared that for "some countries" the protocol was a "pretext to place new obstacles in the way of efforts by developing countries to develop their economies."[18] And some officials of developing countries viewed the efforts of industrialized countries to bring them into a global climate-change convention as a ploy to constrain economic development in the South so that the developed countries could dominate the world's remaining oil resources.[19]

Developing countries, many of which were already subject to macroeconomic policy conditions on loans from multilateral banks, reacted strongly to the suggestion that industrialized countries would also impose environmental conditions on economic assistance or restrict their exports on environmental grounds. The Conference of the **Non-Aligned Movement,** held in September 1998, although subscribing to the values of environmental protection, labor standards, intellectual property protection, sound macroeconomic management, and the promotion and protection of human rights, rejected all attempts to use these issues as conditionalities and pretexts for restricting market access or aid and technology flows to developing countries.[20]

Despite growing disparities among the developing countries between rapidly industrializing countries, such as China, India, Malaysia, and Brazil, and debt-ridden countries that have experienced little or no growth since the 1980s, such as most of sub–Saharan Africa, Myanmar, and Haiti, developing countries share a common view of the relationship between global environmental issues and North-South economic relations. They insist that the industrialized countries, because of their historical dominance in the production and consumption of CFCs and combustion of fossil fuels, are responsible for the thinning of the ozone layer and global warming. More generally, they identify wasteful Northern patterns of excessive consumption as a key cause of global environmental degradation. According to UNDP's 1998 *Human Development Report,* the 20 percent of the world's people in the highest-income countries account for 86 percent of total private consumption expenditures; the poorest 20 percent for a minuscule 1.3 percent. More specifically, the richest fifth

- consume 45 percent of all meat and fish; the poorest fifth, 5 percent
- consume 58 percent of total energy; the poorest fifth, less than 4 percent

CARTOON 5.1   "And may we continue to be worthy of consuming a disproportionate share of this planet's resources." Drawing by Lorenz 1992, *The New Yorker Magazine,* Inc.

- have 74 percent of all telephone lines; the poorest fifth, 1.5 percent
- consume 84 percent of all paper; the poorest fifth, 1.1 percent
- own 87 percent of the world's vehicle fleet; the poorest fifth, less than 1 percent[21]

Based on such comparisons, developing-country officials as well as NGOs began to demand in the early 1990s that industrialized countries reduce their share of what they call "environmental space"—the use of the earth's limited natural resources and environmental services—and permit developing countries to use more of that environmental space for raising their living standards.[22]

Southern concerns about environmental space and resource transfers have led to the institutionalization of several principles that emerged in Rio and have become a feature of all post–Rio environmental negotiations, including the Convention to Combat Desertification, the Cartagena Protocol on Biosafety, and the chemicals conventions. The first of these principles is "additionality," which arose out of the Southern concern that environmental issues would attract international aid away from traditional developmental issues. Developing countries were concerned that instead of raising new funds for dealing with global environmental issues, the North and international finance institutions would simply divert resources previously targeted for development towards the environment. Thus, the principle of additionality sought to ensure that new monies would be made available to deal with global environmental issues.[23]

Despite assurances given to the South, however, this principle suffered a setback soon after UNCED, during the negotiation of the Desertification Convention. Early in these negotiations, it became clear that no new funds would be made available. This development dismayed developing countries, particularly those in Africa, and became a major source of contention during the negotiations. Ultimately, the Global Mechanism was established under the CCD, its role essentially being to use existing resources more efficiently to meet the action needs of the convention.[24] Even though in 2002 the GEF decided to include desertification activities in its funding, the desertification negotiations and the lack of new and additional financial resources to combat desertification severely damaged the principle of additionality.[25]

Developing countries also believe that the North should bear the financial burden of measures to reverse ecological damage. This is often referred to as the principle of "common but differentiated responsibilities." This principle acknowledges that because some nations have a greater and more direct responsibility for having created environmental problems, they have a greater responsibility for addressing them. Although global environmental problems are the concern of all nations, and all nations should work toward their solution, responsibility for action should be differentiated in proportion to the responsibility for creating the problem and the financial and technical resources available for taking effective action.[26] The willingness of Northern countries to give developing countries a relatively long grace period before they have to comply with the ozone and climate change conventions reflects the general acceptance of this principle. But the North generally emphasizes the responsibility of all countries to contribute to solving global environmental problems, which implies a need for developing countries to avoid duplicating the unsustainable historical development patterns of the industrialized world.

Although this principle enjoys broad support and has been explicitly acknowledged in nearly all international environmental agreements since Rio, it does face a challenge in the UNFCCC, with the U.S. call for developing nations, especially India and China, to reduce their greenhouse gas emissions. However, developing countries have become increasingly articulate about industrialized-country responsibility for the problem and the implications for commitments to emissions reductions. During the negotiations of the Kyoto Protocol, for example, Brazil presented an analysis that compared the relative responsibility of Annex I (industrialized) countries and of non–Annex I (developing) countries for climate change, not just in carbon dioxide emissions in a given year, but in carbon dioxide concentrations from historical emissions. It showed that the responsibility of non–Annex I countries for accumulated emissions would not equal that of Annex I countries until the middle of the twenty-second century.[27]

The principle of common but differentiated responsibilities has also led to demands from the South for "new and additional" funding for developing countries' implementation of environmental agreements. However, a sharp reduction in ODA levels in the 1990s and the failure of wealthy countries to amend trade policies that harm the interests of poor countries has increasingly irritated the developing countries. In response, developing countries started to use the threat of retreating from previous consensus agreements on global environmental issues as leverage on the donor countries. At the Earth Summit +5 (the 1997 Special Session of the UN General Assembly to review the implementation of Agenda 21 and the other Rio agreements), the G-77 and China refused to oppose proposals by oil-exporting states to delete all references to reducing consumption of fossil fuels. This tactic failed, however, to shake the veto exercised by donor countries on targets for ODA.[28] Commitments made at the UN Conference on Financing for Development, in March 2002, reversed the ODA decline in 2003 and 2004; however, the current and projected levels of ODA still fall far short of the estimates of what is necessary to achieve internationally agreed development goals.

The third principle is the "polluter pays principle," which seeks to ensure that the costs of environmental action, economic and other, will be borne by those who created the need for that action. As with other aspects of these Rio principles, the South has argued that the polluter pays principle has been steadily diluted. They point to an increasing pattern of pushing treaty implementation steadily southwards, including in the climate, desertification, and biodiversity regimes, by seeking relatively fewer changes in behavior patterns in the North and relatively more in the South—even though it was Northern behavior that gave rise to many problems in the first place.[29]

Another consistent theme in developing-country views of global environmental issues is the inequality in governing structures of international organizations such as the World Bank, which allows a minority of donor countries to outvote the rest of the world. Developing countries have demanded that institutions making decisions on how to spend funds on the global environment should have a "democratic" structure, that is, one in which each country is equally represented. Thus, developing countries did some of their toughest bargaining in negotiations relating to the environment when they resisted the donor countries' proposed governance structure for the Global Environment Facility.

The South also has demanded that transfer of environmental technologies on concessional or preferential terms be part of all agreements and treaties. In the Montreal Protocol negotiations, for instance, developing states demanded a guarantee from the industrialized countries that corporations would provide them with patents and technical knowledge on substitutes for CFCs. In 1990, India tried unsuccessfully to have language included in the amended protocol that would make the obligations of developing states to phase out CFCs subject to the private transfer of technology.

Needless to say, developing countries remain frustrated with global environmental politics. This attitude is clearly related to convictions that the global economic system has always been, and continues to be, skewed in favor of the advanced industrialized countries. On the one hand, one can argue that the developing countries, which had largely rejected the global environmental agenda in the 1970s, have accepted most of that agenda. The concept of sustainable development has allowed developing countries to incorporate long-standing concerns about economic and social development into the environmental agenda; by doing so, they have influenced the nature of global environmental discourse.[30]

At the same time, the South claims few benefits from its continuing involvement in global environmental politics. Much of the focus of North-South environmental relations since Rio has been focused on what the South sees as the failure of the North to deliver what had been promised or implied at Rio—new and additional financial resources, technology transfer, and capacity building. As the concept of sustainable development loses its policy edge, and as the key principles of additionality, common but differentiated responsibilities, and polluter pays are steadily eroded (at least from the view of South), developing countries have a diminishing interest in staying engaged in global environmental politics. Although Southern disenchantment may not turn into total disengagement, it is certainly not conducive to meaningful North-South partnerships for what remain pressing global environmental challenges.[31]

TRADE AND THE ENVIRONMENT

The effects of trade policy on the environment have often been an issue in global environmental politics. However, the global trade system evolved for decades without a thought about its impact on the environment. When the General Agreement on Tariffs and Trade (GATT), the central pillar of the international trading system, was negotiated just after World War II, there was no mention of the word *environment*. At that time, no one saw much connection between trade liberalization and environmental protection. In fact, for the next forty years, trade and environmental policymakers pursued their respective agendas on parallel tracks that rarely, if ever, intersected. The wake-up call for environmentalists was the U.S. ban on tuna from Mexico and Venezuela on the ground that their fleets did not meet U.S. standards for minimizing dolphin kills in tuna fishing. In 1991, the GATT declared that the U.S. ban was illegal under the rules of international trade. U.S. environmentalists were alarmed that a national environmental law could be overturned by the GATT and began to take seriously the environmental implications of trade.[32]

But it was not until the United States began to negotiate a free trade agreement with Mexico that U.S. environmentalists saw a way to influence the process. By 1992, trade and environment had become a high-profile international political issue. The North American Free Trade Agreement (NAFTA) was seen as a symbol of economic integration between countries at different stages of economic development. There was a concern among environmentalists and organized labor that a trade agreement with Mexico might trigger a downward spiral in environmental and labor standards on both sides of the border as industry claims of competitive disadvantage induced governments to relax their environmental and labor regulations.[33] U.S. environmentalists worked closer than ever before with organized labor in the United States and with Mexican environmental groups and workers' organizations. It marked the beginning of a broader and mutual understanding among labor, environmentalists, and consumers. The result was the first international trade agreement that included supplemental agreements on labor and environmental issues.

The GATT and the World Trade Organization (WTO) constitute a regime that seeks to promote a common set of international trade rules, a reduction in tariffs and other trade barriers, and the elimination of discriminatory treatment in international trade relations.[34] The WTO, which was created in 1995 pursuant to the Uruguay Round trade agreement, has the mandate to rule on a broad spectrum of issues from trade in goods and services to intellectual property rights, including issues affecting human health, the use of natural resources, and the protection of the environment.

The preamble to the 1994 treaty that established the WTO recognized that the organization should ensure "the optimal use of the world's resources in accordance with the objective of sustainable development."[35] This was a last-minute victory for environmentalists, although the statement is nonbinding. With this in mind, and with a desire to coordinate the policies in the field of trade and environment, when trade ministers approved the results of the Uruguay Round negotiations in Marrakesh in April 1994, they also decided to begin a work program on trade and environment in the WTO. Their decision, which established the WTO's Committee on Trade and Environment (CTE), ensured that the subject would be given a place on the WTO agenda. The CTE has been mandated to address key trade and environment issues, including eco-labeling, the WTO's relationship with multilateral environmental agreements, and the effects of environmental measures on market access. However, the Committee cannot make binding recommendations and has generally proven ineffective in making progress on substantive issues.

In November 2001, the WTO held its fourth Ministerial Conference in Doha, Qatar, where ministers set the current round of trade liberalization negotiations in motion. They had attempted to start a new round of trade negotiations two years earlier at the third Ministerial Conference in Seattle, but the organization was unable to agree on the agenda amid protests against the WTO and its policies by thousands of environmental, labor, and human rights activists. The Doha Ministerial Declaration launched a broad-based round of multilateral trade negotiations on nine topics—eight of which were supposed to be completed as a single undertaking by 2005: implementation, agriculture, services, industrial tariffs, subsidies, antidumping, regional trade agreements, and the environment. The Declaration contained more language on both economic development and environmental issues, including fisheries subsidies, than any of its predecessors. Yet controversy and lack of transparency still surround the WTO.[36] This section will examine some of the key issues along the trade and environment nexus within the context of the WTO; specifically, the relationship

PHOTO 5.1   Protests at the Ministerial Conference in Seattle, Washington, in 1999. Photo by Al Crespo.

between environmental treaties and the WTO, the dispute settlement process, eco-labeling, and subsidies.

Relationship Between Multilateral Environmental Agreements and the WTO

Some multilateral environmental agreements (MEAs) use trade measures to promote cooperation or otherwise achieve their goals. For example, an MEA may use trade measures to regulate trade among parties and non-parties of the product that is considered a major contributor to the environmental degradation the agreement seeks to curtail. Of the hundreds of MEAs currently in existence, more than twenty incorporate trade measures to achieve their goals.[37] This means that the agreements use restraints on trade in particular substances or products, either between parties to the treaty or between parties and non-parties, or both. Although this is a relatively small number of MEAs, they are some of the most important, including CITES, the Montreal Protocol, the Basel Convention, the Rotterdam Convention, and the Cartagena Protocol on Biosafety. Under all five of these treaties, trade in the specified products (endangered species, controlled ozone depleting substances, hazardous wastes, toxic chemicals, and genetically modified organisms) is banned between parties and non-parties.

CITES, which was negotiated in the early 1970s, before trade became an issue for environmentalists, uses a number of different trade measures to promote compliance. It invokes trade restrictions against parties and non-parties to protect listed species of animals and plants threatened with extinction and endangerment. CITES also uses a permit and listing system to prohibit the import or export of listed wildlife and wildlife products unless a scientific finding is made that the trade in question will not threaten the existence of the species. These trade provisions are designed to severely constrict the market demand for wildlife and wildlife products and, it is hoped, reduce the international market demand for the products and thereby discourage the initial taking of the wildlife.

The Montreal Protocol prohibits trade in ozone-depleting substances with non-parties unless the non-party has demonstrated its full compliance with the control measures under the protocol. The Montreal Protocol seeks to restrict the global market in the consumption and production of ozone-depleting substances; it uses trade provisions to encourage the phaseout of these substances and to discourage the establishment of "pollution havens" in which parties shift their manufacturing capabilities to non-parties. In reducing market demand, the protocol reduces the release of these substances into the atmosphere and provides an incentive for the development of benign substitutes.

The Basel Convention uses trade measures to limit the market for the transboundary movement and disposal of hazardous waste between OECD and non-OECD countries. The agreement's trade provisions encourage the management of waste in an environmentally sound manner and with prior informed consent. The convention also provides that a party shall not permit hazardous waste or other wastes to be traded with a non-party unless that party enters into a bilateral, multilateral, or regional agreement.[38]

Under the Rotterdam Convention, parties can decide, from the convention's agreed list of chemicals and pesticides, which ones they will not import. When trade in the controlled substances does take place, labeling and information requirements must be followed. Decisions taken by the parties must be trade neutral; if a party decides not to consent to imports of a specific chemical, it must also stop domestic production of the chemical for domestic use, as well as imports from non-parties.[39]

The Cartagena Protocol on Biosafety states that parties may restrict the import of some living genetically modified organisms as part of a carefully specified risk management procedure. Living GMOs that will be intentionally released to the environment are subject to an advance informed agreement procedure, and those destined for use as food, feed, or processing must be accompanied by documents identifying them.[40]

Trade-restricting measures in an environmental agreement may serve one of two purposes. First, they may control trade itself, where trade is perceived to be the source of environmental damage that the convention seeks to address. CITES, which requires import and export licenses for trade in endangered species, is a good example. Another is the Rotterdam Convention, which calls on parties to notify other parties before certain types of exports, and allows parties to ban some imports. Second, trade-restricting measures play two types of enforcement roles: (1) They provide an additional incentive to join and adhere to the MEA by barring non-parties from trading in restricted goods with parties. Non-parties to the Basel Convention, for example, cannot ship waste to any of the parties, nor can they import it from them. And (2) these measures help ensure the MEA's effectiveness, again by restricting trade with non-parties. This prevents "leakage," that is, situations where non-parties simply increase production of the restricted good and ship it to the parties that have restricted their own production.[41]

The problem is that such measures might conflict with WTO rules. An agreement that says parties can use trade restrictions against some countries (non-parties), but not against others (parties), could violate Articles I, III, and XI of the GATT (provisions addressing most-favored nations and national-treatment principles, as well as provisions on eliminating quantitative restrictions). Such trade-restricting measures might be used in two ways. First, a party could use them against another party (for example, the prior informed consent system of the Rotterdam Convention is used just among parties to the convention). Most analysts argue that this is not a problem because both countries have voluntarily agreed to be bound by the MEA's rules, including the use of trade measures. This may be true where the trade measures in question are spelled out in the agreement, but problems can arise when the agreement spells out objectives only and leaves it to the parties to make domestic laws to achieve them. Parties to the Kyoto Protocol, for example, may fulfill their obligations (spelled out in the protocol) to lower greenhouse gas emissions by any number of trade-restrictive measures (*not* spelled out). Although WTO members have expressed hope that disputes between parties might be settled within the MEAs themselves, a party complaining about the use of such *non-specific trade measures* would almost certainly choose to take its case to the WTO.[42]

Second, a party could use trade measures against a non-party if both are WTO members. Here, the non-party has *not* voluntarily agreed to be subjected to the MEA's trade measures. As with party-to-party measures, the trade-restricting party may be violating the non-party's rights under WTO rules; but here the non-party might take the matter to the WTO even if the measures are spelled out specifically in the MEA.

The relationship between the WTO and MEA trade measures has been part of the CTE's agenda since its establishment in 1995. Current discussions in the CTE are taking place under the mandate of paragraphs 31 and 32 of the Doha Ministerial Declaration, which deals with the relationship between existing WTO rules and specific trade obligations set out in MEAs.[43] Thus far, parties have not made much progress. One group, which includes Argentina, Australia, Canada, India, Malaysia, and the United States, would like to keep the discussions focused on a limited number of MEAs and on the mandatory and explicit trade obligations that they contain. The EU, on the other hand, prefers a broader, conceptual approach, which, in addition to discussing specific MEAs, would also elaborate basic principles underlying the MEA-WTO relationship. The EU submitted a paper on the relationship between WTO rules and MEAs that outlines basic principles for the relationship between WTO rules and MEAs in this regard. These could include the recognition of the importance and necessity of MEAs; that multilateral environmental policy should be made within MEAs; the need for close cooperation and information exchange to enhance the mutual supportiveness between international trade and environment policies; and the recognition that MEAs and the WTO are equal bodies of international law. Although some supported the EU paper, many others, and developing countries in particular, felt it went beyond the scope of the CTE mandate.[44]

Environmental Trade Measures and Dispute Resolution

Many environmental laws authorize restrictions on trade for a variety of policy objectives related to the environment, both domestic and international. Such laws have been called environmental trade measures (ETMs) and include import prohibitions, product standards, standards governing production of natural resource exports, and mandatory eco-labeling schemes.[45] But exporters disadvantaged by such environmental measures sometimes charge that they are intended to protect domestic producers from foreign competition; sometimes, the governments of the exporting countries have brought such complaints to the WTO's dispute resolution panels.

The United States has taken the lead in defending the right to use ETMs for domestic and international environmental objectives, and it is no accident that it has been the target of cases brought before WTO dispute panels.

As the largest single market in world trade, the United States enjoys a unique capability to exert pressure on the environmental and trade policies of other countries, and it has been pressured by U.S. environmental NGOs to do so, especially in marine conservation issues. The United States used trade restrictions in conjunction with its leadership role to end commercial whaling and to protect dolphins from excessive killing by tuna fishermen and marine mammals generally from the use of destructive drift nets. The U.S. threat to ban South Korean fish products from the U.S. market and to prohibit Korean fishing operations in U.S. waters persuaded South Korea to give up whaling as well as drift-net operations in the Pacific Ocean.[46] The United States also banned wildlife-related exports from Taiwan in 1994 after finding that that country had violated CITES by failing to control trade in rhino horn and tiger bone. Although environmentalists see these as justifiable protections, less powerful countries view the United States as throwing its weight around.

Developing countries are concerned about the use of ETMs by industrialized countries, even for domestic environmental purposes, because they view them as potential barriers to their exports. Rapidly industrializing countries fear that the United States and Europe could use ETMs to protect domestic industries.

Environmental NGOs have argued that basic trade rules and institutions have been systematically biased against the environment: The GATT was created in the 1940s when the environment was not an issue; trade rules and mechanisms that are used to handle disputes between trading partners have long been geared primarily to removing barriers to free trade; and the deliberations of GATT/WTO dispute panels are carried out in secret with no opportunity for nongovernmental testimony or briefs. All this adds up to a secret trial (for that is what these deliberations are) without benefit of expert witnesses and observers; and, because there is no appeal, the full weight of its authority prevails. It may be the only international agent that can tell the United States what to do.

GATT/WTO dispute resolution panels have the authority to determine whether a particular trade measure is compatible with the GATT articles based on a complaint by a state alleging that its market access has been unfairly restricted by the measure. These panels consist of trade specialists from three or five contracting parties with no stake in the case or issue and who have been agreed to by both parties to the dispute. Dispute panel rulings are normally submitted to the WTO Council (which includes all parties to the agreement) for approval. Under the old GATT dispute resolution rules, a ruling could be vetoed by one member of the GATT Council. However, the

Uruguay Round agreement provides for automatic acceptance of a dispute panel ruling by the WTO Council within sixty days unless there is a consensus within the council to reject it. Decisions carry real weight. If a country fails to bring its law into conformity with the decision, its trade partners could take retaliatory trade measures against it. This is more threatening to small countries than large trading countries such as the United States or the EU, although it is doubtful that smaller countries will risk taking such measures against the United States or the EU. One example of a small country threatening retaliatory trade measures is when Ecuador, in November 1999, said it would seek WTO approval for retaliatory sanctions against the EU for the EU's failure to comply with the WTO ruling on its banana-import regime, which discriminated against a number of South and Central American banana-exporting countries. As a developing country and a relatively small importer of EU goods, to impose punitive tariffs on EU imports would have little impact on the EU but would have a devastating effect on Ecuador's consumers. Instead, Ecuador said it would be likely to target intellectual property rights and services for retaliation.[47]

The GATT/WTO dispute resolution panels have been a focal point of political contention over the legitimacy of specific ETMs. In several cases it was an action by the United States, mandated by national law to protect the environment, that was challenged.

The first such dispute panel report, the 1991 panel decision on the U.S.-Mexican tuna-dolphin dispute, was a major factor in shaping the politics of trade and environment issues in subsequent years. As a result of the dispute, developing countries became even more determined to create international rules against what they regarded as unfair trade pressures. Meanwhile, the GATT panel decision prompted many environmental NGOs in the United States to press even harder for changes in the GATT, including provision for ETMs covering issues beyond the jurisdiction of the importing country.[48]

Mexico had filed a complaint with the GATT charging that the U.S. embargo against Mexican yellowfin tuna—imposed under an amendment to the 1972 Marine Mammal Protection Act (MMPA) because the Mexican fleet killed dolphins at twice the rate of the U.S. fleet when catching tuna—was a protectionist measure on behalf of the U.S. tuna industry. Mexico and Venezuela asked why they should forgo export earnings and a low-cost source of protein for their own people to reduce the incidental impact on a marine mammal that was not an endangered species.[49]

The GATT panel found that the U.S. ban was a violation of the GATT because it was concerned only with the process of tuna fishing rather than with the product. It also ruled that GATT Article XX, which allows trade restrictions for human health or the conservation of animal or plant life, cannot justify an exception to that rule because the article does not apply beyond U.S. jurisdiction. This was a historic decision. The GATT panel's ruling on the tuna-dolphin issue reflects the tendency of most trade specialists to view restrictions on trade for environmental purposes as setting a dangerous precedent that could destroy the world trade system. That eight governments or agencies spoke against the U.S. tuna ban before the panel and not one party spoke for it may also have had an influence.[50]

The decision came at an embarrassing moment, when the United States and Mexico were negotiating NAFTA. Because both governments really wanted the agreement, the United States was able to work out an agreement with Mexico that prevented the GATT panel decision from being presented to the GATT Council. But in 1994, the European Union brought a second complaint on the U.S. tuna ban to a GATT dispute panel to secure resolution on the principle of extraterritorial unilateral actions. The EU charged that its exports of tuna were adversely affected by the MMPA's "secondary embargo" against imports of tuna from intermediary nations that fail to certify they do not buy tuna from nations embargoed under the law.

The GATT panel found the U.S. ban incompatible with the GATT articles, but it accepted two key contentions of environmental critics of the GATT. It rejected the EU's arguments that dolphins are not an exhaustible natural resource and that Article XX applies only to the protection of resources located within the territory of the country applying the trade measure in question. But it held that such measures could be used only to conserve those resources directly and not to change the policy of another state—a distinction that is difficult, if not impossible, for policymakers to apply in practice—and thus found the U.S. MMPA incompatible with the GATT.[51]

In two other cases, the EU challenged U.S. laws meant to increase fuel efficiency in automobiles sold in the United States—the 1978 "gas guzzler" tax and the **CAFE (Corporate Average Fuel Economy) standards.**[52] The "gas guzzler" tax levied taxes on auto models with fuel efficiencies below 22.5 miles per gallon, with the size of the tax depending on how far the model's rate was from the minimum. The EU argued that treatment of its cars under the measure was discriminatory, since the tax fell disproportionately on cars of European origin, and that it was not effective in conserving fuel because only a small proportion of cars in the U.S. market were subject to the tax. The GATT panel found that the gas guzzler tax did not unfairly protect U.S. auto manufacturers, and that although the measure may not be as effective in fuel conservation as a fuel tax, it has had the desired effect. So here we have a GATT panel with no environmental expertise whatsoever making a judgment about what is the best strategy.

On the CAFE standards, the GATT panel ruled slightly differently. The CAFE legislation, passed in 1975, was aimed at doubling the average fuel efficiency of the automobiles sold in the U.S. market within ten years. It requires that automakers' domestic fleets average at least 27.5 miles per gallon of gasoline and that the total fleet of foreign-made automobiles sold in the U.S. market must meet the same average. Failure to meet the fleet average results in a fine of $5 for every tenth of a mile per gallon below that average multiplied by the number of automobiles in the manufacturer's fleet. U.S. manufacturers can average their large fuel-consuming vehicles with smaller, more fuel-efficient models; European manufacturers, who sell almost entirely larger luxury automobiles in the U.S. market, cannot. The EU argued that the law worked to the disadvantage of limited-line car producers concentrating on the top of the car market and that individual foreign cars are treated differently from domestic cars. The United States insisted that the CAFE legislation is based on objective criteria and was not aimed at affording protection to domestic production.

The panel found that CAFE was intended to promote fuel efficiency. But the requirement that foreign fleets must be accounted for separately, based on ownership and control relationships rather than characteristics of the products themselves, was found to give foreign cars less favorable conditions of competition than domestically produced cars. The panel also found that the requirement was not aimed at conserving fuel. It concluded that the separate foreign fleet accounting could not be justified under the exceptions in Article XX(g) and recommended that the United States be requested to amend the CAFE regulation to eliminate that requirement, which it did.[53]

Two other complaints about environmental trade measures have been brought under WTO dispute settlement rules operating since 1995. In each case, the complainant state challenged national environmental protection measures, and, in each, the WTO ruled against those measures. In the Venezuela Reformulated Gasoline Case, Venezuela and Brazil claimed to be discriminated against by a U.S. EPA rule under the Clean Air Act that required all refineries to make cleaner gasoline using the 1990 U.S. industry standard as a baseline. Because fuel from foreign refineries was not as "clean" in 1990 as that from U.S. refineries, the importing countries were starting their clean-up efforts from a different starting point. The WTO panel ruled in 1997 for Venezuela and Brazil, and EPA set about revising its rules.[54]

In a second case, in January 1997, India, Pakistan, Malaysia, and Thailand charged that a U.S. ban on the importation of shrimp caught by vessels that kill endangered migratory sea turtles violates WTO rules that no nation can use trade restrictions to influence the (fishing) rules of other countries. The United States argued that relatively simple and inexpensive turtle excluder devices (TEDs) can be placed on shrimp trawlers to save the turtles. To implement the U.S. Endangered Species Act, the U.S. Court of International Trade, in response to a lawsuit brought forth by an NGO, the Earth Island Institute, ruled in December 1995 that to export mechanically caught marine shrimp to the United States, countries that trawl for shrimp in waters where marine turtles occur must, from June 1996, be certified by the U.S. government to have equipped their vessels with TEDs. TEDs have been mandatory on all U.S. shrimp trawlers since December 1994. If properly installed and operated, TEDs, while minimizing loss of the shrimp catch, permit most sea turtles to escape from shrimp trawling nets before they drown. The United States argued the trade measure was necessary because sea turtles were threatened with extinction and the use of TEDs on shrimp nets was the only way to effectively protect them from drowning in shrimp nets.

In April 1998, the WTO dispute settlement panel held that the U.S. import ban on shrimp was "clearly a threat to the multilateral trading system" and consequently was "not within the scope of measures permitted under the chapeau of Article XX." The United States appealed the decision, and in October 1998 the appellate body found that the U.S. ban legitimately related to the "protection of exhaustible natural resources" and thus qualified for provisional justification under Article XX(g). This decision represented a step forward for the use of unilateral trade measures for environmental purposes. But the decision also found that the U.S. import ban was applied in an unjustifiably or arbitrarily discriminatory manner and cited seven distinct flaws in the legislation. It found, for example, that the requirement that all exporters adopt "essentially the same policy" as that applied by the United States had an unjustifiably "coercive effect" on foreign countries. It also found that the United States had not seriously attempted to reach a multilateral solution with the four complaining countries, and that the process for certification of turtle protection programs was not "transparent" or "predictable."[55]

The ruling thus left open the possibility that a unilaterally imposed trade ban in response to foreign environmental practices, and based on nonproduct-related issues, could be implemented in compliance with the GATT. But some trade law experts believed the procedural criteria in the ruling were unrealistic. The case underlined once again the problem of a WTO panel, which lacks either environmental expertise or mandate, passing judgment on trade measures for environmental purposes.

In response to the appellate body decision, the United States issued new guidelines on the issue in July 1999. The new guidelines still prohibited the import of shrimp harvested with technology adversely affecting the relevant sea turtle species. But instead of requiring the use of TEDs by the exporting country, it allowed the exporting country to present evidence that its program to protect sea turtles in the course of shrimp trawling was comparable in effectiveness to the U.S. program. The guidelines noted, however, that the Department of State was not aware of technology as effective as the TED.[56]

Eco-Labeling

Eco-labels are labels indicating that certain products are better for the environment. They help consumers exercise preferences for environmentally sound production methods for products, for example, wood harvested from sustainably managed forests, not clear-cutting. Although some eco-labels are conferred by firms on themselves and others by trade associations on their members, the ones that have credibility with consumers are "third-party" eco-labels awarded by independent entities. The eco-labels that are important to the environment are those that use criteria based on process and production methods (PPMs); that is, they make judgments on the ecological efficacy of the methods by which a product is made/grown/caught—not on the product itself—such as tuna-fishing practices that kill large numbers of dolphins, or unsustainable logging practices. Some governments have sponsored their own eco-labels, but some of the most important are private, voluntary schemes. Third-party eco-labels have already demonstrated their potential for attracting the attention of producers where international policymaking has failed, as shown by the case of the Forest Stewardship Council and timber products.

Certification and labeling became an international issue after the establishment in 1994 of the Forest Stewardship Council (FSC), an independent NGO that created the world's first third-party eco-labeling scheme for wood products. By 1995, the FSC had begun to set standards for sustainable forest management and criteria for potential certifiers to meet and had released a label that could be used to show that a product is certified by FSC standards. FSC hoped to create a market for certified forest products among consumers and to use that market to leverage more sustainable forest management. Today, FSC's governing body is comprised of its more than 617 member organizations and individuals equally divided among environmental, social, and economic voting "chambers." FSC members include environmental organizations such as WWF, Greenpeace, and Friends of the Earth, as well as companies such as IKEA and Home Depot.

FSC has the support of a large and growing number of companies that have united themselves in various countries into "buyers groups" committed to selling only independently certified timber and timber products within three to five years. The FSC-labeling scheme is the preferred scheme for buyers groups in Austria, Belgium, Brazil, Germany, Japan, the Netherlands, Switzerland, the United Kingdom, and the United States. This unprecedented alliance of major companies, NGOs, and other supporters has resulted in dialogue and answers to previously irresolvable forest management challenges and has changed forest management practices worldwide.

Similarly, the London-based Marine Stewardship Council (MSC) has developed an environmental standard for sustainable and well-managed fisheries. It uses a product label to reward environmentally responsible management and practices. Consumers who are concerned about overfishing can choose seafood products that have been independently assessed against the MSC standard and labeled to prove it. The MSC, which was established by Unilever, the world's largest buyer of seafood, and WWF in 1997, has been operating independently since 1999 and has succeeded in bringing together supporters from more than one hundred organizations in twenty or more countries. By the end of 2004, eleven fisheries had been certified.[57]

However, in spite of the success of the FSC and the MSC, eco-labeling can be unfairly discriminatory and has become a focus of international conflicts and debate in the WTO on whether and how that body should address eco-labeling schemes. Since 1994, labeling and related issues have been discussed in many WTO bodies; however, until Doha, which gave the CTE its mandate to address eco-labeling, no WTO body had a formal mandate to make recommendations, including possibly calling for new negotiations.[58] Developed and developing countries have expressed justifiable concerns about some government-sponsored eco-labeling schemes that are skewed in favor of domestic producers and against foreign competitors. An eco-labeling scheme may convey an advantage to a domestic industry by virtually mandating a particular technology or production process; that another technology or process may be equally or more environmentally sound and more suitable in the country of origin is ignored. Some countries are also hostile to private eco-labeling schemes because they threaten to reduce markets for a domestic industry guilty of unsustainable practices. The transparency of official and private voluntary eco-labeling schemes and the ability of affected exporters to participate in their development thus emerged as an issue in the WTO.

Discussions on labeling within the WTO are being affected by the issue of labeling genetically modified organisms (GMOs). Because it encapsulates so many of the relevant issues, it is appropriate that so many delegations are developing their approach to labeling on the GMO issue. Were WTO rules to be considered consistent with the restriction of GMO imports, this could have an enormous impact on global agricultural trade. When assessing the rationale behind a delegation's position on the eco-labeling question, it may be important to place it within the context of their domestic agricultural policies and their adoption of GMO technologies. Exporters of genetically modified (GM) crops, including the United States, believe that the European Union and other countries that do not use GM technology, or do not have access to it, are using GMO-labeling as an unjustified form of protectionism. Countries seeking to restrict imports of GM crops say that doubt remains regarding the health and environmental impact of GM technology and that the scope of possible impacts justifies taking actions in the absence of conclusive scientific information. At the foundation of many of the differences in the GMO debate is the difference among national approaches to regulation.[59]

The current discussions on eco-labeling requirements show some areas of consensus and several areas of divergence. There appears to be consensus that voluntary, participatory, market-based, and transparent environmental labeling schemes are potentially efficient economic instruments for informing consumers about environmentally friendly products. Almost all members agree on the need for transparency in developing and implementing eco-labeling schemes to avoid disadvantaging foreign producers. However, many developing—and some developed—countries remain wary of further discussion in this area because of concerns that stronger eco-labeling regimes could prove a barrier to their market access.[60]

Subsidies and the Environment

Another issue on the trade and environment agenda is what the CTE calls "the environmental benefits of removing trade restrictions and distortions"—a lengthy trade euphemism for subsidy elimination and the environment. A subsidy may be defined as a government-directed intervention, whether through budgeted programs or other means, which transfers resources to a particular economic group. Subsidies distort markets by sending signals to producers and consumers that fail to reflect the true costs of production, thus misallocating financial and natural resources. And subsidies to goods traded internationally give unfair advantages to exports that are subsidized over others.

Subsidies can also have negative impacts on the environment, especially in the commodity sectors (agriculture, forests, and fisheries). They draw a higher level of investment into these sectors and exacerbate the overexploitation of land, forests, and fish; they also make technologies that exploit natural resources more intensively cheaper to acquire, such as flood irrigation or excessive use of pesticides.[61] Thus eliminating subsidies to these sectors represents a rare example of a clear-cut win-win solution in which trade liberalization benefits the environment. The Uruguay Round represented the first substantial step toward subsidy removal in agriculture, and the United States and the "Cairns Group" of industrialized and developing countries supportive of agricultural trade liberalization persuaded the EU to agree to a 20 percent reduction in total support compared to a 1986–1988 base period. But subsidies to fisheries and forests remained outside the agreement.

Fisheries subsidies are one of the factors that have led to massive overfishing (see the fisheries case in chapter 3). A 2002 WWF report estimated that fisheries subsidies total at least $15 billion per year worldwide (roughly 20 percent of the value of global fish catches); this not only has an environmental impact on the world's fish stocks but also affects developing countries as they confront the excess capacity exported from the mostly depleted fisheries of richer countries.[62] Since the establishment of the CTE, some members have focused on the elimination of fisheries subsidies as possibly *the* greatest contribution the multilateral trading system could make to sustainable development. In particular, the lead state coalition known as the Friends of Fish (Australia, Chile, Ecuador, Iceland, New Zealand, Peru, the Philippines, and the United States) have pointed to the "win-win-win" nature of such action: good for the environment, good for development, and good for trade. Their major argument is that subsidies are at least partly responsible for the alarming depletion of many fish stocks because much of the money is spent in commissioning new vessels or in enhancing the efficiency of older boats.[63] But a veto coalition consisting of heavily subsidizing members (EU, Japan, and South Korea) argued that empirical evidence that subsidy elimination would benefit the environment was still weak. Japan and South Korea insisted that poor fisheries management, rather than subsidies, was the root cause of stock depletion, and the EU also took a cautious approach to potential rules.

Subsidy elimination was one of the most hotly contested issues in the preparations for the Seattle Ministerial Conference. The Friends of Fish pushed for the inclusion of a paragraph in the draft ministerial declaration for the Seattle WTO summit calling for a working group on fisheries subsidies. And a disputed paragraph in the draft called for "further substantial reductions in export subsidies, including commitments resulting in the elimination of such subsidies." At the December 1999 Seattle WTO Ministerial Conference, the issue of agricultural subsidies was one of the major stumbling blocks to agreement on a framework for the trade negotiations. While protestors were stealing the headlines, the EU and Japan agreed with the United States on language endorsing the aim of ending agricultural subsidies in return for U.S. concessions on other trade issues; but the two sides could not agree on a timetable for eliminating subsidies before the talks collapsed.

The Friends of Fish, however, didn't give up and were finally able to put the issue of fisheries subsidies on the WTO agenda in Doha. The Doha Ministerial Declaration explicitly calls for negotiations aimed at clarifying and improving WTO rules on fisheries subsidies. The mandate reflects the concerns of the potentially harmful trade, developmental and environmental effects of subsidies to the fisheries sector, and the benefits that stronger WTO rules would achieve. The WTO negotiations on fisheries subsidies since Doha have taken place in the WTO's Rules Committee.[64] After languishing for several years, the discussions took off in June 2004, when Japan made its first proposal to the committee; this development is a breakthrough in that it recognized the need for rules. Since then, the different negotiating groups have submitted proposals and counterproposals on how to proceed. In general, the Friends of Fish have focused on the negotiation of a "negative list" of exceptions to exempt environment-friendly and other subsidies as well as to include special and differential treatment for developing countries. Japan, supported primarily by South Korea and Chinese Taipei (Taiwan), has supported a bottom-up—or "positive list"—approach to defining harmful fisheries subsidies. Japan opposed a blanket ban on subsidies and proposed that each type of subsidy be evaluated and placed in a "box" according to its effect. Permitted subsidies supportive of sustainable development would end up in a "green box." These would include subsidies that promote the conservation and sustainable utilization of fisheries resources, including specific measures such as management plans, environmentally friendly fishing gear, surveys, research and monitoring, measures to enhance stocks and preserve habitats, and the development and diffusion of new technologies. In addition, the "green box" could include measures that, as long as an adequate management plan was in place, did not have harmful effects. Subsidies supporting illegal, unregulated, and unreported fishing or overcapacity would be placed in a "red box."

The two groups have gone back and forth, amending their proposals. In February 2005, a new proposal by Japan, South Korea, and Chinese Taipei was seen as a significant improvement with fewer qualifications on "red box" subsidies. Members generally recognized the need to address the special concerns of developing countries, in particular small and vulnerable states as highlighted in an earlier submission by the Small Island Developing States. However, some developed countries expressed concerns that special and differential treatment provisions could be used by some of the bigger developing countries to create major fleets, thereby undermining the objectives of the disciplines. In this context, Brazil noted that the rules should not prohibit the country to build its own fleet to exploit its national waters within sustainable limits.[65] Although the WTO has not yet finalized new rules on fisheries subsidies nearly four years after Doha—and no deadline was set for these negotiations—the agreement by each side that subsidies pose a threat to the environment, development, and trade is seen as a small step in the right direction.

The Outlook for Trade and Environment

Fisheries subsidies are not the only subsidy issue currently on the WTO's agenda. In fact, negotiations on agriculture subsidies—a key part of the Doha Round—led to the collapse of the fifth WTO Ministerial Conference in Cancún, Mexico, in September 2003. Developing countries viewed the EU-U.S. position on agricultural subsidies, put forward in their pre–Cancún proposal paper, as inadequate because it failed to address developing-country calls for the elimination of export subsidies and substantial reductions in domestic support and tariffs in the North—measures that would undercut local production in poor countries, suppress world prices, and prevent efficient exporters in poorer countries from selling their produce.[66] Developing countries reacted to the EU-U.S. proposal by forming a coalition, the G-20, which included Brazil, China, India, South Africa, and others with significant agrarian populations and large growing markets of interest to the North.[67]

The tension in Cancún increased even more with the presentation of the Sectoral Initiative on Cotton by a group of West African countries (Benin, Burkina Faso, Chad, and Mali) that described the damage caused to them by cotton subsidies in richer countries, particularly in the United States. The proposal asked that subsidies be eliminated and compensation be paid to the four countries. Despite great sympathy for this initiative, the draft Ministerial text that eventually appeared offered no real concessions; instead, it reflected the U.S. position, namely, that affected countries should diversify their production away from cotton.[68]

Although the Cancún Ministerial did not give new direction to the environmental issues under the Doha Agenda, several developments in Mexico may have a major influence on future trade and environment negotiations. First, most of the developing countries refused to go along with the demands made by the developed nations that have been running the show. As one observer pointed out, "It was the first time that the World Trade Organization began to feel like a truly global organization—not just an extension of the U.S. government's foreign and domestic economic policy."[69] This was the first time that developing countries led and maintained negotiating coalitions in the WTO, even though the specific national interests of coalition partners differed. This was a shift in the balance of power in the WTO and could have far reaching implications in other fora, including in the negotiation of regional trade agreements, such as the proposed Free Trade Area of the Americas,[70] and in the environment and development arenas.

The improving relationship between governments and NGOs within the WTO was another aspect of the Ministerial. While protests of WTO policies continued on the outside, NGOs and **civil society** groups provided much needed technical analysis and political support on the inside, especially to smaller-staffed developing countries that face a severe disadvantage during the multilateral negotiating process in keeping up with the blizzard of proposals and frenzy of meetings.[71]

This is not to say that NGOs and civil society are now supportive of the WTO. Environmental, labor, and human rights groups' continuing protests reflect a range of complaints about the WTO and globalization of the economy. One common theme is that the world's trade officials reach agreements without sufficient transparency and participation by civil society. Environmental NGOs had been advocating greater WTO transparency, including dispute panels, since the early 1990s, but with little success. They called for meetings open to the press and the public, NGO input in the selection of experts on the dispute panels, and more NGO input into WTO decisions; but these calls fell on deaf ears. The United States, under pressure from its own NGOs, has pushed for greater transparency in the WTO. But WTO delegations from developing countries and other industrialized countries alike rejected the participation of environmental NGOs generally because they perceived the worldwide NGO movement as being dominated by U.S. NGOs.

They also rejected proposals to breach the confidentiality of the dispute resolution process.

As the Doha Agenda continues to inch its way through the WTO's various committees and negotiating fora, several issues are likely to remain on the top of the trade and environment agenda in the coming years, particularly the relationship between trade rules and MEAs, labeling for environmental purposes, reducing fisheries subsidies, sustainable agriculture, and liberalizing trade in environmental goods and services. The roles that developing countries and NGOs have within the context of the WTO will continue to evolve, as will the emphasis given to the relationship between trade and environment.

ENVIRONMENT AND DEVELOPMENT

Global environmental politics has been shaped since the 1970s by various factors, including increased awareness of environmental issues, improved scientific understanding of the issues, the increased number of countries involved in the negotiation of environmental treaties, the North-South debate, the relationship between trade and environment, and the relationship between environmental protection, economic development, and social development—the so-called three pillars of sustainable development. From the historic Stockholm Conference in 1972 to the Johannesburg Summit in 2002, the international community has been pursuing the goal of sustainable development. The 1972 Stockholm Conference on the Human Environment was the first major event to address environmental deterioration. Fifteen years on, the 1987 Brundtland Report, *Our Common Future*, first brought the idea of sustainable development to the public's attention. Just five years later, the United Nations Conference on Environment and Development achieved a pact, underpinned by a set of core principles, between countries of the North and South linking environment and development concerns.

Rio also launched a new round of global development conferences that would lead to the Millennium Assembly in 2000 where heads of state committed themselves to tackle poverty, malnutrition, and a host of other problems by 2015. The Millennium Assembly was soon followed by a second round of world conferences dealing with the difficulties faced by the world's least-developed countries as well as challenges in global trade and finance. The thirty-year process reached its culmination with the World Summit on Sustainable Development (WSSD) in Johannesburg, South Africa, in 2002.

The Johannesburg Summit marked a key juncture in the multilateral process initiated all those years ago in Stockholm. Johannesburg represented a crucial step in the efforts of the international community to deal with humankind's relationship with the natural environment. The WSSD was designed to bring the curtain down on a decade-long process aimed at establishing a global agenda for development. It was at Rio and the many meetings held since that the multilateral agenda for achieving sustainable development emerged. At Johannesburg, the goal was to turn this agenda into something more.

Most interesting about this period of summits and world conferences is how the sustainable development agenda has advanced. In the earlier years—up through Rio—the discussion was sectoral, that is, the environmental issues were discussed in parallel to issues of social and economic development, such as population, human settlements, education, health, poverty, trade, and finance. *Agenda 21* illustrates this point in that it contained eight chapters on social and economic issues and fourteen chapters on environmental issues. However, by the time delegates arrived in Johannesburg ten years later, the scope had changed and the economic and social development pillars received much greater emphasis, as can be seen in the structure of the Johannesburg Plan of Implementation (JPOI), which contained one chapter on environmental issues and four chapters on economic and social development (see table 5.1). The JPOI also contained three chapters on regional sustainable development issues, which also illustrates another trend—this one toward regionalization rather than globalization. This section will look at these trends and how they affect global environmental politics.

Agenda 21 was negotiated primarily by government delegates who had expertise in environmental issues. Therefore, the one chapter on economic development and issues such as trade, debt, and macroeconomic policies did not receive as much attention during the negotiations. However, the changes in the global economy in the years following the Earth Summit—the rise of globalization being a dominant concern—as rapidly increasing trade and capital flows, coupled with the revolution in information and communication technologies (such as the Internet), made the world more independent and interconnected than ever before. Since 1990, the value of world trade has tripled, and the flows of foreign direct investment (companies investing in other countries) have increased by fourteen times.[72] Absolute priority has been given to expanding the scope for trade and investment in line with neoliberal economics (a political-economic movement, increasingly prominent since 1980, that de-emphasizes or rejects government intervention in the

TABLE 5.1   The Evolving Three Pillars of Sustainable Development

Agenda 21*	Johannesburg Plan of Implementation**
Chapters on Environmental Issues <ul><li>Protection of the atmosphere</li><li>Planning and management of land resources</li><li>Combating deforestation</li><li>Combating desertification and drought</li><li>Sustainable mountain development</li><li>Sustainable agriculture and rural development</li><li>Conservation of biological diversity</li><li>Environmentally sound management of biotechnology</li><li>Protection of the oceans and seas</li><li>Protection of the quality and supply of freshwater resources</li><li>Environmentally sound management of toxic chemicals</li><li>Environmentally sound management of hazardous wastes</li><li>Environmentally sound management of solid wastes and sewage</li><li>Safe and environmentally sound management of radioactive wastes</li></ul> *Chapters on Social and Economic Issues* <ul><li>Economic development and trade</li><li>Combating poverty</li><li>Changing consumption patterns</li><li>Demographic dynamics</li><li>Protecting and promoting human health</li><li>Sustainable human settlement development</li><li>Integrating environment and development in decision making</li></ul>	*Chapters on Environmental Issues* <ul><li>Protecting and managing the natural resource base of economic and social development</li></ul> *Chapters on Social and Economic Issues* <ul><li>Poverty eradication</li><li>Changing unsustainable patterns of consumption and production</li><li>Sustainable development in a globalizing world</li><li>Health and sustainable development</li></ul> *Chapters on Regional Issues* <ul><li>Sustainable development of small island developing states</li><li>Sustainable development for Africa</li><li>Other regional initiatives</li></ul>

*This does not reflect all 40 chapters of Agenda 21, including chapters on means of implementation and major groups.

** This does not include the two chapters on means of implementation

economy and focuses on achieving progress, and even social justice, through promoting free-market methods and emphasizing economic growth). For example, neoliberals argue that the best way to protect the environment is by overcoming poverty via increasing privatization, foreign direct investment, and free trade. As a result, the institutions governing the global economy have grown stronger, but those promoting social equity, poverty alleviation, and environmental cooperation remain weak. The barriers to trade and investment began to fall, and the belief that poor countries could grow themselves out of poverty by boarding the liberalization express train took on almost a religious force—at least in the rich countries.[73] In other words, if poorer countries supported trade liberalization, many of their economic development problems would be solved.

The trend towards globalization—the rapid growth and integration of markets, institutions, and cultures—is viewed by some as a threat, by others as an opportunity. Many policymakers and industrialists in the developed world were positive about the phenomenon. However, a majority of those living in developing countries or engaged in a variety of NGOs worried that environmental and labor standards were in a "race to the bottom" and that social and economic disparities were being exacerbated. Many NGOs were concerned that developing countries would eliminate or ignore environmental and labor standards in their efforts to attract foreign direct investment. There was a fear that if a host country demonstrated that it did not have strict pollution standards and did not condemn child labor or support an eight-hour work day, it would attract more corporate investment.[74]

In a speech delivered to the UN General Assembly in April 2000 to launch the Millennium Report, UN Secretary-General Kofi Annan tackled the globalization issue. Observing that the opportunities provided by this phenomenon were not being equally distributed, he called for a candid debate on the positive and negative consequences of globalization and for discussions about how to make globalization work for all people in all countries. "How can we say that the half of the human race which has yet to make or receive a telephone call, let alone use a computer, is taking part in globalization?" he asked.[75]

In the first three years of the new millennium, major international events focused on the various challenges in achieving sustainable development while taking into account the impact of globalization. Those organizing these events sought to provide a blueprint for global development through a new round of international obligations focusing on quantitative targets and means of implementation. The most influential of these events was the Millennium Assembly.[76]

The Millennium Assembly

To help prepare the United Nations to meet the challenges of the twenty-first century, the UN General Assembly decided to designate its 55th session, starting on 6 September 2000, as the "Millennium Assembly," and to hold a "Millennium Summit" of world leaders to address the pressing challenges faced by the world's people. At the Millennium Assembly, world leaders agreed to a far-reaching plan to support global development objectives for the new century. The world's leaders reaffirmed their commitment to work toward peace and security for all and a world in which sustainable development and poverty eradication would have the highest priority. The agreement, set out in the Millennium Declaration, addressed a wide range of core international issues relating to fundamental values and principles; peace, security and disarmament; development and poverty eradication; the protection of the environment; human rights, democracy and good governance; the needs of the most vulnerable; the special needs of Africa; and the strengthening of the UN. Set against a backdrop of widespread concern about the social and ecological implications of globalization, the Millennium Assembly placed the relationship between poverty, environmental decline, and economic development firmly in the international spotlight.[77]

The following year, Secretary-General Annan presented his report, which was titled *Road Map Towards the Implementation of the UN Millennium Declaration* (UN document 56/326). The report contains, in an annex, eight development goals containing eighteen targets and forty-eight indicators, which are commonly known as the Millennium Development Goals (MDGs). The first seven goals are directed toward eradicating poverty in all its forms: halving extreme poverty and hunger; achieving universal primary education and gender equity; reducing the mortality of children under five by two-thirds and maternal mortality by three-quarters; reversing the spread of HIV/AIDS; halving the proportion of people without access to safe drinking water; and ensuring environmental sustainability. The final goal outlines measures for building a global partnership for development. The goals, targets, and indicators were developed following consultations held among members of the UN Secretariat and representatives of IMF, OECD and the World Bank in order to harmonize reporting on the development goals in the Millennium Declaration and the international development goals (see fig. 5.1).

In a relatively short period of time, the Millennium Development Goals gained tremendous currency, primarily in development circles, but increasingly in related trade and finance spheres. Many actors are now counting on the MDGs to galvanize disparate and sometimes competing development agendas. Increasingly, stakeholders are viewing the MDGs as a powerful political tool to hold governments and international institutions accountable. A

FIGURE 5.1   The Millennium Development Goals

By 2015, all UN member states have pledged to:

Eradicate extreme poverty and hunger
- Reduce by half the proportion of people living on less than a dollar a day.
- Reduce by half the proportion of people who suffer from hunger.

Achieve universal primary education
- Ensure that all boys and girls complete a full course of primary schooling.

Promote gender equality and empower women
- Eliminate gender disparity in primary and secondary education, preferably by 2005, and to all levels of education no later than 2015.

Reduce child mortality
- Reduce by two thirds the mortality rate among children under five.

Improve maternal health
- Reduce by three quarters the maternal mortality ratio.

Combat HIV/AIDS, malaria and other diseases
- Halt and begin to reverse the spread of HIV/AIDS.
- Halt and begin to reverse the incidence of malaria and other major diseases.

Ensure environmental sustainability
- Integrate the principles of sustainable development into country policies and pro-grammes and reverse the loss of environmental resources.
- Reduce by half the proportion of people without sustainable access to safe drinking water.
- Achieve a significant improvement in the lives of at least 100 million slum dwellers by 2020.

Develop a global partnership for development
- Develop further an open trading and financial system that is rule-based, predictable and non-discriminatory. This target includes a commitment to good governance, development, and poverty reduction – both nationally and internationally.
- Address the special needs of the least developed countries. This includes tariff- and quota-free access for their exports; enhanced debt relief for heavily indebted poor countries; cancellation of official bilateral debt; and more generous ODA for countries committed to poverty reduction.
- Address the special needs of landlocked countries and small island developing states.
- Deal comprehensively with the debt problems of developing countries through national and international measures in order to make debt sustainable in the long term.
- In cooperation with developing countries, develop decent and productive work for youth.
- In cooperation with pharmaceutical companies, provide access to affordable essential drugs in developing countries.
- In cooperation with the private sector, make available the benefits of new technologies – especially information and communications technologies.

Source: United Nations, "Millennium Development Goals," http://www.un.org/millenniumgoals/.

key reason for this is that the Millennium Declaration and its MDGs clarify the shared and individual roles and responsibilities of key stakeholders. The declaration sets out the responsibilities of governments to implement various specific goals and targets. It instructs the network of international organizations to marshal their resources and expertise in the most strategic and efficient way possible to support and sustain the efforts of partners at global and country levels. And it urges citizens, civil society organizations, and the private sector to bring to the table their unique strengths for motivation, mobilization, and action.[78]

The momentum achieved with the adoption of the MDGs was reinforced over the next two years by other major international meetings. In Brussels at the third UN Conference on the Least Developed Countries in May 2001, governments addressed the needs of the least-developed countries; and in Doha at the fourth WTO Ministerial Conference in November 2001, they expressed the need to link sustainable development and trade. Meanwhile, in March 2002, the International Conference on Financing for Development in Monterrey, Mexico, supported the mobilization of resources to finance development; the World Food Summit: Five Years Later, in Rome in June 2002, confirmed the global commitment to eradicate hunger; and a series of special sessions of the UN General Assembly promoted issues relating to women, social development, human settlements, and children.

The World Summit on Sustainable Development

All these issues came to a head at the World Summit on Sustainable Development in Johannesburg, South Africa, to map out a detailed course of action for the further implementation of Agenda 21. Once again the issue of "sustainable development" was on the negotiating table, but the series of development-focused conferences over the previous two years definitely had an impact. The Johannesburg Summit did not aim to renegotiate Agenda 21, but it did attempt to fill some key gaps that have impeded its implementation and the shift to sustainable development.

The WSSD took place in a difficult international climate. The 1992 optimism of a large "peace dividend" that could be reallocated to sustainable development had deflated along with the rest of the world economy, especially in the year before the summit. The U.S. government, being preoccupied with the war on terrorism, was generally "hostile" to environmental causes and multilateralism. The developing countries were wary of the industrialized countries and also frustrated with them. The failure to implement the Rio

PHOTO 5.2   NGOs reminding governments about their responsibility to future
generations in Bali, Indonesia, during WSSD PrepCom IV. Courtesy IISD/*Earth
Negotiations Bulletin.*

agreements effectively had cast a long shadow and raised questions about the
credibility and accountability of global conferences.[79]

The Johannesburg Summit opened on Monday, August 26, 2002, and
brought together government representatives from more than 190 countries,
including one hundred world leaders. An estimated 37,000 people attended
either the summit or one of the many other gatherings held alongside the
main event.[80] The difficult negotiations that followed focused on an ambitious plan of implementation that would address poverty eradication, how to
change unsustainable patterns of consumption and production, and the protection and management of natural resources. As in Stockholm and Rio before it, there were divergent views among governments on how to tackle
issues ranging from water and sanitation to desertification, climate change,
biodiversity, oceans, health, education, science and technology, trade and finance. Indeed, there were moments when negotiations came to a standstill
and when skeptics questioned the negotiators' commitment to sustainable
development.

After ten days of hard work in Johannesburg, the negotiations concluded. The summit produced three key outcomes: The first was the Johannesburg Declaration, a pledge by world leaders to commit their countries to the goal of sustainable development. The second was the Johannesburg Plan of Implementation, which sets out a comprehensive program of action for sustainable development, and includes quantifiable goals and targets with fixed deadlines. Finally, the summit produced nearly three hundred voluntary partnerships and other initiatives to support sustainable development. Unlike the Johannesburg Declaration and the Plan of Implementation, this outcome was not the result of multilateral negotiations involving the entire community of nations. Instead, it involved numerous smaller partnerships composed of private-sector and civil-society groups, as well as governments, which committed themselves to a wide range of projects and activities.

Many of the commitments and partnerships agreed to in Johannesburg echoed the Millennium Development Goals. For example, countries agreed to commit themselves to halve the proportion of people who lack clean water and proper sanitation by 2015. These commitments were backed up by a United States announcement of an investment of $970 million in water projects over the next three years, and a European Union announcement to engage in partnerships to meet the new goals, primarily in Africa and Central Asia. The UN received twenty-one other partnership initiatives in this area and at least $20 million in extra resources.[81]

In energy, countries committed themselves to expanding access to the two billion people who do not have access to modern energy services. In addition, although countries did not agree about a target for phasing in renewable energy (e.g., a target of 15 percent of the global energy supply from renewable energy by 2010), which many observers said was a major shortcoming of the summit, they did commit to green energy and the phaseout of subsidies for types of energy inconsistent with sustainable development. And to bolster these commitments, a group of nine major electric companies signed agreements to undertake sustainable energy projects in developing countries. In addition, the EU announced a $700 million partnership initiative on energy, and the United States announced investments of up to $43 million for energy in 2003.[82]

On health issues, in addition to actions to fight HIV/AIDS and reduce water-borne diseases and the health risks caused by pollution, countries agreed to phase out, by 2020, the use and production of chemicals that harm human health and the environment. There were also many commitments made to protect biodiversity and improve ecosystem management. These include commitments to reduce biodiversity loss by 2010; to restore fisheries to their maximum sustainable yields by 2015; to establish a representative network of marine protected areas by 2012; and to improve developing countries' access to environmentally sound alternatives to ozone depleting chemicals by 2010. These commitments are supported by thirty-two partnership initiatives submitted to the UN, with $100 million in additional resources, and a U.S. announcement of $53 million for forest management in 2002–2005.[83]

Yet among all the targets, timetables, commitments, and partnerships that were agreed upon at Johannesburg, there were no silver bullet solutions to aid the fight against poverty and a continually deteriorating natural environment. In fact, as an implementation-focused summit, Johannesburg did not produce a particularly dramatic outcome—there were no agreements that will lead to new treaties, and many of the agreed targets had already been agreed upon at the Millennium Assembly and other meetings. As UN Secretary-General Kofi Annan told the press on the last day of the summit, "I think we have to be careful not to expect conferences like this to produce miracles. But we do expect conferences like this to generate political commitment, momentum and energy for the attainment of the goals."[84]

Was the World Summit on Sustainable Development a success or a failure? This question will most likely be debated long into the future, but the answer depends on one's goals and expectations. For the most part, the success of the WSSD will be evaluated in the future, when the results of the negotiations and other events are visible. Many people left Rio in 1992 with a great sense of disappointment, only to state ten years later that Rio was a high point for the sustainable development agenda.

Among the summit's legacies was a shift in the balance of the three pillars of sustainable development. During the previous decade, sustainable development more often than not equaled protection of the environment. Johannesburg was the first true summit on sustainable development in the sense that advocates of all three pillars were under one roof arguing their cases, raising real issues, and confronting those with different interests and perspectives. It was not a social summit dealing only with poverty, exclusion, and human rights. It was not an economic and globalization summit addressing only trade and investment, finance, and the development and transfer of technology. And it was not an environmental summit focusing only on natural resources degradation, biodiversity loss, climate change, and pollution. Johannesburg was instead a summit about the intersections of all these issues.[85]

But what does this mean for global environmental politics? Some believe that the tide has turned away from the environment and towards the economic and social development pillars of sustainable development. The MDGs focus on these areas and with it a large part of the United Nation's agenda, along with bilateral and multilateral aid. Most of the environmental regimes have been struggling to place their priorities in line with the MDGs so that they will continue to receive attention within the larger development agenda that has overtaken the international community since the Millennium Summit and has been seen in the global conferences as well as the work of the World Bank, the IMF, UNDP, and even the G-8. It is possible that "global environmental politics" has become "global sustainable development politics." However, as the balance between the economic, social, and environmental pillars of sustainable development continues to evolve—along with the attention of policymakers—one thing is clear: Global environmental politics can no longer be examined in isolation.

CONCLUSION: THE PROSPECTS FOR GLOBAL ENVIRONMENTAL POLITICS

The stakes in global environmental politics continue to increase as the costs of environmental degradation and measures to reverse it grow, and as global environmental regimes require greater changes in economic and social development strategies and production techniques to be effective. At the same time, however, because the globalization of investment and the liberalization of trade have accelerated, the effectiveness of global environmental policy is increasingly threatened by global economic forces and the policies that support them. Thus, the ambitious agenda of sustainable development is in danger of being overwhelmed by the economic forces that threaten the health of the planet.

   In the context of these larger economic forces, is the international community on a path that will bring effective cooperation in reversing the main threats to the global environment? The case studies presented in this book show that, on some issues, states have been able to take collective actions that have stopped or significantly reduced specific environmental threats, such as the taking of endangered species of whales and the poaching of African elephants. In the case of the ozone layer, states have devised a regime that has been innovative in its rule making and effective in phasing out products responsible for the damage.

   But the successful regimes have had favorable circumstances. In the ozone case, there were a relatively small number of economic actors whose interests were involved and substitute technology that turned out to be cost effective for the companies. In the whaling case, only a few countries wanted to continue to hunt whales, and there was no large worldwide market for whale products. The ivory case was successful in that a few major countries were able to shut down the market for elephant ivory. The European air pollution regime has been successful because of the availability of cleaner technologies.

In some cases, the international community has not yet been able to reach an effective agreement on global environmental issues involving major economic and social interests, notably forests. The lack of progress toward a forest regime has reflected the veto power wielded by a loose coalition of key developing and developed countries. But potential lead actors have also failed to define the issue in a way that could contribute to an effective regime, in large part because they are unwilling to do anything that would restrict the global trade in forest products. Slowing the hemorrhaging of the world's forests will require that wealthy countries consider what value the remaining forests have to present and future generations worldwide.

The Kyoto Protocol and the climate regime face another set of major economic and social interests, including the requirement of major changes relating to energy production and use. Challenges to the science of global warming by one veto coalition led by the United States and a desire to uphold the principle of common but differentiated responsibilities by a second veto coalition, led by some of the larger developing countries, has delayed not only effective implementation of the protocol but also detailed discussion of emissions reductions beyond 2012.

This book has outlined the importance of continued efforts to improve the effectiveness of environmental regimes even after they are adopted. We have shown how parties can strengthen regimes by tightening the requirements for regulating activities that are causing the environmental disruption or resource depletion, by improving compliance with those requirements, or by broadening state participation in the regime. The regimes for biodiversity, desertification, and fisheries will need different kinds of strengthening in the next several years to become effective in reversing their respective threats. Each of these issues is at a different stage of development and has a unique combination of political and economic dynamics. But for each threat, it will take unprecedented political commitments by major states to create an effective regime.

The biodiversity regime has now initiated work on seven thematic work programs addressing marine and coastal biodiversity; agricultural biodiversity; forest biodiversity; island biodiversity; the biodiversity of inland waters;

dry and subhumid lands biodiversity; and mountain biodiversity. Work has also been initiated on protected areas, access to genetic resources, traditional knowledge, innovations and practices (Article 8(j)); intellectual property rights; indicators; taxonomy; public education and awareness; incentives; and alien species, not to mention the implementation of the Cartagena Protocol on Biosafety. With so many working groups and programs, many are concerned that the regime may become overextended and, therefore, its effectiveness further minimized.

The desertification regime faces considerable administrative and financial problems in fulfilling its mandate of combating desertification and mitigating the effects of drought. Although nearly universal ratification of the convention can be seen as recognition of the problem of land degradation in the drylands, the issue is complicated by the fact that combating desertification has to work hand-in-hand with efforts to address poverty eradication, water resources management, agriculture, deforestation, biodiversity conservation, climate change, and population growth. The success or failure of this regime is a key indicator for the overall success or failure of sustainable development.

The fisheries regime needs strengthening primarily in the compliance system and in participation. The regime for global fisheries management is more complex than any of the others discussed in this book. It consists of a legally binding regime governing the management of straddling fish stocks and highly migratory fish stocks, and the nonbinding FAO Code of Conduct for Responsible Fisheries and the FAO International Plan of Action on Managing Fishing Capacity, which apply to all fisheries under national sovereignty as well as numerous regional treaties. The Fish Stocks Agreement lacks a conference of the parties, relying entirely on regional fisheries organizations to track compliance, and most of the major fishing states have failed to ratify it. The Code of Conduct, adopted in 1995, has strong and relatively concrete norms for sustainable fisheries management, but has a weak system of accountability. The FAO is responsible for reporting on progress in implementing the norms in the agreement, but states feel little or no pressure to conform to the norms because it has no mandate to monitor and report on the implementation of the norms by individual states. The FAO Plan of Action on Managing Fishing Capacity, which could be the most important part of the regime for overfishing, has the same problem.

But environmental regimes are not the only forces that influence the global environment. The world's global trade and financial institutions—the WTO, the IMF, and the World Bank—have often pursued policies that run counter to the needs of effective global environmental regimes. WTO dispute panels have rendered decisions against unilateral trade measures for environmental purposes that seemed to rule out such measures even in cases of endangered species, not because these measures were protectionist but because they would restrict trade. The WTO's decision on the shrimp/turtle issue suggests the possibility of an accommodation between global trade rules and carefully crafted environmental trade measures, but the issue remains a potential conflict among states and between trade specialists and environmentalists. Also still unresolved is whether the WTO will accommodate the use of trade measures by multilateral environmental agreements.

The IMF and the World Bank have similarly been driven by economic interests that are often in conflict with global cooperation on environmental threats. The Indonesian structural adjustment episode of 1998–1999 demonstrates the unwillingness of those institutions to use their considerable financial power to curb even the most egregious national policies damaging to the global environment when the economy in question is of interest to the world's trade and finance systems. Similarly, the World Bank's refusal to consider phasing out financing traditional fossil fuel development projects reflects the predominance of the same interests in shaping its policies. These institutions cannot be expected to change their policies unless the finance ministries of the world's major industrialized countries are forced by domestic political pressures to do so.

Multilateral institutions have also helped create global environmental regimes by agenda setting (UNEP, CSD), bringing states together to negotiate (CSD, UNEP, FAO), by monitoring the state of the global environment (UNEP), or by providing financial support for environmental activities (GEF, World Bank, UNDP). But these institutions have generally lacked the resources and the mandate to promote strong regimes. The GEF has funding that can accomplish only a small fraction of what is needed to support effective international cooperation in biodiversity, climate, ozone protection, international waters, land degradation, and POPs. UNEP and the CSD are both subject to the veto power and weak political will of powerful states.

Some observers have argued that global environmental regimes will not be effective until the ability of individual states to veto action is finally overcome. They have proposed a new Global Environmental Organization, paralleling the World Trade Organization, which, like a global legislature, could impose binding decisions on all member states, and even impose sanctions on those that fail to comply with global policies.[86] Such proposals appear to put the cart of effective global regimes ahead of the horse of adequate politi-

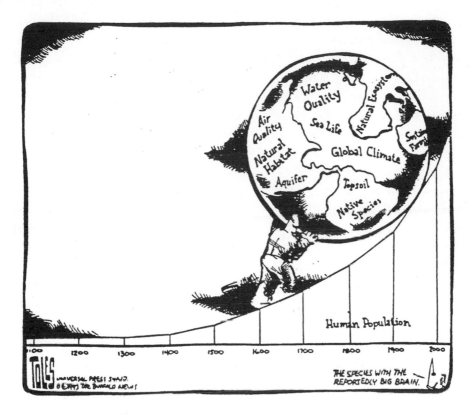

CARTOON 5.2   Global environmental problems and human population. Tom Toles, The Buffalo News © 1993.

cal will. Without the political will to make greater sacrifices to reverse global environmental degradation, it is clear that the world's major states will not agree to give up their power to choose which regimes to adopt. The real problem that must be addressed is how to raise concern for the importance of effective international cooperation on these issues to a significantly higher level in each society. That cannot be accomplished by establishing a new international organization.

The leadership of the highly industrialized countries, beginning with the United States, is a key to effective regimes. The United States is the one state actor without whose leadership any environmental regime is certain to be much weaker. When the United States has been actively engaged in trying to achieve consensus on stronger institutions or actions, it has often been able to overcome reluctance on the part of other industrialized countries, as in the negotiations on ozone depletion, African elephants, whaling, and fish stocks. When the United States has been a veto state, as in the case of climate change and the hazardous waste trade, or has played a much lower-profile role, as in cases of desertification and biodiversity, the resulting regime is weaker. The U.S. executive branch wavered on these issues during the Clinton and Bush administrations and Congress has remained a force for reducing U.S. leadership and enforcing a veto role, especially in the climate change negotiations, the Cartagena Protocol on Biosafety, and the POPs and PIC conventions. And the United States has consistently been a veto state on the issue of committing adequate funding to global environmental threats.

The Group of Eight industrialized countries must also give greater weight to the global environment in their foreign policies and global economic policies than in the past. The United States has prevented the G-8 from taking a strong position on climate change, and the EU countries and Japan have not even ratified the Fish Stocks Agreement. Without leadership from the key industrialized states, there is little hope for effective global regimes for these key issues.

Developing-country governments, too, must move beyond simply demanding technology transfer and financial assistance and must participate fully in global environmental regimes, particularly those for biodiversity, forests, climate change, chemicals, and fisheries. But it may be unrealistic. They need to take new initiatives for North-South bargains in which developing countries accept new commitments in each of the major areas in return for financial or other forms of compensation. In the case of the fisheries regime, for example, key developing-country fishing states might agree to ratify and implement the Fish Stocks Agreement in return for commitments by other distant-water fishing states to give them a larger share of the catch in regional fisheries organizations.

There is increasing awareness among business groups of the implications of global environmental threats and global environmental regimes for their interests. As a result, more and more corporations and trade associations have been playing an active role in global environmental politics. With the realization that many environmental treaties could impose significant new costs on them or otherwise reduce expected profits, they have recognized that early involvement in the negotiating process will often bring long-term benefits once the regime is in place. This involvement can sometimes have a beneficial impact on the outcome. For example, during the Montreal Protocol negotiations, U.S. chemical companies that manufactured CFCs saw the writing on the wall and started to develop CFC alternatives. The chemical companies thus enabled the U.S. negotiators to take a stronger position and emerge as a lead state in the negotiations. On the opposite side, however, corporations and industry associations can also work to defeat strong international environmental measures. Exxon/Mobil has been funding reports that minimize the seriousness and scientific proof of climate change. The agro-industrial complex in the United States along with the chemical companies producing methyl bromide have worked to prevent the phaseout of methyl bromide under the Montreal Protocol.

In a political arena in which both regime negotiations and the policies of global economic institutions are determined by states, and especially their trade and finance ministries, domestic political support for new political commitments on global environmental issues will have to be built state by state. None of this will happen without environmental movements that can influence national opinion in those countries. The worldwide NGO movement continues to become more sophisticated in cooperating across national boundaries and regions, especially through the use of the Internet. International NGO networks on climate change, chemicals, biodiversity, and desertification are mapping strategies for monitoring treaty implementation in every country and ensuring popular participation in national action programs and strategies. TRAFFIC continues to monitor the international trade in endangered species. The global climate network is continuing to develop its technical expertise in analyzing climate action plans. International NGOs such as Greenpeace and WWF are contributing substantial ideas on land-based sources of marine pollution, whales, and fisheries. Nevertheless, the most important challenge to the NGO movement will be to build political pressure on reluctant states to support participation in, or strengthening of, global environmental regimes. This has become increasingly challenging as fundraising for global environmental activities has become more difficult for NGOs, forcing more NGOs to focus on domestic priorities rather than global environmental problems.

In spite of the apparent tension between economic health and ecological health, many experts agree that in the long run economic health is dependent on ecological health. The economy cannot thrive in the face of the total devastation of the biospheric envelope. If we accept that fact, then there are only two ways to resolve that tension between economy and ecology: We can let the tension continue until the integrity of the ecology and the economy deteriorate and snap like old rubber bands, releasing all tension; or we can make the economic, political, social, and cultural changes—the fundamental paradigm shift—that will be supportive of sustainable development. This paradigm shift may be under way, but it is far from complete, and the most difficult political decisions still lie ahead. The challenge is for governments to have the political will to make this shift happen and for the people of the world to demand change.[87]

DISCUSSION QUESTIONS

1. In what ways are the interests of developing countries and industrialized countries at odds over global environmental issues? In what sense are they compatible?
2. Explain how developing country concerns about economic growth might affect their position on ozone depletion or climate change. Why would their position on the Basel Convention be different?
3. Explain how trade and environmental issues affect each other. What is the nature of this relationship?
4. Compare the trade/environment issue with other global environmental issues in the regimes discussed in Chapter 3. Is the WTO/GATT an environmental regime in any sense? Why or why not?
5. Why are developing countries concerned about eco-labeling? How does this differ from the concerns of developed countries?
6. How has the concept of sustainable development evolved since the 1980s?
7. What changed in the world between the Earth Summit in 1992 and the World Summit on Sustainable Development in 2002? How did these changes affect the Summit in Johannesburg?

Notes

Chapter 1

1. World Resources Institute (WRI), *Wasting the Material World: The Impact of Industrial Economies* (Washington, D.C.: WRI, 2001), http://earthtrends.wri.org/pdf_library/features/ene_fea_materials_complete.pdf.

2. The facts and figures in this paragraph are from A. Adriaanse et al., *Resource Flows: The Material Basis of Industrial Economies,* a joint publication of the World Resources Institute (WRI); the Wuppertal Institute; the Netherlands Ministry of Housing, Spatial Planning, and the Environment; and the National Institute for Environmental Studies (Washington, D.C.: WRI, 1997).

3. Worldwatch, *State of the World 2004* (New York: W. W. Norton, 2004), 5.

4. Food and Agriculture Organization, *World Agriculture Towards 2015/2030: An FAO Perspective* (London: Earthscan, 2003).

5. Nick Robins, "Sustainable Consumption: The Way Ahead," presentation at the International Conference on Clean Technologies, February 12–13, 1999, New Delhi, India, http://www.iied.org/smg/pubs/cii-spee.html.

6. Worldwatch, *State of the World 2004,* 10.

7. United Nations Population Division (UNDP), *Human Development Report 1998* (New York: UNDP, 1998).

8. UNDP, *World Population Prospects: The 2002 Revision,* document ESA/P/W180 (February 26, 2003), http://www.un.org/esa/population/publications/wpp2002/WPP2002-HIGHLIGHTSrev1.PDF.

9. Ibid.

10. World Bank, *2004 World Development Indicators* (Washington, D.C.: World Bank, 2004), 114. Worldwatch, *State of the World 2004,* 26.

11. Worldwatch, *State of the World 2004,* 26.

12. Ibid.

13. International Energy Agency, *World Energy Outlook 2004* (Paris: International Energy Agency, 2004).

14. A hectare is 10,000 square meters.

15. World Bank, *2004 World Development Indicators.*

16. Food and Agriculture Organization, *State of the World's Fisheries and Aquaculture* (Rome: Food and Agriculture Organization, 2005).

17. Ibid.

18. World Meteorological Organization, *Comprehensive Assessment of the Freshwater Resources of the World* (Geneva: WMO, 1997), 9.

19. United Nations Environment Programme, *Vital Water Graphics: An Overview of the State of the World's Fresh and Marine Waters* (Nairobi: UNEP, 2002).

20. Ibid.

21. United Nations, *World Urbanization Prospects: The 2003 Revision* (New York: United Nations, 2004), 3, http://www.un.org/esa/population/publications/wup2003/WUP2003Report.pdf.

22. Ibid.

23. Ibid., 7.

24. UN-HABITAT, *State of the World's Cities 2004/2005: Globalization and Urban Culture* (Nairobi: UN-HABITAT/Earthscan, 2004).

25. Andrew Hurrell and Benedict Kingsbury, *The International Politics of the Environment* (Oxford: Clarendon Press, 1992), 2; Pamela S. Chasek, *Earth Negotiations: Analyzing Thirty Years of Environmental Diplomacy* (Tokyo: UNU Press, 2001).

26. For an early effort to categorize the different types of international environmental problems, see Clifford S. Russell and Hans H. Landsberg, "International Environmental Problems: A Taxonomy," *Science* 172 (June 25, 1972): 1307–1314.

27. Robert Dorfman and Nancy S. Dorfman, eds., *Economics of the Environment* (New York: W. W. Norton, 1993), 75.

28. Garrett Hardin, "The Tragedy of the Commons," *Science* 162 (1968): 1243–1248, as cited in Chasek, *Earth Negotiations.*

29. Oran R. Young, *International Governance* (Ithaca: Cornell University Press, 1994), 19–26.

30. Ibid., 23.

31. Ibid., 25.

32. Agreement on the Cartagena Protocol on Biosafety was reached in Montreal in January 2000. See chap. 3.

33. See Susan Strange, "Cave! Hic Dragones: A Critique of Regime Analysis," *International Organization* 36 (Spring 1982): 479–496.

34. Compare the definition and use of the term *regime* in John Gerard Ruggie, "International Responses to Technology: Concepts and Trends," *International Organization* 29 (1975): 557–583; Ernst Haas, "On Systems and International Regimes," *World Politics* 27 (1975): 147–174; Robert Keohane and Joseph Nye Jr., *Power and Interdependence: World Politics in Transition* (Boston: Little, Brown, 1977); Oran Young, "International Regimes: Problems of Concept Formation," *International Organization* 32 (1980): 331–356; Stephen Krasner, *International Regimes* (Ithaca: Cornell University Press, 1983), which includes an earlier version of the definition used here; Robert Keohane, *After Hegemony* (Princeton: Princeton University Press, 1984); Jack Donnelly, "International Human Rights: A Regime Analysis," *International Organization* 40 (1986): 599–642; Stephan Haggard and Beth Simmons, "Theories of International Regimes," *International Organization* 41 (1987): 491–517; Thomas Gehring, "International Environmental Regimes: Dynamic Sectoral Legal Systems," in *Yearbook of International Environmental Law,* vol. 1, ed. G. Handl (London: Graham and Trotman, 1990); David Downie, "Road Map or False Trail: Evaluating the Precedence of the Ozone Regime as Model and Strategy for Global Climate Change," *International Environmental Affairs* 7 (Fall 1995): 321–345; and David Downie, "Global Environmental Policy: Governance Through Regimes," in Regina Axelrod, David Downie, and Norman Vig, eds., *Global Environmental Policy: Institutions, Law, and Policy,* 2nd ed. (Washington, D.C.: Congressional Quarterly Press, 2004), 64–82.

35. For discussions of this tradition, see and compare: Friedrich Kratochwil and John Gerard Ruggie, "International Organization: A State of the Art on an Art of the State," *International Organization* 40 (1986): 753–776; James Dougherty and Robert Pfaltzgraff, *Contending Theories of International Relations*, 3rd ed. (New York: Harper and Row, 1990), chap. 10; and Joseph Grieco, "Anarchy and the Limits of Cooperation: A Realist Critique of the Newest Liberal Institutionalism," *International Organization* 42 (1988): 485–507.

36. Constitutionalists believed "international governance is whatever international organizations do; and . . . formal attributes of international organizations, such as their charters, voting procedures, committee structures and the like, account for what they do" (Kratochwil and Ruggie, "International Organization," 755). The Institutional Process approach examines influence, how information is produced and digested, who speaks to whom, how decisions are made, and so on. It argues that the outputs of international organizations do not always reflect their charters or official procedures. A classic example is Robert Cox and Harold Jacobson, eds., *The Anatomy of Influence* (New Haven: Yale University Press, 1973).

37. For example, Richard Falk, *A Study of Future Worlds* (Princeton: Princeton University Press, 1975).

38. Important examples and discussion of functionalism include David Mitrany, *A Working Peace System* (Chicago: Quadrangle Books, 1943); David Mitrany, *The Functional Theory of Politics* (London: M. Robertson, 1975); and A.J.R. Groom and Paul Taylor, eds., *Functionalism: Theory and Practice in International Relations* (New York: Crane, Russak, 1975).

39. Compare discussions in Kratochwil and Ruggie, "International Organization," 756–763; Dougherty and Pfaltzgraff, *Contending Theories of International Relations*, chap. 10; and Groom and Taylor, *Functionalism: Theory and Practice in International Relations*, chap. 1.

40. Leading examples and discussion include: Ernst Haas, *Beyond the Nation State* (Stanford: Stanford University Press, 1964); Ernst Haas, "The Uniting of Europe and the Uniting of Latin America," *Journal of Common Market Studies* 5 (1967): 315–343; Philippe Schmitter "Three Neo-functional Hypotheses About International Integration," *International Organization* 23 (1969): 161–166; Ernst Haas, "The Study of Regional Integration: Reflections on the Joy and Anguish of Pretheorizing," *International Organization* 24 (1970): 607–646; Joseph Nye, *Peace in Parts: Integration and Conflict in Regional Organization* (Boston: Little, Brown, 1977); Kratochwil and Ruggie, "International Organization," 757–759; and Dougherty and Pfaltzgraff, *Contending Theories of International Relations*, 431–447. Influential comparisons of functionalism and neofunctionalism include Haas, *Beyond the Nation State*, and Groom and Taylor, *Functionalism: Theory and Practice in International Relations*, chaps. 11–12.

41. An example is Ernst Haas, "On Systems and International Regimes," *World Politics* 27 (1975): 147–174; and Ernst Haas, *When Knowledge Is Power: Three Models of Change in International Organizations* (Berkeley: University of California Press, 1990).

42. Robert Keohane and Joseph Nye, *Transnational Relations and World Politics* (Cambridge, Mass.: Harvard University Press, 1972); Robert Keohane and Joseph Nye, "Transnational Relations and International Organizations," *World Politics* 27 (October 1974): 39–62.

43. Keohane and Nye, *Power and Interdependence*. Complex interdependence and turbulent fields share important concerns and insights.

44. John Gerard Ruggie, "International Responses to Technology: Concepts and Trends," *International Organization* 29 (1975): 570.

45. Haas, "On Systems and International Regimes," 147–174.

46. Robert O. Keohane and Joseph S. Nye, *Power and Interdependence* (Boston: Little, Brown, 1977), 5, 19.

47. Stephen Krasner, *International Regimes* (Ithaca: Cornell University Press, 1983), 2.

48. This paragraph is adapted from I. William Zartman, *The 50% Solution* (New Haven: Yale University Press, 1983), 9–10.

49. Oran Young, *International Cooperation* (Ithaca: Cornell University Press, 1989), 13–14.

50. M'Gonigle and Zacher, *Pollution, Politics and International Law* (Berkeley: University of California Press, 1979), 58–59, 84–85, 93–96; Jan Schneider, *World Public Order of the Environment: Toward an International Ecological Law and Organization* (Toronto: University of Toronto Press, 1979), 33, 92–93.

51. For an early analytical overview of these theoretical approaches, see Stephan Haggard and Beth A. Simmons, "Theories of International Regimes," *International Organization* 41 (Summer 1987), 491–517.

52. Keohane and Nye, *Power and Interdependence*, 50–51.

53. For the former approach, see Robert Gilpin, *The Political Economy of International Relations* (Princeton: Princeton University Press, 1987); Joseph M. Grieco, "Anarchy and the Limits of Cooperation: A Realist Critique of the Newest Liberal Institutionalism," *International Organization* 42 (Summer 1988): 485–508; and Strange, "Cave! Hic Dragones," 337–343. Susan Strange, "The Persistent Myth of Lost Hegemony," *International Organization* 41 (Summer 1987): 570, argues that the erosion of international regimes has been caused by inconsistency in U.S. policy rather than the loss of U.S. global hegemony.

54. Oran R. Young, "The Politics of International Regime Formation: Managing Natural Resources and the Environment," *International Organization* 43 (Summer 1989): 355.

55. Fen Osler Hampson, "Climate Change: Building International Coalitions of the Like-Minded," *International Journal* 45 (Winter 1989–1990): 36–74.

56. Robert O. Keohane, Peter M. Haas, and Marc A. Levy, "The Effectiveness of International Environmental Institutions," in Robert O. Keohane, Peter M. Haas, and Marc A. Levy, eds., *Institutions for the Earth* (Cambridge, Mass.: MIT Press, 1993), 4–5.

57. See Peter M. Haas, "Do Regimes Matter? Epistemic Communities and Mediterranean Pollution Control," *International Organization* 43 (Summer 1989): 378–403.

58. The issue of ocean dumping of radioactive wastes, in which scientific evidence was explicitly rejected as the primary basis for decisionmaking by antidumping states, is analyzed in Judith Spiller and Cynthia Hayden, "Radwaste at Sea: A New Era of Polarization or a New Basis for Consensus?" *Ocean Development and International Law* 19 (1988): 345–366.

59. Robert Putnam, "Diplomacy and Domestic Politics: The Logic of Two-Level Games," *International Organization* 42, no. 3 (Summer 1988): 427–460.

60. The description of paradigm shifts is not offered as a new theory to compete with existing theories of international regimes. Rather, this is supposed to represent a supplementary set of lenses through which to discuss environmental issues.

61. Harold and Margaret Sprout, *The Ecological Perspective in Human Affairs* (Princeton: Princeton University Press, 1965); Kenneth Boulding, "The Economics of the Coming Spaceship Earth," in H. E. Jarrett, ed., *Environmental Quality in a Growing Economy* (Baltimore: Johns Hopkins University Press, 1966).

62. For an analysis of neoclassical economic assumptions as they bear on environmental management, see Daniel A. Underwood and Paul G. King, "On the Ideological Foundations of Environmental Policy," *Ecological Economics* 1 (1989): 317–322.

63. See Michael E. Colby, *Environmental Management in Development: The Evolution of Paradigms* (Washington, D.C.: World Bank, 1990).

64. John McCormick, *Reclaiming Paradise: The Global Environmental Movement* (Bloomington, Ind.: Indiana University Press, 1989), 67.

65. See Clem Tisdell, "Sustainable Development: Differing Perspectives of Ecologists and Economists, and Relevance to LDCs," *World Development* 16 (1988): 377–378.

66. Donella H. Meadows et al., *The Limits to Growth* (New York: Universe Books, 1972); *Global 2000 Study, Global 2000 Report* (New York: Pergamon Press, 1980).

67. Julian Simon and Herman Kahn, eds., *The Resourceful Earth* (Oxford: Basil Blackwell, 1984).

68. For an account of the background of the sustainable development concept, see United Nations Center for Transnational Corporations, *Environmental Aspects of the Activities of Transnational Corporations: A Survey* (New York: United Nations, 1985).

69. See World Commission on Environment and Development, *Our Common Future* (Oxford: Oxford University Press, 1987).

70. See Jim MacNeill, "Sustainable Development, Economics and the Growth Imperative" (paper presented at the conference "The Economics of Sustainable Development," Smithsonian Institution, Washington, D.C., January 23–26, 1990).

71. See Edith Brown Weiss, "In Fairness to Future Generations," *Environment* 32 (April 1990): 7ff. See similar arguments made in *Our Own Agenda,* report of the Latin American and Caribbean Commission on Development and Environment (Washington, D.C., and New York: Inter-American Development Bank and United Nations Development Programme, 1990).

72. See Alan Durning, "How Much Is Enough?" *Worldwatch* 3 (November-December 1990): 12–19.

73. See Yusuf J. Ahmad, Salah El Serafy, and Ernst Lutz, eds., *Environmental Accounting for Sustainable Development* (Washington, D.C.: World Bank, 1989). For a concrete example of how natural resources accounting would work, see Robert Repetto et al., *Accounts Overdue: Natural Resources Depreciation in Costa Rica* (Washington, D.C.: World Resources Institute, 1991).

74. See Partha Dasgupta and Karl Goran Maler, "The Environment and Emerging Development Issues" (paper presented at the World Bank Conference on Development Economics, April 26–27, 1990), 14–20; Herman E. Daly, "Toward a Measure of Sustainable Social Net National Product," in Yusuf J. Ahmad, Salah El Serafy, and Ernst Lutz, eds., *Environmental Accounting for Sustainable Development* (Washington, D.C.: World Bank, 1989), 8–9; and Herman E. Daly and John B. Cobb, Jr., *For the Common Good: Redirecting the Economy Toward Community, the Environment and a Sustainable Future* (Boston: Beacon Press, 1989), 368–373, 401–455. A similar effort to rate the distributive effects of national policies is embodied in the United Nations Development Programme's human development indicators in its annual Human Development Report, http://www.undp.org/hdro/.

75. See Karma Ura and Karma Galay, eds., *Gross National Happiness and Development: Proceedings of the First International Seminar on Operationalization of Gross National Happiness* (Thimpu, Bhutan: Center for Bhutan Studies, 2004), http://www.bhutanstudies.org.bt.

76. For information on the Environmental Sustainability Index, see http://www.yale.edu/csi/.

77. See, for example, Dasgupta and Maler, "The Environment and Emerging Issues," 22; and Sander G. Tideman, "Gross National Happiness: Towards a New Paradigm in Economics," in Ura and Galay, eds., *Gross National Happiness and Development,* 222–246.

78. See Robert Repetto, *Promoting Environmentally Sound Economic Progress: What the North Can Do* (Washington, D.C.: World Resources Institute, 1990); and Daly, "Toward a Measure of Sustainable Social Net National Product."

79. *Economic Policies for Sustainable Development,* ministerial brief, Conference on Environment and Development in Asia and the Pacific, October 10–16, 1990, Bangkok, Thailand (Manila: Asian Development Bank, October 1990); Latin American and Caribbean Commission on Development and Environment, *Our Own Agenda*; and Organization of American States, Permanent Council, *Status Report Submitted by the Chairman of the Special Working Group on the Environment* (Washington, D.C.: General Secretariat of the OAS, February 6, 1991).

80. Al Gore, *Earth in the Balance: Ecology and the Human Spirit* (Boston: Houghton Mifflin, 1992), as cited in Gary C. Bryner, *From Promises to Performance: Achieving Global Environmental Goals* (New York: W. W. Norton, 1997), 329.

81. *Agenda 21, Rio Declaration, and Forest Principles* (New York: United Nations, 1992), chaps. 23–32: the final text of agreements negotiated by governments at the UNCED, June 3–14, 1992, Rio de Janeiro, Brazil. "Major groups" include women, youth, indigenous peoples, NGOs, local authorities, unions, business, the science and technology community, and farmers.

82. Ibid. See especially chap. 8 of *Agenda 21.*

83. Ibid.

84. Tideman, "Gross National Happiness," 229.

85. Martin Khor, "Globalisation and sustainable development: Challenges for Johannesburg," *Third World Resurgence* 139/140 (March-April 2002), http://www.twnside.org.sg/title/twr139a.htm.

86. Ibid.

87. James Gustave Speth, "Two Perspectives on Globalization and the Environment," in James Gustave Speth, ed. *Worlds Apart: Globalization and the Environment* (Washington, D.C.: Island Press, 2003), 12.

88. Ibid., 13.

89. Paul Raskin et al., *Great Transition: The Promise and Lure of the Times Ahead* (Boston: Stockholm Environment Institute, 2002), x.

Chapter 2

1. David Day, *The Whale War* (Vancouver and Toronto: Douglas and MacIntyre, 1987), 103–107.

2. Michael M'Gonigle and Mark W. Zacher, *Pollution, Politics and International Law: Tankers at Sea* (Berkeley: University of California Press, 1979).

3. See Peter Dauvergne, *Shadows in the Forest* (Cambridge, Mass.: MIT Press, 1997), 59–98; David W. Brown, *Addicted to Rent: Corporate and Spatial Distribution of Forest Resources in Indonesia* (Jakarta: Indonesia-UK Tropical Forest Management Programme, 1999).

4. Richard Benedick, *Ozone Diplomacy* (Cambridge, Mass.: Harvard University Press, 1991), 59.

5. John McCormick, *Acid Earth: The Global Threat of Acid Pollution* (London: Earthscan, 1985), 88–90.

6. The German Green Party lost all of its parliamentary members in the first all-German elections since 1932 because it opposed reunification, but it had begun to rebound by mid-1991, when polls showed it had the support of 6 percent of the voters—above the 5 percent

needed to achieve representation in the parliament. The Green Party won thirty-four seats in the German Parliament in 1998 and made history by becoming part of a coalition government with the Social Democratic Party. In 2002, the Green Party won fifty-five seats and continued its role in the coalition government with the Social Democratic Party.

7. Brian Wynne, "Implementation of Greenhouse Gas Reductions in the European Community: Institutional and Cultural Factors," *Global Environmental Change Report* (March 1993): 113, 122.

8. *Earth Summit Update,* no. 7 (March 1992): 3.

9. Detlev Sprinz and Tapani Vaahtoranta, "The Interest-based Explanation of International Environmental Policy," *International Organization* 48, no. 1 (1994): 77–105.

10. Carolyn Thomas, *The Environment in International Relations* (London: Royal Institute of International Affairs, 1992), 228.

11. On EU ambitions for global leadership on the environment, see Wynne, "Implementation of Greenhouse Gas Reductions," 102; Paleokrassas is quoted in *Energy, Economics and Climate Change* (July 1994): 14.

12. *Washington Post,* June 9, 1992.

13. Philippe Le Prestre and Evelyne Dufault, "Canada and the Kyoto Protocol on GHGs," *ISUMA* 2, no. 4 (Winter 2001): 40.

14. Andrew Buncombe, "American Mayors Unite to Implement Kyoto Goals on Carbon Dioxide Levels," *The Independent* (United Kingdom), May 16, 2005.

15. Ibid.

16. The Climate Group, "US Climate Change Progress (Kyoto) Unsigned But not Forgotten," December 6, 2004, http://www.theclimategroup.org/index.php?pid=574.

17. For additional information, go to the Regional Greenhouse Gas Initiative Web site at http://www.rggi.org/.

18. For a similar discussion that uses different terms, see David Downie, "UNEP and the Montreal Protocol: New Roles for International Organizations in Regime Creation and Change," in Robert V. Bartlett, Priya A. Kurian, and Madhu Malik, eds., *International Organizations and Environmental Policy* (Westport, Conn.: Greenwood Press, 1995).

19. "Summary of the Intergovernmental Consultation on Strengthening the Scientific Base of the United Nations Environment Programme: 14–15 January 2004," *Earth Negotiations Bulletin* 16, no. 31 (January 16, 2004): 1.

20. Richard Elliott Benedick, "The Ozone Protocol: A New Global Diplomacy," *Conservation Foundation Letter,* no. 4 (1989), 6–7; and *Ozone Diplomacy* (Cambridge, Mass.: Harvard University Press, 1991), 109–110.

21. "Discussion of Major UNEP Priority Activities with Executive Director," n.d.

22. For more details on the challenges that UNEP faced in the latter half of the 1990s, see David L. Downie and Marc A. Levy, "The United Nations Environment Programme at a Turning Point: Options for Change," in Pamela S. Chasek, ed., *The Global Environment in the 21st Century: Prospects for International Cooperation* (Tokyo: UNU Press, 2000).

23. UNEP, "State of the environment and contribution of the United Nations Environment Programme to addressing substantive environmental challenges: Report of the Executive Director," UNEP/GC.23/3, October 21, 2004.

24. Felix Dodds et al., *Post Johannesburg: The Future of the UN Commission on Sustainable Development,* Stakeholder Forum for Our Common Future (paper 9, November 2002), 5, http://www.earthsummit2002.org/es/issues/governance/csdfuture.pdf.

25. Peter H. Sand has described these soft-law alternatives to treaties in *Lessons Learned in Global Environmental Governance* (Washington, D.C.: World Resources Institute, 1990), 16–17.

26. See Khalil Sesmou, "The Food and Agriculture Organization of the United Nations: An Insider's View," *Ecologist* 21 (March-April 1991): 47–56, and other critical analyses in this special issue on the FAO.

27. See "Researchers Score Victory over Pesticides—and Pests—in Asia," *Science* 256 (May 29, 1992): 1272–1273.

28. Michael Hansen, *Sustainable Agriculture and Rural Development: FAO at the Crossroads* (Yonkers, N.Y.: Consumers Union of the United States, 1993), 16–18.

29. For more information about UNDP's Energy and Environment Group, see http://www.undorg/energyandenvironment/.

30. See Gareth Porter et al., *Study of GEF's Overall Performance* (Washington, D.C.: GEF, 1998), 47–51.

31. Documentation and Statistics Office, Bureau for Programme Policy and Evaluation, United Nations Development Programme (UDNP), *Compendium of Ongoing Projects,* UNDP/Series A/nos. 22–27, 1992–1996.

32. UNDP, *Compendium of Ongoing Projects as of 31 December 1996,* Series A/no. 27, 43.

33. UNDP, *Development Effectiveness Report 2003* (New York: UNDP Evaluation Office, 2003), 21.

34. See UNDP, "LP Gas Rural Energy Challenge," http://www.undorg/energy/lpg.htm.

35. See World Bank, "Energy Sector Management Assistance Program," http://wbln0018.worldbank.org/esmap/site.nsf.

36. This formulation is used in the context of a different conceptualization of the role of IOs in global environmental policymaking in Marc A. Levy, Robert O. Keohane, and Peter M. Haas, "Improving the Effectiveness of International Environmental Institutions," in Peter M. Haas, Robert O. Keohane, and Marc A. Levy, eds., *Institutions for the Earth: Sources of Effective International Environmental Protection* (Cambridge, Mass., and London: MIT Press, 1993), 400.

37. For a critical analysis of the environmental impacts of various multilateral development bank loans, see Bruce Rich, *Mortgaging the Earth: The World Bank, Environmental Impoverishment, and the Crisis of Development* (Boston: Beacon Press, 1994).

38. Jim Douglas, "World Bank Involvement in Sector Adjustment for Forests in Indonesia: The Issues" (unpublished paper, 1998).

39. World Bank/World Wide Fund for Nature, "WWF/World Bank Forest Alliance Launches Ambitious Program to Reduce Deforestation and Curb Illegal Logging," news release, May 25, 2005.

40. Ibid.

41. Porter et al., *Study of the GEF's Overall Performance,* 44.

42. Ibid., 38–43. Note that it takes two to three years for a project to go from initial development to final approval by the Executive Board, so 1994 is the first effective year for comparing Bank lending after its new commitments to the GEF.

43. Kathy MacKinnon et al., *Ensuring the Future: The World Bank and Biodiversity* (Washington, D.C.: World Bank, 2004), 3.

44. Loan totals are from Hagler Baily, Stockholm Environment Institute, and IIEC, *The Effect of a Shadow Price on Carbon Emissions in the Energy Portfolio of the Bank: A Backcasting Exercise.* Final report to the Global Climate Change Unit, Global Environment Division,

World Bank, June 13, 1997, I-1; impact on emissions from the Institute for Policy Studies and the International Trade Information Service, *The World Bank and the G-7: Changing the Earth's Climate for Business, 1992–1997* (Washington, D.C.: IPS, 1997), http://www.seen.org/wbreport1/index.html.

45. See World Bank, Environment Department, Land, Water and Natural Habitats Division, *The Impact of Environmental Assistance: The World Bank's Experience* (Washington, D.C.: World Bank, 1996), xv.

46. World Bank, "World Bank Tells UN Earth Summit of New Action to Safeguard Environment," news release 97/1401/S, June 25, 1997.

47. Sustainable Energy and Economy Network/Institute for Policy Studies, "The World Bank and Fossil Fuels: A Clear and Present Danger," policy brief, September 2002, 3, http://www.seen.org/PDFs/wb_brief_sept02.pdf.

48. Ibid.

49. For a defense of the IMF's macroeconomic policy prescriptions in environmental terms, see Ved P. Gandhi, "The IMF and the Environment" (Washington, D.C.: IMF, 1998).

50. David Reed, ed., *Structural Adjustment and the Environment* (Boulder: Westview Press, 1992), esp. 161–178.

51. "IMF Reviews Its Approach to Environmental Issues," *IMF Survey* (April 15, 1991): 124.

52. For more information about the HIPC initiative, see Anthony R. Boote and Kamau Thugge, *Debt Relief for Low-Income Countries; the HIPC Initiative,* Pamphlet Series no. 51 (Washington, D.C.: IMF, 1999), or http://www.imf.org/external/np/exr/facts/hipc.htm.

53. See International Monetary Fund, "The IMF and Environmental Issues," IMF Issue Brief 00/04 (April 13, 2000), http://www.imf.org/external/np/exr/ib/2000/041300.htm.

54. Gandhi, "The IMF and the Environment."

55. See *Jakarta Post,* October 4, 1997.

56. This account of the adjustment loans to Indonesia in 1998–1999 is based on interviews by Gareth Porter in Jakarta in April 1999.

57. Ibid.

58. Ibid.

59. WWF-Macroeconomics Program Office, "Poverty Reduction for the Poor, Not the Privileged" (Poverty Reduction Paper 1, May 30, 2003), http://www.panda.org/downloads/policy/povertyreductionpaper1.doc.

60. Ibid.

61. Belgium, West Germany, Luxembourg, France, Italy, and the Netherlands formed three organizations: the European Economic Community, the European Coal and Steel Community, and the European Atomic Energy Community.

62. European Union, "Environment," *Activities of the European Union: Summaries of Legislation* (Brussels, European Community, 2001), http://europa.eu.int/scadplus/leg/en/s15000.htm.

63. Ibid.

64. APEC, "APEC Economic Leaders' Declaration," Kuala Lumpur, Malaysia (November 18, 1998), http://www.apec.org/apec/leaders__declarations/1998.html.

65. Adil Najam, "The View from the South: Developing Countries in Global Environmental Politics," in Regina S. Axelrod, David L. Downie, and Norman J. Vig, eds., *The Global Environment: Institutions, Law and Policy,* 2nd ed. (Washington, D.C.: Congressional Quarterly Press, 2004).

66. This description is based on the Group of 77, "What Is the Group of 77?" at http://www.g77.org/main/gen_info_1.htm; and Najam, "The View from the South."

67. For more information about SPREP, see the organization's Web site, http://www.sprep.org.ws.

68. For additional information about CCAD, see its Web site, http://www.ccad.ws.

69. See Thomas Weiss and Leon Gordenker, eds., *NGOs, the UN and Global Governance* (Boulder: Lynne Rienner, 1996); Paul Wapner, "Politics Beyond the State: Environmental Actions and World Civic Politics," *World Politics* 47, no. 3 (April 1995): 311–340; Thomas Princen and Matthias Finger, eds., *Environmental NGOs in World Politics* (London and New York: Routledge, 1994); and Barbara Bramble and Gareth Porter, "Non-Governmental Organizations and the Making of US International Environmental Policy," in Andrew Hurrell and Benedict Kingsbury, eds., *The International Politics of the Environment* (Oxford: Clarendon Press, 1992).

70. Greenpeace, "The History of Greenpeace," http://www.greenpeace.org/international/about/history.

71. Ramachandra Guha, "The Environmentalism of the Poor," in Ramachandra Guha and Juan Martinez-Alier, eds., *Varieties of Environmentalism* (London: Earthscan, 1997), 15.

72. See Julie Fisher, *The Road from Rio: Sustainable Development and the Nongovernmental Movement in the Third World* (Westport, Conn.: Praeger, 1993), 123–128.

73. Guha, "The Environmentalism of the Poor," 4.

74. Ibid.

75. See Third World Network, *The Battle for Sarawak's Forests* (Penang, Malaysia: World Rainforest Movement, 1989).

76. For more information about the Green Belt Movement, see its Web site, http://www.greenbeltmovement.org/.

77. For more information about Third World Network, see its Web site, http://www.twnside.org.sg/.

78. For more information on the Center for Science and Environment, see its Web site, http://www.cseindia.org.

79. Interview with Barbara Bramble, National Wildlife Federation, March 1990; Stephen Schwartzman, "Deforestation and Popular Resistance in Acre: From Local Movement to Global Network" (paper presented to the Eighty-eighth Annual Meeting of the American Anthropological Association, Washington, D.C., November 15–19, 1989).

80. David Malin Roodman, "Building a Sustainable Society," in Lester R. Brown, Christopher Flavin, and Hilary French, eds., *State of the World 1999* (New York: W. W. Norton, 1999), 183.

81. For more information on the International POPs Elimination Network, see its Web site, http://ipen.ecn.cz/.

82. Working with Merck and Genentech, the World Resources Institute, the World Wildlife Fund, and the Environmental and Energy Study Institute drafted an interpretive statement and persuaded President Clinton to sign the treaty with such a statement attached.

83. Statement by Craig Van Note before the Subcommittee on Human Rights and International Organizations, Committee on Foreign Affairs, U.S. House of Representatives, September 28, 1989.

84. Robert Boardman, *International Organization and the Conservation of Nature* (Bloomington: Indiana University Press, 1981), 88–94.

85. Patricia Birnie, "The Role of International Law in Solving Certain Environmental Conflicts," in John E. Carroll, ed., *International Environmental Diplomacy: The Management and Resolution of Transfrontier Environmental Problems* (Cambridge: Cambridge University Press, 1988), 107–108.

86. Personal communication from a member of the U.S. delegation to the biodiversity negotiations, February 1994.

87. Kal Raustiala, "States, NGOs and International Environmental Institutions," *International Studies Quarterly* 41 (1997): 728.

88. The *Earth Negotiations Bulletin* was initially published as the *Earth Summit Bulletin* and was created by Johannah Bernstein, Pamela Chasek, and Langston James Goree VI. For more information, see http://www.iisd.ca/linkages/.

89. Raustiala, "States, NGOs and International Environmental Institutions," 730.

90. Laura H. Kosloff and Mark C. Trexler, "The Convention on International Trade in Endangered Species: No Carrot, but Where's the Stick?" *Environmental Law Reporter* 17 (July 1987): 10225–10226.

91. Paul Lewis, "Rich Nations Plan $2 Billion for Environment," *New York Times,* March 17, 1994. Also, see Zoe Young, "NGOs and the Global Environmental Facility: Friendly Foes?" *Environmental Politics* 8, no. 1 (1999): 243–267.

92. This discussion is based on Barbara J. Bramble and Gareth Porter, "Non-Governmental Organizations and the Making of U.S. International Environmental Policy," in Andrew Hurrell and Benedict Kingsbury, eds., *The International Politics of the Environment* (Oxford: Clarendon Press, 1992), 325–346.

93. A. Enders, "Openness and the WTO," working paper, International Institute for Sustainable Development (IISD), Winnipeg, Canada, 1996; Dan Esty, *Why the WTO Needs Environmental NGOs* (Geneva: International Centre for Trade and Sustainable Development, 1997).

94. Marc Williams and Lucy Ford, "The World Trade Organisation, Social Movements and Global Environmental Management," *Environmental Politics* 8, no. 1 (1999): 281.

95. Pew Center on Global Climate Change, "Businesses Leading the Way: GHG Reduction Targets," http://www.pewclimate.org/companies_leading_the_way_belc/targets/index.cfm.

96. Greg Schneider, "Automakers Agree to Cut Emissions in Canada," *Washington Post,* April 6, 2005.

97. See Gareth Porter, *The United States and the Biodiversity Convention: The Case for Participation* (Washington, D.C.: Environmental and Energy Study Institute, 1992). The Industrial Biotechnology Association merged with the Association of Biotechnology Companies in 1993 to form BIO, or Biotechnology Industry Organization.

98. *International Environment Reporter,* June 2, 1993, 416.

99. Julian E. Salt, "Kyoto and the Insurance Industry: An Insider's Perspective," *Environmental Politics* 7, no. 2 (Summer 1998): 164.

100. United Nations Environment Programme, "Extreme Weather Losses Soar to Record High for Insurance Industry: Insurance Industry Facing $35 Billion Plus Bill for 2004," news release 2004/52, December 15, 2004.

101. M'Gonigle and Zacher, *Pollution, Politics and International Law,* 58–62.

102. For more information, see the Global Climate Coalition Web site, http://www.global-climate.org. The Global Climate Coalition was deactivated in 2001 following the election of U.S. President George W. Bush, but their Web site still exists.

103. Day, *The Whale War,* 103–107.

104. Laura Eggerton, "Giant Food Companies Control Standards," *Toronto Star,* April 28, 1999.

105. Interview with William Nitze, Alliance to Save Energy, June 20, 1994.

106. Jennifer Clapp, "Transnational Corporate Interests and Global Environmental Governance: Negotiating Rules for Agricultural Biotechnology and Chemicals," *Environmental Politics* 12, no. 4 (2003): 1–23.

107. Alan S. Miller and Durwood Zaelke, "The NGO Perspective," *Climate Alert* 7, no. 3 (May–June 1994): 3.

108. *Daily Environment Reporter,* August 27, 1992, B2.

109. See, for example, the company profiles on the Pew Center on Global Climate Change Web site, http://www.pewclimate.org/companies_leading_the_way_belc/company_profiles/.

110. Robert L. Paarlberg, "Managing Pesticide Use in Developing Countries," in Peter M. Haas, Robert O. Keohane, and Marc A. Levy, eds., *Institutions for the Earth: Sources of Effective International Environmental Protection* (Cambridge, Mass., and London: MIT Press, 1993), 319.

111. François Nectoux and Yoichi Kuroda, *Timber from the South Seas: An Analysis of Japan's Tropical Timber Trade and Its Environmental Impact* (Gland, Switzerland: World Wildlife Fund, 1989), 94; David Swinbanks, "Sarawak's Tropical Rain-Forests Exploited by Japan," *Nature* 238 (July 30, 1987): 373.

112. Peter Dauvergne, "Globalisation and Deforestation in the Asia-Pacific," *Environmental Politics* 7, no. 4 (Winter 1998): 128.

113. See Stephen Schmidheiny, with the Business Council for Sustainable Development, *Changing Course: A Global Business Perspective on Development and the Environment* (Cambridge, Mass.: MIT Press, 1992).

114. See the World Business Council for Sustainable Development Web site, http://www.wbcsd.org/.

Chapter 3

1. For a more detailed discussion on this dilemma, see Richard Elliot Benedick, "Perspectives of a Negotiation Practitioner," in Gunnar Sjöstedt, ed., *International Environmental Negotiations* (Beverly Hills, Calif.: Sage, 1993), 240–243.

2. This discussion of decisionmaking procedures in global environmental regimes is based on Glenn Wiser and Stephen Porter, "Effective Decision-Making: A Review of Options for Making Decisions to Conserve and Manage Pacific Fish Stocks," prepared by the Center for International Environmental Law for the World Wildlife Fund-US, January 1999.

3. Marc A. Levy, "European Acid Rain: The Power of Tote-Board Diplomacy," in Peter M. Haas, Robert O. Keohane, and Marc A. Levy, eds., *Institutions for the Earth* (Cambridge, Mass.: MIT Press, 1993), 81.

4. Lars Bjorkbom, "Resolution of Environmental Problems: The Use of Diplomacy," in John E. Carroll, ed., *International Environmental Diplomacy: The Management and Resolution of Transfrontier Environmental Problems* (Cambridge: Cambridge University Press, 1988), 128; Harald Dovland, "Monitoring European Transboundary Air Pollution," *Environment* 29 (December 1987): 12.

5. Although the United States was not involved in transboundary air pollution in Europe, it was concerned about a similar situation whereby U.S. emissions were causing acid rain in Canada. See Don Munton, "Acid Rain and Transboundary Air Quality in Canadian-American Relations," *American Review of Canadian Studies* 27, no. 3 (Fall 1997): 327–358.

6. Levy, "European Acid Rain," 83.

7. Don Hinrichsen, "Acid Indigestion in Stockholm," *Ambio* 11, no. 5 (1982): 320–321.

8. Sten Nelson and Peter Druinker, "The Extent of Forest Decline in Europe," *Environment* 29, no. 9 (1987): 7–8.

9. Seven states pledged to reduce their emissions by 40 or 50 percent by various dates. See John McCormick, *Acid Earth: The Global Threat of Acid Pollution* (Washington, D.C.: Earthscan and International Institute for Environment and Development, 1985), 11 (esp. fig. 1).

10. Henrik Selin and Stacy D. VanDeveer, "Mapping Institutional Linkages in European Air Pollution Politics," *Global Environmental Politics* 3, no. 3 (August 2003): 14–46.

11. See Levy, "European Acid Rain," 99–100.

12. See Henrik Selin, "Regional POPs Policy: The UNECE/CLRTAP POPs Agreement," in David L. Downie and Terry Fenge, eds., *Northern Lights Against POPs: Combating Toxic Threats in the Arctic* (Montreal: McGill-Queens University Press, 2003), and Noelle Eckley and Henrik Selin, "Science, Politics, and Persistent Organic Pollutants: Scientific Assessments and their Role in International Environmental Negotiations," *International Environmental Agreements: Politics, Law and Economics* 3, no. 1, (2003): 17–42.

13. Noelle Eckley, "Dependable Dynamism: Lessons for Designing Scientific Assessment Processes in Consensus Negotiations," *Global Environmental Change* 12 (2002), 15–23.

14. See "Targets and Trends," *Acid News* 3 (October 1997): 11, as cited in Jørgen Wettestad, "The 1999 Multi-Pollutant Protocol: A Neglected Break-Through in Solving Europe's Air Pollution Problems," in Olav Schram Stokke and Øystein B. Thommessen, *Yearbook of International Co-operation on Environment and Development 2001/2002* (London: Earthscan Publications, 2001), 36.

15. Wettestad, "The 1999 Multi-Pollutant Protocol," 36.

16. Ute Collier, "Windfall Emission Reduction in the UK," in Ute Collier and Ragnar E. Löfstedt, eds., *Cases in Climate Change Policy: Political Reality in the European Union* (London: Earthscan, 1997), 87–108, as cited in Wettestad, "The 1999 Multi-Pollutant Protocol," 39.

17. Wettestad, "The 1999 Multi Pollutant Protocol," 39. In an overview of the total implementation costs for each country, Germany came out clearly at the top, with 2.15 billion Euro per year, almost twice as much as the number two on the list, the United Kingdom. See "European Union—Commission Proposes National Ceilings for Sulfur Dioxide, NO_x, VOCs, Ammonia," *International Environmental Reporter* 22, no. 13 (1999): 519.

18. Selin and VanDeveer, "Mapping Institutional Linkages."

19. At ground level ozone is a pollutant, a key component of urban smog produced by the interaction in bright sunlight of chemicals from factory emissions and automobiles that can contribute to respiratory problems and damage plants.

20. Mario Molina and F. Sherwood Rowland, "Stratospheric Sink for Chlorofluoromethanes: Chlorine Atomic Catalyzed Destruction of Ozone," *Nature* 249 (June 28, 1974): 810–812.

21. There are a number of detailed discussions of the creation and expansion of the ozone regime. This section draws on David Downie, "Understanding International Environmental Regimes: The Origin, Creation and Expansion of the Ozone Regime" (Ph.D. dissertation, University of North Carolina at Chapel Hill, 1996); Richard Benedick, *Ozone Diplomacy*, 2nd ed. (Cambridge, Mass.: Harvard University Press, 1998); Karen Litfin, *Ozone Discourses* (New York: Columbia University Press, 1994); David Downie, "UNEP and the Montreal Protocol: New Roles for International Organizations in Regime Creation and Change," in Robert V. Bartlettet et al., eds., *International Organizations and Environmental Policy* (Westport, Conn.: Greenwood Press, 1995); and Sharon Roan, *Ozone Crisis: The 15 Year Evolution of a Sudden Global Emergency* (New York: John Wiley & Sons, 1989).

22. See in particular, Iwona Rummel-Bulska, "The Protection of the Ozone Layer Under the Global Framework Convention," in Cees Flinterman et al., eds., *Transboundary Air Pollution* (Dordrecht, Netherlands: Martinus Nijhoff, 1986), 281–296.

23. For detailed analysis of this point, see David Downie, "The Power to Destroy: Understanding Stratospheric Ozone Politics as a Common Pool Resource Problem," in J. Samuel Barkin and George Shambaugh, eds., *Anarchy and the Environment: The International Rela-*

tions of Common Pool Resources (Albany, N.Y.: State University of New York Press, 1999), and "An Analysis of the Montreal Protocol on Substances That Deplete the Ozone Layer," staff paper prepared by the Oceans and Environment Program, Office of Technology Assessment, U.S. Congress, December 10, 1987, 9, table 1.

24. J. Farman et al., "Large Losses of Total Ozone in Antarctica Reveal Seasonal ClOx/NOx Interaction," *Nature* 315 (May 16, 1985): 207–210.

25. For discussion, see Downie, "Understanding International Environmental Regimes," chap. 6; Roan, *Ozone Crisis*, 125–141, 158–188; and Litfin, *Ozone Discourses*, 96–102.

26. Although an historic agreement, the protocol did permit the continued production of ozone-depleting chemicals, neglected to specify that alternatives must not damage the ozone layer, included no provisions for independent monitoring of production and consumption of ozone-destroying chemicals, and contained no real penalties for noncompliance.

27. NASA, *Executive Summary of the Ozone Trends Panel* (Washington, D.C.: NASA, Office of Management, Scientific and Technical Information Division, March, 1988). UNEP and WMO established the trends panel in 1986 as part of a new U.S. initiative, continuing efforts by UNEP. It included more than a hundred scientists from ten countries and examined satellite and ground-based data.

28. World Meteorological Organization et al., *Scientific Assessment of Stratospheric Ozone: 1989*, WMO Global Ozone Research and Monitoring Project, report no. 20 (Geneva: WMO for WMO, UNEP, NASA, NOAA, and U.K. DOE, 1989).

29. For example, at the first Meeting of the Parties (MOP–1) in Helsinki in May 1989, EC members were among eighty nations (along with the United States but not Japan or the Soviet Union), that supported a strong but nonbinding declaration calling for a complete CFC phaseout by the year 2000.

30. Text of the ozone treaties, amendments and adjustments, as well as official reports from each Meeting of the Parties, is available from the Ozone Secretariat's Web site at http://www.unep.org/ozone/.

31. The Fund included $240 million for the initial 1991–1993 period and has been replenished as follows: $455 million for 1994–1996; $466 million for 1997–1999; $477.7 million for 2000–2002; and $573 for 2003–2005. For details on the history and operation of the fund, see the Multilateral Fund homepage at http://www.multilateralfund.org/.

32. HCFCs have shorter atmospheric lifetimes and one HCFC molecule destroys far fewer ozone molecules than one CFC molecule. But ozone destruction by HCFCs takes place sooner. Opponents of HCFCs, therefore, point to its relatively high impact over five years, and supporters highlight its low five-hundred-year impact.

33. "Summary of the Sixteenth Meeting of the Parties to the Montreal Protocol: 22–26 November 2004," *Earth Negotiation Bulletin* 19, no. 40 (November 29, 2004).

34. United Nations Environment Programme (UNEP), "Data Report," UNEP/Oz.L.Pro.16/4, September 18, 2004.

35. Ozone Secretariat, "Press Backgrounder (updated November 2004)," http://www.unep.org/ozone/Public_Information/4_Press%20Releases.asp.

36. For an overview of the state of the science of climate change, see Intergovernmental Panel on Climate Change, *Climate Change 2001: Synthesis Report: Summary for Policy Makers* (Geneva: IPCC 2001), http://www.ipcc.ch/pub/un/syreng/spm.pdf.

37. On the importance of perceptions of cost to early climate policies and absence of accurate cost estimates for the Netherlands, Germany, Japan, and the United States, see Yasuko Kawashima, "A Comparative Analysis of the Decisionmaking Processes of Developed Countries

Toward CO$_2$ Emissions Reduction Targets," *International Environmental Affairs* 9 (Spring 1997): 95–126.

38. See Matthew Paterson, *Global Warming and Global Politics* (London: Routledge, 1996), 77–82.

39. Richard A. Houghton and George M. Woodwell, "Global Climatic Change," *Scientific American* 260 (April 1989): 42–43.

40. Lamont C. Hempel and Matthias Kaelberer, "The Changing Climate in Greenhouse Policy: Obstacles to International Cooperation in Agenda Setting and Policy Formulation" (unpublished paper, April 1990), 6; and Daniel Bodansky, "The United Nations Framework Convention on Climate Change: A Commentary," *Yale Journal of International Law* 18, no. 2 (Summer 1993), 461.

41. The IPCC is organized into three working groups: Working Group I on the climate system, Working Group II on impacts and response options, and Working Group III on economic and social dimensions. For more information, see the IPCC Web site, http://www.ipcc.ch.

42. Japan subsequently backtracked by proposing a process of "pledge and review" in place of binding commitments. Individual countries, it suggested, would set for themselves appropriate targets that would be publicly reviewed. Most EC member states and NGOs were cool to the idea. Bodansky, "The United Nations Framework Convention on Climate Change," 486.

43. Intergovernmental Panel on Climate Change, *The Formulation of Response Strategies: Report by Working Group III, Policymakers' Summary,* June 1990, 11, table 2. For country contributions and rankings at the time of the negotiations, see World Resources Institute, *World Resources, 1992–1993* (New York: Oxford University Press, 1992), 205–213, 345–355. For a good discussion of different methods of greenhouse-gas accounting, see Peter M. Morrisette and Andrew J. Plantinga, "The Global Warming Issue: Viewpoints of Different Countries," *Resources* (Washington, D.C.: Resources for the Future), no. 103 (Spring 1991): 2–6.

44. *Earth Summit Update,* no. 9 (May 1992): 1; *Wall Street Journal,* May 22, 1992, 1.

45. "Global Warming Basics: Glossary," *Pew Center on Global Climate Change 2005,* http://www.pewclimate.org/global-warming-basics/full_glossary/index.cfm.

46. In 2005, 189 countries had ratified the convention. UN Framework Convention on Climate Change, "Status of Ratification," May 24, 2004, http://www.unfccc.int/.

47. For a complete summary and analysis of the Kyoto Protocol, see Herman E. Ott, "The Kyoto Protocol: Unfinished Business," *Environment* 40, no. 6 (1998): 16ff.; Clare Breidenrich et al., "The Kyoto Protocol to the United Nations Framework Convention on Climate Change," *American Journal of International Law* 92, no. 2 (1998): 315.

48. See the UNFCCC, "The Mechanisms Under the Kyoto Protocol: Joint Implementation, the Clean Development Mechanism and Emissions Trading," http://www.unfccc.int/kyoto_mechanisms/items/1673.php.

49. Subsequently, the White House revealed that the United States planned to achieve up to 75 percent of the U.S. reduction requirement by purchasing allowances from the Russian Federation and Ukraine. See Christopher Flavin, "Last Tango in Buenos Aires," *WorldWatch* (November-December 1998): 13.

50. "COP 6: US-EU Differences Blamed for Failure of Climate Change Negotiations," *ICTSD Bridges Weekly Trade News Digest* 4 (November 28, 2000), http://www.ictsd.org/html/weekly/story2.28–11–00.htm.

51. For more information on the agreements reached at COP-7 in Marrakesh, see "Summary of the Seventh Conference of the Parties to the UN Framework Convention on Climate

Change: 29 October–10 November 2001," *Earth Negotiations Bulletin* 12, no. 189 (November 12, 2001), http://www.iisd.ca/vol12/enb12189e.html.

52. ICTSD, "EU Attacks Bush's U-Turn on Climate Change," *Bridges Weekly Trade News Digest* 5, no. 11 (March 27, 2001), http://www.ictsd.org/html/weekly/27–03–01/story3.htm.

53. For a variety of different ratification scenarios, see Greenpeace, "How the Kyoto Protocol Can Come into Force Without the U.S.A.," briefing paper, 2001, http://www.climnet.org/EUenergy/ratification/GP-rat_without_usa.pdf.

54. Benito Müller, "Quo Vadis, Kyoto? Pitfalls and Opportunities," key note, presented at the Civil Society Outreach of the G–8 Meeting of Environment and Development Ministers, March 17–18, 2005, Derby, U.K., 4, http://www.OxfordClimatePolicy.org.

55. Ibid.

56. Katharine Kummer, *International Management of Hazardous Wastes: The Basel Convention and Related Legal Rules* (Oxford: Clarendon Press, 1995), 5.

57. In one example, the cargo ship *Khian Sea* went to sea in 1986 in search of a disposal site for 14,000 tons of incinerator ash containing lead and cadmium. The ship spent almost two years at sea, during which it changed its name twice and dumped 4,000 tons of ash on a beach in Haiti and the remaining 10,000 tons somewhere between the Suez Canal and Singapore.

58. The Dutch minister of environment, for example, called it "waste colonialism." *Report of the Ad Hoc Working Group on the Work of Its Fourth Session,* UNEP/WG.190/4, February 13, 1989, 3.

59. Carol Annette Petsonk, "The Role of the United Nations Environment Programme (UNEP) in the Development of International Environmental Law," *American University Journal of International Law and Policy* 5 (Winter 1990): 374–377; *International Environment Reporter,* April 1989, 159–161.

60. For the text of the convention, meeting reports, official documents, updated lists of signatories and ratifications, and other information on the regime, see the Web site of the Secretariat of the Basel Convention at http://www.basel.int.

61. See David P. Hackett, "An Assessment of the Basel Convention on the Control of Transboundary Movements of Hazardous Wastes and Their Disposal," *American University Journal of International Law and Policy* 5 (Winter 1990): 313–322; Mark A. Montgomery, "Travelling Toxic Trash: An Analysis of the 1989 Basel Convention," *Fletcher Forum of World Affairs* 14 (Summer 1990): 313–326.

62. *International Environment Reporter,* April 1989, 159–160.

63. *Greenpeace Waste Trade Update* 2 (July 15, 1989, and December 1989).

64. Two other regional conventions on hazardous wastes have been adopted since 1992. The Convention to Ban the Importation into Forum Island Countries of Hazardous and Radioactive Wastes and to Control the Transboundary Movement and Management of Hazardous Wastes Within the South Pacific Region (Waigani Convention) was adopted on September 16, 1995, in Papua New Guinea. The Acuerdo Regional sobre Movimiento Transfronterizo de Desechos Peligrosas (Regional Convention on the Transboundary Movement of Hazardous Wastes) was adopted by Costa Rica, El Salvador, Guatemala, Honduras, Nicaragua, and Panama in December 1992.

65. *International Environment Reporter,* May 6, 1992, 275.

66. Only the republics of the former Soviet Union, desperate for foreign exchange and willing to disregard the health and environmental consequences, appeared willing to accept signif-

icant shipments of hazardous wastes. See Steven Coll, "Free Market Intensifies Waste Problem," *Washington Post*, March 23, 1994; Tamara Robinson, "Dirty Deals: Hazardous Waste Imports into Russia and Ukraine," *CIS Environmental Watch* (Monterey Institute of International Studies), no. 5 (Fall 1993).

67. Greenpeace, *The International Trade in Wastes: A Greenpeace Inventory*, 5th ed. (Washington, D.C.: Greenpeace, 1990); *Toxic Trade Update*, no. 6.2 (1993): 6, 7, 12–26; "Chemicals: Shipment to South Africa Draws Enviro Protests," *Greenwire*, February 18, 1994; and "Deadly Trade in Toxics," *U.S. News and World Report*, March 7, 1994, 64–67.

68. John H. Cushman Jr., "Clinton Seeks Ban on Export of Most Hazardous Waste," *New York Times*, March 1, 1994; "Basel Convention Partners Consider Ban on Exports of Hazardous Wastes," *International Environment Reporter*, March 22, 1994, A9.

69. Charles P. Wallace, *Los Angeles Times*, March 23, 1994, cited in *Greenwire*, March 23, 1994. For a detailed account of the Geneva meeting, see Jim Puckett and Cathy Fogel, "A Victory for Environment and Justice: The Basel Ban and How It Happened," Greenpeace International Toxic Trade Campaign, Washington, D.C., September 1994.

70. Greenpeace, *The International Trade in Wastes: Database of Known Hazardous Waste Exports from OECD to Non-OECD Countries: 1989–March 1994*, prepared for the Second Conference of Parties to the Basel Convention (Washington, D.C.: Greenpeace, 1994).

71. Jim Puckett, "The Basel Ban: A Triumph over Business-as-Usual" (Amsterdam: Basel Action Network [Greenpeace], October 1997), http://www.ban.org/about_basel_ban/jims_article.html. In mid–2005, the Ban Amendment still needed five more instruments of ratification. For up-to-date information, see the Basel Convention's Web site at http://www.basel.int.

72. In mid–2005, the Liability Protocol had received only five out of the twenty instruments of ratification necessary for entry into force. For up-to-date information, see the Basel Convention's Web site at http://www.basel.int.

73. Thomas R. Dunlap, *DDT: Scientists, Citizens, and Public Policy* (Princeton: Princeton University Press, 1981); J. G. Koppe and J. Keys, "PCBs and the Precautionary Principle," in P. Harremoës et al., eds., *The Precautionary Principle in the 20th Century* (London: Earthscan, 2002), 64–78.

74. The Action Plan produced at the conference called for improved international efforts to develop and harmonize procedures for assessing and managing hazardous substances and to make more resources available to developing countries for building domestic capacity.

75. Global agreements include the 1972 International Convention on the Prevention of Marine Pollution by Dumping of Wastes and Other Matter (London Convention); and the MARPOL Convention, which includes the 1973 International Convention for the Prevention of Pollution from Ships and its 1978 protocol. Early regional and river agreements that touched on hazardous chemicals include the 1972 Convention for the Prevention of Marine Pollution by Dumping from Ships and Aircraft (Oslo Convention); 1974 Convention for the Prevention of Marine Pollution from Land-Based Sources (Paris Convention); 1974 Convention on the Protection of the Marine Environment of the Baltic Sea Area (Helsinki Convention); 1976 Convention on the Protection of the Rhine Against Chemical Pollution; 1976 Protocol for the Prevention of Pollution of the Mediterranean Sea by Dumping from Ships and Aircraft; and the 1978 Great Lakes Water Quality Agreement.

76. Jonathan Krueger and Henrik Selin, "Governance for Sound Chemicals Management: The Need for a More Comprehensive Global Strategy," *Global Governance* 8 (2002): 323–342.

77. David G. Victor, "Learning by Doing in the Nonbinding International Regime to Manage Trade in Hazardous Chemicals and Pesticides," in David G. Victor et al., eds., *The Implementation and Effectiveness of International Environmental Commitments: Theory and Practice* (Cambridge, Mass.: MIT Press, 1998), 228.

78. The IOMC includes UNEP, FAO, the International Labor Organization (ILO), WHO, UNIDO, UNITAR, and OECD. Other global institutions active on chemicals include the GEF, UNDP, and the World Bank. Regional institutions active on chemicals include the Arctic Council, European Union, Great Lakes Program, Helsinki Commission (HELCOM), North American Agreement on Environmental Cooperation (NAAEC)/Sound Management of Chemicals Initiative, OECD, and the Oslo-Paris Commission for the Protection of the Marine Environment of the North-East Atlantic (OSPAR).

79. For the text of the Convention, official documents from its negotiation, reports from the Conference of Parties, updated lists of parties, and other information, see the Web site of the Rotterdam Convention Secretariat at http://www.pic.int. Leading analyses of the development and content of the Rotterdam Convention include David Victor, "Learning by Doing in the Nonbinding International Regime to Manage Trade in Hazardous Chemicals and Pesticides," and Richard Emory Jr., "Probing the Protections in the Rotterdam Convention on Prior Informed Consent," *Colorado Journal of International Environmental Law and Policy* 23 (2001): 47–91.

80. Scientists and policymakers usually define POPs as possessing four key characteristics: toxicity, persistence, bioaccumulation, and long-range environmental transport.

81. Of course, extensive variations occur in substances, species, and exposures. For broader discussions of the science of POPs, see Downie and Fenge, eds., *Northern Lights Against POPs*, and Theo Colborn, *Our Stolen Future: Are We Threatening Our Fertility, Intelligence, and Survival?* (New York: Dutton, 1996).

82. For a discussion of the science and politics of this point, see Downie and Fenge, eds., *Northern Lights Against POPs*.

83. Other initiatives also contributed to the process. For example, in November 1995, the Washington Declaration issued from the Intergovernmental Conference to Adopt a Global Programme of Action for Protection of the Marine Environment from Land-Based Activities (GPA) called for talks on a legally binding treaty targeting the dirty dozen.

84. For official proceedings of the workshops, see http://irptc.unep.ch/pops/newlayout/prodocas.htm. For background on the workshops, see http://irptc.unep.ch/pops/newlayout/wkshpintro.htm.

85. The LRTAP POPs Protocol addresses the production and use of sixteen pesticides, industrial chemicals, and unintentional by-products. Analyses include Selin and Eckley, "Science, Politics, and Persistent Organic Pollutants," 17–42; and Selin, "Regional POPs Policy."

86. For official reports and other documents from the negotiations, see http://irptc.unep.ch/pops/newlayout/negotiations.htm. For detailed secondary source reports, see http://www.iisd.ca/linkages/chemical/index.html.

87. For detailed analysis of the convention, see David Downie, "Global POPs Policy: The 2001 Stockholm Convention on Persistent Organic Pollutants."

88. Very small amounts of DDT can also be used as an intermediate in production of the chemical dicoful with the understanding that no DDT would be released into the environment.

89. For a detailed discussion of this process, including the original version of figure 3.3, see Downie, "Global POPs Policy," 140–142.

90. See, in particular Paragraphs 7(a) and 9 of Article 8 of the Stockholm Convention.

91. This compromise followed the path set forth by both the climate change and biodiversity conventions. The parties will review the GEF's performance and do have the option of making a final decision to use or exclude the GEF.

92. A revised version of the Endangered Species Conservation Act passed in 1973 banned whaling in U.S. waters or by U.S. citizens, outlawed the import of whale products, and required that the United States initiate bilateral and multilateral negotiations on an agreement to protect and conserve whales.

93. The effort to build an IWC majority to ban whaling was stymied in the latter half of the 1970s because otherwise anti-whaling states such as Canada, Mexico, and other Latin American states were primarily concerned about protecting rights to regulate economic activities within their own 200-mile (320-kilometer) economic zones and opposed the jurisdiction of an international body over whaling.

94. Statement by Craig Van Note, Monitor Consortium, before the Subcommittee on Human Rights and International Organizations, Committee on Foreign Affairs, U.S. House of Representatives, September 28, 1989.

95. "Whaling: Soviet Kills Could Affect Sanctuary Decision," *Greenwire*, February 22, 1994.

96. Teresa Watanabe, "Japan is Set for a Whale of a Fight," *Los Angeles Times*, April 20, 1993.

97. Paul Brown, "Playing Football with the Whales," *Guardian* (London), May 1, 1993. The Caribbean states cooperating with Japan were Grenada, St. Lucia, St. Kitts and Nevis, Antigua and Barbuda, Dominica, and St. Vincent.

98. Greenpeace, "During Clinton's Watch Global Whaling Triples," news release, May 20, 1997.

99. *Greenwire*, May 28, 1999; WWF, "IWC Steps Back from the Brink," press release, May 28, 1999.

100. Kieran Mulvaney, "The Whaling Effect" (Washington, D.C.: World Wildlife Fund, 1999).

101. These simulations, known as the Catch Limit Algorithm (CLA), use population abundance estimates and data on past and present catch levels to estimate the impact of potential harvests on existing whale populations. See the IWC RMP Web site at http://www.iwcoffice.org/conservation/rmp.htm.

102. Alex Kirby, "Japan Sets 2006 Whaling Ultimatum," BBC News Online, July 19, 2004, http://news.bbc.co.uk/1/hi/sci/tech/3907415.stm.

103. Fisheries Agency head Masayuki Komatsu in an Australian Broadcasting Corporation radio interview. See "Japan 'Buys' Pro-Whaling Votes," CNN news, July 18, 2001, http://edition.cnn.com/2001/TECH/science/07/18/japan.whale/index.html, and "Japan Denies Aid-for-Whaling Report," CNN news, July 18, 2001, http://edition.cnn.com/2001/WORLD/asiapcf/east/07/19/japan.whaling/.

104. In an interview with BBC News Online, the Japanese parliament member Mr. Yoshimasa Hayashi said, "If we do get a simple majority here, that would be a very good sign. It would let us either abolish the conservation committee, or change it to embrace both conservation and the sustainable use of whales." See Alex Kirby, BBC News Online, July 19, 2004.

105. Countries voting for the Japanese Commercial Whaling Proposal in 2005 included Antigua and Barbuda, Benin, Cameroon, Ivory Coast, Dominica, Gabon, Grenada, Guinea, Iceland, Japan, Mauritania, Mongolia, Nicaragua, Norway, Palau, Russia, St. Kitts and Nevis, St. Lucia, St. Vincent and Grenadines, Senegal, Solomon Islands, Suriname, and Tuvalu. Countries voting against the Japanese Commercial Whaling Proposal included Argentina, Australia, Austria, Belgium, Brazil, Chile, Czech Republic, Finland, France, Germany, Hungary, Ireland,

Italy, Luxembourg, Mexico, Monaco, Netherlands, New Zealand, Oman, Panama, Portugal, San Marino, Slovak Republic, South Africa, Spain, Sweden, Switzerland, United Kingdom, and the United States of America. Countries abstaining included China, Denmark, Kiribati, South Korea, and Morocco.

106. For example, see Dennis Normile, "Japan's Whaling Program Carries Heavy Baggage," *Science* 289, no. 5488 (September 29, 2000): 2264–2265.

107. Sidney Holt, "Is the IWC Finished as an Instrument for the Conservation of Whales and the Regulation of Whaling?" *Marine Pollution Bulletin*, 46, no. 7 (July 2003): 924–926.

108. WWF, "Report from the Third Day of the 51st IWC Meeting—26 May 1999"; United Nations Environment Programme (UNEP), "CITES Maintains Trade Bans on High-Profile Species," UNEP news release 2000/48, April 20, 2000; "Thirteenth Conference of the Parties to the Convention on International Trade of Endangered Species of Wild Fauna and Flora: 2–14 October 2004," *Earth Negotiations Bulletin* 21, no. 35 (October 3, 2004), http://www.iisd.ca/vol21/enb2135e.html.

109. See http://www.cites.org/eng/res/11/11–04.shtml.

110. Ed Stoddard, "CITES Does Not Follow Standard U.N. Divisions," ENN: Environmental News Network, October 14, 2004, http://www.enn.com/today_PF.html?id=180.

111. For detailed and updated information on these figures see TRAFFIC Web site at http://www.traffic.org, and TRAFFIC, *Annual Report 1997–1998* (London: TRAFFIC, 1998), 1, and subsequent annual reports.

112. See Sarah Fitzgerald, *Whose Business Is It?* (Washington, D.C.: World Wildlife Fund, 1989), 3–8, 13–14.

113. World Resources Institute, *World Resources 1990–1991* (New York: Oxford University Press, 1990), 135.

114. Detailed and updated information on CITES, including its history, operation, species covered, current parties, and other issues can be found on the regime's official Web site at http://www.cites.org.

115. For updated lists and other information concerning the species listed in each appendix, see the Convention on International Trade of Endangered Species Web site at http://www.cites.org.

116. See Sarah Fitzgerald, *Whose Business Is It?*, 3–8, 13–14.

117. David Harland, "Jumping on the 'Ban' Wagon: Efforts to Save the African Elephant," *Fletcher Forum on World Affairs* 14 (Summer 1990): 284–300.

118. "CITES 1989: The African Elephant and More," *TRAFFIC* (USA) 9 (December 1989): 1–3.

119. See World Resources Institute, *World Resources 1990–1991* (New York: Oxford University Press, 1990), 135.

120. *New York Times,* June 5, 1990, C2; Raymond Bonner, *At the Hand of Man: Peril and Hope for Africa's Wildlife* (New York: Vintage Books, 1994), 157.

121. In each case the formal proposals were withdrawn prior to a formal vote. World Wildlife Fund, "The Challenge of African Elephant Conservation," *Conservation Issues,* April 1997. Also available at http://www.wwf.org/new/issues/apr_97/trade.htm.

122. "CITES and the African Elephants: The Decisions and the Next Steps Explained," TRAFFIC dispatches, April 1998, 5–6.

123. CITES, "Verification of Compliance with the Precautionary Undertakings for the Sale and Shipment of Raw Ivory," Doc. SC.42.10.2.1, forty-second meeting of the Standing Committee, Lisbon (Portugal), September 28–October 1, 1999.

124. See "CITES, "Amendments to Appendices I and II of the Convention: Adopted by the Conference of the Parties at Its 13th Meeting, Bangkok (Thailand), 2–14 October, 2004," Notification to the Parties, November 2004, 5, http://www.cites.org/eng/notif/2004/073.pdf.

125. "Summary of the Thirteenth Conference of the Parties to the Convention on International Trade in Endangered Species of Wild Fauna and Flora: 2–14 October 2004," *Earth Negotiations Bulletin* 21, no. 45 (October 18, 2004): 16, http://www.iisd.ca/vol21/enb2145e.html.

126. Arthur Blundell, "A Review of the CITES Listing of Big-Leaf Mahogany," *Oryx* 38, no. 1 (2004): 84–90.

127. Guatemala Official Delegation in CITES COP12, "Presentation by Guatemala on the Inclusion of Big Leaf Mahogany in CITES Appendix II," November 2002, http://www.cites.org/eng/cop/12/inf/E12i–33.PDF.

128. "Mahogany-Swietenia maerophylla," TRAFFIC network briefing, June 1998, http://www.traffic.org/briefings/mahogany.html.

129. Guatemala Official Delegation in CITES COP12, "Presentation by Guatemala on the Inclusion of Big Leaf Mahogany in CITES Appendix II," November 2002, http://www.cites.org/eng/cop/12/inf/E12i–33.PDF.

130. "Big-Leafed Mahogany and CITES," TRAFFIC network briefing, October 2001, http://www.traffic.org/mahogany/cites.html.

131. It is difficult to say, however, whether the difference in the position of the major consumer states resulted from differences in approach (assuring that products were legally obtained vs. protecting commercial interests), or from differences in the listing itself (an Appendix I listing places much more stringent restrictions on trade than does an Appendix II listing).

132. Arthur G. Blundell and Bruce D. Rodan, "Mahogany and CITES: Moving Beyond the Veneer of Legality," *Oryx* 37, no. 1 (January 2003): 85–90.

133. For discussion and examples of this argument, see Le Prestre and Peter Stoett, "International Initiatives, Commitments, and Disappointments: Canada, CITES, and the CBD," in Karen Beazley and Robert Boardman, eds., *Politics of the Wild: Canada's Endangered Species* (Toronto: Oxford University Press, 2001), 190–216, and Joshua Ginsberg, "Enhancement of Survival or Abandonment of the Endangered Species Act?" *BioScience* 54, no. 3 (2004): 180–181. However, neither work nor any other of which we are aware provides clear empirical evidence to support this view.

134. Millennium Ecosystem Assessment, *Ecosystems and Human Well-Being: Synthesis Report* (Washington, D.C.: Island Press, 2005).

135. National sovereignty over one's natural resources implies that a government has control over its resources, such as oil, minerals, and timber. Common heritage implies that no one can be excluded from using natural resources, except by lack of economic and technological capacity; and, conversely, everyone has a right to benefit from the exploitation of the resources. This concept has been used for fisheries and mineral resources found in the high seas and more recently in the debate about genetic resources. See G. Kristin Rosendal, "The Convention on Biological Diversity: A Viable Instrument for Conservation and Sustainable Use," in Helge Ole Bergesen, Georg Parmann, and Øystein B. Thommessen, eds., *Green Globe Yearbook of International Cooperation on Environment and Development 1995* (Oxford: Oxford University Press, 1995), 69–81.

136. Kenton R. Miller et al., "Issues on the Preservation of Biological Diversity," in Robert Repetto, ed., *The Global Possible: Resources, Development and the New Century* (New Haven and London: Yale University Press, 1985), 341–342; IUCN, "Explanatory Notes to

Draft Articles Prepared by IUCN for Inclusion in a Proposed Convention on the Conservation of Biological Diversity and the Establishment of a Fund for That Purpose," pt. 1: General Comments, 1.

137. The main interest of the Reagan administration in making this proposal was to create financial and logistical synergies by bringing the multiplicity of species-specific or region-specific conservation conventions already in existence under one convention so that there could be a single secretariat instead of several. Personal communication from E. U. Curtis Bohlen, former assistant secretary of state for oceans, environment, and science, Washington, D.C., February 2, 1994.

138. "Report of the Ad Hoc Working Group on the Work of Its Second Session in Preparation for a Legal Instrument on Biological Diversity of the Planet," UNEP/Bio.Div2/3, February 23, 1990, 7.

139. Personal communication from a member of the U.S. delegation to the biodiversity convention negotiations, April 12, 1994.

140. For contrasting analyses of the text of the convention regarding intellectual property rights, see Melinda Chandler, "The Biodiversity Convention: Selected Issues of Interest to the International Lawyer," *Colorado Journal of International Environmental Law and Policy* 4, no. 1 (Winter 1993), 161–165; and Gareth Porter, *The United States and the Biodiversity Convention: The Case for Participation* (Washington, D.C.: Environmental and Energy Study Institute, 1992), 13–21.

141. Personal communication from a member of the U.S. delegation to the biodiversity convention negotiations, October 21, 1994. See also Fiona McConnell, *The Biodiversity Convention: A Negotiating History* (London: Kluwer Law International, 1996).

142. A coalition of NGOs with major interests in biodiversity got together with several companies to pressure the Clinton administration into signing the treaty. The Clinton administration dealt with the objections to the text that had been raised by the Bush administration by announcing that it would issue a statement asserting that it interpreted the treaty's provisions on intellectual property rights and the financial mechanism to be compatible with U.S. interests. See U.S. Congress, Senate, Convention on Biological Diversity: Message from the President of the United States, November 20, 1993, Treaty Document 103–120 (Washington, D.C.: U.S. Government Printing Office, 1993).

143. For updated information on the status of signatures and ratifications, see the official CBD Web site at http://www.biodiv.org/.

144. Convention on Biodiversity Web site, "Thematic Programmes," http://www.biodiv. org/programmes/default.shtml.

145. Australian Wheat Board Web site, "The Cartagena Protocol on Biosafety," http://www.awb.com.au/AWBL/Launch/Site/AboutAWB/Content/FactsIndustryInformation/PublicPositionPapers/GMCropTrials.

146. For a summary of the negotiations and a synopsis of the protocol, see "Report of the Resumed Session of the Extraordinary Meeting of the Conference of the Parties for the Adoption of the Protocol on Biodiversity to the Convention on Biological Diversity: 24–28 January 2000," *Earth Negotiations Bulletin* 9, no. 137 (January 31, 2000), http://www.iisd.ca/ biodiv/excop/.

147. "Summary of the First Meeting of the Ad Hoc Group on Liability and Redress and the Second Meeting of the Parties to the Cartagena Protocol on Biosafety: 25 May–3 June 2005," *Earth Negotiations Bulletin* 9, no. 320 (June 6, 2005), http://www.iisd.ca/vol09/enb09320e.html.

148. Article 1 of the CBD states: "The objectives of this Convention, to be pursued in accordance with its relevant provisions, are the conservation of biological diversity, the sustainable

use of its components and the fair and equitable sharing of the benefits arising out of the utilization of genetic resources, including by appropriate access to genetic resources and by appropriate transfer of relevant technologies, taking into account all rights over those resources and to technologies, and by appropriate funding."

149. The Like Minded Group of Megabiodiverse countries (LMMC) was formed in February 2002 in Cancun, Mexico. The founding members of the LMMC were Bolivia, Brazil, China, Colombia, Costa Rica, Ecuador, India, Indonesia, Kenya, Malaysia, Mexico, Peru, Philippines, South Africa, and Venezuela. Later, Madagascar and the Democratic Republic of Congo joined the group. Together, the member countries of the group hold 70 percent of the world's biodiversity.

150. FAO, *Review of the State of World Marine Fishery Resources* (Rome: FAO, 2005), 10.

151. Ibid., 2–3.

152. See Gareth Porter, *Estimating Overcapacity in the Global Fishing Fleet* (Washington, D.C.: World Wildlife Fund, 1998).

153. Stefania Vannuccini, *Overview of Fish Production, Utilization, Consumption and Trade Based on 2002 Data* (Rome: FAO, 2004), 6.

154. According to European law, the European Commission, on behalf of the EU, negotiates fisheries agreements with third countries.

155. See, for example, Commission of the European Communities, "Fishing on the High Seas: A Community Approach," Communication from the Commission to the Council and the European Parliament, SEC (92) 565, April 2, 1992, 5.

156. On Canadian mismanagement, see Raymond Rogers, *The Oceans Are Emptying* (Montreal: Black Rose Books, 1995), 96–147; on EU allocations and Spanish and Portuguese catch, see background document by Bruce Atkinson, Canadian Department of Fisheries and Oceans, Northwest Atlantic Fisheries, Centre St., Johns, Newfoundland.

157. "Canada Hits EU's Atlantic Overfishing," *Washington Times,* February 19, 1995, A11.

158. Marvin Soroos, "The Turbot War: Resolution of an International Fishery Dispute," in Nils Petter Gleditsch, ed., *Conflict and the Environment* (Dordrecht, Netherlands: Kluwer Academic Publishers, 1997), 248.

159. "Summary of the Fifth Substantive Session of the UN Conference on Straddling Fish Stocks and Highly Migratory Fish Stocks: 24 July–4 August 1995," *Earth Negotiations Bulletin* 7, no. 54 (August 7, 1995), http://www.iisd.ca/vol07/0754000e.html.

160. To date there are five technical guidelines relevant to data in fisheries management: #1—Fisheries Operations (1996) and Supplement 1 VMS (1998); #2—Precautionary Approach to Capture Fisheries and Species Introductions (1996); #3—Fisheries Management (1997); #4—Indicators for Sustainable Development of Marine Capture Fisheries (1999); and #5—Implementation of the International Plan of Action to deter, prevent and eliminate, illegal, unreported, and unregulated fishing (2002). Martin Tsamenyi, Lara Manarangi-Trott, and Shilpa Rajkumar, "The International Legal Regime for Fisheries Management" (paper presented at the UNEP Workshop on Fisheries Subsidies and Sustainable Fisheries Management, Geneva, April 26–27, 2004), 14, http://www.unep.ch/etu/Fisheries%20Meeting/FM2004SubPap.htm.

161. The other International Plans of Action are the 1999 International Plan of Action for Reducing Incidental Catch of Seabirds in Longline Fisheries and the 1999 International Plan of Action for the Conservation and Management of Sharks. For more details, see Tsamenyi, Manarangi-Trott, and Rajkumar, "The International Legal Regime for Fisheries Management," 14–16; FAO, *Fisheries Information Center,* http://www.fao.org/fi/default.asp.

162. Tsamenyi, Manarangi-Trott, and Rajkumar, "The International Legal Regime for Fisheries Management," 17.

163. United Nations, "Third Informal Consultations of the States Parties to the Agreement for the Implementation of the Provisions of the United Nations Convention on the Law of the Sea of 10 December 1982 relating to the Conservation and Management of Straddling Fish Stocks and Highly Migratory Fish Stocks," (ICSP3/UNFSA/REP/INF.1), August 19, 2004, 4–5.

164. United Nations Environment Programme (UNEP), *Desertification: The Problem That Won't Go Away* (Nairobi: UNEP, 1992); Ridley Nelson, "Dryland Management: The 'Desertification' Problem," working paper no. 8, World Bank Policy Planning and Research Staff, Environment Department, September 1988, 2.

165. *Crosscurrents,* no. 1 (March 2, 1992): 5. For a more detailed later report on these findings, see William K. Stevens, "Threat of Encroaching Deserts May Be More Myth Than Fact," *New York Times,* January 18, 1994, C1, 10.

166. UN Governmental Liaison Service, "Second Session of Desertification Negotiations, Geneva, 13–24 September 1993," *E and D File* 2, no. 13 (October 1993).

167. "A Convention for Africans," *Impact* (Nairobi), no. 6 (September 1992): 3.

168. United Nations Environment Programme, *Desertification Control Bulletin* (Nairobi), no. 20 (1991); Dr. Mostafa K. Tolba, "Desertification and the Economics of Survival," statement to the International Conference on the Economics of Dryland Degradation and Rehabilitation, Canberra, Australia, March 10–11, 1986.

169. *World Bank News* (May 27, 1993): 4; *Crosscurrents,* no. 5 (March 16, 1992): 13.

170. E. U. Curtis Bohlen, deputy chief of the U.S. delegation, recalls that he made the decision personally without consulting with higher U.S. officials. Private communication from Bohlen, August 15, 1994. On the earlier suggestion by African countries of a possible bargain linking African support for a forest convention with U.S. support for a desertification convention, see *Crosscurrents,* no. 5 (March 16, 1992): 13.

171. *Earth Summit Bulletin* 2, no. 13 (June 16, 1992): 3.

172. "Summary of the First Session of the INC for the Elaboration of an International Convention to Combat Desertification, 24 May–3 June 1993," *Earth Negotiations Bulletin* 4, no. 11 (June 11, 1993): 2–6.

173. "Summary of the Fifth Session of the INC for the Elaboration of an International Convention to Combat Desertification, 6–17 June 1994," *Earth Negotiations Bulletin* 4, no. 55 (June 20, 1994), 7–8.

174. "Summary of the Second Session of the INC for the Elaboration of an International Convention to Combat Desertification, 13–24 September 1993," *Earth Negotiations Bulletin* 4, no. 22 (September 30, 1993): 11.

175. "Summary of the Fifth Session," 9–10.

176. For more information on the challenges faced by the Convention, see "Summary of the Second Conference of the Parties to the Convention to Combat Desertification, 30 November–11 December 1998," *Earth Negotiations Bulletin* 4, no. 127 (December 14, 1998).

177. Marc Debois and Marco Morettini, "Meeting on Desertification in Cuba," *ACP-EU Courier,* no. 200 (September-October 2003): 5.

178. "Summary of the Sixth Conference of the Parties to the Convention to Combat Desertification, 25 August–6 September 2003," *Earth Negotiations Bulletin* 4, no. 173 (September 8, 2003).

179. Dirk Bryant, Daniel Nielsen, and Laura Targley, *The Last Frontier Forests: Ecosystems and Economics on the Edge* (Washington, D.C.: World Resources Institute, 1997), 1.

180. FAO, *State of the World's Forests 2005* (Rome: FAO, 2005), 135–137.

181. FAO, *The Challenge of Sustainable Forest Management* (Rome: FAO, 1993), 9.

182. Even prior to the formation of the United Nations, forests had been discussed as an international issue between Canada and the United States as early as the late nineteenth century. See Peter Gillis and Thomas Rich, *Lost Initiatives* (Westport, Conn.: Greenwood Press, 1986). There is also a long history of international conferences on forestry convened by the British under the banner of "Empire Forestry." See Gregory Barton, *Empire Forestry and the Origins of Environmentalism* (London: Cambridge University Press, 2002).

183. FAO, "History of the Committee on Forestry," COFO/2005/INF/8, http://www.fao.org/docrep/meeting/009/j4566e.htm.

184. David Humphreys, "The Elusive Quest for a Global Forests Convention," *Review of European Community and International Environmental Law* 14, no. 1 (April 2005), 1–10.

185. Non-legally binding authoritative statement of principles for a global consensus on the management, conservation, and sustainable development of all types of forests (Rio de Janeiro, June 13, 1992).

186. *Agenda 21*, 1992 report of the UNCED, I (1992), UN Doc. A/CONF.151/26/Rev. 1, chap. 11.

187. David Humphreys, "The UNCED Process and International Responses to Deforestation" (paper presented to the Inaugural Pan-European Conference on International Studies, Heidelberg, Germany, September 16–20, 1992), 34–35.

188. Malaysia openly charged that industrialized countries were using the issue of conserving tropical forests to prevent rapidly industrializing countries from achieving developed-country status. Claude Smadja, "Malaysia: Objective 2020," *World Link* (Geneva), no. 3 (1991): 26–29.

189. *Earth Summit Update*, no. 8 (April 1992): 7.

190. These initiatives included the Conference on Global Partnerships on Forests organized by Indonesia, the India-UK initiative to establish reporting guidelines for forests to the Commission on Sustainable Development (CSD), and Intergovernmental Working Group on Global Forests, convened jointly by Malaysia and Canada, which met twice in 1994.

191. Jag Maini, "Introduction," in A. J. Grayson and W. B. Maynard, *The World's Forests-Rio+5: International Initiatives Towards Sustainable Management* (Oxford: Commonwealth Forestry Association, 1997), ix. Also see David Humphreys, "The Global Politics of Forest Conservation Since the UNCED," *Environmental Politics* 5, no. 2 (Summer 1996): 231–256.

192. Ans Kolk, *Forests in International Politics: International Organisations, NGOs and the Brazilian Amazon* (International Books, 1996), 162.

193. Malaysian Timber Council, "Global Forests Convention" (MTC, 28 January 2002), http://www.mtc.com.my/publication/series/series1/mtc8.htm. See also H. C. Thang, "Need for a Global Forests Convention?" (paper presented to the GTZ Kick-off Workshop on Knowledge Management, Pulau Pangkor, Malaysia, October 26–29, 2003), and Humphreys, "The Elusive Quest."

194. For a summary of the international initiatives in support of the IPF process, see Grayson and Maynard, *The World's Forests-Rio+5*, 29–46.

195. The IPF's report to the Commission on Sustainable Development (E/CN.17/1997/12) can be found at http://www.un.org/documents/ecosoc/cn17/1997/ecn171997–12.htm.

196. *Practitioner's Guide to the Implementation of the IPF Proposals for Action*, prepared by the Six Country Initiative in Support of the UN *Ad Hoc* Intergovernmental Forum on Forests, 2nd rev. ed., May 1999.

197. See "Americans, Canadians at Odds over 'Sustainable Forestry' Plan," *Ottawa Citizen,* February 1, 1997.

198. NGO briefings on developments in IPF and the Convention on Biodiversity at BIONET, January 26, 1996, and December 5, 1996.

199. Humphreys, "The Elusive Quest."

200. Ibid.

201. William Mankin, Global Forest Policy Project, interview, fourth session of the United Nations Forum on Forests (Geneva, May 11, 2004), as cited in Humphreys, "The Elusive Quest."

202. "Summary of the Nineteenth United Nations General Assembly Special Session to Review Implementation of Agenda 21: 23–27 June 1997," *Earth Negotiations Bulletin* 5, no. 88 (June 30, 1997), 5–6; David Humphreys, "The Report of the Intergovernmental Panel on Forests," 219–220.

203. FAO, *State of the World's Forests, 2003* (Rome: Food and Agriculture Organization), 24.

204. The CPF is currently comprised of fourteen international organization members: Centre for International Forestry Research (CIFOR); Food and Agriculture Organization of the United Nations (FAO); International Tropical Timber Organization (ITTO); International Union of Forestry Research Organizations (IUFRO); Secretariat of the Convention on Biological Diversity (CBD); Secretariat of the Global Environment Facility (GEF); Secretariat of the United Nations Convention to Combat Desertification (UNCCD); Secretariat of the United Nations Forum on Forests (UNFF); Secretariat of the United Nations Framework Convention on Climate Change (UNFCCC); United Nations Development Programme (UNDP); United Nations Environment Programme (UNEP); World Agroforestry Centre (ICRAF); World Bank; and World Conservation Union (IUCN).

205. For more information about the work of the UNFF and its expert groups, see the UNFF Web site at http://www.un.org/esa/forests.

206. For more information on UNFF–5, see "Summary of the Fifth Session of the United Nations Forum on Forests: 16–17 May 2005," *Earth Negotiations Bulletin,* 13, no. 133 (May 30, 2005), http://www.iisd.ca/download/pdf/enb13133e.pdf.

207. See, for example, Wynet Smith, "Undercutting Sustainability: The Global Problem of Illegal Logging and Trade," *Journal of Sustainable Forestry* 19, no. 1–3 (2004): 7.

208. For more information about the Forest Law Enforcement and Governance initiatives, see the World Bank's Forest Governance Program's Web site at http://lnweb18.worldbank.org/ESSD/ardext.nsf/14ByDocName/ForestGovernanceProgram.

209. World Bank, "Forest Governance Program," http://lnweb18.worldbank.org/ESSD/ardext.nsf/14ByDocName/ForestGovernanceProgram. For additional information, see the Center for International Forestry Research, "Forest Law Enforcement, Governance and Trade Research at CIFOR," http://www.cifor.cgiar.org/docs/_ref/research/flegt/index.htm.

Chapter 4

1. This number is derived from a comprehensive collection of legal instruments that includes agreements with important provisions relating to the environment. The commonly cited figure of about 150 multilateral environmental agreements is taken from UNEP data and includes only multilateral agreements totally directed to environmental issues. See Harold K. Jacobson and Edith Brown Weiss, "A Framework for Analysis," in Edith Brown Weiss and Harold K. Jacobson, eds., *Engaging Countries: Strengthening Compliance with International Environmental Accords* (Cambridge, Mass.: MIT Press, 1998), 1, 18.

2. Broader discussions of issues related to implementation and compliance include Weiss and Jacobson, eds., *Engaging Countries;* Edward Miles et al., *Environmental Regime Effectiveness* (Cambridge, Mass.: MIT Press, 2001); and Michael Faure and Jurgen Lefevere, "Compliance with Global Environmental Policy," in Regina Axelrod, David Downie, and Norman Vig, eds., *Global Environmental Policy: Institutions, Law & Policy,* 2nd ed. (Washington, D.C.: Congressional Quarterly Press, 2004).

3. This discussion draws explicitly on research and publications by one of the coauthors. See in particular David Downie, "Global Environmental Policy: Governance Through Regimes," in Regina Axelrod, David Downie, and Norman Vig, eds., *Global Environmental Policy: Institutions, Law & Policy,* 2nd ed. (Washington, D.C.: Congressional Quarterly Press, 2004).

4. Classic examples include Thucydides, Machiavelli, and Hobbes. Influential modern examples include Hans Morgenthau, *Politics Among Nations,* 5th ed. (New York: Knopf, 1973); Robert Jervis, "Cooperation under the Security Dilemma," *World Politics* 30 (1978): 167–186; Kenneth Waltz, *Theory of International Politics* (Reading, Mass: Addison-Wesley, 1979); and Glenn Snyder, "The Security Dilemma in Alliance Politics," *World Politics* 36 (1984): 461–495.

5. For an excellent discussion of the impact of positional concerns on cooperation, see Joseph M. Grieco, "Anarchy and the Limits of Cooperation: A Realist Critique of the Newest Liberal Institutionalism," *International Organization* 42 (1988): 485–507. Subsequent references in this subsection also refer to theoretical discussions of the structural obstacle, not a specific discussion of its impact on environmental cooperation.

6. Jervis, "Cooperation Under the Security Dilemma"; and Kenneth Oye, ed., *Cooperation Under Anarchy* (Princeton: Princeton University Press, 1986), 1–22.

7. Mancur Olson, *The Logic of Collective Action* (Cambridge, Mass.: Harvard University Press, 1965).

8. J. Samuel Barkin and George Shambaugh, eds., *Anarchy and the Environment: The International Relations of Common Pool Resources* (Albany, N.Y.: State University of New York Press, 1999).

9. Robert Keohane, *After Hegemony* (Princeton: Princeton University Press, 1984).

10. Robert Jervis, *Perception and Misperception in International Politics* (Princeton: Princeton University Press, 1976).

11. Downie, "Global Environmental Policy," 71.

12. United Nations Document A/CONF.48/14, 118. This principle later became Principle 2 of the Rio Declaration, but with the words "and developmental" inserted before "policies," thus making it even more self-contradictory.

13. Gary Bryner, *From Promises to Performance: Achieving Global Environmental Goals* (New York: W.W. Norton, 1997), 59.

14. Peter Sand, *Lessons Learned in Global Environmental Governance* (Washington, D.C.: World Resources Institute, 1990), 21.

15. Daniel C. Esty, "Economic Integration and Environmental Protection," in Regina Axelrod, David Downie, and Norman Vig, eds., *Global Environmental Policy: Institutions, Law & Policy,* 2nd ed. (Washington, D.C.: Congressional Quarterly Press, 2004).

16. Peter Haas, Robert Keohane, and Marc Levy, eds., *Institutions for the Earth: Sources of Effective International Environmental Protection* (Cambridge, Mass.: MIT Press, 1993).

17. For extended discussion of these two obstacles, see Lawrence E. Susskind, *Environmental Diplomacy: Negotiating More Effective Global Agreements* (New York: Oxford University Press, 1994); and Sand, *Lessons Learned in Global Environmental Governance.*

18. This point is also made by Susskind, *Environmental Diplomacy,*" 156.

19. Elaine M. Carlin, 2002, "Oil Pollution from Ships at Sea," in Edward L. Miles et al., eds., *Environmental Regime Effectiveness,* 336.

20. Ibid., 345.

21. As with similar discussions in this book, the categories presented in this subsection should also be seen as indicative and heuristic rather and exhaustive and exclusive.

22. Downie, "Global Environmental Policy," 75.

23. Ibid., 76.

24. Ibid., 74.

25. See Knut Midgaard and Arild Underdal, "Multiparty Conferences," in Daniel Druckman, ed., *Negotiations: Social-Psychological Perspectives* (Beverly Hills, Calif.: Sage Publications, 1977), 339; and Pamela S. Chasek, *Earth Negotiations: Analyzing Thirty Years of Environmental Diplomacy* (Tokyo: UNU Press, 2001), chap. 3.

26. Barkin and Shambaugh, eds., *Anarchy and the Environment.*

27. Jacobson and Weiss, "A Framework for Analysis," 4.

28. Edith Brown Weiss, Daniel B. Magraw, and Paul C. Szasz, *International Environmental Law: Basic Instruments and References* (Dobbs Ferry, N.Y.: Transnational, 1992), 696.

29. Abram Chayes and Antonia H. Chayes, "Compliance Without Enforcement: State Behavior Under Regulatory Treaties," *Negotiation Journal* 7 (1991): 311–330.

30. In addition to those already cited, prominent examples of this literature include Peter H. Sand, ed., *The Effectiveness of International Environmental Agreements* (Cambridge: Grotius Publications, 1992); Ronald B. Mitchell, *Intentional Oil Pollution at Sea* (Cambridge, Mass.: MIT Press, 1994); Weiss and Jacobson, eds., *Engaging Countries;* David G. Victor, Kal Raustiala, and Eugene Skolnikof, eds., *The Implementation and Effectiveness of International Environmental Commitments: Theory and Practice* (Cambridge, Mass.: MIT Press, 1998); Michael J. Kelly, "Overcoming Obstacles to the Effective Implementation of International Environmental Agreements," *Georgetown International Environmental Law Review* 9, no. 2 (1997); and Michael Faure and Jurgen Lefevere, "Compliance with Global Environmental Policy," in Regina Axelrod, David Downie, and Norman Vig, eds., *Global Environmental Policy: Institutions, Law & Policy,* 2nd ed. (Washington, D.C.: Congressional Quarterly Press, 2004).

31. Sand, ed., *The Effectiveness of International Environmental Agreements,* 82.

32. Kelly, "Overcoming Obstacles," 462–463.

33. For example, in an experiment conducted by WWF, volunteers declared or displayed a cactus to customs officials in several countries, including the United Kingdom, Switzerland, Germany, Sweden, Denmark, and the United States. Although virtually all cacti are protected under the CITES agreement, no questions were asked by officials in any of these countries about the species of the plant or its origins. See Bill Padgett, "The African Elephant, Africa and CITES: The Next Step," *Indiana Journal of Global Legal Studies* 2 (1995): 529, 538–540, as cited in Kelly, "Overcoming Obstacles," 469–470.

34. David Mulenex, "Improving Compliance Provisions in International Environmental Agreements," in Lawrence E. Susskind, Eric Jay Dolin, and J. William Breslin, eds., *International Environmental Treaty-Making* (Cambridge, Mass.: Program on Negotiation at Harvard Law School, 1992), 174.

35. Andrew J. Heimert, "How the Elephant Lost His Tusks," *Yale Law Journal* 104 (1995): 1473, as cited in Kelly, "Overcoming Obstacles," 465.

36. Environmental Investigation Agency and Telepak, *The Final Cut: Illegal Logging in Indonesia's Orangutan Parks* (London: 1999); David W. Brown, *Addicted to Rent: Corporate and*

Spatial Distribution of Forest Resources in Indonesia: Implications for Forest Sustainability and Government Policy (Jakarta: Indonesia-UK Tropical Forest Management Programme, 1999).

37. Vogel and Kessler, "How Compliance Happens and Doesn't Happen Domestically," in Edith Brown Weiss and Harold K. Jacobson, eds., *Engaging Countries: Strengthening Compliance with International Environmental Accords* (Cambridge, Mass.: MIT Press, 1998), 35.

38. For specific and numerous examples, see reports of the ozone regime's Implementation Committee, available at the Ozone Secretariat's Web site, http://www.unep.org/ozone.

39. Delegates from developing countries consistently make this argument during meetings of the parties to most global environmental regimes. For specific examples, see the official reports from such meetings, which can be found on the relevant secretariat Web sites, or in reports by the *Earth Negotiations Bulletin,* http://www.iisd.ca/.

40. Vogel and Kessler, "How Compliance Happens," 24.

41. Ronald B. Mitchell, "Regime Design Matters: Intentional Oil Pollution and Treaty Compliance," *International Organization* 48, no. 3 (Summer 1994): 425–458.

42. Edith Brown Weiss, "The Five International Treaties: A Living History," in Edith Brown Weiss and Harold K. Jacobson, *Engaging Countries: Strengthening Compliance with International Environmental Accords* (Cambridge, Mass.: MIT Press, 1998), 115–116.

43. Ibid., 162.

44. Ibid.

45. Comment from the U.S. Department of State in U.S. Government Accounting Office, "International Agreements Are Not Well Monitored," GAO/RCED–92–3, January 1992, 54.

46. Victor, Raustiala, and Skolnikoff, eds., *The Implementation and Effectiveness of International Environmental Commitments.*

47. For a full discussion, see Basel Convention Secretariat, *Global Trends in Generation and Transboundary Movement of Hazardous Wastes and Other Wastes: Analysis of the Data Provided by Parties to the Secretariat of the Basel Convention,* UN Publication Series, Basel Convention on the Control of Transboundary Movements on Hazardous Wastes and Their Disposal No. 14 (Geneva: Basel Convention Secretariat, 2004).

48. Juan Carlos di Primio, "Data Quality and Compliance Control," in David G. Victor et al., eds., *The Implementation and Effectiveness of International Environmental Commitments: Theory and Practice* (Cambridge, Mass.: MIT Press, 1998), 283–299.

49. European Environment Agency and United Nations Environment Programme (UNEP), "Chemicals in the European Environment: Low Doses, High Stakes?" in *The EEA and UNEP Annual Message 2 on the State of Europe's Environment* (Copenhagen: European Commission, 2001).

50. Weiss, "The Five International Treaties," 112.

51. Jonathan Krueger and Henrik Selin, "Governance for Sound Chemicals Management: The Need for a More Comprehensive Global Strategy," *Global Governance* 8 (2002): 323–342; Jonathan Krueger, Henrik Selin, and David Downie, "Global Policy for Hazardous Chemicals," in Regina Axelrod, David Downie, and Norman Vig, eds., *Global Environmental Policy: Institutions, Law & Policy,* 2nd ed. (Washington, D.C.: Congressional Quarterly Press, 2004).

52. For additional information, see the TRAFFIC Web site, http://www.traffic.org.

53. Including, for example, the UNEP Governing Council, Open-ended Intergovernmental Group of Ministers or Their Representatives on International Environmental Governance, and Global Ministerial Environment Forum.

54. The "strategic approach to international chemicals management" (SAICM) seeks to integrate better chemicals management into all aspects of development activity. One part of this

is to increase coordination among the relevant activities of the various chemical related institutions. For more information see the SAICM Web site, http://www.chem.unep.ch/saicm/.

55. Ronald B. Mitchell, *Intentional Oil Pollution at Sea,* 47–48.

56. There are many good discussions of this problem. See, for example, Sanford Gaines, "The WTO's reading of the GATT Article XX Chapeau: A Disguised Restriction on Environmental Measures," *University of Pennsylvania Journal of International Economic Law* 22, no. 4: 739–858; Steve Charnovitz, "Exploring the Environmental Exceptions in GATT Article XX," *Journal of World Trade* 25 (1991); and Beatrice Chaytor and James Cameron, "The Treatment of Environmental Considerations in the World Trade Organization," in Helge Ole Bergesen, Georg Parmann, and Øystein B. Thommessen, eds., *Yearbook of International Co-operation on Environment and Development 1999/2000* (London: Earthscan Publications, 1999), 55–64.

57. For more information on this, see Martin Khor, "The Proposed New Issues in the WTO and the Interests of Developing Countries," Trade and Development Series no. 14 (Penang, Malaysia: Third World Network, 2001).

58. See, for example, Susskind, *Environmental Diplomacy,* 113–117.

59. Harold K. Jacobson and Edith Brown Weiss, "Assessing the Record and Designing Strategies to Engage Countries," in Edith Brown Weiss and Harold K. Jacobson, eds., *Engaging Countries: Strengthening Compliance with International Environmental Accords* (Cambridge, Mass.: MIT Press, 1998), 527.

60. United Nations Department for Public Information, "Press Summary of the Secretary-General's Report on Implementing Agenda 21," news release, January 2002.

61. OECD, "Official Development Assistance Increases Further—But 2006 Targets Still a Challenge," news release, April 11, 2005.

62. Jim VandeHei, "G-8 Leaders Agree on $50B in Africa Aid," *Washington Post,* July 9, 2005.

63. For example, see International Institute for Sustainable Development, "Financing Climate Change: Global Environmental Tax?" *Developing Ideas,* no. 15 (September–October 1998).

64. UN Commission on Sustainable Development, *Financial Resources and Mechanisms for Sustainable Development: Overview of Current Issues and Developments,* Report of the Secretary-General E/CN.17/ISWG.II/1994/2 (February 22, 1994), 24.

65. The original proposal, by Nobel Prize–winning economist James Tobin, was for a 0.5 percent tax on speculative currency transactions that would raise $1.5 trillion annually and was aimed at deterring such transactions. The UNDP proposed reducing the tax to 10 percent of the original level. See UNDP, *Human Development Report 1994* (New York: Oxford University Press, 1994), 69–70; Martin Walker, "Global Taxation: Paying for Peace," *World Policy Journal* 10, no. 2 (Summer 1993): 7–12.

66. Stephen R. Seidel and Daniel Blank, "Closing an Ozone Loophole," *The Environmental Forum* 7 (1990): 18–20; "Effect of Ozone-Depleting Chemicals Tax Could Be Wide-Ranging, IRS Attorney Says," *Environment Reporter* 21 (November 2, 1990): 1257.

67. Updated information on HIPC can be found on the World Bank and IMF Web sites, http://www.worldbank.org/debt and http://www.imf.org/external/np/exr/facts/hipc.htm.

68. Ibid.

69. Jim VandeHei, "G-8 Leaders Agree on $50B in Africa Aid," *Washington Post,* July 9, 2005.

70. See http://www.jubileeusa.org/.

71. A. De Moor and P. Calamai, *Subsidizing Unsustainable Development: Undermining the Earth with Public Funds* (San Jose, Costa Rica: Earth Council, 1997); V. P. Gadhi, D. Gray,

and R. McMorran, "A Comprehensive Approach to Domestic Resources for Sustainable Development," in *Finance for Sustainable Development: The Road Ahead* (New York: United Nations, 1997).

72. World Bank, *Expanding the Measure of Wealth: Indicators of Environmentally Sustainable Development* (Washington, D.C.: World Bank, 1997).

Chapter 5

1. See Karl P. Sauvant and Hajo Hasenpflug, eds., *The New International Economic Order: Confrontation or Cooperation Between North and South?* (Boulder: Westview Press, 1977).

2. James K. Sebenius, "Negotiating a Regime to Control Global Warming," in Jessica Tuchman Mathews, *Greenhouse Warming: Negotiating a Global Regime* (Washington, D.C.: World Resources Institute, 1991), 87.

3. South Commission, *The Challenge to the South: The Report of the South Commission* (Oxford: Oxford University Press, 1990); Mohammed Ayoob, "The New-Old Disorder in the Third World," *Global Governance* 1, no. 1 (1995): 59–77; Adil Najam, "An Environmental Negotiation Strategy for the South," *International Environmental Affairs* 7, no. 3 (1995): 249–87; Adil Najam, "The View from the South: Developing Countries in Global Environmental Politics," in Regina S. Axelrod, David L. Downie, and Norman J. Vig, *The Global Environment: Institutions, Law and Policy*, 2nd ed. (Washington, D.C.: Congressional Quarterly Press, 2004), 224–243.

4. Dennis Pirages, *Global Ecopolitics: The New Context for International Relations* (North Scituate, R.I.: Duxbury Press, 1978); Hayward R. Alker Jr. and Peter M. Haas, "The Rise of Global Ecopolitics," in Nazli Choucri, ed., *Global Accord: Environmental Challenges and International Responses* (Cambridge, Mass.: MIT Press, 1993), 133–171; Najam, "An Environmental Negotiation Strategy for the South"; Najam, "The View from the South."

5. This was part of a longer-term decline in the real prices of primary products in the world market, caused by slow growth in demand, the development of cheaper substitutes, and over production. See United Nations Development Programme, *Human Development Report 1992* (New York: UNDP, 1992), 59.

6. UNDP, "Financial Inflows and Outflows," *Human Development Report 1998* (New York: Oxford University Press, 1998). The term *least developed countries* (LDCs) was originally used at the UN in 1971 to describe the "poorest and most economically weak of the developing countries, with formidable economic, institutional and human resources problems, which are often compounded by geographical handicaps and natural and man-made disasters." There are currently fifty LDCs.

7. World Bank, *Global Economic Prospects and the Developing Countries* (Washington, D.C.: World Bank, 1992), 13.

8. WTO Committee on Trade and Development, "Participation of Developing Countries in World Trade: Overview of Major Trends and Underlying Factors," WT/COMTD/W/15, August 16, 1996.

9. UNDP, *Human Development Report 1999* (New York: UNDP, 1999), 34; World Bank, "Total GDP 2003," World Development Indicators database, World Bank, April 2005, http://www.worldbank.org/data/databytopic/GDP.pdf. The twenty richest countries are Australia, Austria, Belgium, Brazil, Canada, China, France, Germany, India, Italy, Japan, Mexico, the Netherlands, the Republic of Korea, the Russian Federation, Spain, Sweden, Switzerland, the United States, and the United Kingdom.

10. For the example of the Philippines, see Gareth Porter, with Delfin Ganapin, Jr., *Population, Resources and the Philippines' Future* (Washington, D.C.: World Resources Institute, 1988); Robin Broad, with John Cavanagh, *Plundering Paradise: The Struggle for Environment in the Philippines* (Berkeley and Los Angeles: University of California Press, 1993); Peter Dauvergne, *Shadows in the Forest: Japan and Politics of Timber in Southeast Asia* (Cambridge, Mass.: MIT Press, 1997).

11. "The Price of the Environment," *Environmental News from the Netherlands*, no. 1 (1992).

12. Mark Fritz, "Imports Hurting African Farmers," *Sacramento Bee*, December 20, 1993, A18.

13. "Dumping on the World," Oxfam briefing paper 61, April 2004, 2, http://www.oxfamireland.org/pdfs/bp61_sugar_dumping.pdf.

14. For more information on subsidies, see David Malin Roodman, "Paying the Piper: Subsidies, Politics and the Environment," Worldwatch paper no. 23, December 1996 (Washington, D.C.: Worldwatch); Matteo Milazzo, "Subsidies in World Fisheries," World Bank technical paper no. 406 (Washington, D.C.: World Bank, 1998); Gareth Porter, "Fisheries Subsidies, Overfishing and Trade," UNEP Environment and Trade Series no. 16 (Geneva: UNEP, 1998); World Trade Organization, Committee on Trade and Environment, *Environmental Benefits of Removing Trade Restrictions and Distortions* (Geneva: WTO, 1997); A.P.G. de Moor, *Perverse Incentives: Subsidies and Sustainable Development* (San Jose, Costa Rica: Earth Council, 1997); OECD, *Environmentally Harmful Subsidies Policy Issues and Challenges* (Paris: OECD, 2003).

15. *Development and Environment*, report and working papers of experts convened by the Secretary-General of the United Nations Conference on the Human Environment, Founex, Switzerland, June 4–12, 1971 (Paris: Mouton, 1971).

16. Najam, "The View from the South."

17. *Development and Environment*, 5–6, as cited in Adil Najam, "Why Environmental Politics Looks Different from the South," in Peter Dauvergne, *Handbook of Global Environmental Politics* (Cheltenham, U.K.: Edward Elgar Press, 2005), 111–126.

18. Statement by H. E. Datuk Amar Stephen K. T. Yong, leader of the Malaysian delegation, at the second Meeting of the Parties to the Montreal Protocol, London, June 27–29, 1990.

19. Talk by Mohammed El-Ashry, then vice president of World Resources Institute, at the Egyptian Embassy, Washington, D.C., March 9, 1990.

20. "Final Document of the XIIth Summit of the Non-Aligned Movement," September 2–3, 1998, Durban, South Africa, http://www.nam.gov.za/xiisummit/index.html.

21. UNDP, *Human Development Report* 1998 (New York: Oxford University Press, 1998). For details and illustrations of the developing country point of view, see also Anil Agarwal, Sunita Narain, and Anju Sharma, eds., *Green Politics: Global Negotiations*, vol. 1 (New Delhi: Center for Science and Environment, 1999).

22. Friends of the Earth Netherlands developed the environmental space concept as part of its 1992 Sustainable Netherlands Action Plan. Environmental space is the total amount of pollution, nonrenewable resources, agricultural land, and forests that can be used globally without impinging on access by future generations to the same resources. For additional information, see the report of the Oslo Ministerial Roundtable on Sustainable Production and Consumption, February 6–10, 1995, http://www.iisd.ca/linkages/consume/oslo000.html.

23. Najam, "The View from the South."

24. Pamela S. Chasek, "The Convention to Combat Desertification: Lessons Learned for Sustainable Development," *Journal of Environment and Development* 6, no. 2 (1997): 147–169.

25. Najam, "The View from the South."

26. Ibid.

27. "Proposed Elements of a Protocol to the United Nations Framework Convention on Climate Change, Presented by Brazil in Response to the Berlin Mandate," Ad Hoc Group on the Berlin Mandate, seventh session, Bonn, July 31–7 August 7, 1997, 22.

28. See *Outreach 1997* 1, no. 24 (April 22, 1997).

29. Najam, "The View from the South." See also Anil Agarwal and Sunita Narain, *Global Warming in an Unequal World: A Case of Environmental Colonialism* (New Delhi: Center for Science and Environment, 1991); Agarwal, Narain, and Sharma, *Green Politics*.

30. Najam, "The View from the South."

31. Ibid.

32. Steve Charnovitz, "Environmentalism Confronts GATT Rules," *Journal of World Trade* 28 (January 1993): 37; Daniel C. Esty, "Economic Integration and the Environment," in Norman J. Vig and Regina S. Axelrod, eds., *The Global Environment: Institutions, Law, and Policy* (Washington, D.C.: Congressional Quarterly Press, 1999), 192.

33. John J. Audley, *Green Politics and Global Trade: NAFTA and the Future of Environmental Politics* (Washington, D.C.: Georgetown University Press, 1997).

34. "Agreement Establishing the World Trade Organization (WTO)," GATT/WTO, Preamble, 1994.

35. Ibid.

36. For more information on the Doha Ministerial Declaration, see WTO, "Ministerial Declaration" WT/MIN(01)/DEC/1 (November 20, 2001), http://www.wto.org/english/thewto_e/minist_e/min01_e/mindecl_c.htm. A good analysis of the declaration can be found at International Center for Trade and Sustainable Development, "The Doha Declaration's Meaning Depends on the Reader," *Bridges* 5, no. 9 (November/December 2001), http://www.ictsd.org/monthly/bridges/BRIDGES5-9.pdf.

37. For a matrix of selected MEAs and their trade provisions, see WTO, "Matrix on Trade Measures Pursuant to Selected Multilateral Environmental Agreements," WT/CTE/W/160/Rev.3 (February 16, 2005), http://docsonline.wto.org/DDFDocuments/t/tn/te/S5R1.doc.

38. The description of the trade provisions of CITES, the Montreal Protocol and the Basel Convention is excerpted from Community Nutrition Institute, "Multilateral Environmental Agreements and the GATT/WTO Regime" (paper presented at the Joint Policy Dialogue on Environment and Trade, January 1996).

39. United Nations Environment Programme and the International Institute for Sustainable Development (IISD), *Environment and Trade: A Handbook* (Winnipeg: IISD/UNEP, 2000).

40. Ibid.

41. Ibid.

42. Ibid.

43. WTO, "Doha Ministerial Declaration," WT/MIN(01)/DEC/1 (November 20, 2001), http://www.wto.org/english/thewto_e/minist_e/min01_e/mindecl_e.htm.

44. International Centre for Trade and Sustainable Development and the International Institute for Sustainable Development, "Trade and Environment," *Doha Round Briefing Series* 3, no. 9 (December 2004), http://www.ictsd.org/pubs/dohabriefings/Vol3/V3_09.pdf.

45. The term *environmental trade measures* is used in Steve Charnowitz, "The Environment vs. Trade Rules: Defogging the Debate," *Environmental Law* 23 (Northwestern School of Law of Lewis and Clark College) (1993): 490. Charnowitz lists all these forms of ETMs except mandatory eco-labeling.

46. Sang Don Lee, "The Effect of Environmental Regulations on Trade: Cases of Korea's New Environmental Laws," *Georgetown International Environmental Law Review* (Summer 1993): 659.

47. ICTSD, "Ecuador, U.S. Reject EU Banana Proposal; Ecuador to Cross-Retaliate," *Bridges Weekly Trade News Digest* 3, no. 45 (November 15, 1999).

48. It was widely believed among NGOs that more such disputes over unilateral actions in the future would ultimately force the negotiation of new GATT rules on the issue. See Bruce Stokes, "The Road from Rio," *National Journal* (May 30, 1992): 1288.

49. Daniel C. Esty, *Greening the GATT: Trade, Environment and the Future* (Washington, D.C.: Institute for International Economics, 1994), 188. In an ironic twist, research undertaken by the Inter-American Tropical Tuna Commission found that "dolphin-safe" tuna fishing results in catching tuna at least thirty-five times more immature (because young tuna do not school beneath groups of dolphins as mature tuna do) and thus threatens to deplete tuna fisheries. See Richard Parker, "The Use and Abuse of Trade Leverage to Protect the Global Commons: What We Can Learn from the Tuna-Dolphin Conflict," *Georgetown International Environmental Law Review* 12, no. 1 (1999): 37–38.

50. For environmental critiques of the decision, see Steve Charnovitz, "GATT and the Environment: Examining the Issues," *International Environmental Affairs* 4, no. 3 (Summer 1992): 203–233; Robert Repetto, "Trade and Environment Policies: Achieving Complementarities and Avoiding Conflict," *WRI Issues and Ideas* (July 1993): 6–10. For an alternative view of the decision, see John H. Jackson, "World Trade Rules and Environmental Policies: Congruence or Conflict?" *Washington and Lee Law Review* 49 (Fall 1992): 1242–1243.

51. For an excellent summary, see Donald M. Goldberg, "GATT Tuna-Dolphin II: Environmental Protection Continues to Clash with Free Trade," CIEL brief no. 2 (June 1994).

52. The panel's conclusions were released in GATT, "United States Taxes on Automobiles: Report of the Panel," restricted, DS31/R, September 29, 1994.

53. Ibid.

54. Janet Welsh Brown, "Trade and the Environment," *Encyclopedia of Violence, Peace and Conflict*, vol. 3 (San Diego: Academic Press, 1999), T12–4.

55. The Appellate Body also noted that the United States had failed to sign the Convention on Migratory Species or the United Nations Convention on the Law of the Sea and had not ratified the Convention on Biological Diversity, nor had it raised the issue of sea turtles during recent CITES conferences. These inconsistencies in the U.S. record on protection of endangered species do not prove, of course, that the U.S. intention in the Shrimp/Turtle case was not protecting endangered sea turtles.

56. See "Revised Guidelines for the Implementation of Section 609 of Public Law 101–162 Relating to the Protection of Sea Turtles in Shrimp Trawl Fishing Operations," Public Notice 3086, Federal Register, July 1999.

57. For more information, see the Marine Stewardship Council's Web site, http://www.msc.org.

58. Since 1994, labeling and related issues have been discussed in the WTO's Committee on Trade and Environment, the Committee on Technical Barriers to Trade (TBT), and the Committee on Sanitary and Phytosanitary Measures (CSPS), as well as during two Triennial Re-

views of the TBT Agreement, at various informal WTO symposia, in external conferences attended by WTO Secretariat staff, and in dispute settlement panels and appellate bodies. For more information on this debate, see Tom Rotherham, *Labelling for Environmental Purposes: A Review of the State of the Debate in the World Trade Organization* (Winnipeg: IISD, 2003), http://www.tradeknowledgenetwork.net/pdf/tkn_labelling.pdf.

59. Ibid., 4.

60. International Centre for Trade and Sustainable Development and the International Institute for Sustainable Development (IISD), "Trade and Environment," *Doha Round Briefing Series* 3, no. 9 (December 2004), http://www.ictsd.org/pubs/dohabriefings/Vol3/V3_09.pdf.

61. See World Trade Organization, Committee on Trade and Environment, *Environmental Benefits of Removing Trade Restrictions and Distortions: Note by the Secretariat* (Geneva: WTO, 1997); Gareth Porter, *Fisheries Subsidies, Overfishing and Trade* (Geneva: United Nations Environment Programme, 1998).

62. World Wildlife Fund, *Turning the Tide on Fishing Subsidies* (Washington, D.C.: WWF, 2002), 4.

63. International Centre for Trade and Sustainable Development and the International Institute for Sustainable Development (IISD), "Trade and Environment."

64. The WTO is not the only international organization addressing the issue of fisheries subsidies. Discussions are also ongoing in the OECD, FAO, UNEP, and APEC. For a summary on the activities of these organizations, see Gareth Porter, *Fisheries Subsidies and Overfishing: Towards a Structured Discussion* (Geneva, UNEP: 2002); and United Nations Environment Programme (UNEP), "Fisheries Subsidies and Sustainable Fisheries Management: A UNEP Update" (June 2004), http://www.unep.ch/etu/Fisheries%20Meeting/bulletinPeche.pdf.

65. This summary of the subsidies debate is based on reports from the International Centre for Trade and Sustainable Development and the International Institute for Sustainable Development's *Doha Round Briefing Series* and *Bridges Weekly Trade Digest*, http://www.ictsd.org.

66. Maria Pia Hernandez, "From Cancún to Hong Kong: WTO Update," *Center Focus*, no. 166 (March 2005), http://www.coc.org/pdfs/coc/cf/2005/cf166_2005-03_from.pdf.

67. The members of the G-20 are Argentina, Bolivia, Brazil, Chile, China, Cuba, Egypt, India, Indonesia, Mexico, Nigeria, Pakistan, Paraguay, Philippines, South Africa, Tanzania, Thailand, and Venezuela.

68. Hernandez, "From Cancún to Hong Kong."

69. Mark Ritchie and Kristin Dawkins, "A New Beginning for WTO After Cancún," *Foreign Policy In Focus*, October 10, 2003, http://www.globalpolicy.org/socecon/trade/2003/1010ncw-beginning.htm.

70. For more information about the Free Trade Area of the Americas, see http://www.ftaa-alca.org/alca_c.asp.

71. Ritchie and Dawkins, "A New Beginning for WTO After Cancún."

72. Kevin P. Gallagher, "The Economics of Globalization and Sustainable Development," *Policy Matters: Trade, Environment and Investment, Cancún and Beyond*, no. 11 (September 2003).

73. Mark Halle, "Sustainable Development Cools Off—Globalization Demands Summit Take New Approach to Meeting Ecological, Social Goals," *Winnipeg* (Canada) *Free Press*, July 29, 2002.

74. Pamela Chasek and Marian A. L. Miller, "Sustainable Development in the Twenty-First Century," in Michael T. Snarr and D. Neil Snarr, *Introducing Global Issues*, 3rd ed. (Boulder: Lynne Rienner, 2005).

75. United Nations, "Addressing Inequities of Globalization 'Overarching Challenge' of Times Says Secretary-General, Presenting Millennium Report to General Assembly," UN Press Release SG/SM/7343, April 3, 2000.

76. The international events held between 2000 and 2002 include the Millennium Assembly in New York, the International Conference on Financing for Development in Monterrey, the Third Least Developed Countries Summit in Brussels, the Fourth World Trade Organization Ministerial Conference held at Doha, the World Food Summit+5 in Rome, and the World Summit on Sustainable Development in Johannesburg. For more information on these events, see Pamela S. Chasek and Richard Sherman, *Ten Days in Johannesburg: A Negotiation of Hope* (Cape Town: Struik Publishers, 2004); and International Institute for Sustainable Development (IISD), *Millennium Review Meeting Bulletin* 104, no. 2 (March 16, 2005), http://www.iisd.ca/sd/ecosocprep1/sdvol104num2e.html.

77. Chasek and Sherman, *Ten Days in Johannesburg*, and IISD, *Millennium Review Meeting Bulletin*.

78. Ibid.

79. James Gustave Speth, "Perspectives on the Johannesburg Summit," *Environment* 45, no. 1 (2003).

80. United Nations. "Report of the World Summit on Sustainable Development; A/CONF.199/20" (New York: United Nations, 2002), http://www.johannesburgsummit.org/html/documents/summit_docs/131302_wssd_report_ reissued.pdf.

81. United Nations Department of Economic and Social Affairs, "The Johannesburg Summit Test: What Will Change" (September 25, 2002), http://www.johannesburgsummit.org/html/whats_new/feature_story41.html.

82. Ibid.

83. Ibid.

84. Ibid.

85. Speth, "Perspectives on the Johannesburg Summit," 24–29.

86. See, for example, Daniel C. Esty, "The Case for a Global Environmental Organization," in Peter B. Kenen (ed.), *Managing the World Economy: Fifty Years After Bretton Woods* (Washington, D.C.: Institute for International Economics, 1994); Frank Biermann and Steffen Bauer, *A World Environment Organization Solution or Threat for Effective International Environmental Governance?* (Aldershot, U.K.: Ashgate Publishing, 2005).

87. This paragraph has been adapted from Chasek and Miller, "Sustainable Development in the Twenty-First Century."

Chronology

1800   Atmospheric carbon dioxide and methane concentrations in the atmosphere hover around 270–290 parts per million (ppm) and 700 parts per billion (ppb), respectively. Most scientists today use these numbers as a pre-industrial revolution baseline for comparison.

1857   Svante Arrhenius, a Swedish scientist, identifies enhanced greenhouse effect but fails to link the phenomenon to a cause.

1859   John Tyndal, an Irish physicist, becomes one of the first scientists to study and identify the greenhouse effect as well as the relative radiative forcings of different gases in the atmosphere.

1900 CO_2 concentration in the atmosphere reaches 295 ppm.

1902   The Convention for the Protection of Birds Useful to Agriculture is signed.

1903   First international conservation NGO formed, the Society for the Preservation of the Wild Fauna of the Empire, in the UK.

1911   Treaty for the Preservation and Protection of Fur Seals is signed.

1913   Commission for the International Protection of Nature is founded.

1933   The London Convention on the Preservation of Fauna and Flora in their Natural State is signed.

1938   G.S. Callendar revisits Arrhenius' theory on the greenhouse effect and argues that increases in CO_2 concentration could explain recent warming trends.

1940   Convention on Nature Protection and Wildlife Preservation in the Western Hemisphere is signed.

1945   United Nations established.

1946   The International Convention for the Regulation of Whaling is signed; International Whaling Commission created.

1947   Commission for the International Protection of Nature renamed the International Union for the Conservation of Nature (IUCN), becoming first INGO with a global outlook on environmental problems.

1947   World Meteorological Organization (WMO) created.

1948   International Maritime Organization (IMO) created.

1949   The International Convention for the North-West Atlantic Fisheries is signed.

1950   The International Convention for the Protection of Birds is signed.

1954   The International Convention for the Prevention of Pollution of Sea by Oil is signed.

1956   European Economic Community established.

1956   Revelle and Keeling publish a paper on CO_2, showing the trend of increasing atmospheric concentrations over the past century.

1959   Antarctic Treaty is signed.

1962   Publication of Rachel Carson's *Silent Spring*.

1963   Agreement for the Protection of the Rhine against Pollution is signed.

1967   Supertanker *Torry Canyon* grounds in the English channel resulting in massive oil spill.

1969   National Environmental Policy Act of 1969 (NEPA) is passed by U.S. Congress.

1971   Ramsar Convention on Wetlands of International Importance is signed.

1972   United Nations Conference on the Human Environment is convened in Stockholm.

1972   United Nations Environment Program (UNEP) created.

1972   *The Limits to Growth* report for the Club of Rome is published.

1972   The Convention on the Prevention of Marine Pollution by Dumping of Wastes and Other Matter (London Convention) is signed.

1972   Convention for the Conservation of Antarctic Seals is signed.

1973   Convention on International Trade in Endangered Species of Wild Fauna and Flora (CITES) is signed.

1973   International Convention for the Prevention of Pollution from Ships (MARPOL) is signed.

1973   U.S. Endangered Species Conservation Act banning whaling and whale imports becomes law.

1974   Declaration on the Establishment of a New International Economic Order (NIEO) is issued by the Sixth Special Session of the United Nations General Assembly.

1974   M.J. Molina and F.S. Rowland publish their theory that CFCs threaten the ozone layer.

1974   World Population Conference held in Bucharest.

1974   World Food Conference held in Rome.

1975 UNEP Regional Seas Programme created.

1976 Convention for the Protection of the Mediterranean Sea against Pollution is signed.

1976 United Nations Conference on Human Settlements held in Vancouver.

1976 UNEP International Register of Potentially Toxic Chemicals established.

1977 United Nations Conference on Desertification adopts the Plan of Action to Combat Desertification.

1977 Ad Hoc Conference of Experts convened by UNEP approves the World Plan of Action on the Ozone Layer.

1979 Convention on the Conservation of Migratory Species (CMS) is signed.

1979 Convention on Long-Range Transboundary Air Pollution (LRTAP) is signed.

1979 First World Climate Conference convened by WMO, UNEP and ICSU in Geneva warns of danger of global warming.

1980 Convention on the Conservation of Antarctic Marine Living Resources (CCAMLR) is signed.

1980 World Conservation Strategy launched by IUCN and UNEP.

1980 Global 2000 Report to the President is published.

1981 Montevideo Programme on International Environmental Law launched

1982 Formal Negotiations begin on protection of the ozone layer.

1982 The United Nations Convention on the Law of the Sea (UNCLOS) is signed.

1982 Phaseout of commercial whaling over a three-year period is passed by the International Whaling Commission (IWC).

1984 International Tropical Timber Agreement (ITTA) is signed.

1984 Union Carbide Bhopal Disaster.

1984 Protocol for Long-Term Financing of Monitoring (LRTAP) is signed.

1985 The Vienna Convention for Protection of the Ozone Layer is signed.

1985 Antarctic ozone hole discovery published in *Nature*.

1985 Canadian scientists discover abnormally high levels of persistent organic pollutants (POPs) in some Inuit communities in northern Canada, revealing global transport of toxic chemicals.

1985 The Helsinki Protocol to the LRTAP is signed, committing the signatories to reduce sulfur dioxide emissions.

1985 London Convention meeting of the parties votes to ban all further dumping of low-level radioactive wastes in oceans until it is proven safe.

1985   Conference of climate experts in Villach, Austria, produces consensus on serious possibility of global warming.

1985   Tropical Forestry Action Plan (TFAP) is approved by donor countries at a conference in The Hague.

1985   Montreal Guidelines for the Protection of the Marine Environment from Land-Based Sources are signed.

1986   Major explosion at the Soviet nuclear plant in Chernobyl spreads radioactive cloud across Western Europe and Japan.

1987   The Montreal Protocol on Substances that Deplete the Ozone Layer is signed.

1987   International Tropical Timber Organization (ITTO) holds first meeting in Yokohama, Japan.

1987   The Report of the World Commission on Environment and Development (the Brundtland Report) is published as *Our Common Future*.

1988   British scientists issue report on dramatic decrease in ozone layer over Antarctica; Ozone Trends Panel report documents ozone-layer decreases in Northern Hemisphere.

1988   The Sofia Protocol to LRTAP is signed, committing the signatories to reduce nitrogen oxide emissions.

1988   Convention on the Regulation of Antarctic Mineral Resources Activities (CRAMRA) is signed in Wellington, New Zealand.

1989   Exxon Valdez spills oil in the Gulf of Alaska.

1989   Communiqué of the Group of Seven (G-7) heads of industrial democracies focuses on the global environment.

1989   Twenty-four nations issue The Hague Declaration on the Environment.

1989   The Basel Convention on the Control of Transboundary Movements of Hazardous Wastes and Their Disposal is signed; the European Community reaches agreement with ACP (Africa, the Caribbean, and the Pacific) states to ban hazardous waste exports to countries without the capacity to dispose of them safely.

1989   Ministerial Conference on Atmospheric Pollution and Climate Change issues the Noordwijk Declaration, in the Netherlands, calling for stabilization of carbon dioxide emissions by 2000.

1989   Seventh CITES conference votes to ban trade in African elephant ivory products.

1990   Second meeting of the parties to the Montreal Protocol convenes in London to strengthen the Montreal Protocol.

1990   Communiqué of G-7 heads of state summit meeting in Houston calls for negotiation of an international agreement on the world's forests.

1990   Bergen Ministerial Declaration on Sustainable Development in the Economic Commission for Europe (ECE) calls stabilization of carbon dioxide emissions the first step.

1990   Meeting of Antarctic Treaty Consultative Parties (ATCPs) in Santiago, Chile, agrees to begin negotiations on a convention for environmental protection of Antarctica.

1990   Ban on whaling extended by the International Whaling Commission.

1990   IPCC releases First Assessment Report, asserting that the average global surface temperature has increased by 0.3 to 0.6 degrees Celsius since 1980.

1991   Bamako Convention on the Ban of the Import into Africa and the Control of Transboundary Movement and Management of Hazardous Wastes Within Africa.

1991   Global Environment Facility (GEF) established.

1991   Protocol on Environmental Protection to the Antarctic Treaty is signed.

1991   Volatile Organic Compounds Protocol to LRTAP signed.

1992   United Nations Conference on Environment and Development is convened in Rio de Janeiro.

1992   Framework Convention on Climate Change is signed at Rio de Janeiro.

1992   Convention on Biological Diversity is signed at Rio de Janeiro.

1993   Central American Forest Treaty is signed.

1993   United Nations Conference on Straddling and Highly Migratory Fish Stocks is convened.

1994   United Nations Convention to Combat Desertification is signed.

1994   United Nations Convention on the Law of the Sea enters into force.

1994   GATT Uruguay Round concludes negotiations in Marrakesh, Morocco.

1994   International Conference on Population and Development is held in Cairo.

1994   Global Conference on the Sustainable Development of Small Island Developing States meets in Barbados.

1994   World Conference on Natural Disaster Reduction meets in Yokohama, Japan.

1995   World Conference on Social Development convenes in Copenhagen.

1995   Fourth World Conference on Women convenes in Beijing.

1995   Agreement on the Conservation and Management of Stradding Fish Stocks and Highly Migratory Fish Stocks is signed.

1995   World Trade Organization is established.

320 Chronology

1996 IPCC releases Second Assessment Report that concludes that there is a discernible human influence on global climate.

1997 Montreal Amendment to the Montreal Protocol signed on the tenth anniversary of the Protocol.

1997 UN General Assembly Special Session convenes in New York to review the implementation of Agenda 21.

1997 Tenth CITES conference votes to reopen the ivory trade in Botswana, Namibia, and Zimbabwe.

1997 Kyoto Protocol to the Framework Convention on Climate Change is signed.

1998 Protocols on Heavy Metals and Persistent Organic Pollutants to LTRAP are signed.

1998 Rotterdam Convention on the Prior Informed Consent Procedure for Certain Hazardous Chemicals and Pesticides in International Trade is signed.

1999 Special Session of the General Assembly to review the implementation of the Barbados Programme of Action on Small Island Developing States.

1999 Protocol to Abate Acidification, Eutrophication and Ground-Level Ozone to LTRAP is adopted.

1999 First legal sale of ivory in a decade takes place in Windhoek, Namibia.

1999 Protocol on Liability and Compensation to the Basel Convention on the Control of Transboundary Movements and Hazardous Wastes and Their Disposal is adopted.

2000 Cartagena Protocol on Biosafety is adopted by the Conference of the Parties to the Convention on Biological Diversity.

2000 Millennium Summit held at UN headquarters in New York.

2001 Stockholm Convention on Persistent Organic Pollutants is signed.

2001 IPCC's Third Assessment Report (TAR) concludes that the evidence for humanity's influence on the global climate is stronger than ever.

2002 International Conference on Financing for Development held in Monterrey, Mexico.

2002 UN World Summit on Sustainable Development held in Johannesburg, South Africa.

2003 The African Ministerial Conference on the Environment (AMCEN) adopts the New Partnership for Africa's Development (NEPAD) Environment Action Plan.

2003 Cartagena Protocol on Biosafety enters into force.

2004 CO_2 concentration in the atmosphere reaches an unprecedented 379 ppm.

2004 Rotterdam Convention enters into force.

2004   Stockholm Convention enters into force.

2004   The Nobel Committee announces that Professor Wangari Maathai, Assistant Minister of Environment and Natural Resources of Kenya and founder and chair of the Green Belt Movement, is the 2004 Nobel Peace Prize winner.

2005   Kyoto Protocol enters into force.

2005   Mauritius International Meeting on the Implementation of the Barbados Program of Action on the Sustainable Development of Small Island Developing States.

2005   World Conference on Disaster Reduction, held in Kobe-Hyogo, Japan.

2005   European Union's Greenhouse Gas Emission Trading Scheme (EU ETS) begins operation as the world's first multicountry, multisector greenhouse gas emission trading scheme.

2005   UN General Assembly High-Level Meeting to Review the Implementation of the Millennium Declaration.

Suggested Readings

This section provides an indicative list of additional readings on core issues addressed in this volume. Any such list, especially one so short, must necessarily omit many important and informative works. Thus, we have striven to create a list of accessible and easily obtainable recent works, not a comprehensive bibliography. Please also note that many of the works cited in the footnotes are not listed again here. Finally, many of the edited volumes in the first section of the list below contain chapters that provide detailed case studies of the regimes introduced in chapter 3.

Global Environmental Politics, Law and Institutions

Agarwal, Anil, Sunita Narain, and Anju Sharma, eds. *Green Politics: Global Negotiations.* Vol. 1. New Delhi: Center for Science and Environment, 1999.

Axelrod, Regina, David Downie, and Norman Vig, eds. *The Global Environment: Institutions, Law & Policy.* 2nd ed. Washington, D.C.: Congressional Quarterly Press, 2004.

Barkin, J. Samuel, and George Shambaugh, eds. *Anarchy and the Environment: The International Relations of Common Pool Resources.* Albany: State University of New York Press, 1999.

Biermann, Frank, and Steffen Bauer, eds. *A World Environment Organization: Solution or Threat for Effective International Environmental Governance?* London: Ashgate, 2004.

Bohringer, Christoph, and Andreas Loschel. *Climate Change Policy and Global Trade.* Berlin: Springer Verlag, 2004.

Bulkeley, Harriet, and Michele M. Betsill, eds. *Cities and Climate Change: Urban Sustainability and Global Environmental Governance.* New York: Routledge, 2003.

Caldwell, Lynton Keith. *International Environmental Policy: From the 20th Century to the 21st Century.* Durham, N.C.: Duke University Press, 1996.

Caldwell, Lynton Keith, and Robert V. Bartlett. *Environmental Policy: Transnational Issues and National Trends.* Westport, Conn.: Quorum Books, 1997.

Chasek, Pamela S. *Earth Negotiations: Analyzing Thirty Years of Environmental Diplomacy.* Tokyo: UNU Press, 2001.

———, ed. *The Global Environment in the 21st Century: Prospects for International Cooperation.* Tokyo: UNU Press, 2000.

Conca, Ken, and Geoffrey D. Dabelko, eds. *Green Planet Blues: Environmental Politics from Stockholm to Johannesburg.* 3rd ed. Boulder: Westview Press: 2004.

DeSombre, Elizabeth R. *Domestic Sources of International Environmental Policy: Industry, Environmentalists, and U.S. Power.* Cambridge, Mass.: MIT Press, 2000.

———. *The Global Environment and World Politics: International Relations in the 21st Century.* Continuum Publishing Group, 2002.

Dimitrov, Radoslav S. "Knowledge, Power and Interests in Environmental Regime Formation." *International Studies Quarterly* 47, no. 1 (March 2003).

Faure, Michael, Joyeeta Gupta, and Andries Nentjes, eds. *Climate Change and the Kyoto Protocol: The Role of Institutions and Instruments to Control Global Change.* Northampton, Mass.: Edward Elgar, 2003.

Haas, Peter M., Robert O. Keohane, and Marc A. Levy, eds. *Institutions for the Earth.* Cambridge, Mass.: MIT Press, 1993.

Hampson, Fen Osler, and Michael Hart. *Multilateral Negotiations: Lessons from Arms Control, Trade and the Environment.* Baltimore: Johns Hopkins University Press, 1995.

Houghton, John. *Global Warming: A Complete Briefing.* Cambridge: Cambridge University Press, 2004.

Jeong, Ho-Won, ed. *Global Environmental Policies.* London: Palgrave, 2001.

Kanie, Norichika, and Peter M. Haas. *Emerging Forces in Environmental Governance.* Tokyo, New York: United Nations University Press, 2004.

Kelly, Michael J. "Overcoming Obstacles to the Effective Implementation of International Environmental Agreements." *Georgetown International Environmental Law Review* 9, no. 2 (1997): 447–488.

Keohane, Robert O., and Marc A. Levy, eds. *Institutions for Environmental Aid.* Cambridge, Mass.: MIT Press, 1996.

Litfin, Karen, ed. *The Greening of Sovereignty in World Politics.* Cambridge, Mass.: MIT Press, 1998.

Miles, Edward, Arild Underdal, Steiner Andresen, Jorgen Wettestad, Jon Birger Skjaerseth, and Elain Carlin. *Environmental Regime Effectiveness.* Cambridge, Mass.: MIT Press, 2002.

Najam, Adil, Ioli Christopoulou, and William R. Moomaw. "The Emergent 'System' of Global Environmental Governance." *Global Environmental Politics* 4, no. 4 (2004).

Sands, Philippe, ed. *Principles of International Environmental Law.* 3rd ed. Cambridge: Cambridge University Press, 2003.

Schreurs, Miranda A. *Environmental Politics in Japan, Germany, and the United States.* Cambridge: Cambridge University Press, 2002.

Tolba, Mostafa K. *Global Environmental Diplomacy: Negotiating Environmental Agreements for the World, 1973–1992.* Cambridge, Mass.: MIT Press, 1998.

Victor, David G., Kal Raustiala, and Eugene B. Skolnikoff, eds. *The Implementation and Effectiveness of International Environmental Commitments.* Cambridge, Mass.: MIT Press, 1998.

Weiss, Edith Brown, and Harold K. Jacobson. "Getting Countries to Comply with International Agreements." *Environment* 41, no. 6 (July-August 1999): 16–20, 37–45.

_____, eds. *Engaging Countries: Strengthening Compliance with International Environmental Accords.* Cambridge, Mass.: MIT Press, 1998.

Young, Oran R. *International Cooperation: Building Regimes for Natural Resources and the Environment.* Ithaca: Cornell University Press, 1989.

_____. *International Governance: Protecting the Environment in a Stateless Society.* Ithaca: Cornell University Press, 1994.

International Organizations

Barkin, J. Samuel. *International Organization: Theories and Institutions.* New York: Palgrave, 2006.

Barnett, Michael, and Martha Finnemore. *Rules for the World: International Organizations in Global Politics.* Ithaca: Cornell University Press, 2004.

Karns, Margaret P., and Karen A. Mingst. *International Organizations: The Politics and Processes of Global Governance.* Boulder: Lynne Rienner, 2004.

Martin, Lisa L. and Beth A. Simmons, eds. *International Institutions.* Cambridge: MIT Press, 2001.

Developing Countries and Global Environmental Politics

Chasek, Pamela S., and Lavanya Rajamani. "Steps Toward Enhanced Parity: Negotiating Capacity and Strategies of Developing Countries." In Inge Kaul, ed., *Providing Global Public Goods: Making Globalization Work for All.* New York: Oxford University Press, 2002.

DeSombre, Elizabeth R. "Developing Country Influence in Global Environmental Negotiations." *Environmental Politics* 9, no. 3 (Autumn 2000).

Harris, Paul, ed. *Confronting Environmental Change in East and Southeast Asia: Eco-Politics, Foreign Policy, and Sustainable Development.* London: Earthscan, 2005.

Miller, Marian A. L. *The Third World in Global Environmental Politics.* Boulder: Lynne Rienner, 1995.

Najam, Adil. "The View from the South: Developing Countries in Global Environmental Politics." In Regina Axelrod, David Downie, and Norman Vig, eds. *The Global Environment: Institutions Law & Policy.* 2nd ed. Washington, D.C.: Congressional Quarterly Press, 2004.

_____. "Why Environmental Politics Looks Different from the South." In Peter Dauvergne, ed., *Handbook of Global Environmental Politics.* Cheltenham, U.K.: Edward Elgar Press, 2005.

Srinivasan, T. N. *Developing Countries and the Multilateral Trading System: From the GATT to the Uruguay Round and the Future.* Boulder: Westview Press, 1998.

Nongovernmental Organizations

Betsill, Michele. "Environmental NGOs Meet the Sovereign State: The Kyoto Protocol Negotiations on Global Climate Change." *Colorado Journal of International Environmental Law and Policy* 13, no. 1 (Winter 2002).

Betsill, Michele, and Elisabeth Corell. "NGO Influence in International Environmental Negotiations." *Global Environmental Politics* 1, no. 4 (November 2001).

_____. "A Comparative Look at NGO Influence in International Environmental Negotiations: Desertification and Climate Change." *Global Environmental Politics* 1, no. 4 (November 2001).

Breitmeier, Helmut, and Volker Rittberger. "Environmental NGOs in an Emerging Global Civil Society." In Pamela S. Chasek, ed., *The Global Environment in the Twenty-First Century: Prospects for International Cooperation.* Tokyo: UNU Press, 2000.

Chasek, Pamela S. "Environmental Organizations and Multilateral Diplomacy: A Case Study of the *Earth Negotiations Bulletin.*" In James P. Muldoon, Jr. et al., eds., *Multilateral Diplomacy and the United Nations Today.* 3rd ed. Boulder: Westview Press, 2005.

Charnowitz, Steve. "Two Centuries of Participation: NGOs and International Governance." *Michigan Journal of International Law* 18, no. 2 (1997).

Esty, Daniel C. "Non-Governmental Organizations at the World Trade Organization: Cooperation, Competition or Exclusion." *Journal of International Economic Law* 1 (1998).

326 · Suggested Readings

Raustiala, Kal. "States, NGOs and International Environmental Institutions." *International Studies Quarterly* 41 (1997): 719–740.

Sustainable Development

Chasek, Pamela S., and Marian A. L. Miller. "Sustainable Development in the Twenty-First Century." In Michael Snarr and D. Neil Snarr, eds., *Introducing Global Issues*. 3rd. ed. Boulder: Lynne Rienner, 2005.

Dodds, Felix, ed. *The Way Forward: Beyond Agenda 21*. London: Earthscan, 1997.

Meadows, Donella H., et al. *The Limits to Growth*. New York: Universe Books, 1972.

World Commission on Environment and Development. *Our Common Future*. New York: Oxford University Press, 1987.

Earth Summit and World Summit on Sustainable Development

Chasek, Pamela S., and Richard Sherman. *Ten Days in Johannesburg: A Negotiation of Hope*. Cape Town: Struik Publishers, 2004.

Grubb, Michael, et al. *The "Earth Summit" Agreements: A Guide and Assessment*. London: Earthscan, 1993.

Haas, Peter M. "UN Conferences and Constructivist Governance of the Environment." *Global Governance* 8 (2002).

Najam, Adil, et al. "From Rio to Johannesburg: Progress and Prospects." *Environment* 44, no. 7 (2002).

Sjöstedt, Gunnar, Bertram Spector, and I. William Zartman, eds. *Negotiating International Regimes: Lessons Learned from the United Nations Conference on Environment and Development*. London: Graham and Trotman, 1994.

Speth, James Gustave. "Perspectives on the Johannesburg Summit." *Environment* 45, no. 1 (2003).

Wapner, Paul. "World Summit on Sustainable Development: Toward a Post-Jo'burg Environmentalism." *Global Environmental Politics* 3, no. 1 (2003).

Air Pollution

Selin, Henrik, and Stacy D. VanDeveer. "Mapping Institutional Linkages in European Air Pollution Politics." *Global Environmental Politics* 3, no. 3 (August 2003).

UN Economic Commission for Europe. *Strategies and Policies for Air Pollution Abatement*. Geneva: United Nations, 2004.

Biodiversity

Le Prestre, Philippe G., ed. *Governing Global Biodiversity: The Evolution and Implementation of the Convention on Biological Diversity*. London: Ashgate, 2002.

McConnell, Fiona. *The Biodiversity Convention: A Negotiating History*. London: Kluwer Law International, 1996.

Swanson, Timothy. *Global Action for Biodiversity*. London: Earthscan, 1997.

Millennium Ecosystem Assessment. *Ecosystems and Human Well-Being: Synthesis Report*. Washington, D.C.: Island Press, 2005.

Chemicals and Hazardous Wastes

Carson, Rachel. *Silent Spring*. Boston: Houghton Mifflin, 1962.

Downie, David, and Terry Fenge, eds. *Northern Lights Against POPs: Combating Toxic Threats in the Arctic.* Montreal, London, and Ithaca: McGill-Queens University Press, 2003.

Eckley, Noelle, and Henrik Selin. "Science, Politics, and Persistent Organic Pollutants: Scientific Assessments and their Role in International Environmental Negotiations." *International Environmental Agreements: Politics, Law and Economics* 3, no. 1 (2003).

O'Neill, Kate. *Waste Trading Among Rich Nations: Building a New Theory of Environmental Regulation.* Cambridge, Mass: MIT Press, 2000.

Thornton, Joe. *Pandora's Poison: On Chlorine, Health and a New Environmental Strategy.* Cambridge, Mass.: MIT Press, 2000.

Climate Change

Bodansky, Daniel. "The United Nations Framework Convention on Climate Change: A Commentary." *Yale Journal of International Law* 18, no. 2 (Summer 1993).

Bohringer, Christoph, and Andreas Loschel. *Climate Change Policy and Global Trade.* Berlin: Springer Verlag, 2004.

Bulkeley, Harriet, and Michele M. Betsill, eds. *Cities and Climate Change: Urban Sustainability and Global Environmental Governance.* New York: Routledge, 2003.

Faure, Michael, Joyeeta Gupta, and Andries Nentjes, eds. *Climate Change and the Kyoto Protocol: The Role of Institutions and Instruments to Control Global Change.* Northampton, Mass.: Edward Elgar, 2003.

Houghton, John. *Global Warming: A Complete Briefing.* Cambridge: Cambridge University Press, 2004.

Mintzer, Irving M., and J. A. Leonard, eds. *Negotiating Climate Change: The Inside Story of the Rio Convention.* Cambridge: Cambridge University Press, 1994.

Spence, Chris. *Global Warming: Personal Solutions for a Healthy Planet.* New York: Palgrave, 2005.

Victor, David. *Climate Change: Debating America's Policy Options.* New York: Council on Foreign Relations Press, 2004.

Desertification

Chasek, Pamela S. "Negotiations on the Convention to Combat Desertification." In Gunnar Sjöstedt, ed., *Professional Cultures in International Negotiation: Bridge or Rift?* Lanham, Md.: Lexington Books, 2003.

Chasek, Pamela S., and Elisabeth Corell. "Addressing Desertification at the International Level: The Institutional System." In James Reynolds and Mark Stafford Smith, eds., *Global Desertification: Do Humans Cause Deserts?* Berlin: Dahlem University Press, 2002.

Corell, Elisabeth. "North-South Financial Tensions: Desertification After UNGASS." *Environmental Politics* 7, no. 1 (1998).

Najam, Adil. "Dynamics of the Southern Collective: Developing Countries in Desertification Negotiations." *Global Environmental Politics* 4, no. 3 (August 2004).

Fisheries

Food and Agriculture Organization. *State of the World's Fisheries 2004.* Rome: FAO, 2005.

Porter, Gareth. *Fishing Subsidies, Overfishing and Trade.* Geneva: United Nations Environment Programme, 1998.

Forests

Dauvergne, Peter. *Shadows in the Forest: Japan and the Politics of Timber in Southeast Asia.* Cambridge, Mass.: MIT Press, 1997.

_____. "Globalisation and Deforestation in the Asia-Pacific." *Environmental Politics* 7, no. 4 (Winter 1998): 114–135.

Davenport, Deborah S. "An Alternative Explanation for the Failure of the UNCED Forest Negotiations." *Global Environmental Politics* 5, no. 1 (2005).

Humphreys, David. "The Global Politics of Forest Conservation Since the UNCED." *Environmental Politics* 5, no. 2 (Summer 1996): 231–256.

_____. "Redefining the Issues: NGO Influence on International Forest Negotiations." *Global Environmental Politics* 4, no. 2 (2004).

Oceans and Seas

Haas, Peter M. *Saving the Mediterranean: The Politics of International Environmental Cooperation.* New York: Columbia University Press, 1990.

Mitchell, Ronald B. *Intentional Oil Pollution at Sea: Environmental Policy and Treaty Compliance.* Cambridge, Mass.: MIT Press, 1994.

Ozone Depletion

Anderson, Stephan, and Madhava Sarma, eds. *Protecting the Ozone Layer: The United Nations History.* London: Earthscan, 2002.

Benedick, Richard Elliott. *Ozone Diplomacy.* Cambridge, Mass.: Harvard University Press, 1991.

Chasek, Pamela S. "The Ozone Depletion Regime." In Bertram Specter and I. William Zartman, eds., *Getting It Done: Post Agreement Negotiations and International Regimes.* Washington, D.C.: United States Institute of Peace Press, 2003.

Downie, David. "UNEP and the Montreal Protocol: New Roles for International Organizations in Regime Creation and Change." In Robert V. Bartlett, Priya A. Kurian, and Madhu Malik, eds., *International Organizations and Environmental Policy.* Westport, Conn.: Greenwood Press, 1995.

Litfin, Karen. *Ozone Discourses: Science and Politics in International Environmental Cooperation.* New York: Columbia University Press, 1994.

Parson, Edward A. *Protecting the Ozone Layer.* Oxford University Press, 2003.

Whaling

Baker, C. S., et al. "Scientific Whaling: Source of Illegal Products for Market?" (Letter). *Science* 290, no. 5497 (2000): 1695–1696.

Mulvaney, Kieran. *The Whaling Effect.* Washington, D.C.: World Wildlife Fund, 1999.

Shwartz, Mark. "Whale Populations Are Too Low to Resume Commercial Hunting, Geneticists Find." *Stanford Report,* July 24, 2003.

Economics and Trade

Esty, Daniel C. "The World Trade Organization's Legitimacy Crisis." *World Trade Review* 1, no. 1 (2002).

Finger, J. Michael, and Philip Schuler. "Implementation of Uruguay Round Commitments: The Development Challenge." Policy Research Working Paper Series 2215. Washington, D.C.: The World Bank, 1999.

Gallagher, Kevin P. "The Economics of Globalization and Sustainable Development." *Policy Matters: Trade, Environment and Investment, Cancun and Beyond,* no. 11 (September 2003).

Parker, Richard. "The Use and Abuse of Trade Leverage to Protect the Global Commons: What We Can Learn from the Tuna-Dolphin Conflict." *Georgetown Environmental Law Review* 12 (1999): 1–123.

Repetto, Robert. *Trade and Sustainable Development.* Geneva: United Nations Environment Programme (UNEP), 1994.

_____. *Mortgaging the Earth: The World Bank, Environmental Impoverishment, and the Crisis of Development.* Boston: Beacon Press, 1994.

Runge, C. Ford, with Francois Ortalo-Magne and Philip Vande Kamp. *Freer Trade, Protected Environment.* New York: Council on Foreign Relations Press, 1994.

Williams, Marc, and Lucy Ford. "The World Trade Organisation, Social Movements and Global Environmental Management." *Environmental Politics* 8, no. 1 (1999): 268–289.

Annual Publications

Fridtjof Nansen Institute. *Yearbook of International Co-operation on Environment and Development.* London: Earthscan, 2004. (Published annually since 1997)

United Nations Development Programme. *Human Development Report 2004.* New York: Oxford University Press, 2004. (Published annually)

United Nations Population Fund. *The State of World Population, 2004.* New York: UNFPA, 2005. (Published annually since 1978)

World Bank. *World Development Report 2005.* Washington, D.C.: World Bank, 2004. (Published annually)

World Resources Institute. *World Resources, 2002–2004.* Washington, D.C.: WRI, 2003. (Published biennially since 1990)

Worldwatch Institute. *State of the World 2005.* New York: W. W. Norton, 2005. (Published annually since 1984)

List of Internet Resources

The following list of Internet resources does not represent a comprehensive list of all resources related to global environmental politics. Instead, the list below consists of organizations mentioned in this book and their Internet addresses that are in use as of the date of publication. All Internet addresses are subject to change at any time.

Alliance of Small Island States:
http://www.sidsnet.org/aosis/

Arctic Monitoring and Assessment
Programme:
http://www.amap.no

Asia-Pacific Economic Cooperation:
http://www.apec.org

Asian Development Bank:
http://www.adb.org/

Basel Convention on the Control
of Transboundary Movements of
Hazardous Wastes and Their Disposal:
http://www.basel.int/

Cartegena Protocol on Biosafety:
http://www.biodiv.org/biosafety/

CEE Bankwatch Network:
http://www.bankwatch.org/

Central American Commission on
Environment and Development:
http://www.ccad.ws/

Climate Action Network:
http://www.climatenetwork.org

Commission for Environmental
Cooperation- North America:
http://www.cec.org/

Conservation International:
http://www.conservation.org/

Convention on Biological Diversity:
http://www.biodiv.org/

Convention on International Trade
in Endangered Species of
Wild Fauna and Flora:
http://www.cites.org/

Convention on Long-Range
Transboundary Air Pollution:
http://www.unece.org/env/lrtap/

Convention on the Conservation of
Migratory Species of Wild Animals:
http://www.cms.int/

Convention on the Prevention of
Marine Pollution by Dumping of
Wastes and Other Matter:
http://www.londonconvention.org/

Coordinator of the Indigenous
Organizations of the Amazon Basin:
http://www.coica.org/

Council on Environmental Quality (U.S.):
http://www.whitehouse.gov/ceq/

Environmental Defense:
http://www.environmentaldefense.org/

Environmental Protection Agency (U.S).:
http://www.epa.gov

Environmental Treaties and Resource
Indicators:
http://sedac.ciesin.columbia.edu/entri/

European Environmental Bureau:
http://www.eeb.org/

European Union:
http://europa.eu.int/

Food and Agriculture Organization:
http://www.fao.org

Foundation for International
Law and Development:
http://www.field.org.uk/

Friends of the Earth (UK):
http://www.foe.co.uk/

Friends of the Earth (U.S.):
http://www.foe.org

Friends of the Earth International:
http://www.foei.org

Global Environment Facility:
http://www.gefweb.org/

Greenpeace International:
http://www.greenpeace.org/

Group of 77:
http://www.g77.org/

Inter-American Development Bank:
http://www.iadb.org/

Intergovernmental Forum on
Chemical Safety:
http://www.who.int/ifcs/

Intergovernmental Panel on
Climate Change:
http://www.ipcc.ch/

International Atomic Energy Agency:
http://www.iaea.org/

International Chamber of Commerce:
http://www.iccwbo.org/

International Council for Science:
http://www.icsu.org/index.php

International Development Association:
http://www.worldbank.org/ida/

International Institute for
Environment and Development:
http://www.iied.org/

International Institute for Sustainable
Development:
http://www.iisd.org

International Labor Organization:
http://www.ilo.org/

International Maritime Organization:
http://www.imo.org/

International Monetary Fund:
http://www.imf.org/

International POPs Elimination Network:
http://ipen.ecn.cz/
http://www.who.int/ipcs/

International Tropical Timber
Organization:
http://www.itto.or.jp/

International Whaling Commission:
http://www.iwcoffice.org/

Inter-Organization Programme for the
Sound Management of Chemicals (IOMC):
http://www.who.int/iomc/

IUCN-World Conservation Union:
http://www.iucn.org

Linkages/*Earth Negotiations Bulletin*
(IISD):
http://www.iisd.ca/

Mediterranean Action Plan (MAP):
http://www.unepmap.gr/

Montreal Protocol on Substances that
Deplete the Ozone Layer:
http://www.unep.org/ozone/

Multilateral Fund for the Implementation
of the Montreal Protocol:
http://www.multilateralfund.org/

National Audubon Society:
http://www.audubon.org/

National Wildlife Federation:
http://www.nwf.org

Natural Resources Defense Council:
http://www.nrdc.org

New Partnership for Africa's Development:
http://www.nepad.org/

Oil Companies International Marine
Forum:
http://www.ocimf.com/

Organization for Economic Cooperation
and Development:
http://www.oecd.org

Organization of American States:
http://www.oas.org/

Organization of the Petroleum Exporting
Countries:
http://www.opec.org/

Pesticide Action Network:
http://www.pan-international.org/

Ramsar Convention on Wetlands of
International Importance:
http://www.ramsar.org

Rotterdam Convention on the Prior
Informed Consent Procedure for Certain
Hazardous Chemicals and Pesticides in
International Trade:
http://www.pic.int/

Sierra Club:
http://www.sierraclub.org/

South Pacific Regional Environment
Programme (SPREP):
http://www.sprep.org.ws/

Stockholm Convention on Persistent
Organic Pollutants:
http://www.pops.int/

Stockholm Environment Institute:
http://www.sei.se/

Strategic Approach to International
Chemicals Management:
http://www.chem.uncp.ch/saicm/

Third World Network:
http://www.twnside.org.sg/

TRAFFIC:
http://www.traffic.org/

United Nations:
http://www.un.org

United Nations Fish Stocks Agreement:
http://www.un.org/Depts/los/convention_
agreements/convention_overview_fish_
stocks.htm

United Nations Commission on
Sustainable Development:
http://www.un.org/esa/sustdev/csd

United Nations Conference on Trade and
Development:
http://www.unctad.org

United Nations Convention to Combat
Desertification:
http://www.unccd.int

United Nations Development Programme:
http://www.undp.org

United Nations Development
Programme – Energy and Environment
for Sustainable Development:
http://www.undp.org/energyandenvironment/

United Nations Division for Ocean Affairs
and the Law of the Sea:
http://www.un.org/Depts/los/

United Nations Division for Sustainable
Development:
http://www.un.org/esa/sustdev/

United Nations Economic and Social
Council:
http://www.un.org/docs/ecosoc/

United Nations Environment Programme:
http://www.unep.org

UNEP Chemicals:
http://www.chem.unep.ch/

UNEP: Geneva Office:
http://www.unep.ch

United Nations Framework Convention on
Climate Change:
http://www.unfccc.int

United Nations Global Environmental
Monitoring Systems (GEMS)/Water
Programme:
http://www.gemswater.org/

United Nations Human Settlements
Programme:
http://www.unhabitat.org/

United Nations Industrial Development
Organization:
http://www.unido.org

United Nations Population Fund:
http://www.unfpa.org/

United States Department of State:
http://www.state.gov/

Women's Environment and Development
Organization:
http://www.wedo.org

World Bank:
http://www.worldbank.org

World Business Council for Sustainable
Development:
http://www.wbcsd.ch/

World Health Organization:
http://www.who.org

World Meteorological Organization:
http://www.wmo.ch/

World Resources Institute:
http://www.wri.org

World Summit on Sustainable
Development:
http://www.johannesburgsummit.org

World Trade Organization:
http://www.wto.org

Worldwide Fund for Nature:
http://www.panda.org/

World Wildlife Fund (U.S.):
http://www.worldwildlife.org/

Glossary

Acid rain is precipitation that deposits nitric or sulfuric acids on the earth, buildings, and vegetation.

Biodiversity (or biological diversity) is the variety of organisms, including species of plants and animals, genetic variation within individual species, and diversity of ecosystems.

Biosafety refers to a set of precautionary practices to ensure the safe transfer, handling, use, and disposal of living modified organisms derived from modern biotechnology.

Biosphere refers to the earth's land, water, atmosphere, and living things, or to a particular zone of the whole.

Biotechnology is the branch of molecular biology that studies the use of microorganisms to perform specific industrial processes.

A **blocking** or **veto state** is one that by virtue of its importance on a particular environmental issue is able to block or weaken international agreement.

Boreal forests are those lying between arctic tundra to the north and warmer temperate forests to the south.

Bretton Woods institutions are the international financial institutions, such as the World Bank, the International Monetary Fund, and the International Finance Corporation, named after the New Hampshire resort at which they were negotiated.

By-catch is unintentionally caught fish, seabirds, sea turtles, marine mammals, and other ocean life.

CAFE standards are the Corporate Average Fuel Economy standards, a measure of fuel efficiency, imposed on U.S. auto manufacturers and importers of cars since 1975.

Certification and Labeling is the process of inspecting particular forests or fisheries to see if they are being managed according to an agreed-on set of principles and criteria, and labeling them as such.

Civil society refers to an array of private-sector institutions such as trade unions, business associations, environmental and development organizations, women's and youth groups, cooperatives, and religious groups having an interest in public policy issues and decisions.

The **Clean Development Mechanism** is a procedure under the Kyoto Protocol under which developed countries may finance greenhouse-gas emissions-avoiding projects in developing countries, and receive credits for doing so which they may apply towards meeting mandatory limits on their own emissions.

Climate change refers to the likelihood of increased change in the average weather over a period of time (usually thirty or more years) from natural causes (e.g., ice ages brought on by changes in the earth's orbit around the sun), or as the result of human intervention (e.g., through the release of carbon dioxide and other greenhouse gases).

The **commons** are the natural resources and vital life support services that belong to all humankind rather than to any one country.

A **convention** is a multilateral legal agreement and the most common form of legal instrument used in agreements on international environmental issues.

Desertification is the deterioration of the biological potential of land from a combination of adverse climate and excessive human exploitation, leading ultimately to desertlike conditions.

Emissions trading is a mechanism under the Kyoto Protocol through which parties with emissions commitments may trade units of their emissions allowances with other parties. The aim is to improve the overall flexibility and economic efficiency of making emissions cuts.

Environmental accounting involves various methods of figuring national income accounts that assign value to resources such as soil, water, forests, and minerals and therefore reflect more accurately in the accounting system the depletion of natural resources and the degradation of natural systems.

Environmental services are the conserving or restorative functions of nature, for example, the ability of plants to convert carbon dioxide to oxygen, the ability of marshlands to cleanse polluted waters, or the capacity of a vegetation-covered floodplain to dissipate the destructive power of a river in flood.

Eutrophication is a process whereby water bodies, such as lakes, estuaries, or slow-moving streams receive excess nutrients that stimulate excessive plant growth (algae, periphyton attached algae, and nuisance plants and weeds). This enhanced plant growth, often called an algal bloom, reduces dissolved oxygen in the water when dead plant material decomposes and can cause other organisms to die.

The **exclusionist paradigm** (also known as frontier economics) is the dominant social paradigm in contemporary societies and holds that humans are not subject to natural laws in their use of natural resources and systems for economic purposes.

Exclusive economic zones (EEZs) are the 200-mile-wide (320-kilometer-wide) territorial waters under the jurisdiction of individual nations.

A **framework convention** is a multilateral agreement that establishes common principles but does not include binding commitments to specific actions.

Germplasm is the genetic material that carries the inherited characteristics of an organism.

Global commons are the natural resources and vital life-support services, such as the earth's climate system, ozone layer, and oceans and seas that belong to all humankind rather than to any one country or private enterprise.

Global warming refers to the apparent trend of increasing temperatures on the world's surface and in the lower atmosphere, caused by the entrapment of heat due to the buildup of certain gases (see greenhouse gases).

Globalization is a term used to describe the changes in societies and the world economy that are the result of dramatically increased trade and cultural exchange. In the economic context, it refers almost exclusively to the effects of trade, particularly trade liberalization or "free trade."

Green taxes include a variety of measures that would penalize practices that pollute or degrade the environment or encourage excessive use or waste of a valuable natural resource or service.

Greenhouse gases are certain gases—mainly carbon dioxide, ground-level ozone, chlorofluorocarbons (CFCs), and halons, methane, and nitrous oxide—that build up in the atmosphere and lead to global warming, also referred to as the greenhouse effect.

Gross world product is the value of the total goods and services produced in the world annually.

The Group of Eight (or G-8) industrialized nations includes the United States, Canada, the United Kingdom, Japan, Germany, France, Italy, and Russia.

The **Group of 77** (G-77) is a coalition of developing countries (numbering more than 130) that has pressed for reform of North-South economic structures since the mid-1970s.

A **hegemonic power** is a state that is able to set the primary rules of an international system, usually through a combination of military and economic power.

Intellectual property rights (IPR) are the rights of businesses, individuals, or states to legal protection of their discoveries and inventions.

Intergenerational equity is a norm of state behavior that calls for giving adequate consideration to the interests of future generations, including the enjoyment of a healthy environment and natural resources.

International financial institutions are international organizations such as the World Bank, the regional development banks, the International Monetary Fund, and the International Finance Corporation.

An **international regime** is a set of principles, norms, rules, operating procedures, and institutions usually centered on one or more international agreements, governing particular issues in world politics.

Joint implementation (JI) is a mechanism under the Kyoto Protocol through which a developed country can receive "emissions reduction units" when it helps to finance projects that reduce net greenhouse-gas emissions in another developed country (in practice, the recipient state is likely to be a country with an "economy in transition").

The **Law of the Sea** was adopted in December 1982 by the Third United Nations Conference on the Law of the Sea. The convention comprises 320 articles and nine annexes, governing all aspects of ocean space, such as delimitation, environmental control, marine scientific research, economic and commercial activities, transfer of technology, and the settlement of disputes relating to ocean matters. The convention entered into force on November 16, 1994.

A **lead state** is one that sponsors and asserts leadership on behalf of the most advanced proposal for international regulation on an environmental issue.

Neoclassical economics is a school of economic theory maintaining that free markets will allocate resources so that the greatest number of people will be satisfied.

The **New International Economic Order** is the list of demands made in the 1970s by the Group of 77 (developing nations) for changes in the structure of North-South economic relations.

The **Non-Aligned Movement** is a group of 115 members representing the interests and priorities of developing countries. The movement has its origin in the Asia-Africa Conference held in Bandung, Indonesia in 1955, where Third World leaders shared their similar problems of resisting the pressures of the major powers, maintaining their independence, and opposing colonialism and neocolonialism, especially Western domination.

Nontariff barriers are trade barriers, other than tariffs, erected by a government to discourage imports, for example, quotas (both formal and "voluntary"), outright prohibition of specific imports (such as the Japanese refusal to import rice), discriminatory restrictions, or licensing requirements.

Official development assistance, or foreign aid, consists of loans, grants, technical assistance, and other forms of cooperation extended by developed-country governments to developing countries.

The **ozone layer** is the concentration of ozone in the stratosphere, between 15 and 50 kilometers (9.3 and 31 miles) above the earth's surface, depending on latitude, season, and other factors.

Paradigm refers to a set of assumptions about reality that define and often limit the scope of inquiry in a field of knowledge.

PCBs (polychlorinated biphenyls) are a set of synthetic organic chemicals suspected of causing cancer, endocrine disruption, and other adverse impacts on organisms. Because of their nonflammability, chemical stability, high boiling point, and electrical insulating properties, PCBs were used in hundreds of industrial and commercial applications, including electrical, heat transfer, and hydraulic equipment; as plasticizers in paints, plastics, and rubber products; in pigments, dyes, and carbonless copy paper as well as many other applications. More than 1.5 billion pounds of PCBs were manufactured in the United States prior to cessation of production in 1977.

Persistent organic pollutants (POPs) are a set of toxic chemicals that remain intact in the environment for long periods, can become widely distributed geographically, and accumulate in the fatty tissue of living organisms.

Plantation forests are forests usually created for commercial benefit. Trees are selected for their wood properties, planted (usually as a single species) and encouraged to grow to a useful size as quickly as possible.

Prior Informed Consent procedure (PIC) is a means for formally obtaining and disseminating the decisions of importing countries about whether they wish to receive future shipments of a certain chemical and for ensuring compliance with these decisions by exporting countries. The aim is to promote a shared responsibility between exporting and importing countries in protecting human health and the environment from the harmful effects of such chemicals.

A **protocol** is a multilateral agreement providing detailed, specific commitments attached to a convention.

Soft law refers to nonbinding documents drawn up by international bodies that establish norms; these documents can take on the force of law through customary practice.

The **stratosphere** is the upper part of the atmosphere, approximately 6–30 miles above the earth's surface.

A **supporting state** is one that is willing to publicly support and work for the most far-reaching proposal for international regulation on an environmental issue.

Sustainable development is a perspective on environmental management that emphasizes the need to reconcile present and future economic needs through environmental conservation.

Sustainable forest management is a process rather than a prescribed system of forest management. Elements may include participatory and equitable approaches to decisionmaking geared toward maintaining ecosystem and landscape functions while also meeting economic, social, and cultural needs.

A **swing state** is one that attempts to bargain for major concessions in return for acceding to a global environmental agreement.

Technology transfer is the transfer, usually from highly industrialized to less industrialized developing countries, of the means of producing scientifically or technically advanced goods in the form of patents, machinery and equipment, or the necessary scientific-technical knowledge.

Transboundary air pollution is the emission of pollutants, especially nitric and sulfuric acids, across national boundaries.

A **unitary actor model** is an explanatory concept based on the assumption that state actors can be treated as though they are a single entity with a single, internally consistent set of values and attitudes.

The **Uruguay Round** is the negotiations under the auspices of the General Agreement on Tariffs and Trade on liberalization of world trade that began in 1985 in Uruguay and ended in 1994.

A **veto coalition** is a group of veto states that forms around a given issue.

A **veto** or **blocking state** is one that by virtue of its importance on a particular environmental issue is able to block or weaken international agreement.

Index